THE BEST AUSTRALIAN ESSAYS 2010

THE BEST AUSTRALIAN ESSAYS 2010

Edited by
ROBERT DREWE

Published by Black Inc.,
an imprint of Schwartz Media Pty Ltd

37–39 Langridge Street
Collingwood Vic 3066 Australia
email: enquiries@blackincbooks.com
http://www.blackincbooks.com

ISBN 9781863954945

Contents

Introduction

Robert Drewe

Whenever I see the word 'essay' I'm back in English class again, that pivotal first year of adolescence and high school when the childish 'compositions' of primary school ('What I Did in the Holidays' and 'My Pets' and 'It Was All a Dream!') suddenly turned into 'essays' and became longer, scarier and, it was hoped in those pre-Google days, more informative.

Maybe I'm not alone in piling some high-school freight onto the subject. So even though I'm not keen on literary genre boundaries, I find myself beginning this introduction, as I began the selection process, by trying to establish a precise definition of the essay.

The collator will usually canvass the idea of the essay as falling somewhere between a short story and a reflective piece of journalism. Perhaps. Trying to define an essay is a vague and slippery endeavour. Aldous Huxley noted that 'like the novel, the essay is a literary device for saying almost everything about almost anything.' Huxley then went on to declare, 'By tradition, the essay is a short piece, and it is therefore impossible to give all things full play within the limits of a single essay.' Well, that clears that up! What we're reasonably sure of, however, is that the essay is a shortish piece of non-fiction on a focused subject, often written from a personal point of view.

Huxley made more sense with his view that a collection of essays 'can cover almost as much ground, and cover it almost as thoroughly, as can a long novel.' Anyway, I took that as my objective in the task of collecting and editing the best of many varied pieces for *The Best Australian Essays 2010.* I wanted to showcase those subjects which thoughtful and talented Australian writers were absorbed by in this particular year; indeed (I thought), wouldn't it be good to show what this country, and its culture, was *about* in 2010?

Of course, what this country was largely about was a back-and-forth, ever-changing political landscape of blighted global-environmental hopes, leadership musical chairs, cynical opportunism and party-political shenanigans. Not surprisingly, the puzzled and disenchanted political essays being written as this book went to press, soon after the deadlocked federal election, were mostly manifesto-free and indecisive and merely reflected the weary, sullen bewilderment of the Australian electors. In a genre that depends on clear focus it was understandable that, like the voters, even the best writers were marking time, seemingly numbed by the political gridlock.

So as editor I turned at the outset to the other facets of contemporary culture where politics was central: our current engagement in two wars, and the traditional and increasing power of the mining industry, and the whipped-up anxiety over asylum seekers, not to mention the consciousness shifts in regard to indigenous and foreign-born Australians.

Plenty of material there for an essayist's consideration, as is evident in the on-the-spot writings of the redoubtable war correspondent Paul McGeough, the meticulously wide-ranging Kathy Marks and the always perceptive and incisive Nicolas Rothwell, and in the pungent thoughts on race and belonging of Robert Manne, Sunil Badami and Pauline Nguyen. As for what Australia is and has always been *about,* one could do no better than the clear cultural analysis of Guy Rundle and David Malouf.

But politics isn't all. This is a personal selection and there are several fine essays on Australian literature herein, one of whose subjects, Peter Porter – represented in Clive James's moving obituary – was noted for his generosity to younger writers, myself included, in years past. Speaking of connections, his biographer David Marr brings the young and randy Patrick White, then unknown, unserious, unawarded, unattached and unpolitical, vividly to life. And Gerard Windsor finds an unusually serene connection to dead forebears and in-laws in the Waverley Cemetery.

I was intrigued by writers stepping outside their usual genre: essays by such noted fiction writers as Alex Miller, Carmel Bird and Murray Bail gave insights into their creative workings, as did the cryptic prose offerings of the poets Les Murray and Andrew Sant. But the most affecting essays for me were those on a tragic and familiar incident in my own North Coast neighbourhood, depicted by the novelist Melissa Lucashenko, and on the life of a small girl, by Anne Manne.

I read hundreds of essays for this book, scouring the quarterly journals, serious magazines, national newspapers and British and American publications for writing either by Australians, or on Australia as a topic. There are many well-known names here, and some entertaining and informative new ones. Perhaps surprisingly, I continued to be as impressed at the end of the selection process as I was at the beginning. I'm satisfied that an outsider – a Martian, say – landing in Australia and wanting to know what it was *about*, would at least have an inkling of its culture: its current loves and angers, its art and myths and amusements and gender concerns – and its propensity for bushfires.

My own writing life being a continuous inquiry into what makes Australia tick, I was grateful to be enlightened and/or amused by such varied subjects as the dreaded cultural cringe, vegetarianism, wild animals, menstruation, fair play, outback pubs, painters, marriage, Aboriginal magic, botany, pop music, beauty quests and Australian crime (or the surprising dearth of it). Having previously edited two volumes of *The Best Australian Short Stories*, I was surprised to find that although the short-story entries were more numerous each year than the essays, these non-fiction pieces ranged over a much wider field.

As well as considering previously published material, I also scanned scores of new essays, including some multiple submissions that a lone editor, working in a relatively narrow time frame, could never hope to read in their entirety. Without Black Inc.'s diligent research, suggestions and culling, the task would have been impossible. Some loud and crabby essays were rejected, not because of their controversial nature (far from it), but because they were part of extended passionate exchanges that would have taken up half the book. Life was also too short for over-10,000-word efforts, and many boring and copiously footnoted academic essays failed to make the grade; similarly discounted were long-winded speeches by several well-known public figures and any essays written in verse or green biro.

I feel bad that numerous excellent and sometimes entertainingly droll essays missed out, not that they lacked quality but because the collection required a certain literary balance of light and shade and, of course, reflected my own sometimes quirky taste. I could easily have produced another two or three anthologies with the material I received.

Once more, the *Best Australian* literary series created a sort of postal history at Evan and Chris Connick's General Store and Post Office ('For Civility and Service'), the only commercial building in the tiny Northern Rivers hamlet of Tintenbar, New South Wales, where my post-office box regularly overflowed onto the counter near the pie-warmer, and I would leave the building clutching a pile of genuinely hot copy. I apologise again to this good-humoured and patient couple for crowding their store for six months with parcel upon parcel of Australian literature.

Robert Drewe

Peter Porter 1929–2010

Clive James

If the eternal life in which Peter Porter did not believe had granted him permission to check out the action shortly after his demise, he would have been interested in his obituaries. Self-deprecation having been his characteristic mode both in art and in life, he was always reluctant to claim a victory even when weighed down by the arrival of yet another van-load of laurels. But he might have been pleased to see how, in both Britain and Australia, those deputed in the media to lament his passing nearly all hailed him not just as an Australian poet, but as a poet of the English language. A matter of contention had finally been settled, simply because he had spent so long being the man and artist that he was. His early poetry was so brilliant that the argument should have been over immediately, but sometimes the obvious answer can take a lifetime to become common wisdom.

He had spent much of his career caught in a fork, punished in Australia for trying to please the Poms, and punished in the UK for being an Aussie expatriate with a frame of reference above his station. Later on, he won acceptance in both camps, and by the time of his death he was a living example of the old country's culture reinforcing itself with the energy of the new, and of the new country's culture gaining scope from an expanded context. From the Australian viewpoint, if Les Murray was still the king of the stay-at-homes, Porter was the king of the stay-aways, the position of expatriate artist having at last come to be seen as a contribution rather than a betrayal. For the British, his work and stature added up to a powerful reminder that the old empire lived on as an intellectual event. In both countries, after his death, those who wrote about him awarded him so much admiration that even he would have been obliged to believe it, although undoubtedly he would have described it as part of a scheme to have his estate taxed twice.

Born in Queensland to a family in reduced circumstances, the young Peter was shunted off to a boot-camp boarding school just to get him out of the way, and was denied any university education because in those days if your father couldn't pay, you didn't go. (A bit later on, the often mocked conservative prime minister R.G. Menzies changed all that with the Commonwealth Scholarship Scheme, but too late to save Peter from discovering Brisbane's shortcomings as a cosmopolitan metropolis.) His upbringing was scarcely the blacking factory, but he couldn't be blamed for looking back on it as a non-event. To a painful extent, his character was shaped by what didn't happen: nobody, as he later complained, was ever kissed less often. From that experience, or lack of it, grew his strange conviction that women found him negligible. (He was notorious for saying that there really were two nations, but they were the attractive and the unattractive.) At several stages in his life, before the advent of his second wife Christine removed his credibility as a victim of deprivation, I knew plenty of women who complained that they would have very much liked to kiss him but he wouldn't stop telling them about Scarlatti.

Thus habituated from his earliest years to believing that even his good luck must be bad luck in disguise, Peter, established in London, had the grace to turn his own mental disposition into a joke, and many of us who knew him were glad to join in, sometimes making stuff up to boost the legend. He would come back to London from some Australian literary festival and recount how the Australian headliner poet had been given the luxury hotel's penthouse suite with resident chef and dancing girls, whereas he, Porter, had been allotted a motel room on the fringe of town with one towel and a stale cheese sandwich. Glad to be at the same rocking table, we evoked, with his delighted participation, what would happen when he was awarded the

Nobel Prize for Literature. Instead of receiving it from the hands of King Carl XVI Gustaf in Stockholm, he would be asked to pick it up from Sweden's assistant cultural attaché in the car park of Stevenage railway station.

Possibly he took too much pleasure in running himself down. When you are speaking to the media, the trouble with modesty is that the reporters tend to agree with it, just as, when someone has a high opinion of himself, the reporters tend to agree with that. As I tried to tell him by way of a parable, a certain famous writer who wore dark glasses indoors did the right thing when he assured a journalist it was because his nervous system was so sensitive. The famous writer's putative sensitivity had been the first characteristic discussed in any profile written about him ever since. A lover of literary gossip, Peter revelled in this information, but did not change his ways. Speaking to an interviewer concerned with the eternal non-question of which of his two nations he felt nationalistic about, Peter said 'patriotism and allegiance are small matters in comparison with my egotism.' He was lucky that 'Aussie Poet Admits Ego' was not the headline of the piece.

In truth, he had very little egotism, and might have been better off if he'd had more. Instead, at the core of his nature was generosity, to the extent that it sometimes threatened to be his undoing. Though his financial position was always parlous and could scarcely be saved by his industry as a first-string critic for the *Times Literary Supplement*, the *Observer* and the BBC – only a culture gets enriched by that kind of effort, not the contributor – he would give time he didn't have to any demands from the poetic world, immolating his energies in symposia, conferences and doomed readings in the upstairs rooms of penniless literary societies. This particular form of generosity would often extend to inviting Australian poets visiting London to billet themselves in his flat. Apart from judging a poetry competition, I couldn't imagine anything more likely to ruin the concentration necessary to write poetry. Peter, however, didn't think that way. He had no idea of rationing his energies, and anyway, as his prolific output of verse proved, he didn't believe in the jealous nurturing of a few fine things, Flaubert-style. Indeed his role models were not from literature at all: they were from music. He was fond of saying that Bach's cantatas would have been no more marvellous had there been fewer of them.

Peter already knew a lot about classical music before he first left home and he wasn't far into his London residency before he had learnt everything. The geology of his flat in Bayswater altered in recent years when the ranks and banks of LPs were supplemented by rows of CDs. But though he often told interviewers that he rated music above literature, it is important, once again, for us to watch his words. He loved literature as much as anyone can who takes pains in adding to it. At our last meeting, during that strange period when the sky was silent and we were all ruled by the moods of an Icelandic volcano, he was typically eloquent about the arts, about which he had always had the rare gift of speaking with unapologetic enthusiasm. He was frail, and sometimes his speech came slowly, but we still had our usual fight about the later Wallace Stevens, whom Peter revered and I find suspect, and somewhere in the conversation, casually but strikingly, he let slip the remark that he thought nothing could beat the feeling of writing a poem at that moment when the poem takes over and starts to write itself.

Even though there would clearly not be much more of it, this was magic talk of the kind that I, like all his friends, had grown so used to over the years that we tended to take it for granted. I often had to remind myself that hardly anyone could speak like this. Alive a long time and active all over the cultural map, Peter joined several literary groups together, but in one of them I was lucky enough to be included, and when the gang now known as the Friday Lunch used to meet each week, often he and I would be the last two left at the end, and the subject of the conversation was almost always the arts. He was a walking university, except that you rarely encounter his kind of range in a university. As time went by I got better at playing feed-man in a routine that I could see was a stage show in the making. This was proved true one year at the Melbourne Festival, when, at short notice, Peter and I were pushed on stage by the tridents of the organisers, having been told to improvise an hour's conversation. As usual we both quoted reams of poetry from memory. It caused a sensation among the young people in the audience, not because what we remembered was so unusual, but because for them it was so unusual to find someone remembering anything.

The ABC arts producer Jill Kitson was in the audience and she suggested that we might, when we got back to London, go into the ABC's studio in Great Portland Street and record a set of six broadcasts along the same lines. Eventually there were six seasons of them recorded at the rate of one season a year, and in Australia they became a staple of arts broadcasting, with Peter's knowledge and easy eloquence remarked on by thousands of listeners. Though he never knew, in my opinion, how to read his own poetry aloud, Peter was an ace broadcaster from a script. But he was even better off the cuff, and in those shows he is at his dazzling best, as fluent and entertaining as he was in real life. (On behalf of his reputation, if not of mine, I might suggest that it would be good if the BBC picked them up. They are all on my website – an enterprise he rather approved of, because it took endless labour and made no money, a pattern he recognised – but his contribution deserves a far wider audience than that.) His *The Rest on the Flight: Selected Poems*, which was published in May 2010 and which he lived just long enough to see, will doubtless provide the core of his heritage. I hope it will sell the way Philip Larkin's *Collected Poems* did, like snow-cones in the Sahara. Wedded to tumultuous simultaneity and sometimes, it seemed to me, to outright obscurity, Peter was rarely as approachable as Larkin, but he had the gift of the phrase that lodged in the reader's head. At its best, his poetry spoke the way he did. 'Auden didn't love God, he just found him attractive.' I can hear him saying it now. In the broadcasts, he proved that he could say things like that all the time. Dr Johnson might have talked for victory, but Peter seemed to talk for posterity.

When we last met, it was the only thing I said that was good enough to match him. Complaining away as hilariously as usual about the injustice of the literary world, he said he didn't care about posterity. 'You don't have to,' I said. 'For you, it's already here.' Surely I was right for once. While he lived, so many people thought he was great that not even he could have believed they were in league to do him down. But he could never have played the hero, because for him it was creativity itself that had the heroic status, beyond politics, beyond patriotism, beyond even personal happiness. His poetry, so wonderful when it is really flying, is not trying to tell you how much he knows. It's giving thanks for how much there is to be known.

The Times Literary Supplement

The Inferno

Christine Kenneally

Earlier this year, on the day now known as Black Saturday, when the worst wildfires in modern Australian history incinerated more than a million acres of the state of Victoria and killed 173 people, Bruce Ackerman left his house in Marysville to meet up with his regular Saturday lunch group. Marysville, a small town some sixty miles northeast of Melbourne, sprang up in the 1860s as a stopover for miners on their way to the gold-rush towns farther north. Situated in a cool valley of the Great Dividing Range, the mountainous spine that dominates eastern Australia, the town is a popular tourist destination. Ackerman, a bluff fifty-year-old, is proud of being a fourth-generation inhabitant, and told me that his work as a plumber had taken him inside every house there except one. Over the years, he had served on the water board, the cemetery trust, the school council, the ambulance service, and the volunteer fire brigade.

The lunch group broke up earlier than usual; three of Ackerman's friends, a fire captain and two members of his team, were about to be placed on standby because of the risk of bushfire. Two days earlier Victoria's premier, John Brumby, had held a press conference at which he stated that the coming Saturday, near the end of the antipodean summer, would be the 'worst day in the history of the state.' 'The state is just tinder-dry,' he said, and told Victorians that it was time to put their fire plan into action.

After lunch, Ackerman drove some seven miles southwest to the small town of Narbethong and had a drink with some friends. While he was there, he became aware of an unusual amount of activity on the road running through the town. Drivers sped through, asking if Narbethong was safe from fire. Amid the gathering panic, Ackerman smelled smoke. He rushed back north to Marysville against a stream of traffic coming the other way. By the time he was a few miles from Marysville, he could see a colossal firewall coming toward him from the southwest. It was 300 feet high. He raced it all the way back to the town, driving on the wrong side of the road to get through blocked intersections and dodging cars that sped toward him in their effort to flee. The fire behind Ackerman emitted a roar like a jet engine and threw embers and fireballs out ahead of him. Huge patches of trees and grass ignited around the car as he drove. In his mind Ackerman started running through the steps of his fire plan.

Fire plans are a distinctive feature of Australian life. Whereas other regions prone to wildfire, most notably California, typically employ mandatory evacuations to remove citizens from an affected area, Australians are instructed to pick one of two options: leave early or stay and fight the fire. Though risky, the choice to stay is a popular one, both because unprotected houses are often lost to the flames and because of a streak of self-reliance in the Australian character. Australians have had great success saving their homes: a fire front passes in a matter of minutes, during which time the house shields those inside from the heat, and research has shown that houses usually catch fire not as the front passes but, rather, before or after, when wind-borne embers settle on it. Fire plans include removing flammable items from around the house, storing as much water as possible, and being ready to put out flames as a fire front draws near. Many Australians become experts on matters like smoke inhalation and the effects of radiant heat on the body, and public-information ads drive home the importance of wearing long sleeves and trousers and avoiding all synthetic materials, which ignite much faster in radiant heat. The best-prepared people build their houses out of fireproof materials, install sprinkler systems on their roofs, and maintain water tanks attached to professional-grade firefighting pumps and hoses. At the start of this year, a Californian study, pointing to a dramatic increase in the number of buildings lost to wildfire in recent decades, recommended the adoption of 'more effective' Australian tactics representing 'a more sustainable coexistence with fire.' But in the months since Black Saturday the Australian approach to fighting fire has come under question. During an ongoing royal commission, experts have pondered how wildfires should be handled on an increasingly fire-prone continent, and also the extent to which the deaths of Black Saturday were the result not just of the Australian landscape but of an entire mentality.

*

Australia's worst fires have all occurred in its southeastern states, with Victoria often hit the hardest. In the Black Friday fires of 1939, almost a quarter of the state was burned and seventy-eight people died. The Ash Wednesday fires of 1983 killed seventy-five people and destroyed more than 2000 homes. In the past ten years, the risk of catastrophic fire has increased because of a pervasive drought, the severest since records began, which is widely thought to be a result of global warming. Victorians are asked to use less than 155 litres of water per person per day. Gardens can be watered for only a few hours on two days a week, and it is illegal to use a hose when washing your car.

This year, starting on 28 January, Victoria experienced the most severe heat wave in its history. Many elderly people died; steel train tracks buckled; in one Melbourne park a thousand fruit bats fell dead from the trees. By Monday 2 February, Claire Yeo, one of Victoria's two fire meteorologists, noted that all the factors that create extreme fire weather were evident: high temperatures; strong, gusty winds; and very little moisture. On Tuesday, the Bureau of Meteorology predicted that the temperature for Saturday the seventh would be thirty-seven degrees Celsius – ninety-eight degrees Fahrenheit – but Yeo told a fire chief that a temperature upward of 113 degrees Fahrenheit was more likely. 'I think we are going to break records,' she said. By Wednesday, the numbers she was calculating on a system that rates the danger of fire were worse than anything she had ever seen. So terrible was the forecast that, when she had to brief assembled fire chiefs, meteorologists and other specialists on the situation, she stood at her lectern for some time, hanging her head and unable to speak.

Yeo's predictions were accurate. Saturday the seventh was the hottest day in Melbourne since records began to be kept, in 1855. The temperature reached 46.4 degrees Celsius (115.5 degrees Fahrenheit) in Melbourne and 120 degrees Fahrenheit elsewhere in the state. Humidity was at just 6 per cent, and a strong wind was blowing from the northwest. The 600 fires that started that day were not just the deadliest that Australia had ever known but among the worst the world had seen for decades.

At around 3 p.m., a watcher in a fire tower on Mount Despair reported a smoke plume in the Murrindindi state forest, a little more than twenty miles northwest of Marysville. From there, burning embers were carried by the wind to Little Wonder, a point at the top of a ridge in the nearby Black Ranges, and soon there was fire on the other side of the ridge, too. The fire was by now travelling at around seven miles an hour. With the northwesterly wind behind it, it spread southeast toward a popular camping spot. A fire crew raced to get to the campsite before the fire did. The firefighters drove two trucks into a nearby river and gathered nineteen campers into the water. Minutes later, the fire caught up with them. Nine children and an adult were crammed into the cabs, and the other campers sheltered beside the trucks, under wet blankets, while the firemen fought the flames. The campsite was incinerated, but everyone survived.

A little later, a front of cooler weather moved into Victoria. Temperatures dropped eighteen degrees Fahrenheit, and all over Melbourne people spilled from their houses in relief. But, while a drop in temperature can make a fire less likely, it doesn't have much impact on one that is already raging. Worse, the cool front brought about a ninety-degree change in the wind, from northwesterly to southwesterly. Now the long, narrow line of fire that had been spreading southeast became a wide fire front that charged northeast to a string of towns along the Maroondah Highway: first Narbethong, then Marysville, Buxton, Taggerty and Alexandra.

The fire hit Marysville so fast that no one had good information about what was happening. Not long before, it had seemed that the fire would pass the town by. Ian Bates, who was on duty at the State Emergency Services building, recalls standing in front of the building talking to the local fire captain. He glanced over the captain's shoulder and saw the fire coming at the town. He pointed and said, 'Look at that!' At the same moment, the captain pointed over Bates's shoulder and shouted exactly the same thing. Bates looked behind him. The fire was coming at the town from both sides.

Residents, seeing huge clouds of dirty orange-yellow smoke looming over the trees, got in their cars and drove, either to shelter in the local football oval or out of town entirely. The local police, firefighters and emergency workers scrambled to alert people to the danger. Bates and his deputy drove through residential streets with their lights and sirens on, knocking on doors and yelling through the PA system that everyone needed to leave. They put together a convoy that was able to exit the town in less than thirty minutes.

*

Once Bruce Ackerman got home, he called his daughter and his son's girlfriend, both in their twenties and living in Marysville, and told them to leave town. (His son works as a fireman, and his wife was in Melbourne with friends for the night.) Then he phoned an elderly couple next door and told them to go to the football oval, but they were reluctant to leave. The wife walked over to Ackerman's house. 'She was shaking like a dog,' he told me. 'She said, "I'm not scared. I've stood up to bigger men than that bloody bit of smoke." And I said, "Elsa! Get down to the oval."' A little later, her husband came over. 'We went through the same routine,' Ackerman said. 'He said, "I'm tough and I'm not going for no one." And I took him outside and I made him listen to the roar, and I said, "Dudley! Piss off!" And he did.' Ackerman phoned his next-door neighbours on the other side, Liz Fiske and her thirteen-year-old son. Fiske's husband, a fire captain who was away on duty, had been best man at Ackerman's wedding, and Ackerman had been best man at his. Fiske, too, refused to leave her house.

Between phone calls, Ackerman frantically prepared his home. He took his truck out of the shed at the foot of his front yard and parked it in a carport next to the house. He removed all the doormats from the house, stuffed draft-blockers under the doors, checked that all the windows were shut and started the sprinklers on his lawn. He grabbed a ladder and checked that the gutters on his house were clear. The light outside became dimmer and dimmer as the sun was blocked out by an enormous pall of smoke. Ackerman filled eight buckets, two watering cans, the dog's bath, the spa bath, the wheelbarrow and the trash can with water, the house's water pressure falling all the while. He moved out everything that was stored under his veranda, took down the picnic umbrellas in the garden, and removed the gas tank from the barbecue. He turned off the gas to the house. Then the house's electricity failed, everything went dark, and the water supply petered out. Ackerman called Liz Fiske again, hoping that there might still be time for her and her son to leave. This time, her son answered the phone. He told Ackerman that his mother was in the yard, fighting the fire. Ackerman said to him, 'Be brave for your mum. You'll be all right, mate. You're a strong man.'

At around half past six, the fire front hit Ackerman's house. The fire shone as brightly as daylight, illuminating everything – 'red, just red, pure bright light, red raw,' Ackerman said. As the fire burned around his house, Ackerman was in constant motion. 'I was upstairs, downstairs, in and out of every room, back and forth, to and fro, looking where the fire was spotting, popping in and out with buckets, dousing it down. The fire came right up to the house, and it was catching,' he told me.

The front passed in minutes, but to Ackerman it seemed like days. 'I was a volunteer fireman in Ash Wednesday. I've seen a lot, but I've never, ever seen anything like this,' he told me. All night, Marysville was lit by a dull, smoky glow as its buildings burned down. Explosions and flares went off constantly as gas tanks, paint cans and other flammable objects ignited. Just after the front went through, Ackerman was outside again to put out spot fires that had started around his house. Liz Fiske's house was on fire, and he couldn't find her or her son. 'I hoped to Christ they had got out,' he said. He drove down to the football oval, where his elderly neighbours had taken refuge, along with fifty or so other residents who had missed the convoy out of town. Everyone there was alive, and the grass on the oval had stayed green, even though all the trees that circled it had burned. Then he drove back through the town to check on friends whose house had begun to burn. By the time he got there, the piping to their water pump had melted, their tanks were leaking, and the pump itself had vaporised. They were trying their hardest, Ackerman said, but they were absolutely exhausted. Ackerman put on gloves and pulled a flaming trellis off a wall, saving their house. He went back to Liz Fiske's house, which had burned down completely, and then drove three miles to check on an uncle and aunt: their house was destroyed, too, but, as there was no sign of their car, he felt confident that they had managed to leave. Around half past three in the morning, Ackerman ran into a firefighter who had a satellite phone, and he called his wife to tell her he was alive.

*

Six days after Black Saturday, I drove to the town of Alexandra, twenty miles north of Marysville, to meet Geoff McClure of the Department of Sustainability and Environment, and to see the fire, which had now joined up with another large fire and was heading toward Alexandra. McClure was affable and solicitous, but he looked tired. Over the week, the fire had burned through almost 300,000 acres, and he had been working fourteen hours a day. He lent me some flame-retardant overalls and a helmet made from plastic with a melting point above 320 degrees Fahrenheit. Then we drove out toward the fire line.

As we left Alexandra, we saw the Great Dividing Range framed by a mass of smoke that looked like a giant cumulus cloud. The fire was heading downhill in a fire line about twenty-five miles across. Because the wind that day was blowing back against the fire, the smoke spiralled up from within the burning vegetation. The darker the plume and the fuzzier its boundaries, McClure explained, the more intense the fire.

Some eucalyptus, of which Australia has more than 700 species, produces significantly more radiant heat when burning than the wood of other trees, and the growth of eucalyptus forests is naturally punctuated by fires. Fire promotes rejuvenation, by removing the buildup of ground litter, opening the canopy, and eliminating competitive species. It is also a crucible in which the buds of many eucalyptus species sprout. Currently, Victoria's Department of Sustainability and Environment is responsible for controlled burning to reduce fuel loads. This doesn't prevent fires, but it does decrease the intensity of the fires that occur.

We passed a police roadblock, and drove up a tree-lined dirt track in the direction of the fire. The goal, McClure explained, was to stop the fire from coming out of the forest; there was little anyone could do to stop its descent down the hill. Hundreds of firefighters were being deployed; in recent days, they had used bulldozers to establish containment lines of bare earth that could interrupt the progress of the fire. In the bush, the bulldozer is as essential to firefighting as the fire truck. The containment lines, only ten feet wide, looked precarious, but although embers carried on the wind can sometimes enable fire to jump a line, the absence of fuel at the line prevents the fire front itself from burning through. We drove to where two young firefighters were strengthening a containment line by back burning – starting a controlled fire that would burn back toward an approaching fire front, depriving it of fuel. Using fuel cannisters with long nozzles, they had established a line of flames some two feet high and intensely hot. My eyes stung as we stood watching, fifteen feet away.

Strange cataclysmic phenomena occur in a huge wildfire. Kevin Tollhurst, a fire ecologist in Melbourne, told me that fires as hot as the one at Marysville – which is thought to have reached a temperature of 2200 degrees Fahrenheit – can produce their own weather. Fires generate convection columns of gas, which may rise as much as 40,000 feet and form pyrocumulus clouds. The clouds can create lightning, which may then start more fires downwind of the original fire. The sound of the gas – like a twig popping in a fireplace, but exponentially louder – creates a wildfire's distinctive roar. The Marysville fire was so hot that gas flared out laterally, acting as a wick, along which the fire caught quickly, crossing the ground in sudden, unpredictable pulses. In the face of such a fire, it is possible to be looking at a front more than a thousand feet away and then, in an instant, to be surrounded by flames. Firefighters described the Black Saturday firestorm as 'alive,' and said that its behaviour was completely unprecedented. In some areas it was apparently cyclonic, coming at them from all sides, burning up a road in one direction and then, minutes later, burning in the opposite direction. Tollhurst told the royal commission that the energy from all the fires that day was the equivalent of 1500 Hiroshimas.

Later, McClure took me to see some of the damage to a cluster of properties just off the road south of Alexandra. The buildings looked as if they had imploded. Glass that had melted like toffee was draped around their edges. In the yard next to the remains of one building, the blackened branches of a tree stretched out and up, and from them dangled pitch-black round baubles. I picked one up from the ground and pushed my thumb through the charcoal outer layer to the yellow core, which was leathery and desiccated. It still smelled faintly of apple.

*

The devastation of Black Saturday became clear only over many days, unfolding for survivors as a disorienting nightmare and extending across Victoria. In places where the fire had passed, the countryside was completely silent, with no sign of animal life. In Marysville, Bruce Ackerman's house was one of only fourteen left standing. The town had been annihilated in an afternoon. Police set up roadblocks around the worst affected places, and three towns, including Marysville, were declared crime scenes, after arson, a surprisingly common cause of wildfires, was suspected. No one was allowed back into Marysville for weeks.

The death toll rose from fifteen to 173. It was clear that some bodies would never be recovered, having been effectively cremated. Others were found unburned in positions that suggested that they had simply dropped dead while running from the flame; the radiant heat of a bushfire, which can ignite mattresses and curtains through closed windows, can kill at a considerable distance more or less instantaneously. Survivors emerged with ever more excruciating stories. As people escaped, they had seen their neighbours' bodies lying charred in the streets. A few days after the fire, police found a house with the remains of nine bodies: eight adults had formed a protective huddle around a baby.

Nearly two weeks after Black Saturday, I drove from Alexandra to the Marysville golf course, just outside the town, to meet with Bruce Ackerman, who, because his house was intact, had been allowed to stay in Marysville, alongside the army, the police and emergency-services crews. As I waited in the parking lot, I walked over to a semi-trailer that looked as if it had been detonated from within. The exhaust stacks drooped outward, and thick rivulets of melted aluminium lay congealed in the gutter beneath. When I tapped one with my foot, it clanged loudly. Ackerman arrived, and we sat on the porch of the clubhouse. In front of us, many trees were burned, but the links were still green. A tiny bird with a long tail and a glowing blue face hopped about on the grass.

For eight days after the fire, Ackerman told me, he had helped the police as they searched for bodies in collapsed houses. During a fire, he explained, people usually take shelter in the bathroom: 'And who would know where the bathroom is? The plumber.' Thirty-nine people in Marysville lost their lives; Ackerman's neighbours Liz Fiske and her son were among the dead.

Not until six weeks after Black Saturday was Marysville reopened for residents, and a few days later Ackerman took me on a tour of the town, which was still closed to the public. Wire fencing had been erected along most streets, cordoning off the destroyed buildings. We drove along the river to a waterfall, which, like many things in Marysville, had once been invisible through thick foliage but could now be seen from hundreds of yards away. We stopped at Ackerman's house, a large, rustic two-storey home, incongruously intact and attractive amid the devastation. Trees that must have been fully alight stood no more than twenty feet from the house. Ackerman's front yard was green and inviting, but a big tin shed at the foot of the lawn was splayed everywhere, as if another tin shed had been dropped on it from a great height. Farther down the hill, the army had created a car yard, neatly lining up nearly a hundred skeletal cars and buses.

While we drove around the town, Ackerman's phone rang constantly. It sometimes seemed that there was little in the town that he wasn't doing. He had helped reinstate water service, refilling the depleted reservoir. He was head of a committee to establish a temporary village nearby to house residents who were rebuilding their homes. That morning, he had dug a grave.

*

Nine days after Black Saturday, Victoria set up a yearlong commission to investigate the cause of the fires and 'all aspects of the government's bushfire strategy.' The commission delivered an interim report in August, in time to influence preparations for the coming fire season, which begins next week. The public hearings, streamed live over the internet, have been avidly followed, and the sense that many Victorians had that they can manage the risks of fire has started to seem dangerously close to complacency.

The commission asked people how they had heard about and tracked the fire. Had they used mobile phones or landlines? Were they listening to the radio or watching the TV? Did they text their neighbours, or check official web sites, or dial 000 (the Australian equivalent of 911)? Despite a bristling network of communications technology across the state, when the fire came many people found themselves completely alone. Witnesses described emergency calls that were never answered, and one that was answered by an operator a thousand miles away in Queensland, who had no idea that there even were bushfires in Victoria. Communication failures also occurred between agencies and up and down lines of command. Fire crews repeatedly called for backup that never came. A radio station of the Australian Broadcasting Corporation became a kind of emergency information service, but a number of its broadcasts were based on official reports that were inaccurate or obsolete by crucial minutes, or even hours. People checked their televisions and radios for news of a fire that they – and in many cases *only* they – could see coming toward them.

Victoria's administration is now grappling with new ways of alerting its citizens to large-scale danger. One expert has suggested making fire information available in real time via Twitter. Australia has one of the highest cell-phone-user populations in the world, and, in early March, I (along with millions of other cell-phone users in Victoria) received a text message from the Victorian police, warning of extreme fire weather over the next two days. But other government-level inefficiencies remain. For instance, the Department of Sustainability and Environment is supposed to conduct controlled fires to lower fuel loads in dense forests, but some witnesses described the incineration of streets that had seen no controlled burning for more than forty years. Residents complained that local councils required them to get permits before uprooting native plants, even trees overhanging their houses, despite fire guidelines which state that all houses in fire-prone areas need large cleared areas around them. (New laws allow Victorians to clear any plants within ten metres of their houses.)

Throughout the commission's earliest hearings, one issue dominated: the 'stay or go' policy. Culturally, this is a sensitive issue; protecting a home against fire has been an aspect of Australian life in the bush for 150 years. But over weeks of testimony it became apparent that many residents treat 'stay or go' more like 'wait and see,' either because they are complacent or because they panic once they hear the fire's roar and see the sky go dark. Leaving at the last minute is the worst possible strategy. By the time you can see the firewall, your exits may be blocked, and by fleeing you forfeit the heat shield of your home. Often, bodies are found between house and car, keys waiting in the ignition. Before Black Saturday, a study of deaths in a hundred years of Australian fires showed that the majority occurred during late evacuation. The experts behind this study told the commission that they still believed in 'stay or go' – that, as one slogan has it, 'houses protect people, and people protect houses.' But police testimony given at the royal commission indicated a worrying reversal of the usual trend: of the 173 deaths, 113 occurred *inside* houses. No evidence has yet been released to indicate whether these people were actively defending their homes or passively sheltering from the fire. If the latter, the option of staying and fighting remains at least theoretically viable. But, if investigation reveals that many people died while still fighting the fire, Black Saturday's most significant legacy may be to have exposed a fundamental limitation of the 'stay or go' policy. In California, officials currently preparing for the height of fire season have backed away from their consideration of 'stay or go,' and unanimously advocated evacuation. Even in Australia, 'stay or go' now finds fewer supporters: recently, a new scale for rating fire danger was announced, and, at the highest rating – 'code red (catastrophic)' – people are told that the safest option is simply to leave.

According to some experts, even if all systems had worked perfectly on Black Saturday, many houses might have been undefendable. The fire ecologist Kevin Tollhurst, giving evidence before the commission, said that Australian fire science tends to be based on observation of smaller fires, but that it seems increasingly likely that fire behaviour is partly a function of scale. Many experts predict that global warming – an issue that the commission will formally examine – will make fires on the scale of Black Saturday's more and more common. If that turns out to be the case, it may be that models for understanding a fire as large as the one that destroyed Marysville don't yet exist. On my last day with Ackerman, as he left me in the clubhouse of the golf course, I asked him whether his own experience defending his home had changed his opinion about the feasibility of staying to fight a fire. He turned to me. 'Should I stay or should I go?' he said, and held up a finger. 'Go! Believe me, next time I'll be the first one out.'

The New Yorker

Shoulder-Deep in the Entrails

Shane Maloney

It's four on Wednesday afternoon and I'm wandering the corridors of Parliament House trying to figure out where I am. The place is vast, a world entire, and its navigation presents a considerable challenge for the non-denizen on a temporary visa.

I arrived yesterday, come for a bit of a sniff around, collecting background for a novel way beyond deadline. I've already got what I came for – a few minutes with a handful of members, people who can draw diagrams of processes and describe situations that will become grist to my fictive mill – and I'm wondering if I can trade my cut-price ticket for an earlier flight back to Melbourne. What I don't yet know is that an accident of timing has put me in the dress circle for the biggest show in town.

Anthony Albanese is coming towards me, flanked by a pair of suits. I've met Albo, eaten with him. Something about him makes me think of a kid with a slingshot and scabby knees and a billy-cart you wish you were game enough to ride, a big winner in the marbles ring, bit of a jostler. He gives me a nod as we pass, not quite placing me. He doesn't look like he's plotting a coup, but what do I know?

My spirit-guide finds me. A repository of Labor Party history, a fountain of discretion, he wheels me around, introducing me, identifying the invisible proprieties, minding my manners, borrowing from the library on my behalf. He knows where my interests lie, in the nooks and crannies of potential happenstance that can be woven into a plot. He smooths my path into the offices of ministers and the cubicles of invisible minions, those messengerial attendants who pass unremarked through the sealed doors of confidential conclaves.

It's sixish now and I'm back in Lindsay Tanner's office, my temporary *pied-à-terre.* This is ministerial row, heavy-hitters territory, and not a mouse stirs in the corridor. If skulduggery is afoot, it treads very softly indeed.

The day is winding down and the staff in the office engine room are keeping an amused eye on the television monitors streaming Sky News. Reports of an imminent spill are getting more feverish by the minute. Journalists are interviewing journalists about what other journalists think might be happening. Arms are shoulder-deep in the entrails; reports arrive of a calf born with two heads; flights of vultures have been sighted in the evening sky.

Tanner's chief-of-staff shambles into the room, watches for a while, shrugs, joins the general badinage, does a little light job-allocation, wanders out. Mary Day, his political major-domo, lends me her desk to check my email. Nothing to see here, folks.

The television commentators keep gnawing their bone. The South Australian Right is organising the numbers, the Victorian Left ... Julia Gillard has been seen going into Kevin Rudd's office. The PM and deputy PM are having a meeting. Hold the presses.

In breaking news, Lindsay has joined Kevin and Julia in the PM's office. Not bad, considering he's three metres from me and we're off to dinner. If something doesn't happen soon, the Australian media will burst like a festering boil. Time to get out of there.

So it's down to the basement car park and into the Prius and off to a pub in O'Connor. Lindsay's driving, letting his phone go unanswered. By now, it's vibrating like a blowfly with the DTs.

We join Maria Vamvakinou, the member for Calwell, and a crew of young staffers. Lindsay does a quick check of his messages, somebody wanting to know if he'll be attending the press conference. Shrugs all round. What press conference? Lindsay doesn't bother to reply. For the next two hours, we talk about ... books. Recent reads, swapped recommendations, shared authors, the problem of finding enough time for history and fiction. He helps me shape a particular scene in the novel that I've been sweating.

Lucky he's only the federal finance minister. Back in Brumbyland, this amount of frontbench face-time would cost me thousands.

He gives me a lift to my rented room. On the way, I quiz him about the Greens' challenge to his seat. He triangulates the electoral demographics, won't be drawn on tactics. I leave him parked at the kerbside, phone to his ear.

The Victor Lodge has neither TV nor radio but the coin internet has ten minutes left on the meter. While his finance minister was helping me plot a chapter, Rudd had announced a caucus meeting for the next morning. Lindsay's car is no longer at the kerb.

So now it's nine-thirty the next morning and I'm standing behind the media scrum outside the party room. Feral cats at a mouse hole, they await their prey. Bob Ellis, X-ray visionary, is framing his cadences into a dictaphone: '… an atmosphere of desolate pity …' The door opens and the pack lunges at the party's emissary. Gillard, unopposed. Swan, deputy.

Hurble-burble, hurble-burble. No further information is forthcoming. Heave and surge. The caucus doors open on an empty room. They've escaped, gone out the other door. The flackery departs, stringing out along the corridor, bound I know not where. I'm not in the loop.

Ah-ha. The prime minister's courtyard. Security men are checking passes. Press only, and PH staff. My day visitor tag won't cut it. I pull out my notebook, merge into a cluster of pundits and sidle through. We wait in the damp air, voices muted. A historic moment. I seek portents and symbols. On cue, the cawing of a crow pierces the winter sky.

Michelle Grattan and Paul Kelly join the crowd, waxy and wrinkled as exhibits in some glass case at Madame Tussauds. What ponderous platitudes must Kelly's gigantic intellect be distilling from this moment, I wonder? What quotidian punditry is Grattan incubating? Polonius and old lace.

Rudd appears. He looks numb. He speaks slowly. The lip quivers. We watch, transfixed. He has a list, dot points of his achievements. Let it be recorded that he made worthwhile things happen, that he helped people, improved and prolonged lives. I'm proud of this, proud of that. He tries to speak from the heart. It is too late. The carapace of jargon cannot be thrown off so easily. His voice catches. The pauses grow longer. His eyes moisten. His ticker falters, replaced valve and all. We gotta zip, he finishes. Zip? Zip?

There is scant satisfaction in this. Not much pity, either. It's too late. Anyway, it's Gillard's turn. Toward the waterhole lumbers the herd.

Eleven o'clock and the party room is chockers. Press, MPs, you name it. Julia sweeps in. Swan combines the gravity of a cardinal with the air of a man who just found a $50 note on the footpath.

Gillard speaks, ticks all the boxes in our bright and admirable democracy of alarm clocks and open minds, harnessed talent and harnessed wind, teamwork and hard work, surplus budgets and brave soldiers, pulled government advertising and invitations to reciprocity. There's mention, too, of sanctuary.

A very elastic word, that.

And now the press are shouting, baying like brokers in the bourse. Fran Kelly is a corgi, straining at the leash. Barking, barking. 'Juliagillard, juliagillard, juliagillard.'

Each must have a turn, no matter that the question has already been asked and answered. Every child wins a prize. Nobody cares if the lolly has already been sucked. Gillard's full sentences are chopped into bits. It's the only language these people understand. Then it's Julia's turn to zip. She's off to see the GG, get her chit signed.

Back in Tanner's office and everybody is closeted in a meeting. Next thing we're staring up at the office television, watching Lindsay call it quits. Nobody can doubt his explanation because he is, quite simply, exactly what he appears to be. A mensch.

On the plane back to Melbourne, I find myself sitting beside a Channel Ten news presenter and her producer. They'd arrived too late for the Kevin and Julia shows and spent the afternoon doing live links to camera.

I hope I'm home in time for the late news so somebody can explain it all to me.

Inside Story

Patrick White's London

David Marr

For a time Patrick White credited a Romanian crank in the Sydney suburbs with saving his life. Dr Herman Morgenstern was treating his asthma with calcium injections and long sessions under blue lights. The results seemed miraculous. One afternoon in April 1958, White turned up at the Romanian's surgery wanting a little something to help him through the ordeal he faced that evening. Morgenstern gave him a pill and a lift to Martin Place where, at the headquarters of the Rural Bank, Patrick White was to be given the Miles Franklin Award for *Voss*. 'As it was the first time awarded,' he wrote to his friends David and Gwen Moore, 'the bull that went with it was most alarming.'

Among the television cameras and literary bores gathered in the bank's conference room was the prime minister, Bob Menzies. Genial, huge with the dewlaps of a sea lion, Menzies had been prime minister for nearly a decade. The two men shook hands. This seems to be the only time these two legends – the nation's most honoured writer and most durable prime minister – came face to face.

White's late, radical reputation might suggest this meeting was fraught with difficulty. Not at all. Though he had toyed with revolution during the war – 'We must destroy everything, everything, even ourselves,' Lieselotte cried in the Jardin Exotique of *The Aunt's Story* – such ideas had died on his return home. Revolutions were for elsewhere – particularly the Greece of his partner Manoly Lascaris – but not for Australia. Once settled in Sarsaparilla with his vegetables and dogs, the conservative instincts of his family reasserted themselves and he quickly absorbed the deep suspicion of the Left held by the Jewish refugee intellectuals who were to be another of his lifelines to civilisation.

'My political convictions do not burn,' he confessed to his cousin Peggy Garland in May 1956. Then came Suez six months later. 'It is difficult to concentrate for the stink of history just at present,' White wrote to his New York publisher Ben Huebsch on the eve of the September ceasefire. 'With the exception of a few imbeciles, everyone here is very shocked at recent events. Menzies may be supporting Eden's policy at the UN, but we most definitely are not.'

Even so, on the night they met, Menzies still had White's vote and would have it for at least another poll. White could not bring himself to support Labor's Bert Evatt, a rumpled figure of some international glamour who had also turned up at the Rural Bank to celebrate what was, at the time, one of the richest literary prizes in the world. 'I feel I would like to know Evatt,' he later confided to his friend Molly McKie. 'Menzies is, of course, showier, but one wonders how much of it is part of an act.'

The three men posed with *Voss*. Of the thousands of photographs taken of White in his long life, this is among the most gruesome. Menzies and Evatt appear to be awestruck at the sight of the novel: Menzies points and Evatt grips its spine. Between them, petrified despite all Dr Morgenstern had tried to do for him, stood Patrick White.

Menzies' enthusiasm for literature was not all show. Early in his career he had wanted to establish academies to promote Australian writing and painting. These plans foundered but from the prime minister's seat on the Commonwealth Literary Fund he promoted writers who shared his old-fashioned taste and sabotaged the prospects of modernists and leftists. Menzies considered those vices went hand in hand. At his direction the Australian Secutity Intelligence Organisation, ASIO, vetted all who sought assistance from the fund. Menzies discreetly vetoed grants to communists, fellow travellers and radicals – particularly radical Aborigines.

A fortnight before the shindig at the Rural Bank, Menzies had scuppered support for a writer thought, by the fund's literary assessors, to show 'brilliant promise.' But ASIO had detected evidence of communist sympathies in his university years. Menzies decided the issue for himself. He read the man's first, fine novel, *Boys in the Island*, and declared it had 'all the worst defects of what is called, I believe, "the modern idiom."' Christopher Koch would win the Miles Franklin twice, but while Menzies remained in office he was denied all official support.

Luckily White never had to go cap in hand to the Commonwealth Literary Fund. The cause of modernism in Australia – not that White saw it as a cause or called it modernism – drew strength from the fortune of White's family. His writing always rode on the sheep's back. He welcomed the £500 cheque from Miles Franklin's trustees and told the press he would spend it on a hi-fi set and a stove. But he didn't need the money. He could not be touched by the guardians of Australia's official taste. Menzies had no hold over him.

The old fraud had not read *Voss*. I've searched the Menzies archive for any trace of the speech he made that night. There are notes for his address a few days earlier marking the centenary celebrations of the NSW Cricket Association and a speech he gave a few days later to businessmen in Hobart. But nothing for the Miles Franklin. It seems he was speaking off the cuff. 'Mr Menzies said Australia was achieving some degree of maturity in the novel,' reported the *Sydney Morning Herald*. 'It was growing away from an excessive attention to earthy humour and an emphasis on the Australian scene, and beginning to explore the psychological aspects of character.'

If *Voss* is not an exploration of 'the Australian scene,' *Moby-Dick* is not about whaling. But misjudged as Menzies' remarks were, they point to a determination both men shared not to be bound by the Australian scene. They knew the country in their bones. It was the deep subject matter of their lives. But they were patriots committed to a wider word. Both were members of an unacknowledged tribe: Australians who loved England and saw themselves as Londoners.

Menzies had the romantic affection of a man who did not see the white cliffs until he was forty-one. Years later he would note in his diary 'the usual palpitations' at seeing the coast of Britain once more after a voyage from Australia. Patrick White, on the other hand, was born in England, went to school and university there; discovered sex in London and had his first literary triumphs there. His affection was not sentimental. He complained about London all his life, with the love and despair of a native.

A few days after collecting his prize winnings – and writing half a dozen letters about the occasion to friends all over the place – White set off with Lascaris on a long journey which had London as its final destination. He had not seen the city for a decade. 'I wonder how I succeeded in living in it for so long, overlooking so much,' he wrote to the Moores. 'It is so terribly dirty, ugly, the people so drab – also ugly and dirty – the women like uncooked dough, the men so often suggestive of raw veal.'

White never doubted that returning to Australia after the war was of fundamental importance to him as a man and an artist. The alternative, he wrote in his endlessly quoted essay 'Prodigal Son,' was 'remaining in what I then felt to be an actual and spiritual graveyard, with the prospect of ceasing to be an artist and turning instead into that most sterile of beings, a London intellectual.'

That he made such a fanfare of his escape, and grizzled so much every time he visited the city later in his life, has encouraged us to overlook the importance London always had in White's life and writing. This mistake is encouraged also by an odd quirk of Australian multiculturalism. We pride ourselves on recognising the enriching benefits of Italian Australians maintaining links with the Venetia or Sicily of their families even some generations on. Ditto Chinese Australians keeping in touch with Guangzhou and Hong Kong. But when Britain is the old home, Australians who keep such contact alive are thought a little odd: snobs perhaps, relics of a lost age, empire sentimentalists like Menzies.

Even in his most reclusive years in Sarsaparilla, White never lost contact with London. He used a London bookshop and each week a rice-paper edition of the *Observer* arrived at the house on Showground Road. Piles of rustling airmail *Observers* were a mark of civilisation in the better houses of Australia. White's was one. His letters were alive with references to stories read in the *Observer.* He loved the photographs.

'Thank you for letters and the Asprey catalogue,' he wrote to Geoff and Ninette Dutton in the 1970s. 'It is really surprising that such expensive toys are made in present-day England; one wonders who would buy them: perhaps some of those faces one sees in the business section of the *Observer*. However, I must say some of the jewels appeal to me. I shall always be a sucker for jewels and furs; if I were a woman I expect I should have become the most rapacious kind of cocotte, and probably would have got stoned for wearing bird-of-paradise plumes on top of everything else.'

It irked White enormously that the most hostile reviews of his work in England always seemed to appear in the *Observer*. It seemed a poor way to repay a loyal reader on the far side of the world. He saw plots, even the malignant hand of Clive James, behind these unhappy notices. Angus Wilson's review of *The Twyborn Affair* in 1979 was an exception. It was, he told his New York publisher Alan Williams, 'the first time in decades that I haven't been done dirt in the *Observer*.'

His return in 1958 was followed by visits every three or four years for the next twenty years, experiencing growing delight while making the same old complaints: plain faces, poor food, shocking prices, ugly streets and nosey journalists. That he felt so at home in London he confessed freely in letters to friends and publishers, but he chose a remarkable occasion to make his feelings plain to the world. The day after the news broke that he had won the Nobel Prize – as Australia was claiming Patrick White as its own – he told the press: 'I feel what I am, I don't feel particularly Australian. I live here and work here. A Londoner is what I think I am at heart but my blood is Australian and that's what gets me going.'

He put it less politely in private. After not hearing from his old lover Pepe Mamblas for twenty-five years or more, the now Duke of Baena wrote to congratulate him on the prize. White replied: 'Two years ago we were in Europe, but like it less and less. London, parts of the French provinces, and the mountains of Greece are all I want to see again. I am at heart a Londoner, only by fate an Australian; I imagine it's like being born with a hump or a clubfoot: one has to put up with it.'

*

White believed the time and place of births mattered for everyone: to be born a Gemini, for instance, gave him in his own mind an affinity with Pushkin, Henry Lawson and Marilyn Monroe. That he was born in London meant a great deal to him and he declared his few months there before he embarked with parents and nanny for Australia in September 1912 were 'a formative period.'

His childhood was spent among Australians of a certain class who believed themselves as at home in London as they were in Sydney or Melbourne. For most it was a delusion – a delusion White would explore in his novels – but for many it was absolutely true. Their lives were spent in big houses in Australia and big houses over there. Marriages were made. Australian money put lead on British roofs. White's mother Ruth would set up home in London after the war and pour a little of her fortune into Glyndebourne. Being Australian and being children of the empire was not thought the least contradictory in those years. At least in the white dominions, the ethos of the British empire was an empire of equals.

The boy was back in London at the age of thirteen on his way to school. The 1920s was the last decade in which the Australian rich in large numbers gambled with the lives of their children in English boarding schools. Young Patrick was one of those damaged by the experience and emerged with a wary suspicion of the human race and a connoisseur of bullying in all its nuances.

'My four years at boarding school in England were such hell, I shouldn't wish it for any child I know,' he told his niece Alexandra Bishop. 'The only thing I can say in favour of them is that, when anything particularly awful was happening during the war, like the Blitz in London, or when one was being shot up or bombed in the Western Desert, or escaping into Tobruk in the dark, I used to tell myself: at least none of this is quite so bad as the years at Cheltenham, because the enemy is only trying to destroy one's body, not the part that matters.'

Australian boarding schools in the 1920s were as capable as Cheltenham College of breaking a boy. White never saw that the philistine values he so despised in his schooldays were one and the same with the philistine values he would excoriate back home.

Along with the language, the crown, the Westminster system and the common law, those Philistine instincts are Britain's enduring legacy to Australia. It's a common bond we strangely fail to celebrate.

What only London could give the boy was theatre and it was through the West End that White fell in love with the city while he was still a schoolboy. With Ronald Waters, a stage-struck friend in the same boarding house, White spent hours concocting shows, designing stage sets, and writing away for the autographs of actresses. One of their contemporaries in the house, Ragnar Christophersen, remembered the boys gathering after the Christmas holidays one year to boast how many shows they'd all seen. 'We asked Paddy once and I remember he had been to thirty, which meant he must have been to the theatre or cinema on some days at least twice.'

White's first and enduring literary ambition was to have a great success in the West End. Though he bitched all his life about his family's malign attitude to his career, he finally admitted to me, as he read through the manuscript of my biography – in front of me, slowly, over nine agonizing days – that being a playwright had also been his mother Ruth's ambition for him: to be another Somerset Maugham, the next Galsworthy. After Cheltenham and a couple of years jackerooing in Australia – to see if, indeed, he might be suited for the land – and then three years in Cambridge, White came down to London in 1935, found a room in Ebury Street and began to write plays.

We know so much more – perhaps too much – of his early efforts now that his notebooks from that time have reached the National Library of Australia. *Miracle* was perhaps his first:

> A child in the East End claims to have seen the virgin and can show stigmata. After some time the child, tormented by her conscience, confesses to fraud. The effect on the various personages. The cabinet minister who has given up his career for a life of contemplation as a result. His mistress who has also converted. How are they to react?

There was a handsome Jesuit involved somehow in the plot and a rather blowsy upper-crust woman wearing mauves and purple who would wander in and out of White's work for the next fifty years.

Nothing came of the unknown number of plays he wrote in his Ebury Street years: *Marriages Are Made in Hell*, *It Is a Pity He Is Blind*, *How Many Virgins*, etc. But his love of theatre survived all setbacks and disappointments. He saw everything. After Ralph Richardson came to lunch at his house in Sydney in the 1970s, White wrote to his publisher, Tom Maschler: 'All these old actors grow quite pop-eyed when they hear all the plays I have seen them in, because of course I was in London all through the Thirties, and not somewhere like Goondiwindi as is commonly thought.'

A couple of his poems appeared in magazines but his first success of any note was a revue sketch called 'Peter Plover's Party,' a monologue for a flibbertigibbet performed by Cyril Richard for over a year in *Nine Sharp*:

> I read your last. It was such fun. Though personally, I don't think the woman would have eaten the potato. She would have kept it as a souvenir. Just a psychological point. And of course, your style's becoming a joy. So delightfully raw.

Early success in revue marked for life his writing for the stage. He had seen Strindberg and Wedekind, admired the German expressionists and absorbed Racine, but from *The Ham Funeral* all the way to *Shepherd on the Rocks*, his plays were flavoured by the spirit and conventions of revue: knockabout figures, song and dance, and direct address in the unmistakeable voice of the writer himself.

White's London was a few blocks round Ebury Street, not a celebrated address, but somewhere convenient and quite respectable, within walking distance of more distinguished quarters of the town where its population of writers, actors, harlots, painters, aristocrats, antique dealers and refugees aspired to live on the way up or once lived on the way down. A handful of the characters around Ebury Street – most, as it happens, refugees – would inhabit the Jardin Exotique of *The Aunt's Story* and the grey world of that grey second novel, *The Living and the Dead*.

Where should the blue plaque go? Not in Ebury Street itself but round the corner on 13 Eccleston Street – now a bar – where he had taken a flat above the studio of the Australian modernist and fabulist Roy de Maistre. Though something like twice White's age, the painter was both his lover and mentor. He had a way of seducing then persuading young men of artistic bent to take themselves seriously. Francis Bacon was another of his protégés. De Maistre encouraged Bacon to abandon furniture design for painting. White, meanwhile, turned the top two floors of the house into a small modernist triumph with furniture all by Bacon.

Here is an important point for biographers: that two famous gay men knew each other in their early lives is not proof they have ever leapt into bed together. As far as I have been able to discover, neither White nor Bacon ever claimed to have had that pleasure with each other. They were friends for a long time until White became overawed by Bacon's fame. He wrote unforgettably of Bacon having in these early London years 'a beautiful pansy-shaped face and rather too much lipstick. He lived in a house at the Chelsea end of Ebury Street, not far from the Mozart house, with an old Nanny who used to shoplift when they were hard up.'

The transformation de Maistre worked on White was to persuade him to put aside his ambition to be the next Galsworthy to work on a novel sketched in his jackerooing years back home. This was *Happy Valley*, the novel that made White's name. 'I began to write from the inside out when Roy de Maistre introduced me to abstract painting,' White told Geoffrey Dutton. 'Before that I had only approached writing as an exercise in naturalism ... Then came the terrors of abstract painting. As far as I was concerned, it was like jumping into space, and finding nothing there at first (the same thing when one first plunges into Zen). Then gradually one saw that it was possible to weave about freely on different levels at one and the same time.'

On a rather self-consciously literary jaunt to the Atlantic coast of France to work on the final draft of *Happy Valley*, White began an affair with Pepe Mamblas, an apparently charming Fascist, later an envoy for Franco, who would introduce him to another London altogether: the London of rich and immensely snobbish homosexuals.

The role of young men from the colonies in this little world has not, I believe, had the anthropological attention it deserves. I know a little of it and recognise it in White's writing because I had an uncle Adrian who went over – after the war, as it happens, not before – and was soon living in Belgrave Place. My father was not fooled but it puzzled my mother, when she visited in 1954, that her brother was living there with a number of servants, a Rolls and no particular source of income. Adrian later told me: 'The trip wires were always out at Victoria for fresh men just off the boat from Australia and South Africa.'

White's rich gay existence revolved round the house of Malcolm Bullock MP who, after the death of his wife, the daughter of the Earl of Derby, devoted his life to theatre, gossip and the company of young men. White told me of eating opulent meals *à deux* with Bullock while the Russian empire chairs bit into his kidneys.

To Mamblas, who was leading a shadowy existence in France down near the Spanish border, White sent sharp sketches of the figures he encountered in this society. Little masterpieces like his report to Mamblas of meeting Sybil Thorndike and Lewis Casson suggest this London world is where he found a taste for social comedy that was with him for life. Indeed, this might have been its heyday. He wrote:

> I have never met an actress who acted so hard off the stage, and yet with it all, a lot of sincerity – that was what I could not understand – the queer mixture of sincerity and technique. The conversation was mostly political. They are very ardently Left. Sybil works herself into a frenzy which one suspects may develop into an epileptic fit. She sits on the edge of her chair, trying to bring out words which refuse to come, and clutching at the air as a substitute. The uncomfortable part was that I found myself also straining to sit on the edge of my chair and could almost feel my face growing into the shape of hers. Lewis Casson sat there like a block of granite against which, occasionally, she cannoned, to quiver off again. By the end of the evening I was in a state of complete awe and exhaustion.

White was not in love. There was a good deal of sex associated with this existence, but no love. He was never in love in London, not even with Mamblas. The city never represented that for him. He fell deeply in love in America in the summer of 1939 – not once but twice – when he went over to find a publisher for *Happy Valley*. Rather to his surprise, he landed Ben Huebsch of the Viking Press. Most of White's finest novels were written for this man, a New York Jew of great intellectual and moral clarity. The one thing London took a very long time to provide White was a publisher of stature. That was the role of New York for thirty years.

He fell so hard for his first American lover – a poet in Taos called Spud Johnson – that White decided he would abandon London and live in America. In this mood of farewell, he began to sketch a novel set in London which he thought would share the scale and ambition of Joyce's portrait of Dublin in *Ulysses*. He would make a quick dash back to pack his belongings and attend rehearsals for what promised to be his first play staged – *Return to Abyssinia* starring the great French actress Françoise Rosay – but then return forever to America.

War broke out. The play was cancelled but he took the berth he had on the *Vandyck* and reached England in late autumn. 'Wartime London also has its advantages,' he told Mamblas. 'Most of the rich, upholstered bores have fled into the fields, and altogether the secondary, mechanical relationships have disappeared out of one's life.'

The novel was proving long, shapeless and murky. Years later he realised he had dived into it far too soon, thinking to himself: 'Ah, I am a writer now! Quick, I must write another.' He blamed the war only partly for what he rated his worst novel. The real fault, he told the novelist Thea Astley many years later, was haste. 'The idea had been in my mind for some time. I wanted to write a book about London and the characters were more or less assembled. But if I had hatched the thing for several more years, it might have become the book of London, instead of just another novel, and several of the characters who remained shadowy, flickery creatures might have become living human beings.'

Almost word for word he put into the novel a little speech Mamblas had delivered as they left Malcolm Bullock's house one foggy night after a tedious dinner, a speech complaining about gay high society in London that ended with the Spanish attaché offering White 'the choice of the two ways, of the living and the dead.' He told Mamblas that would be the novel's title.

Asthmatic and Australian, not yet wanted for the war and still free to travel, White returned to New York to be reunited with his second great American passion, a Manhattan doctor from the Deep South. He finished the deliberately abbreviated version of the novel and gave it to Huebsch in June 1940. White still imagined himself living the rest of his life in America but he had to face the war. It was another of the defining decisions of his life. Auden, whom he never met and always disliked, stayed on in New York. White returned to fight, not to Australia but to London.

*

'The Blitz in Patrick White' would be a great Ph.D subtitled something like: 'A Redeeming Fire.' The bombing of London was one of the great imaginative events of his life, in which he formed a new and deeper attachment to the city. He was no longer a dilettante observer – or not only that – but a survivor among the craters, immensely stimulated by the fire raining from the sky.

White was at the Café Royal with a young director, John Wyse, the night the bombing began. 'The eastern sky was ablaze, fire engines clanging,' White wrote in *Flaws in the Glass*. 'It was not yet dark. The west was a cold ice-green as opposed to the Wagnerian glow eastwards, the play of light paradoxical as our world was turned upside down ...' He and Wyse were thrown to the ground on Ebury Street as a bomb hit Victoria. A soldier offered them his helmet as shelter. The two fops made it to Eccleston Street and fucked under the bed. Wyse told me he had never seen White so carefree.

They had survived the blaze that destroyed the Jardin Exotique and spared Himmelfarb 'the amazed Jew' who 'walked unharmed beneath the chariot wheels.' This was the same fire that consumed the ex-bawd Eddie Twyborn – back in trousers but with too much make-up like the early Francis Bacon – crossing London to join his mother at the Connaught.

And the blitz gave birth to *Voss*. At some point in those apocalyptic weeks, sitting in his room swigging Calvados as the bombs fell, White read the journal of the explorer Edward John Eyre, a young man who walked across the Nullarbor in the early 1840s. Eyre was a name known from White's childhood, but he was now 'electrified' by this account of a romantic's journey through a landscape set on destroying him. The journal gave White an itch to see Australia again and the vague ambition to write a novel about an explorer.

'We now live almost exclusively in the cellars and basements at night,' he wrote to Spud Johnson. But most nights he also walked the streets. 'The alternative seemed to be extinction by staying in, and the deserted streets have been very beautiful, in a white moonlight and a yellow flashing of guns.' He and the city lost their inhibitions together, for any night might be for any of them the end of the world. This was the territory of White's late masterpiece, *The Twyborn Affair.* He wrote: 'I learned a lot about the whore's mentality, and the variations on her one client, in fact the whole tragi-comedy of sex.'

The war that took White to Africa and Palestine washed him up in London again in January 1946, a civilian once again with a new suit and a new suitcase. The city was in ruins, he was hungry, his friends were stuck in ruts. De Maistre had turned into a high-society Catholic with delusions of royal connection. But here was yet fresh evidence for the 'redeeming fire' thesis: de Maistre lost a cousin when a buzz bomb hit the Chelsea Barracks. His painting *The Aunt* was based on a photograph he found of her in the rubble. The painting helped clarify the purpose of White's next novel, one he had been planning in one form or another for ten years. He bought the painting and began *The Aunt's Story.*

The novel was his companion and shelter as he began another of his epic explorations: a visit to Australia to see whether that was where he and Lascaris might live. 'I landed here after fourteen years' absence, and immediately realised how Australian I have been all the time underneath,' he told Mamblas. 'Even the uglier aspects of the place have their significance and rightness to me, though I expect if you came here, a real European, you would be rightly appalled. But I am enjoying relaxing with my instinct after a long session with my reason.'

But something compelled him to return to London. This expensive, complicated journey was made ostensibly to sell his furniture and collect his dogs. But I believe he wanted to see the city one more time to be absolutely sure of his decision. He felt no happy palpitations when he arrived after a long journey in the hold of a troop ship. 'It costs a fortune just to exist – doing nothing and eating filth in what used to be the cheap restaurants – though from the one meal I ate at the Ritz, I should say filth prevails. Most of the people one sees look ill, tired, hopeless, or just dull and apathetic. There seems to be a restriction on everything one attempts to do. And it is not as if one felt there was an end to it, and that one would get somewhere someday. I can see no future at all for England, and advise anyone I know to leave it.'

The one oasis in London was the West End and it rekindled his old ambition to be a playwright. Waiting to get out of England once again, he wrote *The Ham Funeral.* It was his farewell to London, and to the callow young man he had been before the war: a poet growing up and fighting his way out of the smothering embrace of his landlady, Alma Lusty, and her great, damp, crumbling house. 'Send us a pitcher post-card now and agen,' she calls as he makes a break for freedom. 'Let's know you're alive and kickin! But write plain.'

*

White's ambitions were huge. What he found on his return to the other side of the world was crucial to everything that followed. But so was everything he brought in his luggage: London standards and taste, and the ambition to be a writer who would speak not to Australia alone but to the world. He brought all he had learned of the human heart in war and peace on Ebury Street, in Belgravia and the West End. He saw himself as a man of understanding in a country that did not understand. Though he felt both immediately at home and a stranger in Sarsaparilla, he was – like so many figures in the novels that would come – the stranger in the know.

He had also absorbed into his own imagination the history of the Lascaris family, a history of ruin after ruin, exile after exile. Counting the Byzantium of Manoly's supposed ancestors, the family had been expelled centuries ago from Constantinople and Nicea, a generation earlier from their rich existence in Smyrna and in the late 1940s from the disappearing Greek city of Alexandria. Both men were exiles from cosmopolitan cities they loved, an exile from which, frankly, they took a certain masochistic pleasure. And distance would allow White to imagine Smyrna, Nicea, Alexandria and London more freely than had they lived there still.

He stuck it out. Survived miserable years of doubt. Renewed his name in the literary world with *The Tree of Man* and became famous with *Voss*. He returned to London on that first visit in 1958 a literary celebrity. White feared fame but allowed himself in London to live briefly every few years the life of a literary celebrity: being feted by publishers, 'fending off' the press, throwing himself into the 'whirl' of the city from which he sent home reports of meetings with the famous and curious. This to the Duttons in 1971:

> We lunched with the Charles Johnstons ... and in addition to the Princess Bagration had Princess Aly Khan and Diana Duff Cooper! The latter still has a very blue stare, but by now is rather crippled and wafty: she told us a long and tangled story about a pair of gorillas having sex in a private zoo for the entertainment of a number of Bright Old Things.

London delighted both White and Lascaris as a city of amazing stories and strange encounters. A passion for gossip and human peculiarity was one of the strong bonds in their marriage. But Lascaris found other aspects of their visits less entertaining. It irritated him that his partner, so mean in Sydney, would spend so lavishly in London. He thought it a little vulgar, with the taint of the colonial made good. And White's determination to go to London every time they travelled also irritated him. White could say the next trip would be devoted to exploring Greece or spending time with the Lascaris family and friends in America, but London was always the real objective.

London meant theatre. Every visit rekindled passions Lascaris would like to see wither and die. He feared theatre as a distraction from White's real mission as a novelist. But with the appetite of a schoolboy, White dragged him to everything. He never returned to the city without a play or a film to sell.

In 1958 he brought from his desk drawer *The Ham Funeral*. No luck. He revised it a little before their next London visit in 1963. No luck again. With him on that visit he had also brought the scripts of *Night on Bald Mountain* and *The Season at Sarsaparilla* hoping to snare a London management. Still no luck. White was surprised and hurt when at the last minute the Mermaid Theatre rejected *Sarsaparilla* as indecent. Australians would gasp at the decadence of London theatre, he told his old friends the Moores. 'They have just no idea what goes on – if it isn't adultery, it's incest, abortion, up-your-jacksie Queen Elizabeth – and the language – by this time the bloodys have given way to the fucks.'

White never bothered with London cinema on the grounds that good films always reached Australia – but not those that might fall foul of Australia's long night of censorship. So in London one year he took himself off to see Joe Dallesandro in Andy Warhol's *Flesh*. 'For the first time I saw a nude erection on the screen,' he wrote to an old queen in the bush. 'And a very handsome one it was.'

One of White's great fears when he went out to Australia was that he would, without knowing it, lose the absolute standards he had absorbed in London. Books reached Sarsaparilla, of course, but not London conversation and only rarely the writers in whose company White placed himself. London visits reassured him that his standards weren't slipping. He held off beginning new novels – *Riders in the Chariot* was boiling up in 1958 – or beginning second drafts of novels – *The Eye of the Storm* in 1971 – until he had tested himself once again in London.

The Eye of the Storm was another of his works born in London. The sombre purpose of the 1963 visit had been to see his ailing mother for what he knew would be the last time. Ruth was dying, in state, in a luxurious flat in Rutland House, nearly blind but still ruling the staff from her bed. The hostility between them died away. They had wonderful long conversations. It came to White as he was crossing Kensington High Street one day that this would make a novel he must write. *The Eye of the Storm* would be set in Sydney – in his own house above Centennial Park – but later he also turned this last reconciliation of mother and son into the 'many delightful conversations, others more disquieting' of Eadie and Eadith Twyborn in the wartime Connaught Hotel.

White had it in for the Connaught. One year, with great care, his publisher had booked a table for lunch. It was at a time when the hotel was hugely fashionable and the booking had been made months in advance. But Manoly Lascaris was wearing a skivvy under his jacket. The headwaiter offered 'sir' a tie. White declared: 'You are not going to treat my friend like a dog on a lead' and led the party out.

London, dirty in 1958, filthy in 1963, squalid in 1968 – the formula White used in dozens of letters was 'filth almost equal to Istanbul' – seemed miraculously spruce in 1971. The new prosperity of Britain was not the only explanation. White was feeling particularly wonderful about the city because he had at last found a great London publisher.

Back before the war, his first had rejected *The Living and the Dead*. The second refused to take *The Tree of Man*, which was rejected by about twenty publishing houses before Ben Huebsch fixed him up with Eyre & Spottiswoode. Try as they might, the E & S team never excited White. Rumours in the late 1960s that he was looking for a new publisher provoked an orgy of flattering attention. White toyed briefly with the idea of finding an Australian publisher, but he was just making mischief. With the Commonwealth publishing cartel still firmly in place, London houses ruled the Australian market. White had no patriotic objections.

Harold Macmillan called at Centennial Park to recruit him for the family firm. The two men spent an hour talking about Mount Athos. But Macmillan was pipped at the post by Jonathan Cape. 'I can't think of a living author I would rather publish than Patrick White,' Cape's Tom Maschler told White's agent. 'If you gave me the choice between publishing Graham Greene and publishing Patrick White, I would choose Patrick White any day – and then the statement is almost an insult to White.'

Maschler and then his colleague Graham Greene (the *other* Graham Greene) became the demanding audience for whom he wrote his last – and some of his finest – novels, beginning with *The Vivisector* in 1970. Maschler and Greene opened the highest reaches of literary London to him. The old claim of his class proved true for Patrick White in the Jonathan Cape years: he had never felt so at home in London. In that mood he made the rather shocking admission, when the good news came through from Stockholm in 1973, that he was, at heart, a Londoner.

He was reasserting his ambiguous vision of himself: prophet and gossip, novelist and playwright, man and woman, Australian and Londoner. He was drawing on a fundamental conviction – as a patriot and an artist – that chauvinism is bad. Ever since Australian critics had condemned his early novels as un-Australian, White mocked literary nationalism. Now at this moment of triumph he was asserting his absolute freedom as an artist. No fashion, no literary school and no country could claim him as its own.

White won the Nobel Prize and Bob Menzies became Lord Warden of the Cinque Ports with an admiral's uniform and an apartment in Walmer Castle. Menzies couldn't have been happier. After a few years and a couple of strokes he retired from public life while remaining an active adviser to his party in the looming constitutional confrontation with the new prime minister, Labor's Gough Whitlam. White had long since given his vote to Labor. As for so many, his breach with the conservatives had come with the Vietnam War. The breach was angry. Whitlam was his political hero. On one last issue, White and Menzies saw eye to eye: to the eternal credit of the former prime minister, he advised his party not to block supply in 1975. He was ignored.

*

White was not done with London. There was one more book and one more visit in the spring and summer of 1976. 'London is still my favourite place for living,' he wrote to Manning Clark. And to Geoffrey Dutton: 'London is in my bones and I can't tear myself away from it.' Early one morning, White left his hotel in Wilbraham Place to explore his old stamping ground: the region between Ebury Street and the Thames where, in an imagined Beckwith Street, the light glimmering off the water, he would place the red-brick façade of Eadith Trist's whorehouse.

The Twyborn Affair is the London novel White had been hatching for forty years, familiar territory revisited with absolute candour and absolute mastery. Here the all-knowing Eudoxia/Eddie/Eadith is pitted against the conventional and timid of two worlds, of here and there, of England and Australia. This was not the London he visited as a literary celebrity but the city in which he had discovered himself so long before, where he might have died, as Eddie Twyborn does, on the blazing first night of the Blitz.

> Down one of the dark tributary streets came a young soldier in battle dress and tin hat. He reached the corner in time to fall head on, making almost a straight line on the pavement, with this character from a carnival or looney bin. The young man seemed to be trying to share the brim of his protective hat with one who could hardly remain a stranger. 'Something happening at last, eh?'

The nurse rang me at 5.45 a.m. on 30 September 1990 to say Patrick had died earlier that morning. Manoly came on the line: he wanted me to ring people. Among them was my friend Anne Chisholm, who was working in London on the biography I had finished only a few months before. What I didn't know at that early hour was that Patrick had made an absurd request that the press not be told of his death until his ashes were scattered. By the time I rang back to beg Anne to keep the news to herself, her husband, the great journalist Michael Davie, had rung Fleet Street. It was on the wires. Though absurd it was somehow absolutely right that the news of Patrick White's death should reach Australia from the city that shaped him, the city he most loved, his other home, London.

The 2010 Menzies Lecture

Ten Myths of Australian Crime

Mark Dapin

Most crime in Australia is spiralling out of control, downwards. Our murder rate is near a historic low. Burglaries have collapsed. Car theft is disappearing. Armed robbers rarely rob banks and drug-addicted street thieves are not stabbing anyone with syringes. Little old ladies living at home alone are among the safest people in society. They are not targeted by roving gangs of feral kids, or anyone else much, apart from overseas internet fraudsters. Our police cells are not clogged with hard-drug users, and haven't been for almost a decade. Horrible, life-shattering, violent events do happen every day, but not to many people and, more crucially, not to many people over twenty-five years old.

The angry old men of talkback radio play up to an ageing audience's fear of crimes that are highly unlikely to affect them. It's crude, cruel and popular entertainment, with only the softest grounding in the reality of risk.

Good Weekend visited the undistinguished but secure-looking headquarters of the Australian Institute of Criminology (AIC) in the public-service ghetto of Griffith, ACT, and spoke to its experts in every field from homicide monitoring to firearms theft, in Sydney, Melbourne and Canberra, to get the real picture of crime in Australia, and address ten myths.

1. The murder rate is rising

It seems as if there is more murder because there is more

media. Every discovered homicide is reported in every available detail. Murder trials last for weeks or months and every claim is tested. The worst media linger over the pornography of death: blood on the bludgeon, the desperate struggle, the final gasp for breath.

But in 2008, only 260 Australians – out of a population of about 21.5 million – were murdered. Although this was a rise of five murders on 2007, numbers have tumbled since 1999, when 344 people were killed. Rates were at their peak in the late '70s and '80s, when two people in every 100,000 could expect to be murdered. The figure is now 1.2 in every 100,000. (By comparison, you are almost five times more likely to be murdered in the US.)

It used to be that most victims were murdered by their friends and acquaintances, but there has been an inexplicable drop in amicicide in Australia, which has left 'intimate partner' homicides at the top of the table.

'Why friends are now suddenly not killing each other as frequently as they were ten years ago is not something we've been able to identify in any meaningful way,' says Jason Payne, of the AIC's national homicide-monitoring and drug-use-monitoring programs.

Payne is a master of AIC speak, which is always heavily qualified and duly weighted, but differs from standard Canberra bureaucratese in that its aim is to illuminate the truth rather than obscure it. Most people here talk in long, considered sentences, with chains of clauses all linked to relentlessly logical, unemotional conclusions. They examine percentages, ratios and deviations to analyse how and why – and indeed whether – Australians are being killed, raped and robbed.

Only 12 per cent of homicides involved the use of a gun. The number of Australians dying of gunshot wounds has decreased since the 1996 National Agreement on Firearms, but the rate was already falling before it was introduced. There is debate as to whether the legislation has contributed to the decline in gun murders, but it has certainly halved the number of firearms reported stolen (from about 4000 a year in the 1990s to about 2000).

'Mind you,' says Samantha Bricknell, author of the AIC's *Firearms Theft* and *Facts and Figures* series, 'we're not really finding any improvements in compliance. We're still finding about

40 per cent of owners are being recorded by police as not being storage compliant.'

Police recover 12 to 13 per cent of stolen firearms. 'But we don't really know what happens to the rest,' says Bricknell. 'Our data, while probably an underestimate, has shown that in any given year, firearms from about 2 per cent of theft incidents are then known to be associated with a criminal offence.' (The 2008 figures include three suicides.)

There are about 765,000 gun owners in Australia, with about 2.5 million registered firearms – and probably the same number of unregistered weapons – but, says Bricknell, 'You're more likely to be killed by someone punching you in the face than being shot. We've got a lot of firearms in the country, but I don't think we're a particularly violent bunch.' Recent events in Sydney and Melbourne show that if you are a professional criminal (that is, you get caught a lot) or an associate, there's a chance you'll be shot at by business rivals, but professionals are generally not interested in targeting outsiders.

2. Little old ladies aren't safe in the streets ...

Our worst fears and deepest sympathies are spared for the most helpless: the frail aged who have already lived through so much – poverty, war, widowhood, grief – only to end up as easy targets for drug-addicted wild boys who'll bash them over their head for the change in their purse.

But most street robbers do not target vulnerable old people, partly because there is not much point. An old lady is unlikely to be carrying an iPod, iPhone or anything else they could easily use or on-sell. Out of the 5228 people who reported being victims of an armed robbery in 2007 – and most armed robberies are reported – only forty of them were women over sixty-five.

Also, older people tend not to be out between 6 p.m. and 6 a.m., when two-thirds of armed robberies occur. Most victims of so-called 'muggers' are not little old ladies but big young men.

'With the exception of kids aged zero to fourteen,' says AIC research analyst Lance Smith, 'the group of Australians that experiences the lowest rates of robbery victimisation is women aged fifty-five and over.'

In 2007, in those states for which the AIC has comprehensive data, only 3 per cent of people robbed at knifepoint suffered a serious injury. The injury – and it is classified as an injury – most often reported by robbery victims is trauma. But if victims had realised how little danger of serious injury they faced, the experience might have been less traumatic.

3. … or in their homes

By global standards, Australian homes seem well defended. People bar the windows of their terrace houses and draw steel shutters across timber fronts. They fear the intimacy of burglary, a stranger assessing their possessions, foreign hands on family heirlooms, crawling noises in the night.

But the rate of reported burglaries in Australia has plummeted by 40 per cent over the past twelve years – and burglary is another crime police usually get to hear about, if only because victims have to fill out a police report to make an insurance claim. Not much time has been spent looking into reasons for the happy decline of burglary (research money tends to flow towards crimes that are rising) but many people have made their homes more secure.

There were never many people in the burgling game, anyway. 'About 5 to 10 per cent of the offending population are responsible for 50 to 60 per cent of property crimes committed,' says Payne. And only a very small proportion would target the elderly. 'If you knew an old person lived in a house,' says Kelly Richards, the AIC's juvenile justice expert, 'you would know that most of their stuff is not actually very desirable. They probably don't have a plasma-screen TV, a great laptop, a digital camera … The sorts of things that get bumped off really don't feature in older people's houses.'

According to the Royal Automobile Club of Victoria, which insures both home contents and cars, the most stolen item in Victoria in 2009 was the digital camera, and the number of claims rose for laptops and games terminals such as PlayStation and Wii. Watches, phones, jewellery and sunglasses were also among thieves' favourites.

And, according to the AIC, although motor-vehicle theft has fallen by 44 per cent in the past twelve years, there were still 68,270 cars, trucks and bikes reported stolen in Australia in 2008.

4. Most criminals are hard-drug users

'You hear that drugs are fuelling a lot of crime out there, the burglaries and other things, because people are trying to fence the material to get money to buy drugs,' says AIC director Adam Tomison, a man who, before he took up his current post, acted as adviser for the Northern Territory's 'Little Children Are Sacred' Board of Inquiry into the Protection of Aboriginal Children from Sexual Abuse. 'But drug-related arrests have come down by 8 per cent since 1996–97.'

The number of criminals caught carrying drugs has fallen, too. For ten years, the AIC's Drug Use Monitoring Australia program has looked at eight different police lock-ups across the country, drug-tested detainees and interviewed them about their recent drug use. The tests are voluntary, the results are confidential, and the researchers sometimes hand out Mars Bars.

'Interestingly enough, the detainees don't mind it,' says Jason Payne. 'There was a lot of scepticism about the number who'd be willing to participate, but we get 70 to 80 per cent of people agreeing to tell us, and then about 80 per cent of those people supply us with urine. So it's huge in terms of compliance rates, and certainly unexpected for a criminal-justice system project.'

The results, says Payne, show that 'heroin [use] nationally is at the lowest it's been for some time'. Early in 2001 – when Australian heroin use was around its historic peak – there was a sudden heroin shortage, which led to an increase in the price and decrease in the purity of the drug.

'Within the space of three or four months,' says Payne, 'the number of our detainees who tested positive for heroin went down from around 40 per cent to 16 per cent. What we've seen in our data since that time is pretty much a stabilisation of roughly 10 to 15 per cent of detainees testing positive to heroin in the Sydney site.'

There was a sudden, unsustained increase in cocaine use, but no one really knows whether heroin users cleaned up or switched drugs. Amphetamine use increased from about 1999 to 2006, but has subsequently declined by about 5 to 10 per cent across most sites.

The AIC study does not distinguish between 'ice' and other amphetamines, so it's difficult to say whether there really is an 'ice epidemic.' 'Fewer people in police custody are using any kind of amphetamine,' says Payne, 'but we don't know what the relative proportion of amphetamine types are within that. We ask our detainees whether they've heard of any new drugs for sale on the street and, even to this day, we get detainees telling us they've heard of a new drug called "ice," but that may be because of the media coverage.'

5. One in two women has experienced sexual violence

'If you want to go for the most sensationalist aspect, you could say one in two women has been sexually assaulted in some sense,' says Tomison. 'That would include non-contact offences.'

Australia suffers from horrific rates of sexual violence, and sexual assault is one of the crimes least likely to be reported. But reported sexual assaults increased by 51 per cent between 1995 and 2008, and in 2009 police recorded 18,800 victims of the crime, 84 per cent of whom were female. Although changes in social attitudes have led more women (and men) to take their attackers to court, these figures are still greatly understated.

The AIC considers prevalence studies more reliable than police figures. A prevalence study is a survey in which respondents are asked if they have experienced certain behaviour over a given period. About one in two women reveal they have been a victim of a sex crime at some time in their lives, and only about a third of those reported the offence.

Tabloid news loves a sexual predator, a loner stalking joggers, a family man abducting random pedestrians in a panel van, a rapist with choking fingers and charcoal eyes. But most victims of sexual assault have not been raped. In NSW, for instance, there is no offence of 'rape.' Rape is seen as part of a spectrum of behaviour that can be classified as sexual assault, the definition of which includes 'non-contact offences,' such as 'flashing' or exposing a child to pornography, as well as gang rape at gunpoint. Contact offences can include being groped in a nightclub.

Tomison stresses that even 'inappropriate touching' can traumatise someone for years, but, says Richards, 'For young women, I think you'd be hard-pressed to find somebody who hadn't been groped at a bar or had their boobs squeezed at a nightclub.'

Kelly Richards grew up in Sydney's western suburbs, haunted

by the gang-rape murders of 26-year-old Anita Cobby in 1986 and twenty-year-old Janine Balding in 1988. It was those hideous crimes that sparked her interest in criminology, but she stresses most sexual assaults now happen in the home. And between 1995 and 2005, 40 per cent of recorded sexual assaults were attacks on children under fourteen. 'Essentially, once you become twenty-five, your chance of becoming a victim of sexual assault drops dramatically,' she says.

6. Strangers are a danger

When women are raped, it is rarely at the hands of a desperate sadist lurking in an alley. Most victims are attacked by a man they know. 'The fear is all around stranger danger,' says Richards, 'but the relative risk of being attacked by a stranger is minute compared with the risk of being victimised in the home, which is actually quite substantial.' In 2008, 78 per cent of victims were assaulted by either a family member or someone else they knew, and 65 per cent were attacked in a private home (as opposed to only 7 per cent on the street).

Murder victims usually know their killers, too (since the majority are their present or former partners). Strangers commit about 30 per cent of homicides that involve males, and only about 5 per cent of those involving females. 'It's the same as assaults,' says Tomison. 'Often who's assaulting you is someone you know. There are drunken street brawls and the like, but often that's by people they know as well, in some sense.'

In the 1970s, much money and energy was expended in warning children about the risks of associating with strangers. It is now clear that while this was happening, many kids were being systematically sexually assaulted by their relatives, their teachers, their priests and their sports trainers.

So was the stranger-danger campaign an irresponsible waste of time?

'Well, it probably was, to a large extent,' says Richards.

7. All women share the same risk of domestic violence

Throughout the 1970s and '80s, various campaigns stressed that domestic violence can happen to any woman, anywhere. All relationships looked like potential prisons run by angry warders who beat their helpless captives at whim. But, statistically, all women are not at equal risk. 'It isn't just a working-class problem,' says Richards, 'but by and large, it occurs more in more socially disadvantaged communities, and, of course, where it happens the most is in indigenous communities, which are incredibly disadvantaged.'

There is no specific offence of 'domestic assault.' Much violence in the home is reported simply as assault, and assault figures in Australia are rising – between 1996 and 2008, there was a 49 per cent increase in assaults reported – but the majority of those were young men on young men.

'Young people tend to victimise each other,' says Richards, 'and the cohort of young offenders and young victims are not two separate groups at all. You might be an offender one week and victim the next.'

'It's impossible to have a conversation about crime and justice in Australia without addressing the indigenous issue,' says Richards. While the NT has the highest homicide rate per capita, AIC crime-prevention expert Peter Homel says, 'The biggest violence figures these days in NSW remain out in western NSW, particularly north-western NSW, where there is a large concentration of Aboriginal people.' Part of this is simply a question of demographics. Indigenous people tend to have more children, and the indigenous population is, on average, younger, with a lower life expectancy.

Prevalence studies suggest one in three women have survived domestic violence. However, like sexual assault – which, says Richards, 'should perhaps be called "sexual offending"' – domestic violence is now viewed as a spectrum, encompassing yells and threats as well as punches and kicks.

While Tomison is careful not to minimise the potential to intimidate and control another person with angry words, he concedes, 'The definition of domestic violence is quite broad these days. It also includes economic and social violence, if you like. In the public domain, I think the risk is that people will see it all in the one barrel, and therefore feel it's everywhere and everything's happening all the time, and perhaps overstate the situation.'

The huge majority of cases in the courts feature men attacking women, but some estimates from general population surveys show almost as many men as women are injured in domestic disputes. But there is a 'qualitative difference' in men's experience of domestic violence, says Tomison. 'Typically, the male may be assaulted in response to an assault that he's committed.' Men in an abusive relationship are generally less physically vulnerable and less financially dependent, and it's much easier for them to walk away.

8. Alcohol causes violence

Everybody knows that alcohol causes violence, because everyone has seen drunks fight in the pub, or at least heard about it, or seen closed-circuit TV footage of drunken battles on the streets of Surfers Paradise on the news.

The Australian Institute of Health and Welfare's 2007 National Drug Strategy Household Survey asked people if they had been assaulted by somebody under the influence of alcohol in the past twelve months. About 4 per cent of respondents said that, to their knowledge, they had been.

But 'one of the important things about the alcohol–violence relationship is that most people who drink aren't violent,' says Payne. 'Most people go out or drink at home and never end up in a violent altercation of any kind.'

Most people who turn violent when they're drunk are – like the majority of offenders at most levels – men under twenty-five, who tend to drink 'in environments where there is a lot of machismo and a whole range of other environmental and social characteristics which, in and of themselves, are also likely to give rise to violence,' says Payne.

'There's a very unlikely chance that two friends sitting down drinking together at home, watching television, will turn into a violent incident,' he says, 'whereas an alternative environment – loud, pumping music in a nightclub, for example, or a high-paced situation – might be more likely to result in violence.'

A study in Queensland by Ross Homel of Griffith University found that a significant amount of nightclub violence could be avoided simply by employing less aggressive bouncers, replacing glasses with plastic cups and by rearranging the interior of the building so the main thoroughfare from the street or to the toilets did not pass near the bar, so people didn't bump into each other and spill drinks so often.

Drunken violence tends to happen the most around 'entertainment precincts' where there are – unsurprisingly – a lot of pubs and bars. I meet Ross Homel's brother, Peter, in his home in Stanmore, in Sydney's inner west, our conversation awkwardly punctuated by exclamation marks dropped from planes on the Sydney Airport flight path. As the AIC's crime-prevention expert, Peter, like his brother, has given a lot of thought to entertainment-precinct violence.

'Part of the reason people are attracted to these locations is there's an edginess,' he says. 'They're about being in exciting and strange, potentially risky areas. Work my brother did around some of the nightclubs on the Gold Coast did a very good job at reducing the violence, but also made them pretty boring.'

9. Drugs cause violence

Everyone knows people go mad on drugs, leap out of windows believing they can fly, peel their skin because they think they're oranges, or generally express their hatred for the 'straight' world by going on a 'drug-fuelled rampage,' leaving behind the inevitable 'trail of destruction.'

But 'there's not a lot of evidence that links the pharmacological effects of a drug on subsequent behaviour without mediating factors,' says Payne. 'The only definitive biological link that people have identified between amphetamine – which is the main drug people talk about when they talk about violence – and violence is that after long periods of amphetamine use, people can develop a level of psychosis that makes them very paranoid and indeed alters brain chemistry, which arguably has been linked to irrational thoughts, aggressive behaviour and those sorts of things. But actually identifying a direct effect – "Take a tablet, go and commit a violent offence" – it doesn't exist.'

Their drug habit might have increased their 'need' to commit robberies, says Payne, 'but in quite a lot of cases, people who use drugs already had histories of offending, so we cannot definitively say, "Because you're a druggie, you're an offender."'

10. Computer crime is massive and widespread

New technology tends to give rise to new fears and new crimes – or at least new names for old ones. The internet has given birth to a range of potential offences including 'online grooming,' 'cyberstalking,' 'cyberbullying' and 'identity theft.' These sound much scarier than approaching a child, following a woman, throwing stones at the quiet kids or using somebody else's credit cards – but how much of a problem are they really?

Raymond Choo, the AIC's cybercrime specialist, says more than 150 people were charged with online child-sex exploitation (offenders 'grooming' children on the net) in the past financial year. Choo estimates the number of unreported offences as 'between hundreds and thousands.'

I meet Russell Smith, the AIC's authority on computer crime and fraud, at the Qantas Club in Melbourne Airport, a no-man's land of laptop-absorbed business people. 'There's a perception that electronic fraud and credit-card fraud is rife and increasing,' says Smith. 'It's actually very small.'

According to the Australian Payments Clearing Association, out of the 4.5 billion banking and credit-card transactions each year, only about 660,000 are fraudulent. The Australian Bureau of Statistics found that about 5 per cent of the population were victims of phishing scams, 'Nigerian letters' and the like. A smaller number actually gave up any money. Some transactions were huge but most only lost a few hundred dollars.

Computer crimes are relatively easy to commit but 'there's probably only a relatively small proportion of people who want to engage in that sort of stuff anyway,' says Smith. 'The opportunities are there to a greater extent than available criminals.'

The fact of the matter is, Australians are not very criminal at all. 'A good example is the way the Australian Tax Office approaches its compliance activities,' explains Russell Smith. 'They assume that the vast bulk of the population is going to be law-abiding and fill out their tax returns correctly and honestly, and won't try to do anything deceptive. If the vast bulk of the population weren't that honest, the tax system wouldn't be able to operate.'

*

Speaking personally, I have been seriously assaulted twice and hospitalised as a result. Under current definitions, I have also been sexually assaulted twice. A place where I was living has been burgled, I have had my 'identity' stolen in a credit-card fraud, and I once left the front door open and woke up to find a homeless man asleep in my bath. I have known a murderer, a burglar and a rapist. I have had knives pulled on me at least twice. But most of this happened overseas, and I guess I'm just unlucky.

Because, as much as desperate politicians and dishonest radio demagogues would like you to think otherwise, most Australians do not have much to fear from crime and, in many categories of offence, those who are most likely to fall victim to the crime are also those likeliest to commit it.

So does this knowledge help the AIC's criminologists sleep soundly?

'There's no link between people's fear and concern about crime and the reality,' says Richards. 'And I think that is the case even when you understand the reality. I know that my risk of being kidnapped, taken off the street and sexually assaulted, or somebody raiding my house with a gun, are incredibly small, but my fear and concern about that happening is much, much greater than the risk. I think that's justified, because the point for me isn't that it's incredibly unlikely to happen, it's that if it happens – and it does happen – it would have such an overwhelming effect on every aspect of your life, it is, for me, worth avoiding the risk altogether. I know that catching the train home at night is unlikely to end up with my body in a paddock, but I'd still rather stay in a hotel or get a cab.

'Some parents obviously overestimate the risk that their children will be abducted and killed or sexually assaulted, but I think – in fact, I know – even when parents understand that risk is incredibly small, they don't want to be that one in a million. And I think that's totally valid.'

Good Weekend

On Marriage

Andrew Sant

For a few weeks now there has been an entry in my diary to remind me to attend a wedding. That Saturday is now free. I have just crossed the entry out. One or, I hope, both parties have thought better of it: a third party had the job of getting the message through. A headline with, as yet, no full report. This is a personal disappointment because wedding invitations don't often come my way. I mainly seem to knock around with the sorts of people who now shun the institution, or don't give it a thought – which is not to say I don't know and am not fond of married couples. I am. I'm not against marriage outright. Some of them are, I think, happy in the loose sense that word is used to describe people who have not felt the need to untie the knot. But then, you never really know, or want to, what goes on in someone's marriage.

When detail of that kind emerges, over a drink or two for instance, and possibly at great length, the frontline report makes for grim listening. A married person, after the fourth glass of wine, rarely if ever fesses up that, years on, loving kindness, stimulating conversation and great sex reign under the mortgaged roof. The story will take a different turn altogether and, one hopes, the children, privy to the looming bust-up headline, will never, so to speak, have seriously to read on. My younger friends have pre-empted this situation. I'm not sure which requires greater courage: to marry or not to marry, given our needs. Either way, in these more enlightened times, the force of the law will, if necessary, be ready to spring into action if one of the warring parties has changed the locks in a tactical masterstroke and commandeered the assets. So, no wedding to attend, no champagne, no bountiful nosh, no speeches, in fact, possibly no hope. Unless an alternative route to a loving domestic destination has been decided upon. I hope so.

I wonder if there are marriage counsellors who have never fallen in love, never married – rather like priests who have to listen to all manner of things about which they have no personal acquaintance. I myself have lived within the institution of marriage but am no authority. It happened this way – with little fanfare. We made a booking at the registry office in Hobart, Tasmania, and pinned down a witness. Although a weekday, it was quite a busy day for weddings though, luckily, we were able to get a slot near lunchtime on the day we required. This was a day when the witness and the other guest, my father, who lived interstate, could turn up. If this sounds like a mean, though roughly accurate, guest list I should explain: all the other relatives were a hemisphere away, not in Australia – my future wife and I had met in London – and we were new in town. The ceremony was followed by drinks in a pub, we newlyweds the centre of attention, conducted in a similar optimistic spirit towards the future when we raised a glass or two together in the same bar after our divorce. Our relationship was not restricted by legal documents. But I am getting ahead. In the car park, just prior to our entering the registry building, my father took me aside and said, with all of the casualness of someone offering a boiled sweet, 'Why are you bothering to get married?' I was unprepared for this question. It was a hammer blow. As it was, I think, sometime later when, perhaps inappropriately – though truthfully – I mentioned this query of my father's to my wife, one of the most honest and understanding people I have ever met and who was then pregnant.

The answer was that we were doing it for him and the aforementioned non-libertarian relatives who couldn't attend and didn't have the contraceptive pill in their day. It was, under the cheerful circumstances, an obligation, the done thing. We, after all the generations of marriages in our families, didn't want to go it alone, cause upset, be shunned. All of a sudden, minutes prior to signing the marriage certificate, the sense we had of generational coercion appeared to be radically misplaced. It put me off my stride when going up the steps. But too late to say, 'Hey look, it appears that out of the blue we can take an alternative route,' which is what my friends may be considering now, the institution ever being reinforced by politicians, churchmen and other parties with a necessary interest in social order. Besides, those missing relatives who were, in an incorporeal way, present in large numbers, might hold an opposite view and let it be known. There is mercy in very small ceremonies.

My father's next brief words about the marriage were in the form of a statement – some years later. He was of the unswerving opinion that if a marriage ended it had failed. I could only give him half marks for this analysis – or not even that. Failed! I would express the view that an ended marriage or relationship had simply run its natural course. Unless there'd been, say, a death or disappearance. But for reasons that will become apparent I didn't say that. Clearly, in each other's eyes, neither of us was or ever would be an authority on the matter. There is professional training for marriage guidance but not, if you decide to go in for it, marriage itself. So there are a lot of people with the experience of marriage but few who can claim authority on the matter. However, if there's formative experience to be had it comes in twos: parents. Many a child would wish on occasion that a helpful person with authority, if their whereabouts were known, could step in and make sense of what was going on around them at home. I was such a one. Marriage failure was looming, if I'd known it, and its natural course had me stumped. That's how mysterious other people's marriages are, even close at hand, and the character of my parents' marriage even now.

If there is one piece of advice I would have given to my parents at the Anglican St John's church, Hampstead, London, in 1947 it would have been, 'Stop! Don't get married. Think again.' This might sound odd coming from the single issue of that marriage and with all the benefits of being alive, but then plenty of good inexpert advice is never taken. I have scrutinised the flagstones out the front of St John's, stood where my parents stood in the wedding photographs and looked out, as they did, through the main gates – through which they would that day pass into the afternoon. I did this with a real need to get some perspective. It would all end in tears for the groom, and worse for the bride, in a faraway place, in 1962.

They were both good caring people if this is part of the definition of those who voted Liberal in the United Kingdom during the '50s (my mother) or Labour (my father). I was also for those parties. Both on my preferred side of the then Conservative-dominated electorate. On my vague understanding at the time, the Liberals and Labour had a belief in social justice, a concern for the underdog almost wholly to themselves. I was concerned, more particularly, with the condition of my mother when I said to her in 1962, Beaumaris, Melbourne, 'Why are you so unhappy?' We were standing next to the polished oak sideboard that had recently followed us by ship to Australia. The answer from the woman whom I, aged eleven, naturally loved more than any other, was also a question: 'How do you know?' I knew the answer to that was beyond words and, like politics, complex so I just said, 'I know.' I think she realised I was firm in this knowledge, worried too much about how it was affecting me, and this may have played a part in what was to come. She could probably see I was firm too in the way that I would find myself making a choice, based on all the available feeling and knowledge, on which parent in my mind eventually to side with, and cast a secret, unalterable vote.

Some while after the question, weeks, my father and I went out looking for a puppy – the first pet we were to have in Australia. It was a Sunday, so it was window shopping at a pet shop I'd spotted from our new company-provided Holden car. When we got back I felt something was wrong. Or more wrong than usual. Recently, my mother had been found by the window cleaner, collapsed in the garden. Another time she'd been to the cinema with my father, and vomited during the screening. I wasn't meant to be privy to all this but an only child has a lot of spare time to overhear things. For days, or longer, she would be lethargically quiet and then, behind the closed bedroom door, there'd be screaming. Home life was unpredictable. I was concentrating hard on my mother's condition and this no doubt contributed to the sense that my father was remote. As I would later find out, a lot of the behaviour I was witnessing was the product of being English and buttoned-up – my father a slave to good form. We didn't appear to get on well with Australians, who in manner were very different from us. It was only later, much later, when I had undertaken a serious investigation of this marriage, that I discovered that after I was born my mother had been 'mentally ill' and been committed to a hospital. Or as my father would occasionally but concisely put it, she was 'mad.' But that's the kind of extreme, distorted thing a person will say after a few glasses of scotch when attempting to provide some insight into a failed marriage, and get himself off the hook.

It was mid-afternoon. There was a chill in the air – our first Australian version of autumn. My mother had said before we left, not wanting to join us, that she needed an afternoon nap. So it was surprising to find her still up and about when we got back – and she said she was surprised we were back as early as we were. I noticed she was unsteady on her feet and wondered whether my father also noticed this. Soon she said that she'd take her nap. I was puzzled as the rest of the afternoon slowly passed – my father in his study, me loafing around – why she hadn't reappeared. What would we have for dinner? I crept into the master bedroom, as the estate agent had called it, and saw she was still asleep, lying on her side, right arm over her shoulder, at the edge of the bed. I knelt and looked at her serene face – said some quiet things. It was during this time, not long, though ever since it has seemed very long, I realised she was no longer alive. I just knew. It was not only her pallor, but something else too. She was utterly still and unfathomably absent. I didn't move for a while. Then with the self-possession that seems, necessarily, to accompany a crisis, I realised I'd have to rise, leave her, and announce what had happened to my father in his study.

He didn't believe me. Perhaps it was the self-possession. I had on occasion lied to cover my more adventurous tracks, and been found out – it was a severely punishable offence – but I was not equipped to make up a story that meant he no longer had a wife nor I a mother. Lying was an accusation he would continue to level at me too frequently, perhaps because in a subconscious way he remained angry that I'd appeared to take a senior role in this family catastrophe, taken control, initially, out of his hands. Certainly, when the police arrived, my first encounter with police in Australia, they believed my story. Or perhaps, more simply and charitably, he thought I'd made a misdiagnosis. I talked him round and he agreed to come and see for himself. A local GP arrived shortly afterwards. I was blocked from the room. By then the lights were on in the house.

It was the police who, next day, would start the hunt for the suicide note – taking the empty brown bottle of barbiturates as evidence. Though a crime had been committed – suicide is, mercifully, no longer one – and decisions made in the light of a situation for which no one had been remotely prepared, the atmosphere was coolly rational. My father was, after all, an actuary – a person who calculates, mathematically, life expectancy for the insurance industry. I don't think he ever saw the irony of this. Talented and hardworking, he'd been appointed to an important executive position in Melbourne. A professional, even a marriage counsellor, may not bring the wisdom of work home. One decision made was that the nature of her death was not to be talked about – this decision was made unilaterally. We could, we both agreed, still have a dog. We would 'soldier on' in Australia, although I found out many years later, from the papers relating to the coronial inquiry that, in her note, my mother had said she was 'a failure' and wanted me to be looked after by her younger sister back in England. I think my mother had also behaved rationally and, clearly, worked out a strategy. She didn't want to be found by her husband dead in the marriage bed during the night. Nor when she had the most time at her disposal, on a school day. This is consistent with her wanting to cause a minimum of distress. Her one miscalculation, I'm sure, was that it would be her husband who would find her. But since it was also decided that it would be inappropriate for me, being too young, to attend the funeral – a funeral with one mourner in this far-off country – and that I'd be better off at school, I might never have had the chance, finally, to see my mother. If it had been possible for me to realise this then, I would have been thankful for it, as I am, in a way, now.

My father was not a ladies' man, as people of his generation called certain men. In his remaining decades, there would be no other women, no marriage. He wasn't cut out for it. Though I'm not saying he didn't have normal, even considerable, longings. I think he did. No other responsive women came his way.

He, a modestly paid professional without family assets, had entered the marriage contract at the age of thirty-five on the grounds, postwar – he had been in the Home Guard – that a wife was a requirement and, when others might have gone somewhere to dance, he looked no further than the office. There sat my mother, lovely, aged thirty-seven, at a typewriter. She, the eldest sibling of four, who had been exhausted from caring for her – by then deceased – parents, was the only one not 'spoken for.' Recently she'd had to part, painfully, from a married lover. Loneliness consumed her, and the widening prospect of more. For neither of them, just then, was there any alternative but to walk down the aisle.

Meanjin

Culturestate

Guy Rundle

Sydney had a hot summer in 1939, but it was even hotter for Ronald McCuaig. The writer, a fixture of bohemian Sydney, was producing a volume of poetry, *Vaudeville* – the first book of genuinely modernist poetry by an Australian. There was no question of taking it to a printer – the material, mild for our era, was louche in the extreme for a country that had banned, among others, *Madame Bovary*, and would later ban *The Catcher in the Rye*.

So McCuaig did the job himself. He purchased a platen press, a device which prints individual sheets between two flat plates, using a lever. The platen has a history stretching back hundreds of years – it was the cornerstone of the 'pamphlet wars' of the seventeenth century, and of the idea of a free public sphere.

McCuaig took two weeks to print individual sheets, and then put them together, to create a few hundred copies, most of which remained unsold. He would produce three more volumes of poetry, all self-published, before ceasing to write poetry in mid-life. He died in 1993 at the age of eighty-five, the year after a professional edition of his *Selected Poems* had been published.

McCuaig can hit a cool and stylish note in his verse, although much of it dips too far into the twee and whimsical for contemporary tastes – he was, like most 'bohemians' before the Second World War, working off the image of Wilde, Beardsley, Dowson and others of the Café Royal.

Tellingly, McCuaig's greatest contribution to Australian poetry may well be that he encouraged his friend and fellow journalist/poet Kenneth Slessor to a more ambitious aesthetic, thus helping him to bust out of his late Georgianism and into the full modernity of 'Five Bells.' That's how it goes. But what is important here are the dual features of McCuaig's life at the time – his unstinting sense of purpose, written in the muscles he gained pulling the platen down 10,000 times over – and the degree to which his work was genuinely outside any circuit of money, power, or institutional process then available.

In a country that at the time had no state funding for literature, theatre or the other arts, a small national broadcaster and five small universities, principally offering bachelor degrees, events such as the publication of McCuaig's *Vaudeville* were genuine events in what Australia's small group of progressives saw as a transformative process, acting on a society of which it was not a part.

Nothing mediated between the wider society and bohemian culture, and Australia's bohemians were probably the most isolated and numerically insignificant of any country in the world. Alistair Kershaw's memoir of the 1930s, *Hey Days*, described a Melbourne bohemia concentrated in several blocks near Bourke Hill, and all knowing each other. The Ern Malley affair, hatched by two bright lights of Sydney bohemia, had been incubated in the Directorate, effectively a transfer of a large section of the Sydney University chapter into an army psych-ops unit, and drew in everyone from Max Harris to the Reeds and, at one stage, H.V. Evatt (who had been lined up to write an introduction).

Both McCuaig and Kershaw would live long enough – into the 1990s – to see the world of Western culture, and that of Australia in particular, changed beyond measure. From being a byword for philistinism and distance from the known world – Sartre, in *Being and Nothingness*, ponders what it is like to be at other places on a map, the last-named, impossibly distant being Melbourne – in the Australia of today cultural production sits at the centre of economic, political and social life. By the time McCuaig died, poetry and the arts had become part of a web of production and reception intertwined with the state, the education system, tourism and the amorphous notion of 'community activities.' From direct grants at federal, state and local level, to publications support, residency programs and creative-writing courses, the process forms a conventional part of contemporary life. Indeed the debate over whether the arts should be state-funded has been won more decisively than just about any liberal-left victory of the century – parties of both sides now simply assume that the state will fund a degree of cultural production, an idea that parties of both sides would have dismissed as out of the question some decades earlier. The occasional cavilling of the right about funding for this or that terrible Australian movie or little-read poetry collection has a purpose largely as an element in the culture wars, and is undermined by the fact that high peaks of the movement – such as *Quadrant* and Les Murray – have taken large amounts in state funds over the decades.

Cultural production has gone from being an activity outside the mainstream, and often in conflict with the state, to having its entree into the centre of the marketplace facilitated by state programs. Yet in that passage, a strange thing has happened – the idea of the arts as professed by artists has remained centred on the bohemian and avant-gardist idea that animated McCuaig and his compatriots.

McCuaig's arduous self-printing of *Vaudeville* was at the extreme end of the difficulties faced by artists in the 'high modernist' era, but it was not atypical of the times. Joyce's *Ulysses* was printed privately by Sylvia Beach; the early abstract expressionists had their technique formed by the use of cheap house-paint; what modern theatre there was often came from the left subculture centred on the Communist Party, as did early film festivals.

Today, what confronts the questing artist is not the indifference of society and the state, but its embrace, and the requirements associated with it. The process of making art now brings with it induction into the business of grant applications, job applications, CV composition and folio preparation. Most creative writers approach these with intensely ambivalent feelings. Unless completely narcissistic they are grateful for the possibility of getting paid to create art that would otherwise not be commercially viable, for the space of autonomy that art demands. But at the same time, successive transformations of grants-scheme processes have turned artistic life into the very antithesis of that autonomy, asking would-be recipients to unpack a variety of activities – artistic, reflective, spontaneous – into an account of themselves, a form of self-analysis in order to identify their influences and intentions. Would-be artists, fleeing the humdrum, could be forgiven for wondering what they had got themselves into.

This, it should be emphasised, is not a lament about the petty demands of state-authorised philistines on the sovereign imagination. Given that arts grants involve distribution of taxpayers' money to pay for things most of them would not voluntarily purchase, due diligence is required. My point is rather that the entire role of the modernist, avant-garde or difficult artist in contemporary society is transformed when decades of bipartisan political commitment effectively render support of it permanent and ongoing (more so than, for example, manufacturing tariffs and industry protection). Avant-gardism lives off the sense that it is challenging existing understandings, relations, assumptions – including those marshalled by the state as ideology. State support and encouragement bring a contradiction into the heart of that practice. Yet were the contemporary arts en masse to take such a changed relationship to heart and surrender an avant-garde self-conception – to decide instead that they were simply decoration and diversion for a specific class of cultural consumers – the whole project would fall apart.

This dilemma began to arise with some force in the 1980s, when the new left – the last political movement to which the Western avant-garde was attached – had all but collapsed, and a self-consciously nihilistic capitalism had established the core set of values. Though some responded by leaving the avant-garde arts altogether – either to continue avant-gardism through the new adventure of theory, or, in the manner of Julian Schnabel, to create an art practice that was both commercial and ironic in its commercialism – others plugged on, and each year their ranks were augmented by the gradual expansion of creative-arts courses and an arts sector of employment.

Indeed it was in the 1980s that a new, third phase of state–culture relations in modernity was forged. If the first had been one where critical culture remained genuinely outside the influence of the state and economics, and the second was one dominated by grants – to people, companies and arts organisations

– whose beginnings had nevertheless been outside the state-economy process (the roneod poetry magazine, the scratch theatre company), from the mid-'80s onwards the state became not only a support for artists but also a producer of them and a consumer of their product. This was the era when local networks of arts communities became state-funded fringe festivals and other such events; when the hitherto quasi-trade-style culture schools, such as the National Gallery School and Swinburne film school, were drawn into the mainstream tertiary system; when creative writing, editing and publishing departments were established.

The impetus for such developments was various – an old-style commitment on the part of social-democratic governments to high-culture, non-commodified community activities, pressure from the arts community, private culture industries shifting training costs to the state – but increasingly it came to be understood that the arts could be integrated into national economic life for various purposes. National branding on the international market was one – this was the era when the global image of Australia came to be cemented as some sort of mix of Ken Done, Paul Hogan and Olivia Newton-John. Another was the attempt to forge a new national identity in a society no longer satisfied with received notions of being an Anglo Commonwealth nation.

As the millennium turned, the relations between state, culture and personal identity changed substantially, even though old ideas of how they were, or weren't, interconnected, continued. Middle and high-end cultural production, far from being an add-on to a 'real' primary and manufacturing economy, was now an ever-expanding circuit taking in larger areas of state-organised social life. Tourism was one of the first areas in which campaigns became more than simply hiring an artist to create a poster. A whole range of cultural activities, from films to the Venice Biennale, was drawn in to project the country to the world. As education became more consumer-driven, cultural creativity courses expanded significantly, propelled by an increasing focus on questions of personal identity and expression in an era when social identities were increasingly self-created. The expansion of such courses also suited state governments eager to remove school-leavers and young people from the unemployment statistics.

A further extension of the circuit was through federal and state health departments, increasingly willing to directly fund cultural production – from regional educational theatre tours to art therapeutic activities – as part of its expanded notion of 'community.'

The result has been a bizarre reversal of the fate of the bohemian artist living and dying alone and little-read in a garret, sustained only by the purity of her or his passion.

Increasingly one essential quality of the artistic life – its precariousness and contingency, the sense of an unplanned encounter between artist, imagination and world – has met its opposite. The young, genuinely creative person can see a possible and structured future – a life of moving through the stages of small group funding, individual grants, residencies, creative activity teaching positions, and so on. Such a future is hardly secure, but it is achievable, and it has the possibility of rewarding the less talented but more entrepreneurial artist who has aptitude in stringing together funding from an increasingly broad variety of sources. Yet what was once frequently collaborative activity becomes increasingly competitive, individualised and routine.

Perhaps the highest stage of this process occurs when parts of the state become so keen on extending their interaction with avant-garde cultural production that contradictions arise. Thus, in Melbourne, a culture of post-graffiti street stencil art that rapidly became world famous simultaneously attracted local council funding and prosecutions for vandalism. The resulting tussle – in which a traditionally minded premier mused on attracting international visitors through the use of attractive window-baskets in Melbourne's laneways – and the victory of the stencillers, whose status remains ambiguous, said much about a transformed relation between culture and the state.

Successive generations of Australian avant-gardists may have been aware of the ironies and contradictions of state-funded subversiveness, but far less attention was paid to the deeper contradictions of the creative process becoming fused with state processes. In particular, though many are adept at identifying the old-style external state that is characteristic of modernity – witness the endless parade of 'refugee' plays, art and writings during the long-term mandatory detention period of the Howard government – few have seen much of a problem with the transformed method of the state in the contemporary era, one in which more effort is put into the shaping of individual desire and psychologies than the regulation and control of given subjects.

In this process, sometimes known as 'governmentality,' the state is increasingly concerned not with the explicit content of its subjects, but with the forms of their life, and subjectivities. Mobilisation of the population to live in a certain way – to aspire to personal success, participate in a high work, high consumption cycle. Improving health outcomes is seen less as a matter of creating more health facilities or better access to sports facilities and so on, and more as one of shaping people's perception of certain habits – eating, drinking, smoking – as inherently dangerous.

Similar efforts are employed in a wide variety of areas, many of them 'community development,' such as the creation of a sense of Australian identity that at the same time appears to arise spontaneously from the populace. Take for example the Rudd government's effort to create a sense of celebration and meaning around Australia Day. Rather than enunciate an explicit idea of what Australia is, much of the effort centred on a website to which people could submit their ideas about how to celebrate the occasion. The very activity thus drew people into a participatory notion of Australia Day, without actually staging a debate about whether the day should be celebrated at all, or whether the existing process – that of a laid-back holiday with no great symbolic celebratory features – reflects the genuine widespread sentiment about the day.

Broader cultural and political requirements merge seamlessly. When Baz Luhrmann agrees to produce *Australia*, a movie loosely based on Xavier Herbert's *Capricornia*, and funds it by making the film a centrepiece of a tourism campaign, it is the exact opposite of a talented artist selling out to curry political favour. It is rather an inability to acknowledge the manner in which critical art – even that done in a popular idiom – should relate to its audience as autonomous subjects, challenged to be transformed by the content. Instead, fundamental questions that might be posed – whether the dispossession of the Aborigines renders Australia a place to which a sentimental attachment should not be made – are decided in advance by the very nature of the art–tourism collaboration. Cate Blanchett, launching the US season of the Sydney Theatre Company's version of *A Streetcar Named Desire*, announced that the tour was 'practising soft diplomacy.' It is impossible to decide whether this is a joke or a serious remark, because it is both – the idea that art's highest honour is to be part of a state so extended that its boundaries blur seamlessly into social life.

Middle and high culture has triumphed, but by the time it reached the summit, its purpose and justification had evaporated. McCuaig, pulling down the platen press 10,000 times, found strength in the conviction that he was doing something real and important. But it is not only the success of the modernist project that has made McCuaig's ardour appear, on reflection, no longer to apply. Post-Auschwitz, post-Warhol, post-*Simpsons*, the very notion of an authoritative high culture has been replaced, in both reception and production, by a cultural continuum, as the place where people live emotionally and aesthetically.

This is most visible in that paradoxical core of contemporary culture, the creative-writing course. Virtually unknown outside a few elite American universities even two decades ago, it has now become a centrepiece of humanities departments, undergraduate courses and adult education. It serves students, institutions whose funding is now adjusted according to student numbers (rather than an independent evaluation of the course), governments that increasingly use variants of such courses, ostensibly as training for culture industries, and writers, established or otherwise, who obtain teaching jobs in such courses. Yet everyone who has taught these courses has had one signal experience – when one asks the students what books and writers they feel passionate about, who has influenced them, one encounters a vague and unenthusiastic response. Going in, you half-imagine that the class will be a mixture of passionate beatniks, extolling Sartre and Kerouac, intense modernists determined à la Stein or Eliot to reinvent writing, or committed realists inspired by Hemingway and Joyce Carol Oates to nail how it is, man. Instead, by and large, one gets people who do not live in literary culture, often motivated by various ideas of self-expression, of vague creativity, of aspirations towards fame and genius, but who cannot really talk about a world of reading and writing. Frequently, when they do become passionate, it is in discussion of mainstream films, music or genre fiction. They have grown up in a culture where these things are all-encompassing and formative: as we all have. Who, under sixty, can honestly say that key formative texts in their lives have not been a number of three-minute songs and a couple of briefly fashionable movies? But in the creative-writing class, the one question that screams to be asked cannot be voiced: why are you here? For quite aside from any other considerations, the creative-writing teacher knows that the question could as easily be turned on him or her.

The numbers of creative-writing students are small, yet their dilemma – a state-sponsored production of culture whose animating urge, that of the autonomous artwork, contradicts that very activity – catches the way in which culture and the state have developed over the past few decades. Such institutions sometimes have the feel of a Dada *atelier*, dedicated to the relentless production of an output for which there is no demand whatsoever, honing a trade that has no role.

Yet further out from that, it is clear that vast amounts of public culture have the same problem, a multiple disjuncture between public demands, institutional structures and old rationales. Sculpture accumulates in public places, long after the streets in question have come to seem cluttered and unpleasing, a decades-old mission to bring art to the people now jammed on autopilot and with a municipal budget line that demands spending, lest it be cancelled next time round; community festivals – Moomba is one such benighted example – whose rationale, never rock-solid, has been utterly worn away by decades of social and cultural change, yet which is continuously revived not by spontaneous action from below, but by interlocking state processes few artists are keen to openly criticise.

This is not a state controlling culture by crudely dictating terms to it, but one that has surrendered key elements of state power to cultural shaping. One interesting exception was the recent campaign to defend Melbourne's increasingly threatened live music scene. Despite sporadic support for some activities, rock had largely been left alone, because it was simply too wild and sprawling to be harnessed in the manner of other arts. Indeed, its existence as degree-zero culture – something people will just pick up a guitar and do – effectively meant that the state virtually ignored it. Thus when the Victorian government sought to appease tabloid concerns about street violence, it saw no problem in introducing a blanket law requiring all public musical performances – from an AC/DC concert to an open-mike folk night – to employ security. The law placed a burden on music venues already operating on thin margins, and when iconic Melbourne rock pub The Tote announced it would close due to these laws, a public protest movement sprang up. This was effectively outside the 'culturestate' – a genuine political expression based around an activity done by the majority of participants for little or no money and without state funding.

Most people involved in cultural production work in an entirely different framework, far from the commitment of a McCuaig, or the uncompromised pleasure and meaning of the crowd at an Espy Sunday session. Many artists joke ruefully about the round of life that people can enter too easily – the world of grants, teaching, admin jobs and policy work that has become the unintended hinterland of official cultural life. Come application time many wonder aloud if they would not be better off waiting at tables or digging ditches – an expression, in part, at the guilt they feel for ingratitude.

Yet old mythologies of modernism have obscured the price that involvement in the culturestate demands. For many in the culturestate hinterland, the modernist story – from indifference and poverty to a recognition of worth that ostensibly guarantees artistic freedom – is so compelling that the higher unfreedom that results remains unrecognised. In my view, many of those drawn into the culturestate hinterland wear its contradictions in their own bodies and their own lives, often in the form of procrastination, anomie, isolation, psychosomatic illnesses vitiated by ritualised health and dietary regimes, and a persistent low-grade depression.

Most people involved in this recognise the predicament – that a mass and interconnected cultural enterprise has developed from separate policies and intentions, become entwined with a state seeking new modes of social ordering, and developed as a self-perpetuating process. In looking for alternatives, there is no point in returning to a general 'outside' position from which an authentic high or avant-garde culture could be launched. McCuaig's labours were not in vain. Intense, edgy, excellent, non-mass culture is now available to a much wider audience than ever before and that is cause for celebration. But the fact that those battles have been won means that there is all the more need for them not to be endlessly rehearsed as cliché.

The recent Bill Henson furore was a prime example of that – one in which the difficult question of the use of children and teenagers in explicit art was shoe-horned into a simplistic debate about 'free speech.' The most ludicrous aspect of it was the manner in which Henson's supporters were happy to use the art/pornography distinction as some unreflected-upon justification for licensing some individuals to do what others would be jailed for. That the distinction arose from a series of court cases in the 1950s and 1960s, all loaded with assumptions about social worth and artistic intent, bothered Henson's defenders not at all. They were happy to be the most ridiculous of creatures, official state avant-gardists. The companion piece to the Henson furore was the preceding 2020 Summit, in which the virtual courtship of artists to the state had become literal, assembling in Canberra at the court of King Kevin to bend cultural production to the service of the state. The Rudd government's pointed refusal to back Henson soon after the summit was a reminder that the relationship – at the federal level – was one way, but many artists, frozen in a Whitlamite ideology that could envisage no contradiction between the progressive state and cultural producers, didn't see the walloping coming.

So the practice of high or avant-garde culture can't be made meaningful on the grounds that it is outside, resistant, disordering, liberating. It's now another aesthetic in the mix, its state funding defensible on various grounds from cultural (it is good to fund things for which there is no market) to more abstract ones: that poetry, for example, is the central linguistic art, a wellspring for more applied literary culture.

Whether such grounds justify the pursuit of a career in the high arts remains to be seen. This is why so many writers with three or four novels or story collections to their credit, dashing between a stalled novella, a CAE first-fiction class and a consultancy position with the local council's community festival, nurture the notion of avant-garde outsiderism as a raison d'être. Unlike previous cultures, or like current mass-market culture, such a life is not justified by its activities, whose role may well be more regulatory than liberating or enabling.

And that question becomes urgent when one considers the role of teaching, facilitation and policy. Here cultural practitioners need to ask themselves whether they should not take a far more critical stance towards the sort of roles and positions offered by the culturestate. There's nothing wrong with teaching creative writing – unless the program is clearly for a non-cultural purpose, such as removing young people from the unemployment lists. There's nothing wrong with working on community arts – unless the project in question is an aspect of the management of social or ideological energies or the counterfeiting of social energy.

Of course the market has also drawn autonomous culture into its operation too – but part of the enduring myth of the avant-garde outsider tends to make artists aware of the danger of 'selling out' to private interests. Attempts by the state to censor or distort art from the outside rarely come under equal scrutiny. It is where state power facilitates cultural production, with no explicit control over content yet for its own broader formal purposes, that artists often fail to critically assess what is involved. It is my argument that they should, and that this is part of a wider process of reflecting on the role of avant-garde, modernist and high-art practices in contemporary society. Ronald McCuaig's labours are done. The weight that presses these days is not that of the platen, turning out small but revolutionary volumes to widespread indifference, but rather that of state and social processes whose tender embrace of culture is so forceful because it comes from within as much as without.

Meanjin

Something Sacred

Peter Conrad

At the Royal Albert Hall in 1996, Kylie Minogue had an awe-inducing glimpse of the vacuum that she exists to fill. Nick Cave, after clubbing her to death in the video for 'Where the Wild Roses Grow,' one of his *Murder Ballads*, had enticed her into appearing at the Poetry Olympics. Waiting for her entrance, she peeped out at the current performer – a blind, whiskery bard who declaimed a poem that his fingers read in Braille.

'Nick,' Kylie said in a panic, 'God is on stage! How am I supposed to follow that?'

Cave said 'Jesus did an okay job,' then pushed her out to face the gaping arena. Identified by a sticker with her name in capitals, rawly denuded of her usual ostrich feathers and dressed in unglamorous trackies, without the budgie tweet of her singing voice and the rhythmic camouflage of a band, she recited the fatuous lyrics of her song 'I Should Be So Lucky.' She might have been booed for her inanity, but the crowd adored her. It was as if the Second Coming had happened there and then.

Following God is precisely what Kylie does. In place of the doddering Ancient of Days, whose death was long ago announced by Nietzsche and Dostoevsky, we now have a sky full of the twinkling airborne creatures we call celebrities – temporary deities who are up there on sufferance and can be tugged down to Earth whenever we tire of them. With her new album, *Aphrodite*, Kylie launches herself into orbit as a pagan love goddess, chirpily dismissing all her previous lovers, breathily demanding the services of a Cupid boy, and, in a sideways reversion to Christianity, looking for an angel. As always, her music is merely an excuse for a revision of her image, which happens in the video for 'All the Lovers': in the gulf of a Los Angeles boulevard, between cliffs of chilly steel and blank glass, she surmounts a scrum of grappling, entangled bodies, smiling down on an orgy of multicultural, polymorphous copulation.

Is she too cheekily cute, too unthreateningly matey to be in charge of so much venery? Are there still traces of Charlene, the greasy tomboy from *Neighbours*, in Kylie's persona? If you think so, then the white goddess has a darker alter ego in her sister Dannii, an altogether more alarming figure – Parvati perhaps, her four arms flailing as she straddles a lion or tiger, her spiked heels jabbing its flanks. Dannii spoke from between her legs when she did a stint in Eve Ensler's *Vagina Monologues*. But her authority does not end there. She is omnisexual: although Kylie, with her smudged garage overalls or her spangled hotpants, may have the reputation for androgyny, it was Dannii, referring to her adolescent apprenticeship in showbiz, who once gruffly claimed, 'I worked my bollocks off.' For all her wiggling and flouncing, Kylie is endearingly frail; Dannii, like some rampantly fertile matriarch from the Hindu pantheon, keeps company with man-eating animals. In the video for her song 'So Under Pressure' – a self-pitying lament about her stress after Kylie's cancer diagnosis – she accessorises her outfits with a writhing albino python. Her idea of fun, according to Chas Newkey-Burden in his newly released *Dannii Minogue: The Biography*, is to be caged and lowered into a shark tank, where she tantalises the slavering fish with her immaculate, inedible limbs.

Growing up in Melbourne, Kylie and Dannii shared a bedroom, with a border of string hung across the middle to mark the halves that were their small but exclusive realms. Now it's the world that they divide between them, and, since celebrities beam their images around the globe by satellite, they seem to have the sky stitched up as well.

*

White Diamond, a documentary about the resumption of Kylie's

Showgirl tour after her recovery from cancer, begins with a scene in which she squeezes through a birth tunnel. A helper with a torch leads her along dark corridors and up a set of steep stairs; she follows nervously, wobbling on her vertiginous heels, the fronds of her headdress brushing the low ceiling, with another helper crouching behind to hold up her resplendent train. Finally, under her own power, she rises into the light, to be greeted by a roar of gratification. This is what she calls 'my cosmic thing – a collision of energy between the audience and myself': a galactic moment, when our prayers cause the sun to rise and our fervour propels an ordinary, undersized Melbourne teenager to stardom. But apotheosis is hard work. Later in the documentary, voiceless with the flu in Manchester, Kylie croaks apologetically through an *a cappella* medley of her ancient hits, while thousands of customers, refusing to feel short-changed because they can at least enjoy the sight of her, helpfully bellow, 'We love you, Kylie.' Behind the Sydney Entertainment Centre, in another scene, she edges warily towards a wire fence that holds back an old woman armed with a banner.

'I'm legally blind, sweetheart,' says the frumpy fan: is she expecting an autograph or a cure? Either way, Kylie apparently feels obligated. As she says somewhere else in *White Diamond*, 'a tour is a mission.'

In earlier days, her mission was more devious or deviant. During their affair Michael Hutchence bragged that his hobby was 'corrupting Kylie'; the paraphernalia he supposedly used included a set of handcuffs. Anxious to cast off the compulsory niceness of *Neighbours*, Kylie was avid for abuse. Nick Cave killed her, and Sir Les Patterson, having unreeled from inside his trouser leg the phallic equivalent of an anaconda, made her flee screaming from the stage of the Royal Festival Hall. Bottling her as the absinthe fairy in *Moulin Rouge*, Baz Luhrmann turned her into a green pixie who screeches towards Ewan McGregor with fangs bared and febrile wings buzzing like a manic mosquito.

At first Kylie's handlers joked about the religious frenzy she excited. *The Kylie Bible*, a promotional publication from 1994, gave her the opportunity to describe the view from on high. 'What lays [sic] before me is beautiful, dangerous, breathtaking, seductive, challenging and inspiring,' she declared, presumably referring to the world she had created. Ten years later, the waxen Kylie at Madame Tussauds indulged in a little seasonal sacrilege. Her effigy hovered over the Beckhams: Kylie was the annunciating angel, with David and Victoria as the holy family. An enraged visitor lashed out at the blasphemy, beheading Posh in the process. Kylie, dangling high overhead, of course escaped damage.

Since then, her sanctification has progressed beyond parody. 'She wanted to have something sacred,' says the choreographer Akram Khan when rehearsing Kylie's troupe of go-go boys in *White Diamond*; he supplies it in a routine that turns the dancers into worshippers, fluttering around their tiny idol. The religious cult is managed by William Baker who, before he was Kylie's stylist, creative director and cosily connubial 'gay husband,' studied theology at the University of London. As well as fussing over her costumes – he once confided that 'the decision to move into knickers and bras was a long-term ambition for us both' – Baker superintends her mystique or, as he calls it in his introduction to the touring exhibition of her glad rags, 'the Kylie mythos.' For the video of 'Can't Get You Out of My Head,' he wrapped her in a hooded smock sliced open to the thigh; his aim was to evoke 'the whole Virgin Mary thing,' though it's doubtful that Our Lady would have had slits in her smock. At the same time he saw Kylie as a 'modern Venus,' a heathen hoyden who wrapped her legs round a pole as she cavorted. He has dressed her up as a succession of divas, the divinities manufactured by the cinema: Monroe dripping with diamonds, Bardot in heart-shaped shades, Garland balanced on a horned moon singing 'Somewhere over the Rainbow.' Kylie, tirelessly morphing as she sped through forty-second costume changes, adopted Baker's combination of pious iconography and cheeky iconoclasm. 'Believe in the sacred and break every rule,' she sings on the last track of her album *Impossible Princess.* She assumes that it is possible to do those two contradictory things at once because she knows that the sacred is just a trick of light. In *21*, a dance performance choreographed by Rafael Bonachela at Sadler's Wells, her image was projected onto a gauze screen thirty-feet high. She became, as Baker said, 'an ethereal presence made up solely of light particles' – a pixelated illusion, briefly scintillating in the darkness.

Astral beings such as Kylie no longer seem to be composed of flesh and blood; they are light-emission devices, magnified, as by Bonachela, or multiplied, as in the video clip for 'Come into My World,' where she is cloned four times while dancing through a Paris street. Hence the tabloid suggestion that she might be an alien life-form: she treasures an article that seized on her 'elfin features and small breasts,' along with her lobeless ears, to demonstrate that she was the perfect prototype for an extraterrestrial. During her *KylieFever2002* tour she appeared as Kyborg, a humanoid robot swathed in silver armour and attended by a platoon of cybermen with chrome helmets. The chaste exoskeleton peeled off to reveal Kylie in a crystal-mesh bra and miniskirt, strutting lace-up boots. 'A vision of goddess-like perfection,' cooed Baker – or a nightmare in which the demonic dominatrix Silvanemesis took control of the world?

The object of all this hagiographic toil and trouble remains detached from it. Kylie's inventory of the costumes she donated to the Victorian Arts Centre takes care to point out their fault lines: the safety pins, bulldog clips, industrial zips, quick hooks and clingy velcro that allow her persona to be pieced together and ripped apart. She once called herself 'a watery icon.' It is a more interesting and touching phrase than any in her song lyrics, and a sly recognition that the images she projects are a mirage. Gods or goddesses don't have to subscribe to their own religion; belief is for lesser mortals.

*

Being a Gemini, Kylie automatically bifurcates herself. 'You're always dealing with at least two people!' she once wrote in *GQ*. The second person might be Dannii, her shadow side. Although Dannii rails against the assumption that they are 'Siamese twins, some freak circus act,' they began as a composite, interchangeable creature. After the pubescent Kylie left *The Sullivans*, Dannii was drafted in to impersonate her in a retrospective dream sequence; when Dannii surged ahead in popularity on *Young Talent Time*, Kylie did secretarial duty by helping to autograph the pictures sent out to her sister's fans.

They soon set about differentiating themselves. Dannii established their separate identities by casting them in a cartoon:

'Kylie is a fluffy, purring pussycat and I'm like a bulldog.' After seeing Dannii in *Grease*, Kylie said she had done well as the slutty Rizzo, then added that personally she always wanted to play the demure, simpering Sandy, Olivia Newton-John's role in the film with John Travolta. In 1999 they defined their disparity by their choice of Shakespearean heroines. Kylie played the naïve Miranda in a production of *The Tempest* in Barbados, while at the Edinburgh Fringe Festival Dannii played Lady Macbeth, whom she transformed, according to a reviewer, into a 'disco-queen-from-hell.' Kylie sweetly wondered at the brave new world; Dannii relished Lady Macbeth's manipulativeness, admired the careerist's killer instincts and enjoyed the fact that she took the sexual initiative with her henpecked husband. Dannii once said 'I spend all day every day working towards being famous.' Unless everyone had heard of her, she said, explaining her 1988 Kmart clothing range, 'there'd be no way I could ever have my own fashion label.' Imagine a contemporary Lady Macbeth designing drawstring shorts and T-shirts for Kmart, with $17.98 as the top price: luckily the ballistic force of Dannii's ambition was neutralised by the triviality of her goal, which may have spared the world another Margaret Thatcher.

Dannii has always seen herself as a global brand, and by her adolescence she had outgrown Australia. 'The market there isn't big enough,' she said. 'I have to make it happen in Britain and the States.' While attempting to make it happen, she dispensed geopolitical aperçus. 'The bombing in Downing Street freaked me out,' she whimpered in 1991, even though the IRA aimed no mortars at her. At large in New York, she shuddered during a research trip to the Bronx, where she was hoping to learn how to funk up her chirrupy sound. 'There were no white people around,' she reported in alarm. Back home in 2002 she praised the French bigot Jean-Marie Le Pen, tut-tutted that Britain was 'in an appalling state with the muggings and the car-jackings,' and censoriously noted that in Queensland 'some of the street signs are in Asian!' By contrast, Kylie's one recorded comment on international politics had her customary deft evasiveness. In South Africa in 1989, a year before Mandela's release from prison, she was asked about apartheid. 'I think they should stop killing the rhinos,' she said.

Though Kylie admits to being 'a manufactured product,' she lets herself be sold rather than trying to do the selling. A cool irony, signalled by the quizzical arch of her left eyebrow, places her at a giggly distance from Dannii's hustling. She knows that the product is cheap and easy to fake, so she finds herself outnumbered by imitators such as the drag queens who flock to 'Kylie Nights.' 'There are,' she has wearily conceded, 'millions of Kylie clones and even Kylie dolls.' The recording impresario Pete Waterman noted the wistfulness of her own mimicry: 'She was outselling Madonna four to one, but still wanted to be her. Everyone wanted to be Kylie Minogue except Kylie Minogue, who wanted to be Madonna.' When Kylie and Madonna met – of course at an awards ceremony, which is where celebrities constellate – Madonna was wearing a T-shirt that shouted 'Kylie Minogue.' Who knows if it was an act of homage, or a postmodern put-down? There's a kind of masochism to Kylie's pliability, a willingness to suffer or to be derided so that others – Cave, Luhrmann, Sam Taylor-Wood, who filmed her naked mouthing to an aria sung by a male castrato, or Pedro Almodóvar, with whom she longs to work – can make art out of her. In 1996 she offered herself to any indie rockers who might want to use her in a collaboration. 'It would be like giving ten sculptors a piece of rock,' she said. She was the rock, braced for the mallet and chisel. In Melbourne, on the *Showgirl* tour, the sisters appeared together one evening to perform the Robbie Williams hit 'Kids.' Kylie, romping in leopard-skin print, informed Dannii that she was 'dancing with the chairman of the board' and reminded her that 'the purpose of a woman is to love her man.' In slinky black lingerie, Dannii offered Kylie a ride on her 'twelve-cylinder symphony,' cocking a leg in fish-net stockings as if about to mount a motorbike. Kylie looks lovably infantile in the filmed recording of the gig, as if she were wearing her Dolce & Gabbana catsuit for a children's party. Dannii, however, is a feral prowler, dangerous rather than playful.

If you had to choose a body part as a metonym for each of them, Kylie would have to be identified with her loco-motive rear end, so beloved in bottom-fixated Britain. She admired the sculpted buttocks of Jean-Claude Van Damme, with whom she appeared – playing Cammy, a fluffy paratrooper who guards an Asian dictator – in the film *Street Fighter*, and she was flattered when he taught her his exercise routine for callipygian trimming and tightening. But she tends to look over her shoulder at this asset as if it had a life of its own, and disparages its limited repertoire of moves. 'I mean,' she once asked, 'what does my bum do? It's not like it can actually do anything – except wiggle.' Dannii's defining feature is more upfront. In 1996 she allegedly spent more than US$5000 on boob-augmentation in New York. Asked about this by Piers Morgan in a recent television interview, she cupped the glands in question and aimed them at the camera like twin bazookas. 'They're good, aren't they?' she snarled.

Maximising her appeal to all possible markets, Kylie likes to play at being a hermaphrodite. Her pictorial autobiography, *Kylie: Evidence*, includes a nude painting by Simon Henwood, which gives her girlish breasts and a boy's shrinking genitals. In a winking allusion to William Baker, she once said, 'Everyone should have a Willie'; as she well knew, the remark means something different if you lose the capitalisation. Dannii has less tolerance for this flirtatious blurring of identity. During her stint as a judge on *The X Factor*, a contestant called Danyl Johnson, who had outed himself as bisexual in a tabloid newspaper, performed Jennifer Hudson's gynocratic tirade from *Dreamgirls*. Dannii complimented him for his success in 'turning guys into girls,' then added: 'No need to change the gender references, if we're to believe everything we read in the press.' Four thousand viewers, whose lives were presumably otherwise empty, protested at her innuendo. Perhaps Dannii – born Danielle, though she precociously rebranded herself to ensure memorability – was irritated to find a man initially called Daniel encroaching on her self-invented terrain.

The wisecrack could not have been further from Kylie's witty description of herself as 'a very short drag queen' trapped 'in a woman's body.' Dannii has no patience with such self-deprecation; her default mode is attack, and you can often sense a metallic menace as she readies her weapons. After she broke up with Jacques Villeneuve – Homerically described by Newkey-Burden as 'the Formula One hero' – the ribald Jonathan Ross asked her if she had exchanged him for one of his colleagues on the racing circuit. 'I'm not a screwdriver,' Dannii snapped. The exchange occurred on the radio, but I could picture Ross nervously crossing his legs.

*

It all leads to an existential quandary: who or what are these mutant creatures – the products of a collective fantasy, alive only if the image of them is on show and on sale, or if they are gossiped and blogged about by the countless strangers who are their confidants and imaginary best friends? They began as human beings like the rest of us. Then at a certain point, by their own efforts or by our abject need, they were exempted from nature, hoisted off the Earth.

So far Dannii has kept self-doubt at bay. She is currently partnered by the ex-rugby player Kris Smith. He models for Myer while she has a deal to sell her new clothing range through David Jones; the child of this corporate merger was born in July. During her early, brief marriage to Julian McMahon, Dannii was bemused by the biological chores that go with being human. 'Where does a baby fit in?' she asked. 'It's not the kind of thing I can put in the luggage cart on the plane.' Organising the arrival of little Ethan Edward Smith, she announced that she would not interrupt her singing and dancing, her contest-judging and clothes-designing, her Tweeting and self-streaming: 'I've got no plans to stop working and take time off – apart from the actual birth. I've heard I have to be at the birth, right?' Let's hope she found time to put in an appearance at the happy event.

Kylie, meanwhile, just before flying back from London to Melbourne to meet her infant nephew, filled a spare hour by performing 'All the Lovers' atop a pyramid of writhing muscle men on Alan Carr's television talk show. Afterwards Carr asked her about the cancer diagnosis, and the year of invisibility that she spent undergoing treatment (though of course she kept a video diary: for the Minogue sisters, the unfilmed life is not worth living). Kylie, who is thoughtful, paused for a moment. 'It's such a human experience,' she finally said, bearing down hard on the adjective. 'It's a reminder of humanity.' She seemed genuinely taken aback that her body had recalled her to membership of our infirm species, which is made of more perishable stuff than crystal mesh and sequins; afloat on her 'cosmic thing,' Kylie needed to be reminded that she was human.

Watching, I felt suddenly sorry for this ageing waif, and also for the rest of us, so credulously fascinated by Dannii and Danyl, Jacko and Jackie O, J-Lo and SuBo, Posh and Paris. While God was alive, I certainly disliked him. Now that he has been replaced by our own inadequate inventions, I think it might be time to invite him back.

The Monthly

On Botany

Jo Lennan

Brontë-esque moors; *Wind in the Willows* woodlands; the sprawling floral frontispieces of William Morris. One of English literature's tricks is to lull us English-speaking foreigners into a false sense of familiarity with the landscape. I knew British flora before I set eyes on any of it. But it was a hand-me-down knowledge, a botany-by-fiction. I'm a stranger in this country, and this country is strange to me.

I moved to Britain from Sydney in 2008. I've tried to befriend local species in the part of Oxford where I live. It's down in the Domesday Book as meadow, and between buildings there is an unkempt cemetery and a scrap of swamp, choked with Coke cans and cow parsley. My walks trace rivers out of town: the Cherwell to its upper flanks, and fields with signs announcing their Special Scientific Interest. Or the Isis to its neglected elbow above St Aldate's, where the boatyards at Osney now subsume the ruins of the abbey. This path brings me out at Port Meadow, to find slow-grazing cattle and a stretch of water that comes and goes as it fancies.

It's slow going. For one thing, I'm forced to learn these plants back-to-front. We usually see plants as a part of their surroundings, and only later learn their names. Here, however, the names are what I know – from literature, or human namesakes, like Heather and her ilk. My task is to pin the names back on the plants. But names can also confound: England's oaks are utterly unlike the she-oaks ubiquitous in my corner of Australia – Charles II would sooner have sheltered behind a birch than bother with these spindly creatures. The 'she' is no compliment – the early white Australians found its wood a lesser lumber, too soft for sound construction. But why 'oak,' anyway? She-oaks, actually *Allocasuarinas*, have their own, un-oakish virtues: fortifiers of soils and hosts to orchids, they provide shady spots free of snakes. And she-oaks – among the Earth's first evolved trees – have a special, sombre grace. But none of this helps me to pick an English oak from a line-up.

And there's another, thornier issue obstructing the acquaintance. I harbour a visceral dislike for some English species, a feeling stemming from the fact that, in Australia, a vast majority of what are now invasive weeds were introduced from England. The weed invasion closely tracked the human one – about fifteen years after the First Fleet landed in Botany Bay in 1788, Robert Brown found twenty-nine species of European plants growing wild in the region. The number of escapees from English-style gardens has grown spectacularly since, with over a thousand species now naturalised in New South Wales. Australia's weed problem costs it $4 billion a year – a big reason why our quarantine officials come across like petit fascists.

It's unfair, I know, to hold this prejudice against English plants. Especially here, where they're within their native entitlements. But my ambivalence persists, something like that expressed by the late Judith Wright in her poem 'Oaks etc.':

> It isn't that I don't like
> European trees,
> Why my great-grandfather came from …
> Some of my best friends are …

The nub of it is that my eye is trained not to admire these species, but to see them as unlovely and rapacious. Consider common broom. Native to Britain, it's so respectable here that it lent its name from the Middle Ages, 'planta genista,' to the House of Plantagenet. But it is also uniquely adapted for incursions in warmer climes – its pods split open in heat, expelling seeds at speed. It's invasive in many countries, Australia included. There it has spread across the Cumberland plains to the south-western suburbs of Sydney, squeezing out native flora and fauna. In that light, broom doesn't seem so pretty. It's a common tale – Canberra, coveting the look of English garden cities like Letchworth, slapped a decades-long ban on front fences in an attempt to get residents to grow hedges. Now that hedge species run rampant in surrounding forest, the hedge city aesthetic is less appealing.

Last summer brought something of a rapprochement. The brambles started it. Another British native, they're among Australia's worst offenders, and hellishly hard to clear – goats eat them only if nothing else is going, and in unfenced country any infestations tend to be sprayed with poison. The spraying makes the idea of picking wild blackberries foreign to Australians. The day I ate my first few berries from an English vine, I felt the frisson of tempting fate. Would I fall ill from poison-berries, the foolish heroine in a cautionary children's tale? But now I forage freely, my appreciation for the vine growing with each sweet-staining fruit.

What's more, background checks reveal many of the pests to be mongrels, only partly (if at all) British. Plenty of 'cottage garden' plants that went to Australia via England were exotics here, too. Like the bindweed that, in Oxford, masses obscenely on the banks below Magdalen Bridge, erupting in white or purple trumpets – this lush green vine of the Convolvulaceae family is originally of Mediterranean stock. Another exotic with a European backstory is the weeping willow, whose fallen limbs sprout as new trees along riverbanks. The tree is native to China, although legend has it that England's weeping willows all descend from one Spanish twig, planted by Alexander Pope in Twickenham in the early 1700s. Or the sickly-sweet freesias that bedevil the west coast of Australia – cultivated in Europe, they are in fact hybrids of Cape of Good Hope species.

Plants move by intricate routes, with effects that take time to assess. People are the same. In Oxford, I'm only just waking up to the sleeper result of my own relocation. It's a discernible shift in aesthetic sensibility – and certain weeds, I now see, are rather becoming plants.

Intelligent Life

Getting to Know Them

Tim Flannery

Not so very long ago we humans thought of ourselves as a separate creation – the pinnacle of God's work – that had been granted dominion over nature. But then along came Darwin, and we discovered that we are related, through descent, to other animals. Despite this blow to our dignity we long maintained a polite fiction that we're special enough to merit classification in our own scientific family – the Hominidae. In our minds at least, we thus maintained a comfortable distance from the apes. But the analysis of DNA put an end to that, with the demonstration that only 2 per cent of our genetic code differs from that of the chimpanzees. Now we and chimps must share a twig in the family tree, and the Hominidae has been expanded to encompass the other 'great apes' – chimps, gorillas and orangutans.

That being said, we clearly differ from the other great apes in many ways, a fact elucidated in Anne Innis Dagg's *The Social Behavior of Older Animals*. It's a highly unusual work in that it treats an age group of organisms that has received little previous attention. It is also a commendably broad study – covering a diversity of species from parrots to primates. Humans and chimps, it turns out, value age in sexual partners very differently. In our species youth is prized, but among chimps the reverse is the case. Importantly, female chimpanzees (unlike female humans) do not experience menopause, and thus can remain fertile into old age.

Flo was one of the most sexually attractive female chimps in a troop studied by Jane Goodall. By the time Flo was forty, her teeth were worn down to the gums and her time as the dominant female in the troop was over, but she still managed to drive the boys crazy, attracting a string of suitors and mating fifty times in a single day. Researchers, wondering whether Flo was an anomaly, carried out an eight-year study of chimpanzee sex. In what seems to be something of an understatement of their results, they concluded that:

> chimpanzee males may not find the wrinkled skin, ragged ears, irregular bald patches, and elongated nipples of their aged females as alluring as human men find the full lips and smooth complexions of young women, but clearly they are not reacting negatively …

There is great variety in the ways older animals differ from younger ones – in both physical and behavioural manner. Older chimps may go bald and leopards suffer faded spots, but not all creatures bear such badges of seniority. The plumage of geriatric swallows, for example, is indistinguishable from birds in their prime. But old creatures, regardless of species, tend to be less agile than young ones and more likely to suffer from arthritis, diabetes, cancer, heart disease and mental confusion. All of this means that they're unlikely to be top of the pack, and the way they cope with this is intriguing.

Sherlock was a male baboon who, at the age of twenty-four, was about ninety in human terms. While still keen on sex, elders like Sherlock often don't have the status required to assert themselves against other males. So they often befriend individual females instead. Remarkably, such friendships are not about sex alone. They often involve nursing females, who, though rightly nervous of most males (who occasionally kill infant baboons), in a remarkable sign of trust will even leave their babies in the care of their older male friends while they forage.

When the end comes for older animals, they do not always go unmourned. Some species, such as elephants and chimpanzees, show unmistakable signs of grief and mourning at the death of a member of their group, and even grey whales have been observed behaving as if paying their last respects to the dead. Astonishingly, careful disposal of the body is not beyond some, for gorillas have been observed to bury their dead, while elephants have been known to raid a shed filled with the body parts of slaughtered elephants, removing the ears and feet (which were destined to be turned into umbrella stands) and burying them.

In many ways, elephants represent the great 'other' – enormous, highly social and intelligent creatures whose ways on occasion eerily echo our own. G.A. Bradshaw's *Elephants on the Edge* is a remarkable study of elephant–human interactions, whose opening premise is that 'it is not so much that elephants are *like* us. They *are* us, and we them.' This, I fear, the author means literally rather than metaphorically, for she seems to see no difference between the elephant and the human mind. That allows her to attempt psychoanalysis of elephants using methods developed for humans and to diagnose their 'condition' using human criteria. It flows from her premise that elephants should be endowed with all the basic human rights, and that we can expect them to respect our rights in turn. Unfortunately, the implications of Bradshaw's extraordinary opening premise are not fully explored in her book. Instead, it's essentially a catalogue of human abuse of pachyderms, which jumps in an instant from the treatment of elephants in circuses to the experiences of Holocaust survivors.

Very few people would accept Bradshaw's premise uncritically, so it's important that we explore the nature of the relationship between humans and elephants. Taking an evolutionary perspective reveals many similarities, but differences as well. Every now and again evolution throws up a new kind of creature that goes on to colonise most of the world. The landmass of Eurasia, being the largest of the continents, has produced the largest number of these species, including the family that includes sheep, goats and cattle. But North America too has given the world its champions, including the dog, camel and horse families – arguably man's best friends. Africa, while larger than North America, has paradoxically few such champions. Only two are of any note – the families Hominidae and Elephantidae – yet between them elephants and humans have colonised the habitable surface of the Earth. Indeed they are arguably the most successful mammal families ever to have evolved.

In times past the elephants were more successful than people. Dozens of species – from the pony-sized dwarfs that once grazed on the island of Crete to the woolly mammoth and the mastodons of North and South America – colonised the whole habitable world (with the exception of Australia). But then humans spread and climates changed, so today there remain just two species – the African and Asian (though some argue that the pink-tusked, pygmy elephant of the Congo is a third type) – and today all are under siege from a growing human population. Elephants are more truly African than we are, being members of an ancient group known as the Afrotheria, whose ancestors lived in Africa at the time of the dinosaurs. The hominids, in contrast, are only newly African, our ancestors having arrived on the continent from Eurasia a mere 10 million years ago.

These disparate histories mean that the last common ancestor of the elephants and ourselves was a rat-sized creature that lived over 100 million years ago. Yet undeniably we share much in common, perhaps because some of our ancestors were shaped at the same evolutionary forge – the productive, crowded and intensely competitive world of the African savannah. It's this world, in part, that endowed both elephants and humans with exceptional intelligence and a dependence on complex societies for their wellbeing. But for all their sagacity, elephants have been losing the battle for survival for the last 50,000 years – since humans started leaving Africa. As humans have encroached upon their world, one species after another has gone extinct, and Bradshaw argues that, as we endanger the last living species, they have become prey to psychological stresses that they are manifesting in startling ways.

About two hours' drive outside Johannesburg lies the small nature reserve of Pilanesberg National Park, which is plagued by strange goings-on among its elephants. Rangers working there have observed young males harassing older females for sex, and tourists filmed the astonishing spectacle of an elephant copulating with a rhinoceros. Then dead rhinos started to turn up, all gored to death by elephant tusks. Bradshaw thinks that these phenomena have their roots in a 'complex post-traumatic stress disorder' suffered by the elephants. The stress, she believes, was inflicted by human interactions with elephants – and she thinks that the aberrant elephant psychology at Pilanesberg is only an indication of something much larger.

These are important claims, and in order to assess them properly we need to know more about Pilanesberg's elephant population. Prior to its proclamation as a national park, elephants had been long extinct in the Pilanesberg area, and in an attempt to build up the region's biodiversity, park managers accepted two former circus elephants (both female) and a number of juvenile males that were orphaned during elephant-culling operations elsewhere in South Africa. The rhino-raping and killing males, it turns out, originated in Kruger National Park. At the time they were captured, only small elephants could be transported, so no adult male was present at Pilanesberg when they arrived. Among elephants, males and females lead largely separate lives, the females belonging to herds led by a matriarch, and from which males are ejected at puberty. They then join all-male groups, and presumably learn from mature males the recipe for a successful life.

In her search to explain the bizarre behaviour of the young males, Bradshaw focuses almost entirely on the trauma they suffered when their families were shot during the culling. 'Elephant attacks on rhinoceroses … reflect the violence that this otherwise peaceful species has experienced,' she says. But surely the situation is far more complex than that. What about the circus-raised females? Did they have much experience of elephant sex and know how to handle young males? Bradshaw tells us nothing of their reproductive histories, nor their interactions with the males other than that they rebuffed 'behavior not only unbecoming of a young bull but highly irregular.' Such modesty might be fitting in a Victorian novel, but as we seek to understand the Pilanesberg situation, we need facts.

Then there's the matter of the rhinos. Frustratingly, Bradshaw tells us nothing of the histories of Pilanesberg's rhino population, and too little of their fate. It's reasonable to assume that the rhinos, like the elephants, came from elsewhere; but had they any prior experience of elephants? If they had never interacted with elephants before, may they not have been vulnerable to bullying by the larger creatures? And what of the sex? Was it only female rhinos that were sexually penetrated and then pierced with tusks, or was interspecies sodomy practiced as well? Pretty much all we know is that forty-nine white rhinos died at Pilanesberg between 1992 and 1996 from such attacks – and that is far too little, in my view, to accept uncritically Bradshaw's diagnosis of 'complex post-traumatic stress disorder.'

For all its faults, *Elephants on the Edge* deals with a fascinating and little-understood subject, which makes it doubly disappointing to find it so devoid of facts and overstuffed with opinion. Sadly, it seems to be as much about its author's view of human nature as it is about elephants; but even more disappointingly, it has almost nothing useful to say about how humans and elephants might continue to coexist. Bradshaw talks of creating enormous wild areas for the use of elephants – areas large enough for them to migrate in search of food and water. But in an Africa whose human population is growing exponentially, that is a fantasy. It's clear that the millennia-long contest between elephants and humans will only accelerate in the future, and that the elephants can survive only through our good graces, and on our terms. This means that elephant populations will need to be managed. As they overpopulate parks, we can either watch them precipitate collapse of the ecosystem, then starve to death, or we can cull them. In this context, it's hardly helpful to talk, as Bradshaw does, of a 'humane self' and an 'Auschwitz self' in conflict as we try to manage elephant populations.

If the largest of wild creatures present profound moral and physical challenges to us, so too do the domesticated species with which we share our lives. Temple Grandin is a professor at Colorado State University who has devoted much of her career to the humane treatment and slaughter of the cattle, sheep and pigs that feed us. She is also autistic, a disability that she argues allows her a special empathy with non-human creatures. Her latest book, *Animals Make Us Human*, is an amazing tour de force of animal–human relationships, with chapters on our companion animals, as well as on livestock, wildlife and zoos.

Most of us would prefer not to know where the meat on our plates comes from. And indeed when we consider slaughterhouses where animals mean only money, such knowledge is enough to turn one off meat for life. Grandin comes at the problem from a very different perspective from most, asking simply, 'What does an animal need to be happy?' Even creatures raised for meat, she believes, have the right to a happy life – and they can have it if certain 'freedoms' are granted them. Among these are freedom from hunger and thirst, discomfort, pain, injury and disease; and freedom to express normal behaviour and to live free from fear and distress. Yet as she points out, it's far from obvious how such freedoms might be granted, for each species has its own requirements, and conditions that are paradise for one may be purgatory for another.

If we are to grant these freedoms, Grandin argues that we need to understand how animals think, and most of the book is taken up with chapters on the inner lives of our companion animals – from dogs to cows to chickens to wildlife we interact with, and animals in zoos. In each instance Grandin displays an exceptional understanding of beings that, to most of us, remain enduring mysteries. It's hard to know which animals Grandin has the greatest fondness for, but cattle must be high on the list, for she has long experience of them, and has arguably done more than anyone to improve their lot.

Cattle, Grandin argues, aren't tame animals as are dogs or cats, and therefore freedom from fear is a big issue for them. As she puts it, 'A central welfare issue for beef cattle is poor stockmanship. People screaming and yelling at cattle, hitting or punching them, shocking them with electric prods – all of these things terrify cattle.' In arguing against such practices, she poses a series of immensely practical alternatives, such as positive reinforcement with food treats to move cattle into trucks or chutes. Well-cared-for cattle will 'actually *seek* handling procedures,' she asserts, and such cattle can remain relaxed, unstressed and happy all of their lives – right up to the moment of slaughter.

Unfortunately this is not, for reasons both mundane and infuriating, how most cattle live. 'Even when plants [i.e., slaughterhouses] know they're losing money by shocking and yelling at the animals, they still do it,' she says. 'In one slaughter plant I documented $500 to $1000 savings per day after I had trained employees to handle cattle quietly, but when I left, workers quickly went back to their old rough ways.' She feels that the greatest obstacle to the humane treatment of cattle is that 'to be a good stockperson you have to recognize that an animal is a conscious being that has feelings, and some people don't want to think of animals that way.' She also admits that:

> handling untamed, untrained cattle is frustrating ... and frustration is a mild form of rage ... That's why it's easy for people to blow up at farm animals (or at small children). Getting angry at frustrating situations is natural.

There is also a direct relationship between the way a business treats its employees and the way workers treat the animals in their care. Making sure that workers don't get exhausted by working long shifts, and giving them rewards for measurable outcomes, such as less bruising, injuries and noise, can all ensure a better life for the creatures that feed us.

Cats are a big part of my life, so I read Grandin's chapter on felines with unusual concentration. I was a little dismayed, therefore, to discover that 'animal behaviorists and ethologists don't know as much about cats and their emotions as we do about other domestic animals.' I thought I knew my cats pretty well, but Grandin surprised me by having much of great interest to say about these superbly sensual, mysterious creatures. One bare fact that had hitherto escaped me is that there are two basic cat personalities – bold and shy – which are associated with coat colour. Black cats, it turns out, are usually laid-back, while tortoiseshells are the typical 'scaredy cats.' I live with a black and a tortoiseshell cat (known respectively as the Captain and Bernadette), who could be models for this: the Captain is as solid as a rock, his aura of calm spreading far and wide, while Bernadette has been known to take fright at her own tail. Both, incidentally, had identical upbringings from kittenhood.

It turns out that coat colour in cats may be associated with genetic changes that confer a defence against feline AIDS, and that in turn are linked to behavioural traits. In cities, where cat populations are high, the spread of feline AIDS (which is contracted through scratches and bites) is greatly facilitated. Black cats tend to predominate in such environments. Orange toms, found in certain studies to be more aggressive than black cats, die early because they spend too much time fighting (thereby exposing themselves to feline AIDS), while the laid-back black toms just lounge about, waiting for their turn to mate. There is so much in *Animals Make Us Human* that is thoughtful and deeply insightful that anyone who eats meat, or has a pet, would be well advised to read it.

Not all of the creatures we encounter are as readily studied as our pets, and in *The Hidden Life of Deer* Elizabeth Marshall Thomas takes us on an intimate journey into the lives of some of the more obscure. Despite the fact that deer are among the largest animals anyone is likely to see around their homes, they are so secretive that we know very little of them. Thomas, who lives in southern New Hampshire, began feeding the deer near her home in 2007, when a failure of the acorn crop led her to put out corn for the many wild creatures facing a lean time. Despite the admonitions of experts, she continued feeding the deer, and eventually came to be able to identify both individuals and deer families, the most frequently seen of which she named the Deltas. These she follows through the full cycle of the year, learning as much as she can about their travails and triumphs. But what strikes the reader so forcibly is the individual nature of deer lives – from those of the privileged deer with high social status to those lower down the totem pole whose life is one long struggle.

The Hidden Life of Deer is a wonderfully careful and honest account of one person's attempt to get to know the wildlife living around her. Not all goes smoothly, however, as food put out for one species is likely to attract another. Here's what happened to Thomas:

> The full moon was so bright I thought I'd be able to see animals in the field if any were present. Hoping to catch a glimpse of the Deltas, I went to the kitchen door, a glass door, and cupped my hands beside my eyes to take a look. Surprisingly, I saw nothing at all – just total blackness. This seemed impossible. I looked out a nearby window and saw the whole moonlit scene of the fields and woods, every leaf, every grass blade. I tried again at the glass door, and again saw nothing. As I looked harder and longer, as my eyes got used to the solid black wall, I wondered if an unknown person for an unknown reason had draped a black blanket over our door. But then the

blackness began to seem somewhat fuzzy, and I realized I was looking into fur.

You might think that finding yourself just a fraction of an inch from a bear in the middle of the night would be a terrifying experience, especially when, standing upright, your eyes only come up to the level of his ribs. Thomas, however, turned on the porch light, looked into the eyes of the creature just a foot away (which then ambled off), and proclaimed to herself that she'd 'just had the greatest experience of my life.' The bear, it turns out, was known to Thomas. Indeed she had saved its life. When it was young it had been hit by a truck near her house, severely damaging its right hind leg. The police had arrived to put the creature out of its misery, but Thomas had argued that it should be given a chance:

> I told the men they shouldn't shoot him. The men said that the bear was suffering. They also said he was dangerous. He had to be shot, they insisted. I said I wouldn't let them. They told me to go home. I said, 'I am home.' They told me to go back to the house. I said I couldn't. The officer wondered aloud if I might have been drinking ... The officer had not yet taken out his pistol, but he started to cross the road. So before things could go any further, I scrambled up the bank to the bushes and the bear and told the officer to stay where he was. The men looked at each other. The officer said, 'It's not your bear.'
>
> I said, 'No, but it's my land, it's posted, and you'll need a search warrant to walk on it.'

I must admit that at this point I began to fall in love (in an un-chimpanzee like way) with this feisty older lady.

Despite such humane actions, Thomas is not averse to hunting, but she believes that the practice needs to be well regulated, and that hunters need to be disciplined and expert. In search of knowledge about hunters, she accompanies her neighbour, Don, who has Native American ancestry and hunts with a muzzle loader. He's such an expert hunter that for him the hunting season often lasts less than an hour. 'Gaia put the will to hunt deep into our psyches – there's nothing like it,' she concludes as she follows Don, stepping carefully, 'eyes wide, ears open, hardly breathing … an experience of the utmost intensity.'

Through the eyes of this extraordinary woman, a reader slowly loses view of 'the wild' and instead begins to see individual creatures. It's as if we're granted access to an extended family that includes deer, bears, turkeys and all the wild things of New England. *The Hidden Life of Deer* is a glorious achievement, giving new meaning to what it is both to be human and to be alive on this planet of wonders.

The New York Review of Books

Rick Grossman: The Trip Home

Maureen O'Shaughnessy

That is the gods' work, spinning threads of death
through the lives of mortal men,
and all to make a song for those to come ...

—HOMER, *The Odyssey*

On the first day of their 1986 Queensland tour, Rick Grossman and the rest of the Divinyls flew up to Brisbane, then rented a car and drove to the tavern where they were playing that night, had lunch at the bar, unpacked their gear and did a soundcheck, then were shown to their rooms – a motel was attached – where Rick discovered he'd left his dope fit back in Sydney.

Heroin addiction, as it's outlined in the medical guides, interferes with the brain's pleasure systems, affects its ability to perceive pain. Rick's heart swam in bottomless panic. He had to work quickly. He called his manager, told him of an urgent demo tape. The manager delivered it to a courier. Five hours later, Rick was in the tavern toilet, shooting up. He took to the stage, slung his bass on his hip, not seeing the sea of faces at his feet. Like the words to the song they were singing what he saw when he looked down was a fine line, but that line was on his arm, and it was written in blood.

What makes the body want to disappear? I know it's got something to do with the relief of being outside yourself, escaping the bleak maddening boredom of self-involvement. A simple act and you can blot things out, transcend the quiet disgrace of your own consciousness. I have no trouble imagining the wondrous elation of it except that needles make me wince.

'When you stop growing,' writes Burroughs, 'you start dying. An addict never stops growing.' Stoned, the unthinkable becomes bearable.

I pick him out right away, on a park bench under an elm, recognise the long arms and broad forehead from the video clips, the inky eyes set deep in scooped-out sockets. His mouth has the same smooth point of a bird's beak. He wears a bright red shirt, done up at the sleeves. Underneath his collar his neck is very brown. There is a take-away coffee cup and a pair of sunglasses and a set of keys in his hands. The wind is gusting. A smell of earth is lifting from the wet grass and high up in the low sky I hear the turbines of jets whining. He's dark, solid, a Beckman painting. People can't tell at first where he's from. Here, he looks European, bears the kind of plaintive woodenness you see on those in exile. His movements are jerky, he's too sincere, everything's too clean, and yet whenever he's not speaking I realise I'm immediately and indelicately riveted.

The resonances of our decisions.

Before his mother and father came to Australia, they had to hear many reasons why there was no real hope in the possibility of movement. Yet they set their course for the future. Settling in Sydney in the '50s, they refused to talk about the past. She got a job in the theatre, he went into real estate. They bought houses and bore children. Their children saw that they were unhappy but they denied it.

Even the silences grew quickly.

His father spent unnumbered hours taking in the new world around him. The cool blue line of the horizon. The thick waxed-smooth foliage in the yard and the depthless shadows. The vegetation in the yard grew dense like the jungle, crept into paths and walls. Flying with the RAF during the war, his plane had been shot down over Burma. How long had it taken for him to find his way back? These memories were sunk so far down that no act of will could bring them to the surface. Even if he'd wanted to talk he wouldn't have been able, the cast-iron Englishness of him being, after all, basic to his survival.

In the small, cliff-side house music played – the sound of *My Fair Lady, South Pacific* – filling the voiceless quiet. It was like the soundtrack to a film which reached its peak at dinner time. The rooms were dark, the place was foreign; surrounded now by what they'd made for themselves, they weren't interested in reminders of what they'd left behind. The music was as much as they allowed: it flowed relentlessly, like the water in the subterranean stream below their feet.

It was like this for a long time. Fifteen years. His father came and went and finally gave up. From the gloom of the kitchen his family watched the door one June night, waiting for him to come home. They wouldn't see him again for two years.

Growing up, at Scots College and then Sydney Boys High, Rick wasn't comfortable. He was shy. And very very quiet.

He avoided confrontation and he watched girls. Playing music – it was a fantasy and then it became real.

And soon, like his father, he too moves on. As a twenty-year-old living in Melbourne (before he's left with the empty husks of his dreams lying around him, before he's an addict), his mistakes are made by chance.

He says,

This girl, Michelle, was really mixed up with these heroin dealers. They were nineteen and drove Maseratis and I had no idea what was going on. One day she disappeared. I tried finding her. Eventually I tracked her down. Someone said she was in this house across town. I went round to see and sure enough she was living there and – well, I'd know these days exactly what was going on – but it was a place where you buy smack and she was acting really strange. I was like 'Hello there, how's everyone?' Sat next to this guy on the couch who starts chatting. He says, 'Oh, you're that friend of Michelle's, aren't you?' And I say, 'Yeah, yeah.' And he says, 'You play in bands, don't you?' And I say, 'Yeah.' And he says, 'You play guitar, don't you?' And I say, 'Yeah, I play bass.' And he says, 'I guess being a guitarist you'd really value your hands.' I look at him for a minute and then he says, still really friendly, 'Because you know what? We don't think you should see Michelle anymore.'

Lady, white girl, horse, black tar, brown sugar, smack, goods, H, junk, Harry …

And then, one night, in a back room, after a gig, he tries it.
He says,
From the very beginning, it was absolute euphoria.

I ask questions in a voice that is not really mine. He speaks slowly, with long pauses, as if to check that he's not letting himself sail far from the truth.

He says,
One time, I got hepatitis. A friend took me to a doctor in Carlton. I remember he was really shitty with me for coming in so late in the day. He told me to go and piss into a bottle. Then he went away, came back, looked at the bottle and said, 'You've got to go to Fairfield right away.' They said I was glowing in the dark.

He says,
I remember being away for a couple weeks and I hadn't used and my tolerance had gone right down. I came back to Sydney and I had some and I just dropped. All I remember is people hitting me and I'm thinking, *Why are you doing this, this is FANTASTIC. Just leave me alone.* And they're just hitting me in the chest. The next day I rang them and they said, 'You know, you were *DEAD*.' And I said, 'Ohh … isn't there some left?' Because I hadn't used it all.

He says,
When you are using, you'll give up your child for heroin.

He has a musician's faith in transcendence, along with their humbling doubts, the niggling fears of pointlessness and inadequacy, 'Will people want to listen to what I'm doing? Will they like it?' The willingness to commit oneself to the dumb, fantastic alchemy of inspiration. As the writer Milosz puts it, 'To get up in the morning and to go to work, to be bound to people by the ties of love, friendship or opposition – and all the time to realise that it is only meanwhile and make-believe …'

In those years when he's playing with the Divinyls, Chrissie becomes his sister. She bosses him around. Cuts his hair. Brings him food when he's sick. Placid-accustomed, he lets her. In a band, you tend to replay your family dynamic.

So in many ways it is a story of ordinary betrayal and delusion. He cannot rid himself of his habit and while he works on fooling himself, he believes he's fooling her. The hit-ups have become more frequent. His course is driven and precarious. Strung out at the Australian Made concert, he retreats to the narrow airless cave of a port-a-loo because he's unable to go for more than a few hours without injecting.

It has rained all morning. The air is fetid and the place stinks. He is fumbling in the dark with the cigarette lighter and spoon, his pupils are dilated, his skin is bruised, his bicep is pulled into pleats by the leather belt round his arm. There is a snap-lock bag in his pocket, which contains the three further caps he needs to get through the day.

When the drug warms them the veins swell in ropey maps across his body; the loud wash of the crowd outside spills into the cracks.

Opening the door, he moans softly as he falls. For the last time, Chrissie picks him up. She helps to clear his lungs of mud.

The woman in detox, she'd seen it all, he recalls; she had an eagle eye. A friend attends the compulsory group sessions with him. Both clearly struggling from withdrawal, they can barely sit still, and when they do it is as if the ground shakes them, their bodies rock, trembling. The woman (angora cardie, oversized specs – she looks like Edna Everage) sits watching, mulish, bored, untouched by their excuses for using. She won't talk causes. She talks about getting off. She speaks with an authority they haven't had to put up with for years, as if they are fourth-graders. She has a sublime indifference, even as she helps them, a way that's at once knowing and detached, without ever making it seem that they are a disappointment or a burden.

Each day, he is now anchored by the thought of himself as being in recovery.

He says,

I do other things to distract myself. I watch TV series. At the moment it's *Shameless*. I just finished *Breaking Bad*. I just go home and … It's because I'm alone, you know.

Driving his teenaged son to soccer, he slipped his latest CD, *Purity of Essence*, into the player. He was pleased with this new record, and the direction his band, the Hoodoo Gurus, were taking lately. When he asked him what he thought, his son smiled and shrugged, saying it just wasn't the kind of music he listened to.

And yet among the most beautiful things about his life's work is the force and balance he gives to a band, the unconditional generosity of his playing. He is lashed to every song; the underpinning of the tune, the steel in the rhythm. The bass *shapes* whatever's happening and the music, if it wasn't held together by this dark crazy energy, would crumble into formless noise. These particular qualities, the pleasure of creating order, and the passion for intimacy and for expression, are part of who he is: hence the strength of his obsessions and the straight, unflashy commitment he makes to serving his art.

He is one of those people whose mental map of his journey is still so intricately drawn, so well traced, that even after years have passed he can take you to that place, show you the road out, which is what he does for the many who come to him to help them turn their lives around.

The voice-recorder is switched off and he lifts his face to the supple light, wings his elbows across the bench-back. As my eyes follow his to where a blond dog has raised its leg and is pissing against a bin, I hear him take a deep breath.

He waits, then tells me he is in love.

She lives on the other side of the world, he explains. They're working at how to be together. He feels for her in a way he thought never really existed. She is all he needs. The sun breaks through a sky of torn wool. He gazes over the stretch of parkland washed in the watery light as a relieved sailor might on approaching a familiar landscape.

He laughs, knowing that in some ways it's a cliché, that his attachment and dependence has just moved from one thing to another; this kind of devotion, though, is something he is grateful for.

He says,

Addiction is a spiritual problem brought on by an emptiness, a God-shaped hole.

It removes fear.

It is like salvation.

It is like coming home.

'Freud Has a Name for It': A.A. Phillips's 'The Cultural Cringe'

Ian Henderson

This year the Cultural Cringe is sixty years old, ancient enough for us to recognise that the notorious phrase is usually deployed liberally, inaccurately, and without reference to Arthur Angel Phillips (1900–1985), the nationalist critic who coined it in 1950.

As Richard Nile, the professor of Australian Studies at Curtin University, put it recently, Cultural Cringe might be the only phrase in literary criticism to have become 'an icon of Australia's vernacular culture.' So it seems fitting to remind ourselves that, in the end, its concern was not the production but the reception of Australian writing.

Indeed, 'The Cultural Cringe' is underpinned by a reception theory that creates a culturally specific history of reading. By drawing together the history of Phillips's use of the phrase and his characterisation of it in specific psychoanalytic terms, I'll distil that theory here.

Three preliminary points should be made. Firstly, Phillips coined the term nine months before he deployed it as a title in response to Tyrone Guthrie's infamous report on Australian theatre, noting references to the English tradition usually induced a 'characteristically Australian cultural cringe (sometimes thinly disguised behind a front of blather-skite),' and observing further that a 'cringing culture cannot be a healthy culture.'

The Cringe, then, was born a symptom of disease, but one whose effect on Australian artists, not readers, was in the foreground. Secondly, Phillips's original version of 'The Cultural Cringe' appeared as one of four essays in *Meanjin*, volume 9, 1950, under the series title 'Writers on Grub Street.' Again writers, not readers, were the main concern. Thirdly, Phillips made significant changes when he re-worked his essay for publication in 1958 as a chapter of *The Australian Tradition: Studies in a Colonial Culture.* It's here that some of Phillips's most famous descriptions of Australian reading are to be found. Clearly when released from predetermined frameworks, and with the benefit of hindsight, he could tighten the focus on what the Cringe was all about.

In the end Phillips was interested in inner processes of reading. He set out to delineate 'a disease of the Australian mind' which is both engendered by, and expressed as, a neurotic form of reading; to combat that neurosis by provoking a different form of reading; and to identify the sign by which we will know our reading to be cured.

In the process of meeting these objectives Phillips famously represents the ways of consuming Australian culture as three poses of the body, delineating the two stances analogous to neurotic reading – the Cultural Cringe (the 'Cringe Direct') and the Cultural Strut (the 'Cringe Inverted') – and the one which is the physical manifestation of healthy reading: 'relaxed erectness of carriage.'

Phillips's choice of corporeal metaphors to represent psychological states is an inadvertent acknowledgment of his debts to pre-Freudian experimental psychology, with its focus on physiology, and in particular the physiology of the senses. A key sign of this debt in 'The Cultural Cringe' is its upholding the principle that voices in the head are always memories of sound.

It's significant, then, that Phillips, in an essay packed with sound as well as fury, raises the Australian accent three times in the 1958 version, firstly retailing A.G. Mitchell's mistaken observation that 'Australians are the only Anglo-Saxon community which is ashamed of having its own way of pronouncing the English language,' and secondly by referring to an imagined English critic 'interrupting in the wrong accent.' Finally, in noting that

Australians 'cannot shelter from invidious comparisons' with English writing 'behind the barrier of a separate language,' Phillips hints that our national culture – its distinctive qualities and its quality *per se* – is instead encapsulated by, and embodied in, our accent.

In fact voices in the heads of Australian readers are central to Phillips's argument: 'The Cringe,' he writes in both versions, 'mainly appears in an inability to escape needless comparisons. The Australian reader, more or less consciously, hedges and hesitates, asking himself, "Yes, but what would a cultivated Englishman think of this?"' In Australian writing, Phillips argues, we have learned not to ask ourselves such questions; there we possess 'the art of being unselfconsciously ourselves.' It's the relatively slow development of a corresponding capacity in Australian reading that frustrates Phillips. But only in the later version of the essay does he expand on the cause of this predicament, a peculiar entity formed in the psyche:

> The core of the difficulty is the fact that, in the back of the Australian mind, there sits a minatory Englishman ... that Public School Englishman with his detection of a bad smell permanently engraved on his features, who has left a trail of exasperation through Europe and of smouldering hatred through the East, and whose indifference to the Commonwealth is not even studied.

Phillips continues:

> Subconsciously the educated Australian feels a guilty need to placate this shadowy figure. (Freud has a name for it.) His ghost sits in on the tête-à-tête between Australian reader and writer, interrupting in the wrong accent.

This subconscious psychic formation is a Cringe-inducing ghost in the Australian reading machine.

The 'name' that Phillips tells us Freud has for the 'minatory Englishman' formed in Australian minds ('it') is surely the super-ego as expounded in Freud's 'The Ego and the Id.' And the self-evident subordination of this allusion corresponds with the indirect nature of Phillips's references to the Australian accent: that each feature illuminates the other suggests we are at the disguised heart of his reception theory. For by his focus on human sounds, Phillips underscores the special place of auditory memories for the formation of the thinking, speaking, and reading subject in 'The Ego and the Id,' while also pointing to what this later work owes Freud's early monograph *On Aphasia*. Exploring both will clarify the nature, history and treatability of the Cultural Cringe.

*

In 'The Ego and the Id' Freud re-articulates for his theory of psychology the structure of the human mind, substituting for his formerly functioning distinction between the conscious and the unconscious a new 'antithesis between the coherent ego and the repressed which is split off from it.' Freud further posits that while 'all that is repressed is Ucs. [i.e., of the unconscious system],' 'not all that is Ucs. is repressed.' It seems the repressing aspect of the ego is also unconscious.

This leads him to posit that the ego, while undoubtedly modified by the influence of the external world via the perceptions, is also distinguished by being 'a precipitate of abandoned object-cathexes.' That is, identifications have accumulated in the ego forged in the abandonment of prohibited sexual desires (most formatively, Oedipal desires). Through the process of identification, that is, 'the ego makes it easier for the object to be given up'; this may even be the only means by which 'the id can give up its objects.'

That the 'character of the ego' as formed over time therefore 'contains the history of [former sexual] object choices' affords insight into the historiography operating in 'The Cultural Cringe.' But for now I want to follow Freud's subsequent focus on the first identification, namely a child's identification with his (sic) parents. Indeed, it's through the psychological process of replacing Oedipal desire with identification that identity-formation is itself engendered.

The broad general outcome of the sexual phase dominated by the Oedipus complex may, therefore, be taken to be the forming of a precipitate in the ego ... This modification of the ego retains its special position; it confronts the other contents of the ego as an ego ideal or super-ego.

Thus the super-ego, in Freud's words, 'is the heir of the Oedipus complex,' because repressing the Oedipus complex is 'no easy task' and the psyche seeks a model for strength with which to fortify itself. This it finds in the father's superlative ability to obstruct its desires. As Freud puts it:

> The child's parents, especially his father, were perceived as the obstacle to a realization of his Oedipal wishes; so his infantile ego fortified itself for the carrying out of the repression by erecting this same obstacle within himself. It borrowed strength, so to speak, from the father, and this loan was an extraordinarily momentous act.

Thus the father becomes the super-ego which represses the Oedipus complex; and identification with the father becomes the paradigm of identification *per se*. The super-ego is therefore:

> a memorial of the former weakness and dependence of the ego, and the mature ego remains subject to its domination. As a child was once under a compulsion to obey its parents, so the ego submits to the categorical imperative of its super-ego.

This construction of the super-ego as a 'memorial' to 'former weakness' in the face of a domineering parent presents Phillips with a paradigm for a psycho-cultural history of Australia.

*

In exploring potential uses for this paradigm, a distinction might be drawn between rendering individual psychological development an allegory of national cultural development, and exploring the significance of Australia's social history for 'The Cultural Cringe' in terms of Freud's notion of the id as containing 'phylogenetic acquisitions' by which the super-ego has access to species history and ancestral memory.

In the former allegory, the colonised 'child' Australia has set up an identification with the colonising 'father' England and is now experiencing an unconscious sense of guilt as the Cultural

Cringe: Australian culture is to English culture as the ego is to the super-ego, 'subject to its domination,' critically measured against it, borrowing its strength to repress itself.

The trouble with rigidly sustaining this analogy is that it posits the Cultural Cringe as insurmountable. As Freud writes: 'whatever the [ego] character's later capacity for resisting the influences of abandoned object-cathexes may turn out to be, the effect of the first identifications made in earliest childhood will be general and lasting.' Phillips is rather interested in 'curing' his 'disease' of the Australian reading 'mind.'

Thus connecting Australian social history to the Freudian model of phylogenetic history proves more effective for understanding 'The Cultural Cringe.' Just as the id is, for Freud, the reservoir of 'former ego-structures' of our biological ancestors and the super-ego's contact with these 'makes it a reincarnation of former ego-structures which have left their precipitates behind in the id,' the Australian national id is the reservoir of former (colonial) social structures and the super-ego of Australia is therefore a re-incarnation of a specific colonial cultural, political and social hierarchy.

Phillips is arguing that Australians mistake the English accent for the sound of the super-ego's 'voice.'

Needless to say, when Phillips was writing many Australian-born, Australian-accented children's parents were British-born and spoke with English accents. Pursuing its psychological implications, I need to recall another Freudian concept expounded in 'The Ego and the Id,' namely the distinction between 'unconscious' mental processes, which remain forever repressed in the psyche, and 'preconscious' mental processes, which may become conscious again, namely memories of sense perceptions and feelings, sensations which were consciously experienced 'from the start.'

Different types of interior 'thought processes' can also be distinguished by this means. If these are 'carried out on some material which remains unknown' they remain unconscious. But if, 'in addition' these are 'brought into connection with word-presentations' they are preconscious and capable of becoming conscious again.

By word-presentations Freud means memories of 'auditory

perceptions': 'In essence a word is after all the mnemic residue of a word that has been heard.' Following this through, to 'hear' the 'more or less conscious' critical voice in the head of an Australian-accented child of English-accented parents would be to make conscious again memories of sounds once heard in the unmatched accents of the father. The super-ego of the Australian-born child of English parents would indeed 'interrupt in the wrong accent.'

The English accent of the super-ego would have further effects as the child obtained later and supposedly 'higher' forms of language skill. This process invokes Freud's *On Aphasia*, in which he notes that we learn to speak by creating a 'sound-image' which, when we hear our own voice, becomes associated with a prior auditory sensation.

In early childhood the association may not entail matching the sensations; we speak our own language; we babble. Then we 'learn to speak the language of other people by endeavouring to make the sound-image produced by ourselves as like as possible to the one which gave rise to our speech-innervation.' Freud then notes that we learn to spell by 'linking visual images of the letters with new sound-images,' that is by sounding letters. When we join up, say, two letter sounds:

> we discover ... that the two motor images and sound-images which we have received in this way have long been familiar to us and are identical with the images used in speaking. We then associate the meaning which was attached to the primary verbal sounds with the speech-images which have been acquired by spelling.

The most significant point in *On Aphasia* for 'The Cultural Cringe' now rises:

> If what was spoken primarily was a dialect and not a literary language, the motor and sound-images of the words acquired through spelling have to be super-associated with the old images; thus we have to learn a new language – a task which is facilitated by the similarity between the dialect and the literary language.

Phillips has already raised the point that Australians and the English share a language, so ours is less a 'dialect' than an 'accent.' However he has also laid emphasis on 'the ability to hear the cadence of a phrase in a certain way' when reading: Australian writers presume Australian readers of their writing have this ability. But it also means Australian readers, when reading, are used to 'hearing' the 'cadence' of criticism 'in a certain way': in an English accent. An accumulation of hierarchies occurs based on the English-accented super-ego's domination of the Australian-accented ego: reading is later/higher than speaking; criticism is later/higher than literature; the English (critical) accent is higher than the Australian (reading) accent.

The outcome is that Australia is deemed incapable of being literary. This resonates with Freud's comment in 'The Ego and the Id' that the super-ego's:

> relation to the ego is not exhausted by the precept: 'You ought to be like this (like your father).' It comprises the prohibition: 'You may not be like this (like your father) – that is, you may not do all he does; some things are his prerogative.

Thus Australian readers feel Australian literature ought to be English literature but that it may not be English Literature.

The significance of Freud's account of the role of memories of sound in the development of speaking, reading and writing skills, coupled with that of the super-ego, is readily apparent for Australian-accented children of English-accented parents. But the implication of Phillips's use of Freud is that this recurring phenomenon is universalised in Australia. Phillips implies that the universalisation occurs because of the domination of Australian cultural institutions by British-born personnel and British-made products: cultural authority always seemed to speak in an English accent.

This ties 'The Cultural Cringe' to mid-twentieth-century debates about the Australian accent in the theatre (*Summer of the Seventeenth Doll* premiered the year before Phillips published *The Australian Tradition*) and on the ABC. For even if an Australian's parents spoke with Australian accents, Australians took the formative psychic parental identification within them, the super-ego, to be speaking in an English one.

One can impute from 'The Cultural Cringe' that for Phillips this nationally specific mistake harks back to the literally coercive physical power of English jailers over convicts, coupled with their shared loss of mother England, recalling Freud's comment that:

> the more powerful the Oedipus complex was and the more rapidly it succumbed to repression (under the influence of authority, religious teaching, schooling and reading), the stricter will be the domination of the super-ego over the ego later on – in the form of conscience or perhaps of an unconscious sense of guilt.

Phillips certainly implies that the Cultural Cringe derives from an unusually strict form of domination and is experienced as a uniquely strong Australian sense of guilt.

Now in the simple personal/national development allegory, there was no real cure for the Cultural Cringe because the super-ego is ineradicable. But in Phillips's 'socio-genetic' history, his aim is not the obliteration of the super-ego but to outline a treatment against misrecognising its accent. Correspondingly, Phillips is not opposing criticism of Australian culture, quite the opposite, but wants, via a displacement of the English accent, to replace the Australian readership's automatic condemnation of Australian writing with critical discrimination. As he writes:

> The critical attitude of the intellectual towards the community is ... not in itself harmful; on the contrary, it could be a healthy, even a creative influence, if the criticism were felt to come from within, if the critic had a sense of identification with his subject, if his irritation came from a sense of shared shame rather than from a disdainful separation.

In one sense, the critic's 'identification with his subject,' his (sic) 'shared shame,' positions him among those who are subject to the super-ego (experiencing thus a 'sense of guilt'). However, as a 'critic,' one who deploys a critical voice, he remains more like the super-ego than those whose work he assesses critically.

The sense of 'coming from within' derives then not from levelling super-ego and ego but from the fact that the super-ego, and the critic, are no longer 'speaking' in the wrong (English) accent. Achieving this end entailed a talking cure, or rather a hearing cure: a discerning Australian audience would be produced if more Australians read critics whose own cadences were Australian, that is, if they read more local critics on the Australian tradition.

The mere possibility of a cure confirms that it is the 'realist' ego of Freud's 'The Ego and the Id' that Phillips deploys in 'The Cultural Cringe.' As the Australian philosopher Elizabeth Grosz has argued, the super-ego offered psychoanalysis conceptual grounds for 'curing' non-normative conditions, a practice which was heavily criticised by Jacques Lacan in the same decade Phillips re-worked his theory of the Cringe.

Comparing Phillips's and Lacan's uses of Freud, Phillips upholds an outdated and conservative paradigm of socialisation, wishing to make 'better Australians' by changing the accent of the nonetheless patriarchal critic. In doing so he foregoes more sensual, libertarian models of an Australia that is not so much 'cured' of colonial culture as increasingly entangled in its past and open to multiple futures.

He represses more erotic and convoluted poses as potential replacements for the Cringe in favour of advocating the manifestly bourgeois and masculinist 'relaxed erectness of carriage' with which he ends both versions of 'The Cultural Cringe.' And yet while, in 1950s Paris, Lacan may have been justified in lambasting the conservatism of Freud's 'realist' ego, in 1950s Australia Phillips was surely revolutionary in using it to think through ways to combat clearly irritating colonial attitudes in everyday Australian life, to recognise with its aid that this was all a matter of reading's inner voices. Moreover, in the terms of his own essay, that Phillips coined a vernacular phrase suggests he really did find a word-presentation that could bring a collective unconscious mental process to light. He made the realist ego look radical (again).

*

'The Cultural Cringe' also set out to demonstrate qualities of the Australian-accented critical voice which would replace the one engendering the Cringe. Its temper is democratic though at the cost of underplaying the (national) cultural legitimacy of difficult texts, and of conversations about them between educated elites. Freud is, instead, parenthesised. So in Phillips's light tone lie the advantages and the disadvantages of his vision for Australian criticism: it makes a mockery of my convoluted foray into the same terrain – there is little relaxed erectness of carriage here – but it also exacerbates underestimation of the intellectual complexity of his work and of the full implications of his erudition.

By way of a coda let me contemplate the 'whiteness' of 'The Cultural Cringe' via Freud's description of 'certain forms of obsessional neurosis' in the final chapter of 'The Ego and the Id.' In these, he writes:

> the sense of guilt is over-noisy but cannot justify itself to the ego. Consequently the patient's ego rebels against the imputation of guilt and seeks the physician's support in repudiating it. It would be folly to acquiesce in this, for to do so would have no effect. Analysis eventually shows that the super-ego is being influenced by processes that have remained unknown to the ego. It is possible to discover the repressed impulses which are really at the bottom of the sense of guilt. Thus in this case the super-ego knew more than the ego about the unconscious id.

Let me re-present this passage as a hypothetical critico-clinical situation. The patient is an Australian critic, let us call him Mr P, who has an 'over-noisy' sense of guilt which is unjustified to his ego, and which he disputes in a noisy essay. He seeks his physician's support for the repudiation of his sense of guilt. However, the physician suspects there are 'repressed impulses which are really at the bottom of the sense of guilt': it is not 'over-noisy'; rather, the critic has a neurotic obsession with it.

This suggests to the physician that the critic's essay must also be misguided. Having read it, the physician concludes that it is indeed wrong: the issue is not that Australians have mistaken the super-ego's accent for an English one, but that the critic has mistaken accents for compelling distinctions. For elsewhere in the critic's essay, the physician notes, differences of accents are overlooked: a 'most suitable' Englishman can be both a 'rare pukka sahib with his deep still pool of imaginativeness, and his fine urbanity' and a 'common man with his blending of solidity and tenderness.'

In repeating the term 'pukka sahib,' the physician observes, the critic accidentally invokes that which closes the differences between these three white men, the master, the commoner and the critic: the British Empire. The physician speculates: this critic's unconscious sense of guilt actually rises from the imperialist super-ego's measuring of the nationalist ego; the latter does not compare well with the force by which an empire was forged (Governor P vs Mr P); the imperative fulfilment of a now disintegrating empire must remain, as far as this critic's nationalist psyche is concerned, a prerogative of the dead white father.

The physician concludes: wherever this neurosis holds true, all whites can do is chastise black Australians like him ... But the thought is interrupted by an image of his children dancing.

Southerly

Another Universe

Amanda Hooton

In March 2009, Miss Universe 2008, Dayana Mendoza, was 'deployed' to Guantánamo Bay. She had a great time seeing the jail ('where they shower, how they recreate themselves'), the military dogs ('a very nice demonstration of their skills') and the beach ('soooo beautiful!'). All in all, she told her blog readers, 'I didn't want to leave, it was such a relaxing place, so calm and beautiful.'

The following month, Miss Universe Australia held its crowning ceremony. Its purpose was to choose Miss Universe Australia 2009, who will represent the country this month in the world (indeed, the universe) finals in the Bahamas. Miss Mendoza would have found much that was familiar in the Hilton ballroom in Sydney. All the girls were, indeed, soooo beautiful, and they gave a very nice demonstration of their skills. But – unlike Guantánamo Bay – there was nothing either calm or relaxing about it.

*

By 9 a.m., the ante-room of the Hilton ballroom is packed with girls, and there's a sound like the roar of a jet engine coming from the open door. Every now and then there's a sudden shriek, as if a bird is being mangled in a turbine. The roaring is the sound of many, many hairdryers all being used at once, and the shrieks are from the Miss Universe finalists, whose hair extensions are getting caught in the Velcro rollers. There are almost sixty people in this room, and most of them are young women, but the finalists are easy to spot. They are the ones with the endless legs, the tiny shorts, the sculpted faces. And the business pages of the daily newspapers.

I had many preconceptions about the Miss Universe contest. I expected the Bambi eyelashes, the pneumatic boobs, the hyper-lustrous hair. I didn't expect the analysis of the global financial crisis and the discussion of industrial-relations change. I pass two girls sitting on the floor by the doorway. One has violet eyes and hair the colour of ripe wheat, the other is a brunette with skin like caramel. Both are wearing five-inch heels and miniskirts. 'So what's Peter Costello actually doing?' the blonde asks the brunette, poring over the *Australian Financial Review*. 'Looking for attention,' says the brunette.

Miss Universe contestants know a great deal about attention. This is a competition, after all, to find the girl who, through all the endless permutations of bikinis and evening gowns and coordinated dance routines, can keep most of the attention, of most of the judges, most of the time. Abraham Lincoln would have understood Miss Universe.

The Miss Universe contest began – like its rival Miss World, the Eurovision Song Contest, and other truly global competitions that are also truly strangers to changing social norms or the least hint of irony – in the postwar optimism and reclaimed innocence of the 1950s. Its format has changed very little over the years. There's a swimwear bit, an evening-gown bit, a question bit. In between, there are endless cancan lines of beautiful girls, smiling and waving through the dry ice and glitter showers, and trying, not always successfully, not to fall down the stairs.

According to the Miss Universe creed (no longer in active use, alas), the 'young women of the universe believe people everywhere are seeking peace, tolerance, and mutual understanding.' But even in the Miss Universe universe, things are not all sweetness and light. Both winners and contestants have been dethroned or disqualified because they've been discovered to be mothers, or married, or both; or because they've 'brought the contest into disrepute.' In June this year, Donald Trump (classy co-owner of the Miss Universe contest with CBS from 1996 to

2001, NBC since 2002), sacked Miss California USA for 'dereliction of duty,' after several semi-nude photos of her hit the internet. Host countries have also caused scandals. In 1974, Imelda Marcos spent several million dollars of public funds building the competition stadium in Manila, then used the Philippine air force to seed storm clouds when bad weather threatened the contest. And during the 1979 final in Perth, WA, part of the stage collapsed and Misses Malta, Philippines, England and Brazil all fell two metres into the rubble.

Australia's Miss Universe history has always been mixed. In 2000 the national competition here was virtually abandoned as an anachronism, but in 2004 our unsung delegate, Jennifer Hawkins, stunned the world by taking out the crown. She was the second Australian to be crowned Miss Universe (our first, Kerry Anne Wells, was in 1972), and since her win, the contest has become wildly popular. This year some 7000 girls entered, and every one of them did so with the real sense that she too might end up with the $250,000 tiara, the year-long lease on the Trump Tower apartment in New York, and the opportunity to be deployed to beautiful detention camps all over the world.

It's not all tireless acts of charity, however. Miss Universe is also big business. Every country that fields a contestant must pay a yearly franchise fee to Miss Universe headquarters: between seventy-five and eight-five countries compete, and the fees are thought to be as high as $100,000 a pop. Then there are the broadcasting and advertising rights. Miss Universe is televised in 200 countries worldwide, and watched by an audience of close to a billion. Some estimates put the total value of the competition as high as US$1.5 billion. In 2005, Trump estimated his personal stake to be worth between US$40 million and US$50 million.

For franchise holders in each competing country, meanwhile, money is made from entry fees (in the US, state finalists are often asked to pay up to $1000 to enter), sponsorship, advertising and appearance fees. In Australia, the franchise holder is Deborah Miller, of Melbourne's Cosmopolitan Model Management. She is extremely voluptuous, with extremely long blonde hair and extremely pouty lips. 'It's really about sponsorship,' she says. 'The girls don't have to pay to enter here: any money comes from sponsorship.'

Thirty girls have made it to the Australian final this year. They've got here via various routes: some selected directly from their modelling portfolios; some via several rounds of competition at state level. They are, as you'd imagine, mostly models, but there are also surf-lifesaving medallists and professional cheerleaders. One lovely redhead works with the disabled, which may or may not compensate for her unforgivably short hair; many are students. Depressingly, several seem extremely accomplished. Twenty-three-year-old Kim Eckhof from Western Australia has just finished a double degree in commerce and science, can speak fluent German and French, and is a swimming champion as well as an international model.

Eckhof is one of my early favourites. So is Rachael Finch, a twenty-year-old Queenslander who is not only a TV presenter, but a barefoot waterskier. I like them because of their beauty (Finch is a brunette with extraordinary elongated eyes, Eckhof a perfect blonde) and because neither takes herself too seriously. Finch tells me she's 'just going to push through them nerves' when she gets on stage, and Eckhof confesses to a lingering sense of embarrassment about the whole Miss Universe thing. 'My mum and dad and my boyfriend are coming tonight,' she explains, wincing. 'I've never had a boyfriend before, and then somehow I got one, and now he's going to see me strutting round. It doesn't really feel like me. And they made me get hair extensions! I liked my hair. Now I feel like Barbie.'

It must be said, she looks a bit like Barbie, too, mostly in her leg-to-torso ratio, which seems to be about six to one. This is common to all the contestants: that coltish awkwardness you see so much on catwalks. Their bones are prominent, too, especially their shoulders and collarbones, but only a couple seem dangerously thin. I wonder about boob jobs and collagen and nose jobs and Botox, but to be honest, most of them just look like the products of God or the fates or supercharged genetics, rather than cosmetic intervention.

Tonight, the contest will begin with the cocktail-dress opening parade and the swimsuit parade, after which the top ten contestants will be announced. Then there's the evening-gown parade, the shoe parade, the choosing of the final five, and the announcement of the winner. Before any of this, however, there are two hair sessions, two rehearsals and a make-up session. Eleven hair stylists have been brought in by the salon mogul John Brennan, a round middle-aged man who remembers doing Miss USA's hair in the '80s, before she was dethroned for doing a *Penthouse* shoot. Is there a particular look you're after, I ask a stylist. 'Victoria's Secret,' she tells me. 'Messy, just out of bed, big curls, volume. Volume, volume, volume.' This, obviously, is why twenty-eight of the thirty girls have their hair in rollers. Do many of them, I ask, have hair extensions? 'Only about 90 per cent,' she says.

'It's hard, because you don't want to pay a fortune,' a girl with white-blonde tresses says suddenly. For a moment I think she's referring to hair extensions, which can cost up to $2000; then I realise she's chatting to the girl opposite her.

'Are you with an agency?' says the other girl, also blonde.

'I'm with about eight?' The first blonde has one of those voices that goes up at the end of sentences.

'Who's the main one? Bliss?'

'Get them to recommend someone, maybe.'

'I did, but I didn't like them? They were a bit amateur?' She sighs. 'I've had, like, twenty-five test shots.'

The second blonde nods vigorously. 'You've got to keep going. I had some done by George Anthony.'

'What's her name again?'

'George. It's a boy.'

One of the surprises of Miss Universe is the friendliness. There are, no doubt, girls in this room who would stiletto each other in the eye to win tonight, but most have the grace, or the native cunning, to hide it well; the general atmosphere is one of camaraderie. Once they've got their hair in curlers, many of them begin to congregate in groups, swapping newspapers and notebooks.

'What is the biggest issue facing Australia today, and why?' a breathtaking girl with black hair in a Grecian coil (whose name, impossibly, is Aphrodite) asks a cheeky blonde with a little snip of a nose.

'Aieeee!' says the blonde. 'That's so hard!'

'Okay,' says Aphrodite, looking at her notes. 'Who is the woman you most admire, and why?'

Both these questions, of course, are examples of The Question, which is the Everest summit, the Rachmaninov 3rd, the moon landing of Miss Universe. There is nothing friendly about The Question. It is the moment in which contestants must gird their mental loins and reveal what Miss Universe is really all about: rapier wit, sparkling personality. World Peace.

Under this pressure, casualties are inevitable. In 2007, Miss Teen USA South Carolina was asked why so many Americans are unable to locate the US on a map. 'I personally believe,' she said, blonde hair shimmering, blue eyes blinking, 'that US Americans are unable to do so ... because, uh, some people out there in our nation ... don't have maps! And I believe that our education like such as South Africa and uh, the Iraq, everywhere like such as ... and I believe that they should our education over here! In the US should help the US, should help South Africa and should help the Iraq ... and the Asian countries ... so we will be able to build up our future ... for our children!'

Miss South Carolina didn't win the pageant. But she did become famous on YouTube, where her answer has been viewed by 35 million people, many of whom may not own maps (though they may speak in full sentences). By the look of the girls in this room, however, nobody tonight is going to follow in her footsteps. If preparation counts for anything, everyone here is going to sound like Kofi Annan.

By late morning, Hair Phase One is done, and everyone troops to the ballroom for rehearsal. This is run by a female choreographer called Kate, who spends a lot of time saying things like, 'If you need to go to the toilet backstage, one, you have to find me; two, you have to wear a jacket; and three, you can't talk. And four, you shouldn't be going to the toilet in the first place.'

The girls stand and stop and walk and turn. As they come on stage, most seem to enter a kind of trance, posing and turning and smiling fixedly into the empty room. 'Spread out!' shouts Kate. 'Centre! File into one line here. Are you watching? Walk straight down the middle, straight down, straight down. Hello???? It's really easy!'

It doesn't look easy at all, in fact, and is further complicated by the evening's entertainer, Mark Spano, who weaves in and out of the line, smiling and joking and distracting the girls.

'You have to use your brains!' cries Kate amid the confusion.

'No, you don't,' says Spano encouragingly. 'You don't. You just have to look good.'

'I want more blondes in the front row!' calls Deborah Miller. Three stylists are crowded round her doing something to her hair, but she is obviously the sort of woman who can hold her head motionless while shouting at people fifty metres away. 'Where's Nico?' she cries. 'I need him! Where's Bella? Can you tell Man to Man not to kiss them backstage? No kissing!'

Man to Man are the male models being used tonight for vital tasks such as forming a guard of honour on the red carpet and holding the Question bowl. Backstage, the girls seem unlikely to let anyone kiss them.

'I'm exhausted,' says Aphrodite. 'And I'm hungry.'

'I haven't been to the toilet all day,' says Jade Russell, a 22-year-old blonde who is a flight attendant on a corporate jet.

'What about your bra?' says another girl.

'I've got some chicken fillets,' replies a fourth. 'But they're not heaps sticky, so I'm worried they might pop off.'

'I could Hollywood-tape them for you.'

Out on stage, tonight's MC, Pete Lazer, a TV personality with spiky blond hair, is giving a few pointers to girls practising their walks. 'Don't talk if you've got nothing to say,' he says, advice that could be usefully taken by many TV personalities. 'Just say, "Thanks very much," off.'

'What's the time?' cries Miller, from her position in the wings.

'That's going to be nowhere near enough time for the girls to get changed,' says someone.

'That's all the time they've got,' says Kate.

As the afternoon wears on, I try to think deep thoughts about beauty pageants. Mostly, I think how much better-looking these girls are than me – specifically, how much thinner. It's the thinness through the waist and hips and thighs that really strikes you – a kind of mermaid sleekness. But then, all of these girls are under twenty-five; in a moment of sheer meanness I catalogue the hints of body issues to come: heavy thighs, very round bottoms, flaring hips. Then, when they all walk downstage together, I give up. En masse, they are dazzling: so many long legs, so many white teeth, so much hair. They do the classic Miss Universe pose – all standing, one leg to the front and slightly bent, one hand on hip – and smile. Our culture has spent untold centuries revering women for their youth and their beauty. Here are both, and you can't argue with either.

By 6 p.m., things are really revving up in the ante-room, where, in Hair Phase Two, girls are having their hair teased into enormous, bouncing curls. Then they're allocated their cocktail dresses for the opening parade from a great pile of samples. Many of the dresses are absolutely hideous.

'I guess it will be okay,' says Aphrodite, looking dubiously at her pile of frills and ruffles. 'It'll disguise the no-boob factor.'

'Put hairspray on your legs and that'll hold it,' says another to a girl whose skirt is so short it's riding up over her bottom. 'And if it doesn't, just make it a part of your walk.'

Once their hair is done and their dresses allocated, the girls file down to the end of the room for their make-up. Most have fake eyelashes applied, to go with their fake hair, fake tans and bleached teeth. They still manage to look gorgeous, and they're still being nice to each other: I feel a sudden burst of admiration for them, being so sincere in the midst of this ridiculous endeavour.

Once everyone is dressed and teased and eyelashed to the hilt, and before Man to Man open the outer doors to let loose the flood of guests into the ballroom, the girls file backstage. It's incredibly crowded, and dark, and there isn't a single mirror; girls squeeze into their outfits on chairs and pile things on the floor. A few take photos of each other. 'We look like waxworks,' says one, looking at her camera screen. 'Look at this one! We don't even look real!'

Outside, I fight my way through the crush of early arrivals – mostly anxious parent-looking people – and go upstairs, where the judges are having dinner. There are seven of them, ranging from celebrity hair stylist Joh Bailey to media personality Deborah Hutton. Alcohol seems to have been flowing freely, and everyone, head judge Jonathan Westbrook in particular, seems to be feeling pretty expansive.

'What are you looking for tonight?' asks a television reporter.

'Someone who's warm, someone who's healthy. Not too thin,' says Deborah Hutton.

'Savvy,' says Westbrook suddenly. 'Savvy.'

There's a pause, a little discussion, then Westbrook weighs in again. 'Absolutely toned,' he says, dwelling on the word. 'Physically toned.' Another pause.

'That's a personal favourite,' says Hutton, trying to make a joke of it.

'To be able to compete, like Jennifer did, against the other girls and bring the crown home, she has to be absolutely toned from head to toe,' clarifies Westbrook.

'What about somebody who's absolutely outstanding in swimwear but when it comes to The Question they fluff it up?' asks the reporter.

'I'd give them a nine,' says Joh Bailey jokily.

'Nine-point-five,' says Westbrook eagerly, 'if that'd get her over the line.'

'As long as she's toned,' adds Bailey. I think of all the girls downstairs, trying so hard with their notebooks, and feel suddenly furious.

'And she needs good teeth,' says Westbrook.

There's another pause. 'I think you got the message across,' says someone. 'Toned and savvy.' With good teeth.

*

Back downstairs, every seat has an official program on it, with the word 'pageant' misspelt throughout. As the ceremony begins, I watch the girls file on stage. One has applied too much fake tan and glows like neon; one has mis-positioned her chicken fillet, so everyone can see it. Even so, the youth/beauty combination doesn't fail them, and everyone applauds.

They file off stage, then back on again in swimwear. The mermaid sleekness is very much to the fore. 'Go our Rachael!' someone shouts out. Rachael Finch swings round, executing a flawless Zoolander turn. The final ten are announced: both Finch and Kim Eckhof are chosen. Backstage, all the losers have to change into their evening gowns and go on stage again, which seems slightly unfeeling, but I don't hear any complaints, just a quiet, slightly gritted-teeth determination. 'I'm so glad Kim got picked,' whispers another West Australian. 'If she wins, I'll be as happy as if it was me.'

Everyone marches on stage again. There's a perceptible difference between the finalists and everyone else; the finalists seem to zing with adrenalin, lit from within; the others are suddenly just pretty girls in sparkly gowns. Jade Russell, one of the top ten, lifts her evening gown so high her bikini bottoms, which she's still wearing as knickers, are visible on the catwalk. Jonathan Westbrook is interviewed by Lazer: how did he become a top-flight beauty pageant judge?

'Well,' says Westbrook loudly, 'when you're young, get a very good-looking girlfriend, maybe a model or someone like that. Then people think you've got wonderful taste and ask you to judge pageants ...'

'Get your hand off it!' shouts someone in the audience, and I feel like cheering.

The top five are chosen, and Eckhof and Finch are both picked, and I decide that I, too, could become a top-flight beauty-queen judge. Girls file on and off stage, and the music goes on, and Lazer talks, and suddenly it's Question time.

It's like a reality show, watching people you've come to like face terrible humiliation. Finch is asked, you guessed it, what is the greatest issue facing Australia today, and she answers heart disease, because she's a spokesperson for the Heart Foundation. It sounds better in print than it does in person. Then Georgina Moss, a lovely blonde, is asked who is the woman she most admires in the world, and why.

'Umm, I would say Leni Riefenstahl,' she answers. (Later, when I tell a journalist colleague about this answer, there's a pause. 'Maybe she doesn't know who Hitler was,' she suggests.) Then Eckhof is asked how she felt about Australians during the Victorian bushfires. Very proud, says Eckhof.

There's another pause. The girls do one last twirl. I have my fingers crossed for Eckhof. But Finch, with her beautiful eyes and enormous smile, wins. Eckhof, in the weird parlance of the pageant world, is second runner-up, or third; Jade Russell, still wearing her bikini bottoms, is second, or first runner-up.

Finch looks genuinely shocked and delighted, though not as delighted as her mother, whom I am, by sheer coincidence, standing directly beside. 'She's won! She's won,' screams Colleen Zablocki. 'My daughter's won! She's won!!' Up on stage, Finch can't get her sash to pin together, and, like all beauty queens, her tiara won't stay on. She keeps one hand at her hip and one on her head, like a children's dance, and still manages to look completely lovely.

And perhaps, in the end, that's all that matters. Miss Universe is not about The Question, or World Peace, or anything really, except the hypnotic, universal value of human beauty – the oldest of all our pieties, perhaps, and the most persistent.

All day, these girls have clung together and competed together and helped each other out. Now, suddenly, Finch is no longer part of the gang. Backstage, a little ring of empty space has formed between her and everyone else. She makes an odd, arms-out gesture, as if to draw the other girls towards her, but no one moves, and Miss Universe Australia looks suddenly frightened. 'I don't know what to do! What do I do now?' she asks, there in the light on her own.

*

Postscript: true to form, the Miss Universe scandals continue. In recent weeks, controversy has erupted over a leaked email, written by Rachael Finch to the Miss Universe Organisation in New York, in which Finch complained that she was unduly pressured by Deborah Miller into signing a three-year management contract in the midst of the chaos after her win. The contract allegedly locked Finch into a management agreement for three years, long after her reign is over. According to reports, lawyers believe there may be a case to answer under the *Fair Trading Act*, but Miller has insisted that the contract is fair. 'There's no controversy,' she adds now. 'It was blown out of proportion. Everything is resolved.' There's no word from Finch, so we can only hope that as the curtain goes up and the glitter comes down in the Bahamas on 23 August, all is well with the Universe world once more.

Good Weekend

Ebony: The Girl in the Room

Anne Manne

It starts with a triple-0 call at 1 p.m. on 3 November 2007. A distraught father gasps out the words. A child lies dead. When the ambulance officers arrive at the scene – a modest house in Hawks Nest, north of Newcastle – they are waved towards a bedroom. The father says, 'I can't bear to go in there.' As they open the door, his words suddenly take on a different meaning to that of a grieving father, for an overwhelming stench hits their nostrils. In a bare room littered with faeces is a mattress. On the mattress lies the tiny, emaciated body of a child. She looks only about three years old, even though the father says she is seven. Her little face is shrunken, a 'skull wrapped in skin.'

An ambulance officer looks around the room and breathes in the smell. It looks more like the bleakest of prison cells than a little girl's bedroom. There are no toys or furniture – just the mattress. The window is boarded up entirely. There is just one decoration, a poster of a Victorian painting of a sad-faced little girl, turning away from the world, leaning her head against the wall.

He knows that what he has seen is no accidental death.

It is time for the police.

The mother is taken to hospital. She has taken an overdose.

*

The police attending discover that only the room of the dead girl, whom we shall call Ebony,* is in such a foul state. The rest of the house seems all right, what one might expect. The officer asks an older sister, playing on the computer, how she is coping. She says, 'I had a little cry but now I am over it.' He notes the father, too, is 'detached,' 'robotic, no emotion, very monotone.'

The mother tells police she found Ebony dead at 7 a.m. She attempted mouth-to-mouth resuscitation, but gave up because of bull ants and black vomit coming from the girl's mouth. Then she sang lullabies to her dead daughter for hours. She did not tell her husband, nor raise the alarm.

The father tells police he 'thought it was going to be a good day.' This is because when he got up, sometime after 9 a.m., going straight to his computer to put on his first bet of the day, he had a win. Elated, he put on another, then studied the form guide.

After a few hours, at about 11 a.m., he found his wife crying in the toilet. He asked, 'What's wrong? It's not Ebony, is it? She's not dead, is she?'

The mother had already taken an overdose of painkillers, but he gave his wife a few extra Valium and then didn't know what to do. He rang his aunt and screamed at her, 'She's dead, she's dead,' but hung up before telling her who's dead. He sat on the couch for a couple more hours. At 1 p.m. he called the ambulance.

Soon there are journalists swarming all over the story of the starved girl. Television crews turn up at the house. The father becomes talkative. He has a pudgy face, a long, bleached pony-tail and a strange, inward-looking gaze. Police attending the scene have told him that his daughter has died of starvation and dehydration. 'I don't know how this can be,' he tells the cameras. 'She'd eat like anything. Starvation, we didn't starve her, she was born small, she was a tiny kid.' He regales his audience with tales of mountains of food. Huge Chinese soup-bowls full of muesli and Weet-bix, sandwiches, and biccies and chippies all day. She had been sitting on the couch the night before, all

* Ebony was the child's middle name, which Justice Hulme decided could be used so as not to 'perpetuate her abandonment.' Other names were suppressed by court order to protect the identity of her older sisters.

chirpy, watching TV in the bosom of her family, before going to bed about eight. It all sounds so very normal. They are devoted parents, 'who lived for their three children.' 'I love my kids to death, all three of them, and now one of them is gone,' he says.

He is always the victim. He blames the NSW Department of Community Services (DoCS) for inaction. 'Now they are claiming I didn't want anyone to see Ebony because she was sick. I don't know. It is all wrong. Life's not fair.' DoCS used to visit regularly, but no one's checked on them since they moved up the coast, he complains. 'They're disgusting. They should be shut down.' He blames the removalist guy, too, who refused to bring Ebony's toys when he transported the family, two months earlier from Matraville, north to Hawks Nest on the coast, fleeing the 'druggies and drunks' of Sydney. Ebony was depressed, off her food, pining for those long-lost toys.

The father begs police to get to the bottom of the mystery.

'Someone help me find out what happened to my little girl.'

*

At the autopsy, it takes no time for forensic pathologists to find out what happened to his little girl. She has died the most horrible of deaths: of starvation and thirst. In fact, in all their years as pathologists they have never encountered anything so extreme.

Ebony has three pairs of socks on, top layers put on over dirty ones. They have been on so long they have melded to the skin. As they peel off the socks, the skin comes with them. She weighs only nine kilograms, almost three times less than her expected weight of twenty-six kilograms. Her body has so little moisture that the normal process in a dead body – of fluid moving to the lowest point – has not occurred. There is no food in the stomach, no liquid in the bladder, no fat in the bowel. She is so wasted away she does not have enough muscle left for rigor mortis. The black vomit is dried blood mixed with stomach acid. There is no evidence of bull ants. It is likely beads of this mixture that the mother saw. Ebony's limbs are distorted because she suffers rickets, the nineteenth-century bone disease caused by lack of vitamin D, or sunlight. Her lungs are pink, suggesting she had no contact with the outdoors for many months, perhaps years. They have never witnessed a body like it.

We have washed the bodies of the dead since the beginning of time, preparing them for burial. Their forensic work done, the pathologists wash Ebony's body. They cannot rid the body of the stench of urine and faeces.

Relatives organise a funeral for Ebony. Only six people attend, as the tiny coffin is lowered into the ground. The parents don't go. They have been on the run from police. They are found on a railway station with more than $4000. As they are arrested, the father turns on the wife, pointing: 'It was her, all her fault.'

It is like that from then on. At the trial, they never look at each other.

All falls apart.

*

The neighbours start talking. In Matraville, the mother looked all right to begin with. Towards the end of their time there – from 2006 onwards – she was 'thin and pale.' The whole family is reclusive, antisocial and nocturnal. At 11 p.m., the house springs alive. Random people turn up at odd hours. The father comes and goes in the V8 cars he religiously washes and polishes on weekends. He is a gambling addict and is often down at the TAB. The older girls never seem to attend school. Instead, under the cover of darkness, they whiz up and down the street on scooters, dressed in scruffy clothing, often shorts and thongs, even in winter.

Shopkeepers talk too. About the mother who fills her trolley at the supermarket but puts it all back when the father tells her to. They walk out with nothing except for several 24-packs of Diet Coke. The father goes into butchers and asks about different cuts of meat, but always walks out without buying anything. At the bakery, he only buys enough pastries for four people, never five.

No one has seen Ebony outside for a long time, not since she was seen in a pusher. This was odd in itself, given the pretty, red-haired child with the lovely wide smile was then five years old. But she looked healthy, even chubby, in early 2006. A tradesman visiting the house sees a bedroom roped shut. The father says his autistic daughter is in there. A neighbour, Janice Reid, sees Ebony always in her room, alone, with the door firmly shut. She hears Ebony calling for her mummy and her daddy. Her cries are never answered. One day, Reid looks up at the window where she so often sees the little child standing in the frame, peering out, looking at the world she cannot get to. The window is boarded up. She no longer sees the little girl. She can hear her, though, moving about in her room.

When Reid can no longer hear her moving about, early in 2007, she can't bear it anymore and takes action. Reid asks Debbie Jacobsen, an experienced foster carer, to ring DoCS. Jacobsen insists on staying on the line and demands the conversation is recorded. 'If you don't do something about this child she will be dead. And if she dies I am holding you and DoCS responsible for her death.' DoCS tells her they are already acting. But they are not. The energy of Reid and Jacobsen's outrage is quietly dissipated, dissolved by government red tape and inertia.

The removalist taking the family's things to Hawks Nest is probably the last person outside the family to see Ebony alive. He sees a little girl, very, very thin, lying motionless on the floor of the main bedroom, eyes staring. The girl does not move or speak. This is two months before Ebony dies. After the family moves, Reid goes into the Matraville house and finds rubbish knee-deep in every room. The bathtub is full of cigarettes, cockroaches scuttle about in the filthy kitchen and used nappies are lying around. But it is Ebony's room, she later tells the court, which is the worst, with piles of faeces on the floor. She contacts DoCS again. There is still time to save the little girl. Reid's call is filed away.

*

At the trial, we become privy to what happens in one of those families that the poet Randall Jarrell once described as 'God's concentration camps.' A world where the unthinkable becomes thinkable. The story of their life together is mired in the desperate dependency often found in domestic violence, the weird logic of 'I had to kill her so she couldn't leave me.' Estranged from their families, their door has long been slammed shut on the outside world. There is no one who draws them away from their strange, fatal embrace – the scorpions' dance of death.

They meet in 1990, when she is a young and vulnerable teenager, only seventeen, at a complete loss, as her parents' marriage falls violently apart. He is much older, at twenty-nine, and seems a safe haven. In 1992, when she is eighteen, they marry. She thinks he is someone to depend on. Before long, the dark side of that enveloping embrace is revealed; her sanctuary has prison walls. He suffers from agoraphobia, severe chronic anxiety and panic disorder. He has been a Valium addict since he was eighteen. He has never held a job. This is not a man to help her find her feet and join the outside world, but someone who will enclose her in his strange claustrophobic one, shutting off all exits. Any sign of independence is a threat that she will leave him. When she wants to learn to drive, he teaches her. But he won't let her venture out of the driveway. That is the end of that.

He controls everything, where they live and what they buy. Like many violent men, he treats her abusively but is also, paradoxically, completely dependent on her. By the end of their first year together, she attempts suicide as a way out, but fails. By the time of Ebony's death, the mother's suicide attempts number in the double figures. The father, impassive, tells the court, 'She was always doing that.' He is pathologically possessive of his children, too. He tells people, 'My kids are my life. No kids – no life, that's how I see it.' He can't bear them going to school; besides, school represents the interfering authorities. They are all trapped.

The mother writes a sad letter to her estranged mum, blaming her husband for not letting them see each other. She wishes her mum could have played a role in Ebony's life. 'Fifteen years, nearly, married that is. I still can't believe I'm alive really.' She needs her mother, but 'we know that can't happen,' because her husband forbids contact. He blows their joint $900 weekly welfare payments on internet gambling or sits on the couch in a Valium fog. He gives her no help. She testifies that only when she ends up at the doctor's does her husband rouse himself to say: 'he cannot live without me and how much he loves me. Ha!'

It is after Ebony's birth, however, that things really go off the rails. The mother has a fall during Ebony's pregnancy and then suffers chronic back pain. She develops a Valium addiction of her own – fifteen tablets per day – and a painkiller habit of horrifying proportions – more than twenty per day.

Crown Prosecutor Peter Barnett wants to prove to the court

that both parents are culpable, both wanted the girl dead. He shows the court a police video of a rubbish bin at the house, full of photos of the dead girl, along with a man's shirt with a matted clump of red hair.

Ebony disappears from her family photos. They hold a weird birthday party in March 2007, with candles and a cake. But the birthday girl, Ebony, is not present. She stays in that foul room with the door tied shut. The mother explains, 'She would be running around like a mini tornado and getting into everything. And she has broken presents.'

Mark Austin, the father's lawyer, attempts a defence on the grounds of drug addiction clouding his judgment. The father's habit involves a staggering twenty-five Valium tablets per day. It is the worst case of benzodiazepine addiction his doctor has ever seen. He was completely bombed out on drugs in the last weeks before Ebony's death. Austin asks, 'At Hawks Nest, did you have any concerns in relation to (the child)?' 'No,' says the father. 'Were you concerned about anything at Hawks Nest?' 'Tablets. Getting more.' Not Ebony. He admits only sighting her twice in nine weeks.

It is a strange thing to say in his defence. But the point of their case is that responsibility for the child lay elsewhere. He didn't know. It was all the wife's doing. The father looked after the older girls, the mother looked after Ebony. From about 2006, the child avoided him, wouldn't let him wash or feed her. So that was the arrangement. He tells the court that when Ebony is found dead, the mother said, 'We have to get rid of the body.'

The father was indignant, 'That's criminal, that's like we did something.'

He tells the court that the mother insisted, saying, 'If you don't get rid of the body, I'm going back to bed.' Which she did.

The angle of the mother's defence barrister, Dennis Stewart, is the other standard manoeuvre in the denial-of-responsibility stakes: taking orders. She was not responsible for her actions because she was a battered wife to a violent, possessive man, who carried out his will – *Kapo* to the camp commandant.

She alleges he pimps her, dresses her in schoolgirl outfits and invites men round to spank her, sometimes to have sex with her. Witnesses say the whole family is terrified of the father. But evidence goes in the other direction, too. A neighbour hears him berating her about Ebony's state: 'She's not well, what kind of a fucking cunt of a mother are you?' Not the language of conventional moral indignation, but it is a reproach. They have both lied so much it is hard to trust either testimony.

Decisively, the mother admits that she alone cared for the child, and that the father didn't. Now the mother turns to interpretative denial – the facts are not what they seem. Ebony wasn't starved, but sick. The mother tells of a huge last supper of mush – Weet-bix, muesli, rice, vegetables – all mixed together and heated in the microwave the night before she died. But she has stomach flu, so vomits it all up on the living-room floor. Under a spirited cross-examination by Barnett, the Crown Prosecutor, her claims dissolve. She says she walked Ebony to her bedroom, holding her hand. Only that is a lie, too. The child would have been comatose by then. She had no muscle tone left to support eating or sitting, let alone walking. Barnett is remorseless, unremitting. Finally, he gets the mother to admit that she didn't give Ebony enough food. He pounces. 'Hadn't eaten enough to feed a mouse, correct?'

Beaten, the mother agrees. 'Yes. Not enough to feed a mouse.'

Forensic psychiatrist Dr Olav Nielssen tells the Newcastle Supreme Court that the mother displays 'no sadness or anger' in talking about Ebony's death, but describes horrifying things in a flat, bland way. While she has no discernible mental illness, her absence of emotion in response to trauma is 'highly abnormal.' It is possible that this 'restricted emotional range' is the 'battered wife syndrome.' Possible, but not certain.

Stewart does his valiant best to counter the prosecutor's charge: 'It was never your fault, was it – it was always someone else's, wasn't it?' Stewart asks, 'Do you feel responsibility for her death?' This is her only chance at the lesser charge of manslaughter. To finally accept in death what was never accepted in life. Responsibility. The mother blows it. '*Mostly*, yes ...'

Stewart skips bravely over the qualifier and asks about her failure to notice Ebony's increasingly pitiful state. 'I just didn't see it.' He seeks an explanation in all the drugs; how did they make her feel? 'Feel like I was in a dream-like state, like I wasn't there. They slowed me down.' Stewart sums up before the jury;

she was a loving and caring mother whose drug habit has made her 'negligent, foolish, reprehensible,' oblivious to the child deteriorating in front of her. But not a cold-blooded murderer.

The jury doesn't buy it. None of it is enough to counteract the photos of Ebony's body. Ebony's mother is found guilty of murder. Her father is found guilty of manslaughter.

From the bench, Justice Robert Hulme makes his judgment, unleashing a volley at the parents with an exuberant moral fury. They were so 'absorbed in their own lives,' because of 'incompetence, negligence, self-interest and disinterest' that 'they did not care about her.' They had kept this 'skin-covered skeleton' out of photos, out of sight and out of mind. 'A father could show no less love to his child.' Ebony's life of 'abject cruelty' 'was of no concern to him.' Ebony's mother had been 'unimaginably heartless and cruel.' Even in her last hours, the child could have been saved by a triple-0 call, but the mother 'chose not to lift a finger to help her … For a person to do nothing in those circumstances is so morally reprehensible that it could be no more serious if the person intended that the child die.' It is in the 'worst category' of murder.

The mother is sentenced to life without parole. The father gets sixteen years.

*

Reading the scathing report by Bruce Barbour, the NSW Ombudsman, into the 'appalling' failure of no fewer than five government agencies that received notifications of risk of harm to avert Ebony's death is sickening.

In that ominous phrase turning up with alarming regularity in successive child-death cases, the family was 'known to DoCS' since 1993. Despite it being known by the time of her first pregnancy, in 1992, that the mother was suicidal and the father a Valium addict, there is no evidence of any person or agency providing extra support or therapeutic intervention. When Ebony's older sisters become toddlers in the early '90s, the parents struggle to manage their behaviour. There are community reports of risk of harm.

By the time the older girls reach school, in 2000, teachers report concerns about physical neglect, bruises, and the possibility that the mother self-harms and that the threatening father has a 'severe personality disorder.' By November 2007, Ebony's sisters have missed an astonishing amount of school – about two-and-a-half years – and are struggling as a consequence. Apart from a brief six months at a preschool, Ebony never attends school. Ombudsman Barbour is sharply critical of the department's conciliatory approach to the parents in getting the girls to attend school. They should have been prosecuted.

In a pattern repeated in his dealings with every government agency, the otherwise lethargic father is as nimble as an Al Qaeda operative when evading the authorities, ducking and weaving, laying false trails, while the children regularly vanish into thin air. He refuses to answer the phone or door, lies about the children's whereabouts or claims his wife is dying of cancer. Anything to keep authorities from sighting the children.

DoCS involvement escalates after Ebony's birth in 2000. She is small and undernourished. She is diagnosed with 'failure to thrive' – usually the result of a baby not being fed enough. Such severe neglect can have appalling consequences for a child's emotional and physical development. The mother finds Ebony's behaviour uncontrollable; she avoids eye contact and can hardly speak. Ebony is diagnosed with autism. A medical officer marks her file as 'an extremely worrying child.' A fourth child, born in 2002, is removed as a baby by a Children's Court order for 'failure to thrive' and placed in foster care. The parents refuse to accept responsibility for its condition. In an ominous harbinger of events to come, they lose interest in regaining the baby and stop visiting her.

DoCS now tries to persuade the Children's Court that *all* the children, including Ebony, should be removed from the family. For reasons that are unclear, the case fails. Compared to physical abuse, cases of neglect are notoriously hard to prove as grounds for removal. The family does, however, remain under DoCS supervision by a Children's Court order until early 2003. Importantly, there is one diligent DoCS worker who keeps tabs on the family throughout this period. She keeps a careful history and is dogged in her pursuit of the children's welfare, despite the wily and abusive father. The parents do improve their behaviour somewhat. The intensity and continuity of DoCS involvement from 2001 to 2003 shows a beneficial, if decidedly not miraculous, result.

But the family soon spirals downward again and the risk of harm reports multiply. Between 2005 and 2007, there are seventeen reports to DoCS alone. The reports include domestic violence, Ebony's imprisonment, her window being boarded up, the squalid state of the house and each child's lengthy absence from school.

We come now to a stark fact: not one government agency lays eyes on Ebony in the two years before she dies. Despite the many notifications; despite the fact that one child has already been removed; despite a policy released in July 2006 on child neglect, which reflects 'a new focus on the severity of neglect and seriousness of the harm neglect can cause, *including loss of life*.' Many reports are closed due to 'competing priorities' – code for overworked staff.

In 2007, this picture gets even worse. Although Ebony is in child protection, where a case history can be the basis of life and death judgments, a work-experience student is given the job of writing up the case. She botches the job. The sloppiness means Ebony's file history is so inadequate that the implications of Debbie Jacobsen's crucial phone call – warning of Ebony's imprisonment and likely death – fail to be grasped. It is filed away by the helpline as 'information only.' It is thought to simply add to previous reports of dishevelment at the house.

Most decisively, in April 2007, a new caseworker is instructed to visit the house and – imperative in child-protection cases – sight the children. Lacking judgment, or even the ability to follow DoCS protocol, she eventually sights the older girls, but leaves without seeing Ebony. She allows herself to be fobbed off by the father, who says Ebony is asleep in her room. Even more incredibly, her senior manager accepts that, given the description of the older girls, who seem okay, it is unlikely 'there would be anything different with Ebony,' despite reports that the little disabled girl is shut away in a boarded-up room.

The caseworker does not check whether medical appointments to assess the children are actually attended. No doctor lays eyes on Ebony. No case review occurs for twelve weeks. Ebony 'was not a high priority'; other cases are considered more urgent.

The caseworker leaves DoCS at the end of July, but does not properly brief her successor. The third caseworker does not thoroughly acquaint herself with the file, merely briefing herself by looking at the 'last two pages' of the hopelessly inadequate summary by the work-experience student. This last caseworker is often sick and takes several weeks' sick leave. More delays. Towards the end of August, she is instructed to visit the premises at Matraville to sight the children within twenty-four hours. She makes a few phone calls, but no home visit.

After the family moves to Hawks Nest, yet more risk reports are received, including one about Ebony's soiled prison. Surely now they will act? As Ebony's life ebbs away, over September and October, DoCS slowly moves towards finding a forwarding address and contacts the new child-protection office in her area, the Raymond Terrace office. An evaluation of a case, called a 'risk assessment,' is meant to be completed promptly: within twenty-eight days if it is unsubstantiated; within ninety if it is not. It has taken 210 days, but finally, by 30 October, the risk assessment is complete. The case is now officially transferred to the Raymond Terrace office in Ebony's new district. Her case file is marked 'extreme' risk.

Finally.

Four days later, Ebony is dead. Raymond Terrace has not yet allocated Ebony a caseworker.

*

In her famous account of Daniel Valerio, the toddler beaten to death by his stepfather, Helen Garner asks an important question. Of Daniel's mother, she writes: 'What deal did she do with herself to allow her child to suffer the brutality of her boyfriend ...?' We may ask the same question of Ebony's father. How can ordinary people do such terrible things or let them happen? During or after the event, how do they find ways to deny the meaning of what they are doing? These are also questions at the heart of Stanley Cohen's *States of Denial: Knowing about Atrocities and Suffering*.

Cohen draws on an illuminating moment in a Saul Bellow novel. Does the doctor, who is dying, know and face the fact of his imminent death? 'Did he know this? Of course he did. He was a physician so he must know. But he was human, so he could arrange many things. Both knowing and not-knowing – one of those frequent human arrangements.' 'A frequent human arrangement indeed,' remarks Cohen. Perhaps a more precise way of explaining states of denial, however, is to say that knowledge is possessed, but not acknowledged, and therefore its meaning is disavowed.

There are very many forms of denial and disavowal in this case. The father who denies they could have starved their daughter to death because they are not that kind of people, who insists they love their children 'like gold,' giving them new toys, new furniture, the pool table ... Who claims he didn't know. He wasn't there. He never looked at the child or went into 'that room.' Who denies the *meaning* of her starved body by reframing it in the euphemisms 'unwell' and 'thin.' Who locates responsibility outside them both for withholding food, and projects it onto the removalist who makes Ebony pine away for her long-lost toys.

As Cohen says, 'Denial is always partial; some information's always registered.' The father, on finding the mother crying in the toilet, arrives within just two sentences at the possibility that one of his children is dead: 'What's wrong? It's not Ebony, is it? She's not dead, is she?' On finding his wife distressed, a father does not normally move within the space of a mere seven words from the fact of her state to the idea that one of his children is dead. Unless it is already a strong possibility in his mind – that there is every likelihood of his daughter dying.

We speak of being absent-minded, of what's on our mind, or at the top of our minds, or what's furthest from our minds. These are all common forms of speech, which reveal the subtleties and gradations of attention and inattention. The free association on the psychoanalyst's couch depends upon highly charged but repressed emotional content surfacing. What surfaces here, so quickly, is that the father is aware Ebony is near death, even as he determinedly holds away acceptance of that fact.

However, another deeper form of denial lies at the heart of this crime. This is the denial, because of her autism and disability, of Ebony's full humanity.

Consider how Eva Kittay, a moral philosopher and the mother of a profoundly disabled child, writes of her determination that her daughter 'presents a face to the world that is as attractive as possible … so the first response to her is as positive as I can make it.' Kittay makes daily efforts, more than for her able child, to ensure that 'Sesha goes into the world looking clean and fresh and well cared for, and hoping the message that she is worth caring for will be absorbed by others …'

Kittay is rueful that our 'fear and prejudice against those people with a disability means such efforts are necessary.' Another way of putting what Kittay is doing, however, is to say that she is drawing our attention to Sesha as a human person, signalling her rightful place in the human community. So simple, yet so deep, are the little things a loving mother does.

Ebony's treatment carries the opposite logic, an escalating denial of her humanity. Early photos show Ebony plump and pretty in a little dress, smiling radiantly. But over time, Ebony becomes the scapegoat, the receptacle, the dumping ground for all the despair and rage of this toxic family. As Ebony is progressively dehumanised, it becomes more and more possible to do yet worse things to her. What she becomes, as a result of her abuse, is a further invitation to cruelty. She is gradually, step by step, being excluded from the human community and its most intimate representative, her family. The parents gradually reduce her to living in a non-human state. I will not say animal-like state, for so many of those who share the lives of animals treat them with infinitely greater tenderness than this little child was shown – feed them good food, sleep with them, caress them, pay thousands of dollars in vet bills, mourn them when they die.

Around 2005, the mother decides Ebony is not worth schooling. She rebuffs the special-school teachers eager to take her. Ebony can't learn, can't speak, is disruptive and difficult. No point. She becomes ever more difficult. She screams at the sight of water, so she is washed with a flannel, then not at all. She slips into the category of not worth washing. Then she pisses in her clothes and is not worth dressing. She is five, six and seven years old but wears nappies. In that state, she is not worth photographing, so she disappears from the family album. Her birthday is held in her absence. Her existence is quietly being erased.

Then she is not worth changing. The nappies are left off and she pisses and shits all over her room. Now the room stinks and she is not worth visiting. She is characterised as a wild creature in need of more caging, so the door is tied shut. Locked up, she screams and screams the two words she has left, 'Mummy' and 'Daddy.' The room is so foul no one, not even the mother, wants to go in there. Ebony is given less and less food and water. She becomes weaker and weaker. She is now unable to sit or speak, lies lifeless. She has become thing-like, fading out of existence in 'that room' that the father 'can't bear to go into.' She has become the fulfilment of their treatment of her.

But when Ebony dies, as they confront the brute reality of her corpse, they can no longer live in the state of denial of what it is they have been doing. The father dials triple-0. He first fumbles for the words and then he finds them. He tells the operator that his daughter is dead.

The Monthly

All Things Being Equal

Elizabeth Farrelly

'It's not fair,' complained the sister of the jailed Sydney jihadist. 'Twenty-three years, that's half of his life. It's not fair to him, our community or our religion.'

In fact, it was entirely fair, under the law and assuming the man was guilty as charged. But she could hardly yell, 'It's not right,' since that would beg the question of how it can be right to want to kill innocent civilians but not right to punish people for plotting it. Rightness is something on which we no longer agree, even in principle. So she appealed intuitively to the last remaining principle that reliably unites us. Fairness, aka equality, is a necessary underpinning for civilisation but is it sufficient? Is equality everything?

We live in a world where the social values that have shaped history – duty, patriotism, piety (or God, king and country) – have come to seem terribly antiquated. Where our efforts to stretch democracy around multiculturalism have rendered any appeal to biblical principle similarly obsolete. Fairness is what remains, perhaps all that remains, of our shared moral compass.

Fairness is, of course, democracy's undergarment; *liberté, egalité, fraternité,* all that. Although this suggests fairness is a relatively recent arrival on the political scene, it is also one of our most deeply held principles, as five minutes in any school playground shows.

Allan Ahlberg's classic children's poem, 'Colin' (1983), captures the child's intuitive grasp of the fairness principle:

It isn't fair on the football field
If their team scores a goal
It isn't fair in a cricket match
Unless you bat and bowl …
It isn't fair when I give you a job,
It isn't fair when I don't
If I keep you in, it isn't fair
If you're told to go out, you won't ...
When your life reaches its end, Colin
Though I doubt if I'll be there
I can picture the words on the gravestone now
They'll say: IT IS NOT FAIR.

Families with close siblings will be familiar with the 'one cuts and the other chooses' precept. (The key to this principle is to find a halving so precise as to render the choice no-choice, a self-resolving consensus with a native wisdom that echoes Solomon's over the baby – except there the halving was abjured.)

So it is no surprise that studies reveal the equality urge as a primate one. British biologist Sarah Brosnan found that capuchin monkeys refuse to cooperate when the rewards handed out within a group do not match deserts. The 'animals compare their rewards with those of others and accept or reject rewards according to their relative value.' They also stalk out of the game if one animal always wins, so that the game is perceived to be 'unfair.'

Brosnan proposes that 'individuals who have a sense of fairness are more likely to be successful in co-operative interactions,' making inequity-aversion an evolutionary trait. (Later studies with chimps did not entirely bear this out, although you could argue that's why we dominate the world and they, who share 98 per cent of our genome, do not. Perhaps the fairness gene is in that unique 2 per cent.)

British economist Richard Layard – who argues all public policy is ultimately purposed to happiness enhancement – takes a similar line, saying that inequality, even more than poverty, is the greatest cause of human misery. We generally assume that the converse is also true: that equality will produce happiness. But does it?

Communism, which ought to shed some light here, is no real help since real-world communist societies are, if anything, more hierarchical than others, intensifying the misery of inequality with the hypocrisy of denial.

Plus, there's this: communism strives only for material equality and at the cost, many would argue, of stifling opportunity. (Capitalism, you might say, inverts this; pursuing equality of opportunity at the cost of dramatic material inequality.)

What interests me, though, is where the equality principle, increasingly dominant in our society, is leading us.

'Harrison Bergeron' is a Kurt Vonnegut story set in a future where 'everybody was finally equal.' There, the intelligent are forced to wear 'mental handicap' devices that emit sharp noises every twenty seconds to stop them 'taking unfair advantage of their brains' and dancers are weighted by birdshot or scrap-iron calibrated to the size of their talent.

The story is satirical, of course, but every time I see children's basketball or soccer managers handing out gilt trophies to all – yes, all – members of all teams in a tournament, or a drama teacher handing out certificates of participation, which she must know go straight in the bin, I am reminded of it.

Has our fondness for equality gone too far? Not only because smart kids see straight through it and know they're being patronised but also because there comes a point when fairness militates against excellence. For the human urge to excellence, history suggests, must also be hardwired. Excellence is something we desire in itself but most especially as a means to dominate our fellows – a means to hierarchy.

Psychological studies regularly show that faced with a choice between a greater reward that is nevertheless smaller than that of our peers, and a smaller reward that is greater than theirs, we'll take the 'greater than theirs' option every time. Beyond basic survival-level, status matters more to us than wealth. Indeed, such studies suggest, most wealth-seeking is really status-seeking in disguise. As H.L. Mencken famously said, wealth is 'any income that is at least $100 more a year than the income of one's wife's sister's husband.' So perhaps the truth is that equality and excellence are two competing human drives – the warp and weft, if you will, of our mental lives.

A spatial analogy suggests itself here, with equality as the horizontal axis (landscape format) and excellence as the vertical (or portrait). Architecturally, the equality axis is epitomised by the so-called 'prairie houses' of the early twentieth century. Designed by Frank Lloyd Wright and others, who saw them clearly as a part of democracy's polemic, these consciously evoked the endless horizon and the wide-open plains of opportunity. The excellence drive, by contrast, is most strongly manifest in the relentless, yearning verticality of the medieval gothic.

In theological terms, this equality-excellence dichotomy parallels the distinction between the 'immanent' and 'transcendent' views of God.

The immanent god is the god of good works, of the here and now, of the world; the god of charity. The transcendent god, by contrast, surpasses physicality. This is the god of mysticism. It is traditional to see dichotomy here, as if the two views were mutually exclusive, but many thinkers understand them simply as different aspects of the deity, just as science sees the particle and the wave as different aspects of light.

Many ordinary situations can be understood as a tussle between these conflicting urges – the urge to even out the waves of existence, dampening both the peaks and the troughs, and the urge to heighten, to up the amplitude. Town planning, for example, must always choose between a levelling approach (regulating against the worst excesses by enforcing a degree of uniformity) or allowing the best, which also means tolerating the worst.

Tokyo, for instance, takes this approach. Or consider the typical conundrum of a university senate, doling out funding between its faculties. In any university, the faculties range from the dusty and neglected to the glamorous and fashionable. There is never enough money to go around and the university is mindful that its future depends on its reputation for excellence. It also knows, however, that the dowdy disciplines of today are often the fashion disciplines of tomorrow and that (for that reason among others) their reservoirs of scholarship must be sustained.

Does the senate therefore favour the runt of its litter, with its shabby 1950s buildings and demoralised staff, attempting to level the field a little? Or does it reward existing successes by further funding those faculties (business, say, or law) that already luxuriate in a wealth of student fees, research endowments, government grants and well-paid, highly motivated staff? Riches to the rich.

In general, the progress of modern Western history since, say, the French Revolution, has effected a gradual yielding of the vertical to the horizontal. Witness the dissolution of empires, the growth of republicanism, current threats to the British House of Lords and so on. Witness also the corporate trend towards 'flatter structures' and the rearrangement of knowledge.

Twentieth-century modernism saw itself as a socialist push. In some ways this was so (think Esperanto, secular humanism, prefab housing, the universal franchise and free polio vaccines). As a quintessential Enlightenment project, however, modernism clung to patriarchal top-downism. In retrospect, ideas such as the objectivity of knowledge and the omnipotence of the expert may be seen as nobility's last gasp.

By contrast, post-modernism, drawn by the 'French theorists' (Derrida, Foucault, Lyotard and the boys) from the murk of neo-Marxism, ushered in a new epistemological and moral relativism, which had the effect of Balkanising truth, knowledge, goodness and power.

Just as the Soviet bloc crumbled into its constituent parts under pressure from po-mo bottom-upism, so did knowledge crumble. Post-modernism gives each of us our own truth, like an epistemological iPod encapsulating our subjective lived experience, and the blogosphere, that ultimate self-fest, is its perfect manifestation.

Amelia Watkins runs a typical blog:

> Also, today i had a dream that Africa was invading and killing everyone and we were all gonna die. Then i woke up and was like "Okay, it was just a stupid nightmare. GO back to sleep, its only five" and i went back to sleep. Then my nightmare started again and my friends got me killed. It sucked.
>
> Then today in class we talked about how North Korea wants to kill us. Brilliant. Whats with all the weapons of mass distruction? Couldnt we stick with swords and snowballs? That's

about it. I fell down the stairs again and then i fell into the washer (long story). Surprisingly, today has been a good day. Cya, Mia.

Of course, it's perfectly reasonable for Watkins to publish whatever she feels about her life and for anyone so inclined to read it. To that extent the blogosphere is just a super-expanded village well. But what are the consequences of this Balkanisation of culture?

At its most trivial, the fact that we all have our own ringtones means that for the movies of the future, if such things exist, there will be no instantly recognised sound (as there was for Alfred Hitchcock) that instantly snaps the bad guy, and the audience, to attention. That we can all now select and download our own TV programs when and as we choose is a great freedom but suddenly the old 'did you see ... last night?' staple of discussion around the water cooler is gone, casting us back onto that old staple of phatic communion, the weather.

Or take the church. The shift from medieval gothic, so other-worldly and aspirational, to the worldly, often flat-ceilinged churches of the classical Enlightenment, the twentieth century's free-form but usually centred churches, in which God takes his place within the congregation (not above it) as first among equals (to wit, Parramatta's cathedral) to the post-modern version that is indistinguishable from a suburban sports hall, tax office or greasy spoon.

All these exemplify the loss of our shared language. But more dangerous by far is the changing climate around climate change, where the idea that all opinions have equal weight means that some barmy toff such as Lord Monckton has only to say, 'All the scientists in the world are wrong: I for one don't believe them,' to take half the population with him. As though climate change were something you can vote out of existence, a matter not of fact but belief. As though fact and belief were one and the same.

The medievals burnt people for claiming the right to opinion. Now it's the opposite. Now, just suggesting that opinion is not everything is an elitist heresy likely to get you cyber-flogged.

This is blogville, where no one – not a climate expert, not even God – may raise himself above the rabble. Where the commitment to equality blinds us even to the possibility of something bigger than ourselves, rendering us eventually incapable of abstraction and sucking us instead into the backyard mud of subjectivism.

That is the danger and I believe it is real. But pendulums do swing, and never quite back to the same spot. So perhaps this is all just a next twist of the great helix. Perhaps the new Enlightenment, when it comes, will be like the old one, only a couple of chakras higher.

The Sydney Morning Herald

The Smoking Vegetarian

David Brooks

Why do we stand in wonder before the great paintings, the great sculptures? What is that aura that we seek, that even in the slightest works can capture and enthral us – an aura about the margins and between the lines of poetry, that whelms through music, is part of the atmosphere of novels? Is 'wonder' the best term for it? Critics have wrestled with this question for centuries, resorting to such terms as 'the sacred,' 'worship,' 'the spiritual'; others, rejecting such terms, have found, in that feeling of awe, that yearning, a kind of secular substitute – or evidence that art might *be* a kind of secular substitute. Certainly it doesn't seem to be rational, this wonder and apprehension, and this, perhaps, is its perpetual appeal. We might, before the work of art, find our mind racing, but this feeling is what *sets* the mind racing, not the racing itself: a *stilling*, a confounding, something at the tip of the mind, as a word can be at the tip of the tongue, at once so close and so out of reach that it has others writing of depth psychology, infantile states, mourning for pre-linguistic plenitudes. As if we have found in ourselves a deep hole, a chasm. Even if we choose to ignore it, everything, in this place of art, seems to resonate with its presence.

That is not really where this essay begins. In a more practical sense, it starts in Skadarlija, the oldest part of Belgrade, several years ago. I am in the city at an international writers' festival, one of a handful of Australians there. One of the others, in his early seventies, is a man I haven't seen for almost twenty years. In the late 1980s he was a sometime drinking companion when the poets gathered at the university staff centre on Friday evenings. After our reading at the National Library of Serbia, an early evening event, we go into Skadarlija, to a restaurant with outdoor tables overlooking the street. It's a place famed for grilled meats. Our hosts, knowing that my wife and I are vegetarian, are keen to make sure that there is enough on the menu that we can eat. It's clear that they want to go there, and it's hard to be spoilers. We assure them there's always something. Salad. Chips. A plain pasta.

It's twilight, late September, warm, the air and the atmosphere delicious. We are all hungry. We order wine, food, pour a glass, drink as we wait. My wife lights up a cigarette. I think about doing likewise but since none of the others appears to be a smoker (not so: after dinner our hosts *all* light up) decide against it. The man I haven't seen in twenty years seems disgruntled. We make small talk for a few minutes but then he bursts out with it. 'How can you smoke and be a vegetarian?' he asks, whether of my wife or of me isn't clear. A strange question, anyway, since I can remember him smoking heavily, but he has given it up, evidently. We attempt to answer, tell him, though he seems to have trouble believing it, that we are not vegetarians for our own health, but out of concern for animals (we're dissembling already: we're not vegetarians, but vegans, but instinct warns us against mentioning this). He continues, rude and intrusive, long after my wife's one cigarette has been stubbed out. It's not clear what bothers him most, that we are smokers, or that we are vegetarians. It's as if he feels he has caught the whiff of some deep hypocrisy and is determined to ferret it out. The evening begins to turn sour. It seems as if nothing will stop him.

Vegetarians are never popular. Recent converts especially. Vegans far less. It's okay if it's for one's health – indeed one can receive a measure of understanding and sympathy, as presumably one might if it were for religious reasons – but if it's an aversion to animal slaughter, animal cruelty, a *con*version, it unsettles people. One's friends can't stop talking about it. And then most likely complain that it is you who have become obsessive. As if they feel betrayed. Unobtrusive as you try to be, you've become a walking chastisement. Some people can get very vehement indeed. A website I recently consulted quoted the chef Anthony Bourdain (*Kitchen Confidential*) to the effect that 'vegetarians, and their Hezbollah-like splinter faction, the vegans ... are the enemy of everything good and decent in the human spirit.'

'There is nothing new about turning vegetarians into figures of fun,' writes Colin Spencer, in *The Heretic's Feast*:

> disciples of Pythagoras became stock characters in Attic comedy ... But other societies felt such criticism was no laughing matter and the outsiders were reviled. Vegetarians then became criminalised and were considered blasphemers and heretics.

The Catholic church, for example, has always been in two minds. There are vegetarian orders, vegetarian saints, but the church has historically been at pains to point out that vegetarianism is common to most of the major heretical movements it has tried to repress. It is an aspect of Manichaeism. The Bogomils were vegetarian. The Cathars. The Albigensians. Make a case for the inherent vegetarianism of Christianity (as some of these movements did) and you'd have to shoulder a huge weight of contradictory discourse. Christ is the *lamb* of God. 'This is my flesh,' he says, 'Take, eat, in memory of me.' Christianity, arguably, is organised – like the religion from which it evolved – around eating rituals, proscriptions of the consuming of this or that kind of flesh (long lists in Deuteronomy and Leviticus) that are at the same time encouragements to eat other kinds, to *sacrifice* and eat other kinds (horror and shame displaced: the making sacred as a mode of abjection). Indeed the Judaeo-Christian tradition, with its consistent encouragement to eat meat, its denial of souls to animals, its concentration upon man as the pinnacle of creation, has done much to bring about the culture of animal cruelty that flourishes today. Genesis 9 spells it out emphatically: 'And the fear of you and the dread of you shall be upon every beast of the earth, and upon every fowl of the air, and upon all that moveth upon the earth, and upon all the fishes of the sea; into your hand are they delivered. Every moving thing that liveth shall be meat for you.' The 'split,' I call this, the 'scission,' by which the human, upon promise of eternal reward, is led to deny the core of its being.

To a vegan, of course, vegetarianism and such paraforms as 'pescatarianism' seem half-hearted. The less meat one eats the better, yes, whatever the reason: it can't be good for one's overall anxiety level, subliminal or otherwise, to be consuming flesh still flushed with the terror of imminent execution ('Humane' slaughter? Think again). Avoidance of meat is also good for one's weight, blood pressure, cholesterol level, predisposition to diabetes, etc., to say nothing of one's own feeling about oneself and one's relation to the world, although these latter will be factors only if one has changed diet out of compassion for the animals one might otherwise be eating, and it is here that half-measures become less and less plausible. I won't embark upon the cruelties of battery farming or the dairy industry. There are many ways to inform oneself of such. Suffice to say that, if one is determined to minimise one's impact upon animals, then one's diet will eventually be free of eggs and of dairy products. And, if this *is* one's concern, one doesn't stop there. One avoids leather, fur, wool. One avoids products that contain ingredients that come from animals, and products tested upon animals. One avoids *feeding* animals to animals. And initially this regime will seem difficult, for one finds such products everywhere. They are components of the furniture we use; they are in our cosmetics, medications, soaps, shampoos; most clothes contain them; they help to 'clear' most of the wines we drink; they are there even in the ink and spines of the books we consult in order to learn about them – so omnipresent, indeed, that one could speak of very nearly the entire material world of humans as deeply intertwined with and supported by the world of animals, except that 'supported' is woefully misleading: better to say 'dependent upon the cruel treatment and the killing of animals' – riding, as it were, on a tide of suffering.

Is that, then, what this essay is about? Yes, and no. My account of the absolute pervasiveness of the animal in human *material* culture is to preface the point that the suffering, subjugation and debasement of the animal are just as pervasive in the world of thought as in the world of things – a pervasion the apprehension of which, hard enough in the first place, is rendered all the more difficult firstly because it is a matter less of active *thought against*, as in overt proscriptions of the animal or injunctions to animal cruelty, than it is of *blindness to*, brought about by the overwhelming orientation of attention elsewhere (i.e., onto the perpetuation and 'advancement' of the human); secondly because it is, therefore, a pervasive *absence* rather than a pervasive *presence*; and thirdly because, as with all problems-of-thought of this nature, perception of the extent of this pervasion must be done *with a mind already pervaded.*

Although one might want to preface such a statement with the assertion that such divine powers were in the first place invented in order to issue such an injunction (so much of the sacred having been made by humans for human purposes), the assumption of dominion over the animate world was never so clear and simple a matter as (as the book of Genesis presents it) an injunction from God. It is a far more ancient process than anything the Bible might legend, a key factor in the genesis of culture *per se.* A shift, let's say, from hunting for survival, animal amongst animals, to the cultivation of meat alongside one's grain. A set of mental procedures, eventually, consolidating into rituals, and rituals of *thought*, to enable one to deal with and rationalise the killing of creatures that have become part of one's immediate environment and that, if not necessarily loved, one has at least observed the co-creatureness of and recognised something of one's own creatureness in. It is harder, a kind of fratricide, to kill that-which-one-*is* than to kill that-which-one-is-*not*, and so the assumption of this aforesaid dominion entails a denial of that co-creatureness, an emphasis upon difference rather than sameness, and a machinery of thought that exaggerates and consolidates, indeed *invents*, that difference. Metaphysics surely has some part of its origins in this, a shift, in this regard, into bad faith, inauthenticity, a reinvention of oneself as something other than what one is, a denial of one's animal being, a dividing of oneself against oneself, a suppression so deep that it is perhaps best described as a *wound* that we must carry, must attempt to deal with, have been conditioned, ironically, to turn to metaphysics to attempt to soothe and explain, without ever really knowing what it is, or where it comes from.

What do we do to ourselves when we slaughter? What do we do

to ourselves when we eat our own kind (apart from drawing death so deeply into ourselves, into every cell of the mind as well as the body, as if these can be distinguished)? Deny our kindredness, reinvent ourselves, attach ourselves to another place, give ourselves wings as we might, the fact remains that we also brutalise ourselves – that we also know that we *are* animal, *are* kindred, and *have* embarked upon a kind of cannibalism – a long, slow holocaust – and that repressing this and the shame and guilt that attend it – articulating a whole metaphysical complex to give it a specious validation (a complex akin to the way we process, package and describe our meat to disguise its origins) – we have created a deep schism in ourselves. This schism, this Wound, albeit so deeply repressed that we can only begin to guess which of and in what manner our beliefs and institutions are its proxies, is one of the givens of our culture.

This process is not only one of the main currents in the development of human thought; it is alive in each of us, a complex navigated in the enculturation of every individual. We don't, by and large, want our children to see the slaughter that brings meat to their table – indeed it so unsettles *us* that we have developed complicated systems to mask it – but children seem particularly inclined to identify, and to express their horror at such processes. But then, of course, we see them harden into an adulthood in which, rather than outgrow or overcome it, they in some parts suppress, in some parts sublimate their horror, compounded now by a sense of shame, of having betrayed.

Any such position will face familiar arguments. Most common is that, as the human is biologically constructed as omnivore, it is 'natural' to eat meat. This point is as undeniable as it is irrelevant. Our teeth are shaped that way, yes, and our digestive system, but it is true too that our bodies bear organs that we no longer use, and that the presence of a capacity is no obligation to exploit it. We also have the capacity to choose. There is, for most of humankind, no longer any necessity to depend for sustenance upon the slaughter of other creatures. Almost as common is the argument that meat is necessary for a balanced diet. This, while fervently promoted by the meat industry, is balderdash.

A third argument is of a different kind, Protean in its manifestations, but an anecdote should illustrate it clearly enough –

a Greek friend, describing Easter in his native village: the killing and roasting of the lamb ('Take. Eat …'), and the way this ritual becomes a kind of initiation for the children. He too is troubled by the tiers of pre-packaged animal parts on supermarket shelves. The modern urbanite has lost touch with the land, with ritual. Ideally one eats only meat that comes from animals one kills oneself, so that one knows where the meat comes from and what has been done to bring it to the table. Some sense of *taking responsibility* is involved, a sense that the killing is somehow acceptable if one does it oneself, does not delegate it or expect that it not intrude upon one's consciousness, although this, on the other hand, seems to admit that there is a weight, a problem, to be taken responsibility *for*, and that this killing should not be an ordinary or easy thing to do.

The word 'sacred' has been in the air for some time and now, at last, appears, though it is not clear whether what is sacred is the life taken or – as if the one confers its sacredness on the other – the taking of the life. I think – more sceptically than I might once have done (I can think of no reason why 'tradition,' 'belief,' etc. should absolve one culture more than another) – of the Native American tribes who thanked the spirit of the buffalo they hunted. Yes, life *is* sacred, if I can employ that term in a secular sense – there are many things that are sacred in such a sense – but I am uneasy about the term, firstly because it *is* so definitively *non*-secular, so much within the economy of the religious, and secondly because it is so subject to critical misuse.

The term 'sacred' is itself sacred, it seems, and I'm not sure that it should be. All too often it is a sign that something ethically questionable is being placed safely beyond discussion. It also *objectifies* the thing it qualifies – separates and segregates it. We began to need God, the sacred, etc., as separate entities, when we removed something from ourselves, or sought to remove ourselves from where and what we had been: when, with an act – a long, slow act, albeit – of supreme arrogance, we said that what was *here* (the animal, but not only that) was about *us*, was *not* sacred, and could therefore be subjected *to* us.

As to the non-secularity of the term, I have hypothesised already that metaphysics were born out of the need to establish the human as something above or beyond the animal, as a means of asserting and consolidating that *dominion* which the canny makers of the Bible needed to establish before any other human attribute could be presented. But any implication – and it *is* my implication – that such a development is universal, rather than the product of particular culture, must confront the existence of *vegetarian* religions, past and present, that argue the sacredness of all life and proscribe the taking of it in any form. My difficulty with these – mitigated by gratitude for *any* abatement of cruelty – stems from the way that, even in their apparently contrary direction, such religions still have as their basic premise the progressive *extraction* of the human from its animal predicament. If they proscribe the eating of flesh or the taking of life, they do so on the understanding that this is in the individual's best interests. The compassion they advocate is still, as it were, framed as a compassion-under-duress rather than voluntary and a logical product of one's being.

Another anecdote. I am walking through the university on the first day of first semester. The place is teeming with new students looking for their first lectures, for coffee, for the library, for their friends. I am struck as always by their confusion, their wide-eyed, *calf*-like innocence. How many are vegetarian? How many vegan? One in a hundred? Less? I imagine them carrying their sandwiches for lunch – ham, chicken, cheese – or ordering at one or another of the cafeterias: prawn laksa, beef curry, hamburgers. Even if they wished to think differently, how could they? How is this place – this *university* – going to help them? I try to think of a discipline that is not in some way dependent upon dominion and the exploitation of animals, but which would it be? Such disciplines surely exist, but for the moment I can't think of them. Mathematics? Physics? I can think of few others. Certainly not philosophy, where every major figure, meat-eater or otherwise, either oils the sympathetic machinery of metaphysics or prefaces their work on advancement of the human. Certainly not my own discipline, where the entire pastoral tradition turns about an unspoken centre of cruelty; where the greatest novels rely as much upon dinner parties and the carving of beef as they do upon battles and the intensities of human emotion. Certainly not law, medicine, education, psychology. And certainly not art history. The university – my beloved turning (and disappearing) world of knowledge – seems suddenly, to my absolute dismay, but another immense and complicated agency for the unreflective propagation of cruelty, swallowing these students as an abattoir swallows its victims.

Overstatement? Yes, but a reeling vertigo is not unusual before one gets one's bearings in this new place-of-thought. Reorientation toward the Animal demands a deep and extensive *de-centring of the human.* One questions directly the right of *Homo sapiens* to be the point of everything, proposes that the human be *amongst,* not *above,* that it be *one of,* not *the.* Hitherto, one realises, all understandings of value, all standards of good and evil, had been predicated upon the continued dominance of the species. But what if that were *set aside*? If one has not been brought up to it, this new perception can come as a dramatic destabilisation. It can seem, for a time, as if all the edifices of one's previous understanding, their centre-pin gone, list, threaten to topple, their contingency exposed. The noblest expressions of human nature and purpose can appear blinkered and naïve. One can be shocked at what one finds oneself reconsidering. Surrounded by people brought to a veritable standstill by the insurmountable difficulties of their own existence, for example, one can find oneself thinking that the melancholia that seems the keynote of our time is not much more than an immense, endemic narcissism. 'How can you talk about the suffering of animals,' I'm asked, 'when there is so much *human* suffering?' And while one of my answers is clear, that compassion is self-replenishing and without borders, and that there is no need – especially when most of us give so little to anything other than our own immediate interests – to apportion it, I am all too aware that what is given toward the saving or rehabilitation of a human life, while it must, yes, *be* given, is nevertheless almost certainly also extending the life of one who will continue to eat meat, continue to contribute to the suffering of animals.

A dilemma? Or perhaps merely a paradox. It is hard to know. A recent conversation with a friend turned to matters of animal cruelty, then inevitably to veganism:

'So you don't eat *any* meat?'

'No.'

'Fish?'

'No.'

'No meat, no seafood – and eggs? Milk products?'

'No.'

'And this is not for your health but to avoid cruelty.'

'Yes.'

'But where does it stop?'

We talk, then, about 'sentient' creatures. How does one define sentience by anything other than a *human* understanding of the concept? And how can one say that it is unacceptable to kill 'sentient' creatures but all right to kill others? Aren't plants also in some measure sentient? How can we say that they are not?

Vegans often go further, for just these reasons. Some become fructarians, eating only those parts of plants that plants produce to be eaten as part of their own process of reproduction. Some argue that we should only eat *wild* fruits, regarding cultivation itself as a kind of exploitation. My friend and I agree that, following a strict logic in this regard, one might end up living on air, scarcely able to move for fear of hurting some living thing in the process – effacing oneself in order to avoid cruelty to other creatures, while those other creatures show no such compunction. An absurdity, of course, and yet also not. A paradox. A kind of point zero. And yet one cannot – this is surely, like *argumentum ad hominem*, one of the great errors of thought – allow the difficulty and possible absurdity of the extreme to undermine the principle. It is only in the realm of thought-by-itself – thought alone – that thought can be tidy and without paradox. Thought-in-the-body is a different thing.

The conversation tails off. Driving away, I find myself thinking firstly of the logical difficulty (i.e., that it is logical that there would be difficulty) of *de-centring the human* in this way. All of our thought – our Logos – pivots about that axis: the *machinery* of our logic, our language, its grammars, its systems of metaphor. How could one expect anything other than paradox, embarrassment – a kind of radical and systemic *stupidity* – in one's attempt to think into so radically different a place? How *can* one think, against the core of thought? And then, those words 'point zero' still ringing in my ears, realising that what is (now) needed is a Descartes-like return to a kind of point zero of thought, a starting from scratch, with compassion, rather than wound-spurred anxiety, as one's foundational premise.

I am back at the Wound again. As my opening intimated, I want to speak of the animal in literature and art in a sense different from any I might so far have adduced. Neither in terms of its presence, let's say, nor of its absence, but of something as likely manifest in the curve of an archway or the shadow of a chair. Once, at an exhibition of the paintings of Giorgio Morandi, I saw a man in a business suit standing before a still life, weeping. The painting represented a set of glass bottles on a tabletop. Four glass bottles, and an open canister, nothing more. Can it be that people go to art galleries in order to sublimate their pain? Or to seek its reflection, its echo? Could it be that, in each work they pass, the Wound searches for itself (or for balm, for letting)? Just as the artists cannot have known – at least, not many of them – the nature or origin of that intensity they wished to capture or restore, the idea they wished to return to its body? The church and the gallery closely linked, in a complicity that almost passes understanding? But that is perhaps the point, to *pass* understanding: to be a place – places – to keep from the mind what the mind cannot bear.

I've given up smoking, as it happens, or rather smoking has abandoned me. Not for my health, although I feel better for it. A bit like veganism itself. One mightn't do it for one's health, but that might improve nonetheless, and not just the physical. The Wound is so deep that there's probably no fixing it, soothe it as we might, but with the de-centring of the human there can also be (how to put this?) *a de-centring of the self in one's own life*, a shifting of attention away from the needs and wounds of the self – those *lacks* that are, paradoxically, one of the mainstays (the matrices) of contemporary society – toward the needs and wounds of the Animal, in such a way as amounts, ultimately, to a powerful and empowering redefinition of the self, a new and radical kind of wellbeing.

Angelaki

Country and Western

Sunil Badami

'Where you from, mate?'
'Sydney.'
That makes 'em laugh, for some reason.

When people overseas ask me where I'm from, I naturally say 'Australia.' When people interstate ask, I say 'Sydney.' When people in Sydney ask, I say 'Blacktown,' and they look askance, as if to say: *Where the bloody hell is that?*

For some, the western suburbs are some bloody hell, beginning somewhere around Annandale, blurring into a distant, blank space, uncharted territory, a no-man's-land of strange terrors and cultural desolation that evaporates into Emu Plains. With no atmosphere, no culture – and definitely no reason to visit. A place to leave rather than to return to, a place from which to seek asylum.

The Italian writer Aldo Busi says that 'we travel like lobsters, our heads over our shoulders.' Which is to say, we're always looking back, looking away, our eyes fixed not so much on the horizon to which we're heading, but what we left behind around the corner we just passed.

But in Sydney, where 'executive waterfront investment opportunities' grab at the hem of the foreshore, stabbing the skyline like upturned fingers, once-vibrant harbourside neighbourhoods are now silent but for the sound of the security buzzer, everyone as blinded as dazzled by the harbour's glistering, dancing light.

And, unlike the starving colonists of Old Sydney Town, who looked westwards for salvation (and installed the governor in Parramatta Park), it seems, at least from reading the papers or listening to the radio, nobody looks west, least of all those of us who grew up there. I left as soon as I could, moving to Town, where I imagined everything happened, finding myself apologetically justifying my place by doing everything I could not to appear a Westie, even if I was still obviously a darkie.

In Greystanes, where I grew up, and where the only water views were the Beresford Road stormwater drain or the Prospect Reservoir, our gaze was always fixed on Town, as distant as another country. From the milk bar at the top of Ettalong Road, the sky bleached and laundry-dry, our Paddle Pops dissolving into the incandescent asphalt, you'd see the city, so far away, shimmering in the burnt-blue distance, a mirage reminding you how far away you were, despite being so close.

And at night, Town's candy-coloured lights would flicker uncertainly as the humming sodium streetlamps of the Great Western Highway swallowed them up into the stifling night.

'No, where you really from?' they ask.
'Well, I was born in Blacktown,' I reply. 'But don't tell anyone – we don't want to lower property values.'
They laugh a little less.

The Australian academic and critic Stephen Muecke observes that 'a language like English is like a group of textual suburbs,' each with its own character, the differences expressed not just through space and distance, but in a cultural and political geography, crowded with meaning, like, say, the difference between Blacktown and Circular Quay or Greystanes and Girraween.

It's always struck me, Greystanes or Girraween or even Doonside aside, how incongruously the western suburbs are named. The imperious names of posh suburbs like Northbridge or Edgecliff or Palm Beach describe them perfectly: there *is* a bridge there, it *is* on the edge of a cliff, and there *are* lots of expensively transplanted palms within the high-walled gardens of those luxurious weekenders.

But if you've ever been to Merrylands or Pleasure Point or Silverwater, you'd find it hard to see the merriness or pleasure or silveriness over the belch of exhaust fumes and the roar of motorway traffic. The only high walls on the Cumberland Highway are there not to protect the residents from the invasive gaze of outsiders, but from the pollution and noise and collisions that the many smash-repair shops all the way to Smithfield take advantage of. Sometimes it seems, the roller shutters clamped down against the yellow heat, that even Westies don't want to look around them.

Only Blacktown, where I was born, seems apt: named after a school established to educate the natives in 'civilised' English ways, its indigenous Dharug name long lost. Now it's home to Sydney's biggest population of indigenous Australians, immigrant Indians and Sudanese refugees.

A black town, indeed, even if Greystanes did feel, growing up, as it sounded: a regretful smudge, only an incremental shade from darkness.

'No, seriously, where's your family from?'
'Seriously? Actually, Greystanes. I grew up there.'
They stop laughing.

Just as for those who've never ventured any further down Parramatta Road past Annandale, the western suburbs is uncharted territory, written on the blank page of an imaginary map, my geography is an emotional one. The longer you're away, you realise that the landmarks aren't the things you sped past on the way to the Cumberland Highway on-ramp: those mysterious, windowless hangars; the anonymous storage facilities; the cut-price hotel-motels; the shabby shops selling soiled seconds; the heavy machinery yards, the dead skeletons of cranes and earth-movers hung, fossilised, in the still, suffocating air … but the spaces they once were – and more importantly, the people who inhabit those spaces.

Unlike the heritage-listed million-dollar terraces of Paddington or Rozelle, the streetscapes of western suburbs like Padstow or Rosehill are constantly changing, from minty fibro cottages to brick-veneer bungalows; now lurid McMansions and strange glassy-faced apartments thrown onto empty stretches of Parramatta Road staring out at car yards or the acrid remains of the Homebush abattoirs. Could you tell Australia's second white settlement was established at Parramatta, now in danger of being rechristened Westfieldamatta?

Horrified faces seem to ask: *how could anyone want to live there?* As if you only live there because you can't afford to live anywhere else, seeking asylum from even worse places. When I was due back after a couple of years in London, my mother couldn't understand my reluctance to return. 'There's a new Gloria Jean's in the Boral Brick Pit,' she said indignantly, referring to the Pemulwuy development over the spar from the reservoir. 'And the coffee, frankly, is quite *adequate*.'

Unlike the pho, the raw beef larb, the kuttu roti, the bhelpuri or bibimbap, which are phenomenal. Growing up eating chevapi from Fairfield, pastizzi from South Wentworthville, kofte in Auburn, at little lunch, I'd swap my puris and dhal for Marko's csabai roll; after school, Carlo's mum would stuff us with cannoli or we'd gobble devon-and-sauce sangers at Kieran's.

There's a danger, though, in regarding the western suburbs as a kind of food court, like a series of little China- or Viet- or Korea- or Lebanon- or Serbia-towns, enjoying the cuisine but disregarding the cultures that cooked them up, leaving 'them' to deal with the mess between 'authenticity' and 'assimilation.'

And there's a danger in perpetuating the false perception of 'us' and 'them,' East and West, when the borders are always shifting and easily crossed – as long as it takes to get on a train (or, given Western Sydney's unending public-transport woes, just getting on the motorway) – or, perhaps, more importantly, within us.

Yet it seems odd that most of the city's population, coming from the western suburbs, must make the effort to engage, at least culturally, with thousands spending hours on the train or motorway to line the harbour and crowd the Domain every January for the Sydney Festival, as if there was nowhere else to go, when while the road ends at the foreshore, there are countless directions heading the other way going west into Australia's dark heart.

However, for 'native Westies' like my mother, living in the western suburbs is not simply a question of affordability but *community*: the 'ethnic ghettoes' pilloried by those opposed to diversity exist only as new immigrants find their feet in a strange land among friends. It seems that the transformation in public opinion from 'ethnic ghetto' to celebrated 'cultural precincts' like Norton Street or Dixon Street takes only a generation. Just as from Ettalong Road to Centrepoint, it's only twelve miles, even if in Sydney traffic it sometimes feels a world away: another country, as foreign as the past, in these forgotten places where everything seems demolished, where certainties seem erased.

But it's in those places, like the meaning hidden in the spaces between words, where just as much, if not more, is gained in the translation, as was ever imagined lost.

'Where were they born?'
'Well, my parents were born in India—'
'Right, so you're Indian?'

I eat tandoori chicken I do on the barbie; I've read the Mahabharata, but only in English. I'm not sure I'm *really* Indian and yet people aren't really sure I'm *not*. 'Indianness' is a concept as foreign to me as 'Australianness.' Let alone 'Westieness.'

I was born in Australia, I speak with an Australian accent, I don't speak any Indian language, but I look Indian: what you might call a 'coconut,' white inside and brown out. It's funny: when I tell people in India where my parents are from, they laugh and ask me where I'm *really* from. It's only in India that I'm Australian ... and perhaps vice versa.

In more supposedly cosmopolitan quarters I'd find people kindly reassuring me I wasn't really Indian, or Westie for that matter, and being surprised I took such exception.

Such questions don't bother my mother, adjusting her sari defiantly. 'I'm a Westernie and proud of it,' she says, well, *proudly*.

But what would a Westie look like anyway (or, while we're asking, an Aussie)? Who wears flannie shirts with Winnie Blues tucked into the sleeve over an Ackadacka tank top stuffed into skinny jeans – and, most appallingly, with *thongs*?

(Actually, walking down the trendier quarters of Bondi or Surry Hills, it seems *everybody*. It seems strange not just that such privileged young slashies should be copying Westies, but that their Westie contemporaries might imitate them, imitating their own Westie *parents.*)

And it's ironic that with Sydney's exorbitant house prices forcing people further west, many of us who left are now returning – and those same eastern suburbs or North Shore denizens who might wonder who'd live in the west find themselves on its doorstep, newly arrived immigrants in enclaves like Petersham or Ashfield, where the multicultural atmosphere – with older Portuguese and Greek immigrants rubbing shoulders with newer Chinese and Anglo arrivals – is celebrated.

Much is made of Sydney's multiculturality: after all, as Australia's largest city, home to Australia's busiest airport, and the first destination for many immigrants (such as my parents), it has the most – and most diverse – ethnic communities.

But on a recent trip to Bondi, packed with foreign tourists, it struck me that I was the only non-white person on the street: a strange, unsettling feeling I suddenly realised I'd never have back home, out west.

And it occurred to me that the gateway to Australia wasn't at Circular Quay, but somewhere around Parramatta, Sydney's demographic and geographical heart, its streets alive with exotic aromas and unheard-of dialects, offering at once the reality of Sydney today, and its possibilities tomorrow. Lost for words, I thought of Muecke again:

> When we write, we sometimes run out of words. This is because we come to the edge of the city of words, where there are no more words left in the place we find ourselves.

'No, mate, I'm a Westie. And proud of it.'

And it seems, just as the geography of a place is one more of meaning than merely location, so too a nation – especially a nation of immigrants like Australia – is not so much a collection of gazetted borders or place names but an idea, agreed upon by the majority of the people who claim citizenship of it.

But like any idea, like any nation, like any city, like any community, it cannot exist statically in the ghetto of some idealised past or limited to any particular definition: it can only be enriched and strengthened by debating it and expanding it, the changes keeping it alive.

And nowhere is that more true than the western suburbs, constantly demolishing and building and reinventing, its face changing with every new wave of arrivals, building their own ideas of Australia on the foundations of their own imaginary homelands.

Although the Indonesian-Chinese-Australian theorist Ien Ang acknowledges the conflict between questions of 'where you're from' and 'where you're at,' particularly for immigrants and their children, and while the idea of being where you're at is more relevant in finding your place, it shouldn't discount where you're from. Why, as Salman Rushdie asks, should we be excluded from any part of our heritage, whether it's being treated as a full part of society, or drawing on our roots – whether Oriental or Westie – for our art or identity?

In his classic *The Merry-Go-Round in the Sea* (set in, of all places, Western Australia), Randolph Stow's semi-autobiographical protagonist, Rob, whose uncle is Maltese, wonders 'if he would ever go as far as Malta, and hear people talking foreign languages in the streets.'

We needn't travel so far: once we open the shutters and turn towards our hearts, it's there, where it always was, and if we look hard enough, we can see it never really left us – or us it. Just as I cannot disavow my apparent Indianness, how can I deny the role my Westieness has played in my own history, my own personal journey, in my life and writing?

After all, a culture's artists aren't its privileged informants but its outsiders, always on the margins looking in, not offering new certainties but new ways of questioning accepted ones – like Westie Asians, accidental Orientals, from Blacktown to Chinatown, all of us double-outsiders, looking in from the edge of elsewhere, offering new insights, new visions, new illuminations.

And best of all, not just artists or writers. For one marvellous month in Greystanes, we wander once-silent streets, shining with fairy lights and children's laughter and the jingle of carols. The Caruanas, the Browns, the Sabouhs and the Wongs all festoon their front windows with puddings and elves and animatronic Nativity scenes, steaming in the Mr Whippy gloaming, the sky radiant with rosy resplendence, all of us swelling with Christmas spirit and community pride: Catholics, Protestants, Buddhists, Hindus, Muslims. My two little girls, dark-skinned, blue-eyed, half-Indian, half-Anglo and *wholly Australian*, are as enthralled by these Christmas decorations as they are by the Deepavali ones at the Murugan Temple up the road.

The *Parramatta Advertiser* proudly reports how many people come from all over the city to delight at Greystanes, of all places. And, amidst the excited clamour and electric lustre, nobody notices the spray-on snow or sweltering Santas dissolving in the dusk, or the way each of us has added a little of our own traditions and expectations to make something shinier, more colourful, more inclusive: different, but not discrete. Nor, as the rainbow sparkles and tinkling carols shimmer along Cumberland Road, the uncertain glimmer of Town, so far away.

We've no need to look longingly over our shoulders that one marvellous month, for we can see that light right in front of us, where it always was: round the corner from home, in our neighbours' and children's faces, sticky with choc-top and lit with joy.

Edge of Elsewhere

Infinite Anthology: Adventures in Lexiconia

Les Murray

Here is a brief sample of words I have submitted to Australia's *Macquarie Dictionary* over the last two or three years:

pobblebonk – scarlet-sided banjo frog. Large robust frog common in swamps in coastal Queensland and New South Wales.

kiddy-fiddler – child molester, paedophile.

paste – pastry, in the usage of some Australian regions up into modern times. Comes from Lowland Scots and Northern English dialects and is attested as far back as the twelfth century.

rooibos – Afrikaans 'red bush,' an aromatic shrub from which a caffeine-free infusion is made, termed red-bush tea, very popular in Southern Africa.

doctoring – (cf. 'under the doctor') seeking frequent medical treatment or other medical help, e.g. 'He's been doctoring for years.'

Corymbia – new sub-genus of eucalypts, comprising most smooth-barked species; *Eucalyptus gummifera* becomes *Corymbia gummifera* in new botany.

Archie – (military colloquialism) World War I anti-aircraft gun or gunfire of same.

tramp stamp – tattoo pointing to erogenous zones, suggestive of sexual availability. Classic position is on lower back, at jeans line.

GORD – acronym for gastroesophageal reflux disease.

gregarize – said when a solitary green grasshopper turns red to yellow, exudes serotonin and begins to swarm.

jardin – oil, or more recently polymers, added to emeralds to disguise cracks. Produces a coralline appearance under the microscope.

dirty – two fresh meanings: lucky (e.g.) 'Won the Lottery? Geez yer dirty!' and Aboriginal: countryside overgrown with shrubs, grass etc. is said to be *dirty* when in need of burning off.

squib – a fake bullet wound (film term). An older meaning was to duck something, out of cowardice.

bit with a snake – bitten by a snake. Irish conflation of with and by, from Gaelic *le*. Still heard in my region.

petrichor – aggregate of natural oils and terpenes on dry ground; gives off an exhilarating loamy smell when wetted by rain. Said to trigger reproductive cycle in aquatic creatures, fish etc. Discovered by Drs Joy Beard and R.G. Thomas at the Australian National University in 1964.

*

Where I was born, in the coastal hills of New South Wales, everybody milked cows for a living or drew timber to the mills. Most houses were unpainted with no pictures on their walls or radios to turn song into muzak. Arts were storytelling and ballroom dancing, though World War II at its height put a crimp on the latter. We, my parents and I, used to walk a mile down the paddocks to Grandfather's on a Sunday to listen to the war news on his wireless. I learned the looming names of islands to our near north, out of which Japanese soldiers might surge, and I was impressed by the posh, almost religious tones of the newsreaders, with their BBC accents full of words like *advarnce*. That national broadcasting accent would be swept away within the next ten years, thrown into the landfill with hoary British textbooks full of otters and snowy yuletides. The ABC would be turned on to a sober new national confidence that spoke what are known as 'General' and the more precise 'Cultivated' version of our local English. Our family had moved into the General Australian accent over the two or three generations since we stopped speaking Border Scots, but our men regularly spoke

Broad Australian with neighbours who didn't like putting on any sort of dog. Or any but the American twang in which Western and pop songs were just beginning to be sung, driving out the older bush ballads.

I was an only child, and as my parents' poverty deepened through droughts and the stubborn meanness of our landlord, I was not allowed to have other children come and play; our local bush school would only reopen when I was nine. Pop songs did not interest me. I was arrested by the Psalms and the steely eloquence of our Free Kirk ministers. And by swearing. My father was a former bullock driver and fluent in tremendous profanity when stirred. Later I would call this the Black Poetry and play variations on it. I could never fully match the Biblical cadence he was prone to. When a redback spider bit him on the foot, it hurt unmercifully 'for seven days and seven nights.' My dad was not an educated man, but he was witty, with wondrous timing and a fey imagination, at least until my mother's death when I was twelve. That muted his spirit almost into the grave for decades.

Language was plentiful in my world, but it came from adults or from reading. I read my mother's school prize books, especially the eight-volume encyclopaedia; I read comic books and the Alfa-Laval cream-separator manual – *l'écrémeuse*, for it was in French, from Quebec. When I joined the other fifteen bush kids at Bulby Brush Public School, I read its tiny library in weeks: the best book was Mawson's account of his Antarctic expedition to the South Magnetic Pole in the early 1900s, toiling over the crevasses and the *sastrugi* on a diet of boiled dog livers that poisoned him and his companions with an excess of vitamin A. After my mother's death, our existence sank to a sad Huck Finn level, even as books lifted me into unreal feudal fantasies, able to couch a lance but not to use an urban letterbox.

At eighteen, at the end of school, I had just fallen in love with two powerful muses, philology and poetry. During university it was touch and go which one would shape my life. I was writing odd poems, but also devouring the 'teach yourself' grammars of many languages and ransacking the Fisher Library for texts in them. In the event, the philology lasted ten years. One day, when I was a scholarly and scientific translator at the Australian

National University in Canberra, I read a crucial sentence by a famous German linguist who, when asked how many languages he knew, ruefully answered '*Kaum meine eigene!*' – hardly my own. I saw that my knowledge was in each case shallow and hesitant, and that no matter how deeply I went into each modern language, I would be only privately discovering things other people already knew, whereas with poetry I had the chance of discovering, in public, things no one had previously known. I might penetrate the mystery of home and why it was allowed so little dignity. Shortly afterwards, I headed off to Europe and a total dedication to verse-writing which has never flagged.

Even before I got out of translating, I'd developed a passion for the old part-Scottish farm terminology we'd spoken to each other in my region. It went some way beyond farm usage too, especially in the deep drawn-out *o* we often used in words such as God, log, dog, gone: the dorg is gorn. No other Scots Borders vowels survived, but a cow's udder was her *elder* (also the title of a member of the Free Kirk Synod), a milking shed was called the *bails* and *agen* meant 'by the time that' (agen he gets home, the job'll be finished). A *fessloe* was an ulcer, the iron power offtake of a horse's collar was termed the *hames*, which also meant a complete mess ('I made a hames of my best suit' – Flann O'Brien, *At Swim Two Birds*). A cattle grid was a *ramp*, as in Ireland. A *poddy* was a calf, and a bilious stomach felt *squawmish*. All of these terms were still in use a hundred years after settlement on the NSW north coast, and they mingled with other common words not usually heard in other districts – though *muttai*, Aboriginal for a maize cob for eating, and the Scots *press* for a school cupboard were widespread. From forest work came *dozy* for termite-ridden, *snig chain* and *climbing board*, *calabash* for a steel loop to distribute the pull of chains. Since the settlements of poor people, the fishing villages and weatherboard sawmilling camps were typically the scene of intermarriage between Aboriginal and white, it would have been strange if we had not picked up any Aboriginal words, the harmless small *bandi-bandi* snake and the banana-tasting *puddenie* fruit. More unequivocally Aboriginal were *bullrout*, a freshwater fish armed with a poisonous dorsal fin, the *dooligarl* or hairy man of worldwide mythology, and the *gugri*, a small slab hut for lighting a fire to heat branding irons and similar. That turned out to be the ancient local word for 'house' or 'shelter.' Emaciated animals, including humans, were called *poor* and the same word was a kind of title added to the names of the very ill and the dead. Not all words that looked Aboriginal were Aboriginal in origin: the village of *Bundook* bore the Hindi name of a rifle, doubtless lent by some veteran of the British Indian Army. *Pipi*, Maori for a freshwater mussel, would have been a similar case.

In the 1960s, Professor Alex Mitchell, the man who persuaded the ABC to broadcast in Australian accents, became founding vice-chancellor of Sydney's new Macquarie University. He was joined there by Professor Arthur Delbridge, first proponent of what would inevitably be called the *Macquarie Dictionary*, in honour of Governor Lachlan Macquarie, who reigned at Sydney Cove throughout the teens of the nineteenth century and was the first colonial proconsul to see his antipodean Devil's Island as the precursor of a nation. The old governor always dearly loved to see his name on a map or any large venture. Now the moment had come for a dictionary based on our national dialect and usage, for it had been apparent for years that English was a polycentric language fed from a myriad decolonising sources. An 'Australian magpie' was a singing bird, a non-larcenous shrike resembling the Old World bird only in its black-and-white livery, and while 'utility' had as its second definition in American and British dictionaries the meaning of household supplies such as fuel, power, telephone and water, in Australia the word meant a motor car with its rear seat and boot replaced by a carrying compartment, the whole lighter and less powerful than an American pickup truck; in time, our utility truck would become a *ute* even on official *rego* (registration) papers, and yet bear no relation to any American native tribe.

The designer of the *Macquarie* still had to walk a tightrope. For folk with a respect for our culture and achievements so far, it would be essential to stress the Australianness of the work. For those, still numerous then even at home, who equated Australianness with slang and slovenly English, they would stress the book's comprehensiveness and respectability. An early advertisement catches the balance of the enterprise:

> *The Macquarie's Australian character ...*
>
> The Macquarie contains many words which reflect the uniqueness of the Australian way of life, many of which appear in no comparable dictionary. Beanbag, alf, home unit, brickfielder, bombo, wool cheque, boat people and surf club are examples ...
>
> *and its international content ...*
>
> The Macquarie is also a comprehensive modern dictionary containing international words which have recently come into our language. Words like urban renewal, cheque-book journalism, drogue target, intellectual property, buzz word, chirality and dinkus.

In fact *dinkus*, a small drawing intended to break up a page of type, is said to have been invented by an artist on the Sydney *Bulletin* magazine in the 1920s. But the first edition of the *Macquarie* in 1981 sold 50,000 copies in three months, a huge sale on our small domestic market. This proved that people were prepared to accept their own national lexicon. Suddenly the great Australian epithets seemed no longer to be *mate* and *sheila*, but *award wage* and *after sales service.* And after sales was where the new book perforce had to go, turning from a one-off like the *Australian National Dictionary,* a highly scholarly register of Australianisms, to an institution with children's versions, atlases, illustrated editions, *Macquarie*s for every need, every user, every pocket. So far, there have been five editions of the main volume since the first, all of them edited by Susan Butler, arguably one of the world's great lexicographers. She has always preferred Dr Johnson as an ancestor of her book over Noah Webster's polemical model.

To me, from the very start, words were poor people's treasures, infinite in variety and potential at no cost. Combining them came later, extracting their colours and music. I spoke them in tongues around the hills. As well as their loom and resonance, I became fascinated by their etymologies and all the cultural freight they carried. As I see now, I had turned to my foreign languages for more of that, rather than for communication. I had wanted to see and hear and pronounce all of language, get it into my mouth and my bones. When the new national dictionary came out, I reviewed it in exuberant terms, saying that it re-centred our language in the country where we actually lived. I then began, shyly at first, to pester Susan Butler with postcards suggesting items for inclusion in future editions. She was unfailingly polite about my sometimes ungainly advocacies, and gradually a good many of them began to filter into the ever-evolving text. My rural and Scots items went in first, but always a few unrelated ones drifted in too. I was not much of a checker, always: I would exult over some discovery and fail to notice that it was in already. That happened with *gross motor*, which had replaced *physical education* in our schools. Other items pointed to poignant bits of history: the twenty-odd places called *Irishtown* in the nineteenth century suggested to me reservoir-villages to house labour employed on neighbouring pastoral properties. Irish immigrants were the working underclass back then. Just about all of those villages have long since changed their names. The *whipping side* of a sheep, in shearer's parlance, was the right-hand side, the last to be shorn, but it had a bloody history, as the side receiving most punishment when a right-handed flogger lashed a triced-up convict. Shearers carried that memory in their traditions. *Free traders*, split bloomers for wearing under the voluminous skirts of the nineteenth and earlier-twentieth century, came from Nancy Keesing's splendid *Lily on the Dustbin*, a compendium of urban and feminine language. Occasionally I would tease out a knot of comparative idiom: *bushed*, for instance, meant 'tired' in American speech and was taking over from the Australian meaning of 'lost' or the Canadian one of 'suffering from camp fever.' *Wedge*, in my dialect, was often used as a verb to mean forcing the pace, but in youthful costume it was used to signify a lump of fabric in the groin, sometimes causing *camel toe*, or genitals outlined through tight clothing.

The *Macquarie* always had a corps of volunteer word-catchers, as well as its expert consultants. Not having a field of specialised vocabulary, I have always felt insubstantial alongside experts in, say, prison talk or theatre language, botany or marine creatures. Miscellaneous items of vocabulary simply crossed my ken and were submitted before I could forget them again: *rippy* for dangerously jocular, *überveillance*, invented by two social scientists of the married name Michael for the e-tagging of humans which may be imminent on the horizon, *koro* from Japanese, meaning a fear that the penis will retract into the belly and cause death. Not an ethnic joke: TB in the abdomen is very prone to cause such retraction; it is a grave symptom.

It was interesting to watch how the dictionary has evolved. Etymology, for instance, was weak in the early editions, but had since improved markedly. Borrowings from European immigrant sources had been sparse in the first postwar immigrant period. This changed with the opening of the 'Cuisine Age,' coulis of this, infusion of that; it was by way of the kitchen that Australian speech became truly international. Words began to flock in from South Asia and the Pacific Rim and soon they went far beyond food. The realities of international sport began to emerge: *doosra* recently caught my eye, a Hindi cricketing term for an off-spinner's googly that doesn't break toward the bat, but off to leg. That one comes just before *dosa* and *dosha*, which most modern Britons will already know.

I was sad when biographical entries came into the dictionary; they seemed bound to take up a lot of space with vanities and celebrities. With their historical dimension, however, they do tend to restore a sense of Australia as a community, with a core settlers' history that for a while was bitterly fought over. The culture wars of the last few decades have been treated by the *Macquarie* with an unusual equanimity, the rhetoric all simply calmed into lexis. Arranging the representation of underlying topics and emphases of any reference book is a mystery that belongs to its editors and its public; get it wrong, or allow it bias, and the book is apt to founder. The facts of normal Australian usage have always been the gyroscope of the *Macquarie*, and must have served thousands of foreigners and immigrants (*migrants*, as we oddly term them) as a guide to the familiar oddities of a new country: *informal* as a deliberately invalidated vote in one of our now unique compulsory ballots, *electorate* for a constituency, *footpath* for pavement. Even *watertable*, in the country, for a roadside gutter. Authenticity in novels and film requires no less. I still recall the German translator who didn't know a *digger* was a soldier and used the term for an excavator.

A couple of years ago Susan Butler very kindly invited me to come and be a consultant on her beloved dictionary, observing how she and her otherwise all-female team go about constantly upgrading it. I carp at tiny points of usage, and am set small jobs, pruning out entries which may have become otiose, or which never took off. Most recently I checked a large vocabulary of Australian soldiers' vernacular from 1914 to 1918, in preparation for a commemorative volume honouring the centennial of the Great War. I was to eliminate, with the aid of a War Memorial wordlist, all terms from that war which had never really caught on with the diggers, or survived for long afterwards. *Strafe* was a surprising excision. I also left out *cark sucker*, which a few of the first AIF may have picked up from the first Americans but none had dared to bring home to Mum. The *Macquarie* doesn't indulge the Fescennine unduly, but doesn't fear it either. Some years ago Sue innocently started to speak of the then-popular epithet *fuckwit* in an ABC radio interview, and a pulled plug filled the studio with bland music. It is fascinating to watch definitions shrink and expand, and hear the reasons why words may be held over till they perform better, if ever. One perennial problem is with commercial brand names, which may eventually become accepted words, as *kleenex* has done, and *Coke* in the sense of Coca-Cola has not, though *Coke-bottle lenses* are an entry. When I submitted *Incabloc*, partly in order to find out just what part of the watchmaker's art it referred to, it proved to be a proprietary treatment to protect sealed movements, and so not eligible, though *doona*, a former brand name, has got a *guernsey* in the dictionary for having displaced, in Australia, the earlier French term *duvet*. Excessive care to exclude commercial names seems to have peeled away many commonly used titles: the humble edge trimmer is not allowed either its Australian name *whipper-snipper* nor its neater British *strimmer*, though *hoover* is in as an alternative to our cumbersome *vacuum cleaner*. Only British migrant women use the hoover. A sign of impending acceptance of a commercial word seems to be the dropping of its capital initial.

My earlier contributions were perennially invalidated by lack of a printed source. I was sometimes to provide one by writing a poem in which the word appeared, but that was too transparent. My problem was one of class: I drew typically from a level of vocabulary seen as lower even than that used in urban Broad speech. The real oral language of country folk had had few literary outings since the late-nineteenth century. Radio and TV regularly got it wrong, and the main audience for that was country women who may have hoped their men would one day lift up their diction. I wrote a long narrative poem, *Fredy Neptune*, in the rural speech of the 1890s to the 1940s, including enough contemporary German to establish the hero as an Australian-born bilingual. This was praised as a feast of half-forgotten idiom and harvested for the dictionary, but my real allies were the Aboriginal people once widely seen as even lower and more ill-spoken than rural workers, but now rising again in a near-vacuum of respectable renditions of our one real dialect. The classic Aboriginal words in common Australian use had been adopted 150 to 200 years ago; now white people were hearing a distinctive new phonology and words like *ganji*, policeman (from *gangibel*), *land rights* and *spirit country*, as well as small change such as *blackout*, a party to which whites are not invited, *deadly* meaning 'excellent' and *jar* signifying a quarrel. It was beginning to be hard to exclude all this from the national conversation – and if one print-poor group was now to be deferred to, silencing others would grow harder. Black voices were being heard on radio and TV – modern equivalents of print – and I began to argue hard against a purely middle-class dictionary. Not wholly in vain, since the *Macquarie*'s first beginnings had run parallel with postwar educationists' debates about equity issues arising from denigration of home dialects. Students way back then were asserted to be in danger of losing their self-esteem in the face of Imperial posh speech. Nowadays some would assert the same of Americanising influences – but borrowings from Hollywood and Rock sociolects, even modish Black talk and electronic jargon, are regularly buried by the speed of the fashions that carry them. People don't so much adopt as quote items that fly and fade faster than dictionaries can register them. The lack of depth of real understanding of American culture here was illustrated recently when arrangements to protect President Obama on a brief Australian visit were given the code name Operation Blue Gum. This made a perfect fit with Billy Bluegum the cuddly koala, but it took days for anyone to tell the authorities that *bluegum* in Black idiom referred to an indolent African-American person.

A couple of years ago, on ABC radio, the composer Brett Waymark introduced the term *audiation*, a musical equivalent of *ideation*. Instead of a constant play of ideas in the mind, Waymark's word would mean a teeming of tunes and musical structures there. My Nashville cousin instantly took *Audiation* as the title of his next CD. My own variant is what I call *verberation*, deriving from *verba*, words, and only very slightly from *verberas*, the whipping rods of ancient Rome. Escaping from the disciplines of modern life, words and phrases swim in their definitions and free of them, becoming the molecules of sense and suggestion. They descend through surface consciousness to oracular depths, and return fresh and strange. A whole small constellation of them may rise to initiate a poem. It was for this that I came to love vocabulary, the traffic of one-word poemlets, and why I have always hung around dictionaries and the autistic fodder of lists.

The Monthly

Art and Darkness

Janet Hawley

While talking to Barbara Blackman in her appealing Canberra home – her figure framed by haunting early Charles Blackman paintings and drawings – it strikes me that here is one of life's great, sad ironies. The distinguished 81-year-old arts matriarch is blind and lives – indeed eats, sleeps, bathes and completes her toilette – amid walls laden with her former husband's artworks, their faces' huge, absorbing eyes watching her. All of this she's unable to see, yet she knows the intimate detail of every picture.

Into my mind floats the contrasting image of Charles, also eighty-one, living alone with his saintly male carer in a modest rented Sydney cottage, bereft of art or memorabilia. Of all the thousands of pictures this major artist has painted, he no longer owns a single one. The only pieces of Blackman art he has to look at are three minor prints and a reproduction silk scarf hanging on the wall.

Some fifteen years ago, Blackman's once-fine brain and dynamic personality became addled by a form of alcoholic dementia – Korsakoff's syndrome. Conversations with him now are like groping in a maze of fragments and finding the odd tiny jewel. Suddenly he'll be surprisingly lucid, or warm and sharply funny. Or foul-tempered. But mostly it's as if he's stepped through the looking glass to float into a surreal world, just like his masterly paintings inspired by Lewis Carroll's *Alice's Adventures in Wonderland.*

Disjointed monologues flow from his lips, darting from Van Gogh, to World War II, to wanting redhead Julia Gillard for PM. 'If Julia walked in, I'd say, "Get your gear off, I'm going to paint you,"' he chortles seductively, tugging his beret. But his diminished hand today mainly draws simple cats, white rabbits and flowers, in black pen on small pieces of paper.

Blackman's life is an epic journey, both fuelled and burnt by his grand romantic passions for art, women, wine and song. He ranks as 'Australia's greatest literary painter,' says Felicity St John Moore, art historian and curator of major Blackman retrospectives in 1993 and 2006. 'He is the outstanding artist of the feminine psyche – of love, shadow, guilt and vulnerability; of transformation and changefulness; of curiosity and creative vision.' Blackman always painted an inner poetic vision of what was outwardly happening in his life. It's a life mile-posted by his marriages and divorces to three extraordinary, very different women – who bore him six children.

The Blackman caravan's widening trail, while rich in happiness and creative achievement, is also littered with family dramas, deep pain, rifts and gruesome tales. Each marriage initially flowered and then each, disastrously, became a worsening *ménage à trois* with alcohol. Many great and lesser artists have travelled similar paths and been lucky enough to survive the heavy carousing and imbibing, but fate was not so kind to Charles Blackman.

Charles and Barbara Blackman were a formidable couple in the thirty years they spent together from 1949 to 1979. These are critically regarded as Blackman's most powerful painting years, when he joined the ranks of our major figurative painters. Barbara, a poet and writer, also gained an identity as a legendary artist's wife, along with Cynthia Nolan, Yvonne Boyd and Wendy Whiteley. Post-divorce, her identity continues to grow as a major arts benefactor, slowly gifting her large collection of Blackmans, which included nearly all the Alice paintings, to state and national galleries. She's also donated $1 million to music beneficiaries.

'I don't want to be known as the rich bitch sitting on a pile of valuable paintings,' Barbara tells me. 'I've donated some thirty major paintings, and all my remaining artworks are going to designated galleries in my will, so the public can see them.'

I arrive at her home with a basket of strongly scented produce from my brother's organic farm. She expresses delight and fetches yellow and blue jugs and bowls from her kitchen, directing me to place the bunches of sage, rosemary, thyme, rocket and tomatoes 'like a still life on the dining table.'

As she sits fingering the leaves, above her silver-haired head is a painting of a younger Barbara in an introspective pose. Does she ever contemplate the possible works Charles might have gone on to create, if only he'd beaten his demons?

Tears well in her sightless blue-grey eyes, which unnervingly focus right on you. Her other senses are so acute you'd swear she can see you anyway. 'Every time our great old friend Barry Humphries and I meet, we have a huge embrace,' she begins, 'and embedded in that embrace is the most terrible unspoken sorrow. Charles and he were lifelong friends, and so parallel in their careers.

'There is Barry, a recovered alcoholic decades ago, seventy-six, still up on stage performing, still inventive. Why isn't Charles still at his easel painting? Barry promised he'd cross the world at any time if Charles would join Alcoholics Anonymous, but Charles always refused.

'It's a great if-only in my life,' she continues, 'but I wasn't able to stop Charles drinking and self-destructing. He'd say, "I'm a rotten little shit, but I'm a genius artist, so put up with it." As much as I loved him, I had to leave the marriage. Alcohol turned the enchanting, intelligent, witty Dr Charlie Jekyll into the monster Mr Charlie Hyde. It became dangerous for me to stay; I was losing myself. I knew other artists' wives who'd suicided, and I felt I was in suicide country.'

It was a great love story. Charles, a jockey-sized boy with a huge imagination, who was always drawing, grew up in an impoverished, fatherless home with no books or art. His adored mother was a compulsive gambler – he saw violence and profoundly disturbing behaviour and was sometimes placed in children's homes. Leaving school at fourteen, he gained an art cadetship on the Sydney tabloid the *Sun* and discovered his passion for art, attending night drawing classes and devouring art books in libraries. With friend and budding musicologist James Murdoch, also on the *Sun*, Blackman explored the world of classical music.

Barbara Patterson, meanwhile, had enjoyed a sophisticated upbringing, a university education and was in Brisbane's Barjai circle of poets and writers.

Quitting the *Sun* to pursue art, Charles travelled to Brisbane and met Barbara when they were both nineteen, and romance was kindled. 'We merged each other's disparate worlds,' says Barbara. 'We grew each other up.' But a dark shadow hovered – initially a powerful influence in Blackman's art, it would finally descend between them. Barbara's eyesight was seeping away. She was born two months premature, and her optic nerve never fully developed. 'Charles said, "I have enough sight for both of us,"' she says, repeating his promise. 'When we married in 1950, I was legally blind and on a blind pension.'

They moved to Melbourne, mixing in the artistic milieu with Arthur and Yvonne Boyd, John Perceval, John Brack, Sidney Nolan and Joy Hester, and becoming part of the Heide modernist set with arts patrons John and Sunday Reed. Blackman was 'hell bent on becoming a great painter,' and Barbara, highly capable despite her fading sight, adopted the role of wife/model/muse/organiser/treasurer and steered Charles in that direction.

Charles became Barbara's window to the visual world, explaining in vivid detail, and also reading aloud to her the great writers, philosophers, poets. One day he heard *Alice's Adventures in Wonderland* playing on Barbara's new talking-book machine. It excited his imagination. Alice's surreal journey, changing height, encountering the White Rabbit and the Mad Hatter's tea party, fitted with Barbara's visual distortion, and the changing shape of her pregnant body. Charles was also working nights as a cook at Georges and Mirka Mora's busy restaurant, with food and saucepans flying in all directions. This confluence sparked a series of thirty-five iconic Alice paintings, all worth over the million-dollar mark today, if you could buy one.

Winning the Helena Rubinstein prize, Charles set off to London with Barbara in 1961 for almost six years – exciting times, with the Boyds, Whiteleys, Fred Williams, Clifton Pugh and Barry Humphries also there. A gregarious couple and good cooks, the Blackmans and their home became drawcards. 'The party was always on at our house, wherever we lived,' remember Charles and Barbara's two sons, both painters, Auguste, now fifty-three, and Barnaby, forty-seven. 'Lively conversations, many wild parties, happened around our dining table.'

No matter how heavy the carousing the night before, Charles was in his studio working by 6 a.m. His painting discipline was ferocious and his success grew. His paintings often examined the darkening world of Barbara's disappearing sight and the isolation that came with it.

'When we returned to Australia in 1966, Charles was famous,' relates Barbara. 'Collectors all wanted Blackmans, dealers wanted pictures to sell, galleries wanted shows. We got caught up in the high life: parties, media, photographs. Suddenly, we had more money than we needed. Our intensely intimate life within our circle of creative friends was swept away. It stole our old lives – that's when the real darkness set in. Charles thought he was such a genius; he started doing a lot of quick, picturesque, saleable work, as well as his true, thoughtful work. He's such a prolific painter, it was easy for him.'

Increasingly mercurial, in the 1970s Charles began to disappear on painting trips, 'always with some hot chick,' says Barbara. 'Off to Surfers Paradise or three months in Paris with a Japanese girlfriend. He'd come back needing endless attention, get drunk and be verbally cruel and cutting. When I tried to stop his self-destructive path, he'd belittle me, rave on as we sat in restaurants, saying I was lying, spying on him, invading his privacy. I'd weep in public. I remember a waiter wiping my eyes with a long-stemmed carnation.'

Barry Humphries reflects, 'Charles was always a very cheeky, cocky, anarchic, funny fellow and rather angry inside. He underwent a distinct personality change when drinking. He could be extremely sarcastic and vindictive, particularly to people who couldn't strike back. He was always in denial and too arrogant to admit being alcoholic. Much of his anger and depression stemmed from his childhood. It gets into his paintings. At their best, there's a mood of melancholy. At their worst, they are too sweet.'

His daughter Christabel Blackman, now fifty-one, an art conservator who's lived in Spain for more than twenty years, recalls her parents' marriage drifting apart: 'Barbara was increasingly absorbed in her educational projects, especially the alternative secondary school, Chiron College, in Birchgrove. There were terrible fights, which they no longer hid from us. They had different perceptions of the world now, and Barbara's sight was almost gone. I remember one of the last times she could detect something, in 1975. I was knitting a scarf in my brother's football-team colours and she held it up to the corner of her eye and slowly said, "It's striped." She had awful visual sensations, flashing lights, things we sighted people never understand. Ever since we were little, we'd all led our mother around, explaining things to her.'

Barbara says, 'I still had enough sight into the 1970s to see something of what I was looking at, especially if I was helped and had it explained to me. I saw just enough of Charles's great paintings to know them. It's hard to say when I became totally blind. Gradually, I changed from seeing to visualising what I'm looking at – which to me is just as vivid as seeing.'

James Murdoch remembers being fascinated, 'seeing Barbara with her eye held like a magnifying glass against Charles's paintings, slowly travelling up and down, examining each canvas.'

In 1978, Charles and Barbara agreed to spend a year together in Perth, where Barbara was invited to start a radio program for the print handicapped. Christabel's good friend, nineteen-year-old art student Genevieve de Couvreur, was invited to house-sit the empty Blackman residence in Paddington for the year.

Christabel explains, 'I'd left home at seventeen. As children of two very forceful, famous parents, my brothers and I had all struggled to find our own identities, so we all left home early.' Auguste also speaks frankly of his own long battle to overcome drug and alcohol addiction.

While in Perth, the marriage disintegrated. 'Charles was off on another painting trip with another woman,' explains Barbara, 'so I wrote him a letter of resignation, saying the sighted and the unsighted could no longer help each other. The gulf was too wide.'

Barbara remained in Perth for two years; then, at Diane Cilento's Karnak meditation and arts retreat in Queensland, she met Frenchman Marcel Veldhoven. 'A scholarly gypsy' fourteen years her junior, he was married to her for twenty years until 2001.

Charles returned to the Paddington house and asked the very beautiful, gentle Genevieve to stay on. The artist soon had a fresh new love. He was smitten, felt reborn and new doors opened in his life.

Barbara had been his great intellectual love, but Genevieve, with her sun-kissed golden hair, was now his great romantic love. They spent almost eight years together and have two children: singer-songwriter Bertie Blackman, now twenty-eight, and Felix, twenty-six, a graphic-design graduate studying architecture.

To my surprise, Barbara says of Genevieve, 'I'm grateful she was there, to pick up the burden that I put down, and become my successor. We're all part of a Greek tragedy. I tried warning her – be careful of putting your sweet young wine in that old bottle. Genevieve was only nineteen; Charles was forty-nine, an attractive, famous man thirty years older. But they really loved each other; she's a good person, and she extended his good painting years. Charles began doing wonderful ballet sets, opera sets, new ventures he hadn't done with me. But she had a hard time.'

When I contact Genevieve, now fifty, remarried to a doctor and living in Tasmania, her initial reaction is to thank me for the call. She's accustomed to Blackman stories focusing on the Barbara era, with the two subsequent wives and their children never mentioned. Although pleased to hear Barbara's words about her, Genevieve admits, 'It's been a volatile and tricky scenario at times.'

Christabel, while acknowledging the difficulty of accepting her schoolfriend marrying her father, also describes Genevieve in glowing terms: 'She was a beautiful, sensual young woman, an artist herself with a supreme sense of aesthetics. She'd arrange everything in their house like wonderful still lifes … enormous bunches of flowers, music on, delicious food. Charles had a romantic rebirth and did gorgeous, deeply sensitive paintings.'

'Never in my wildest dreams,' declares Genevieve, 'did I think I'd marry someone thirty years older. People tried to say I was a silly little art student who'd taken up with the master, but it wasn't like that. I was his wife, he was gallant and old-fashioned in many ways. I respected and adored him.

'Charles was so unhappy when he returned from Perth, he was drinking heavily. His relationship with Barbara had become very competitive, but I've never been personally ambitious. I was nineteen, a romantic free spirit. I just thought if I wrapped my arms around him and nurtured him, love would conquer all.' After an extended overseas trip visiting galleries and museums, the couple moved to Buderim, Queensland, bought an old house in the rainforest and created their own Garden of Eden.

'Charles loved being in nature. The sounds of waterfalls, hooting owls, strange birds were all around us,' recalls Genevieve. 'He'd often be quiet, thoughtful, then so quick-witted and funny. He's passionately romantic, and wrote me reams of love letters and poems. I'd wake in the morning to find rose petals scattered around my head on the pillows; go into the kitchen and find a love poem stuck on the oven. He'd been awake since 5 a.m., diligently working in his studio.'

Reinvigorated, Blackman was prolific, painting the Midsummer Night's Dream and Orpheus series, rainforests, composers, sublime nudes of Genevieve, self-portraits. 'At night, we'd cook a lovely dinner and Charles would get sloshed and go to sleep early,' says Genevieve. 'He's a little fellow and it didn't take a lot to get him sloshed. He promised to stop drinking when the baby was born, but two greatly loved babies were born, and he was unable to stop. I had a lot to understand about alcoholism, and I now grew up very quickly. Charles denied it was a problem and refused to address it. No matter what I tried, he'd say, "I'm different, I'm not like anyone else."'

For periods they returned to Sydney to live in the old Woollahra house that Blackman had used as his main studio and storehouse since 1966. Things started to run out of control, says Genevieve. Dealers took advantage of Charles being increasingly inebriated to depart with major paintings for minor cash payments. Many people in the Blackman inner circle had keys to the house.

'People would come and go at all hours and many artworks disappeared,' says Genevieve. 'Charles had a lot of work, so it was hard to keep track of it all. Paintings would suddenly turn up at auction with sellers claiming Charles had given them works they'd taken.'

Charles wasn't the only one to mysteriously lose artworks. Barbara says, 'Things have disappeared off my walls for a long time ... People have acquired paintings, I'll put it that way ... then they turn up in some junky gallery ... But we won't go there ... we don't have to go into the grim parts.'

Despairing over Charles's decline, Genevieve was walking her children in the park when four-year-old Bertie ran up to a derelict drunk and called out, 'Daddy.'

'That was a turning point,' confesses Genevieve. 'I thought, I cannot allow my children to be destroyed like this. I told Charles he had to make a choice – it was alcohol or me. I lost.'

She's sad her children never saw Charles in his prime, but shows them his letters, poems, books on his paintings, to reassure them they were born from a great love match with an artist of great talent. Both have inherited the artistic gene and Bertie's animated graphics are used in the video clips of some of her songs.

'Bertie, who's so like her dad in so many ways, recently visited him,' says Genevieve, 'and asked him to draw something on the inside of her forearm. He wrote in thick black pen, *On a hill thier was yow and me. Charles.* Bertie had it tattooed on, telling me, "Now I'll always have part of my dad with me." I found it heart-wrenching.'

Charles and Genevieve separated in mid-1987, and Charles immediately began a relationship with attractive, dark-haired Victoria Bower – also thirty years younger than he – whom he'd met the previous year. She'd studied art and was working on a film proposal.

'I did warn Victoria, "Just you wait,"' sighs Genevieve. 'She replied, "It's going to be different with me." Yes … I'd thought that, too.'

'Dad was crazy about Victoria; she was exciting,' remarks Christabel. 'He'd found a new love and tried to rescue himself again, and began a new burst of fine paintings. We all hoped and prayed for the best.'

Blackman was working well, illustrating two books, one on rainforests with Al Alvarez, another on an Alice theme with Nadine Amadio. He bought a house in Cairns and began a flurry of painting with his young wife and model, a new admirer to listen to his wit and stories. They married in 1990, and their son, Axiom, was born that year, joining Victoria's young daughter from a previous relationship, Aimee.

While many speak kindly of Victoria, a large circle of Blackman bystanders and some family members were initially concerned about another wedding to a young bride and some saw her as an art-world wannabe infatuated with an ageing art star. When Victoria joined the Raëlian religion in 1992, her detractors considered their case won. Raëlians believe in intelligent design, that all life on Earth was created in scientific laboratories by a species of extraterrestrials.

Today, Victoria uses the name Tara Euphoria Infinity Blackman. She and her new partner run a software anti-virus business and live in northern New South Wales. Beautifully groomed when we meet, Tara dismisses all scepticism, maintaining, even though she was only twenty-eight, she was 'determined to love and save Charles Blackman and his awesome talent. Charles is the diamond in the crown of Australian art.'

'I tried very hard to give Charles a family life,' Tara explains, bringing out photographs of their years together. 'I often had the children from his previous marriages come and stay. I'd get them all dressed up in costumes, doing little plays and performances. Charles loved fantasy.' All the children were flown into Cairns for Axiom's christening, and media mogul Kerry Stokes, a Blackman collector and friend, is Axiom's godfather. (Axiom, twenty, is now studying sound engineering.)

It wasn't long, however, before the third Mrs Blackman discovered what she was up against. 'Charles used to say, "Life is how you live with your trauma,"' Tara recalls. 'The morning after our wedding, we had to fly to Adelaide for an exhibition and Charles decided to get absolutely sozzled before we'd even got on the plane. I thought I'd put a stop to that behaviour, but it became painfully evident Charles was in its grip.'

Blackman finally admitted he needed treatment and was in and out of clinics six times in Sydney, relapsing each time. He booked into the Betty Ford Centre in California, 'but when Charles came out after three weeks,' says Tara, 'he raided the minibar in our hotel and came down to the pool announcing, "I feel like a god."'

They'd sold Cairns and were living back in the Woollahra house, but life became increasingly chaotic. Charles was dismissive of the Raëlians, declaring to his friends that 'all cults are only after your money.' He managed to hold himself together for the 1993 retrospective, but by 1994 Tara and her children moved to another house nearby. 'I'd return each day to try to take care of Charles, but he was often falling over and the situation was terrible.'

Meanwhile, Blackman's accountant since 1976, the avuncular Tom Lowenstein – who enjoys legendary status as accountant to a flock of Australian artists – was given Blackman's power of attorney and tried to get more order into his life.

'I had phone calls from neighbours that vans were arriving at Charles's house and paintings and furniture were being carted away,' explains Lowenstein. 'So I immediately put all his remaining artworks into secure storage, had everything catalogued and found a carer to move in full-time.' Fred O'Brien, who'd sold up as co-owner of Sydney's Dendy Theatre, was an admirer of Blackman's art and agreed to move in for three months. 'Sixteen years later, I'm still here,' says O'Brien, a warm man with a kindly smile.

Initially, the almost impossible battle was to stop Blackman getting alcohol, with O'Brien enduring the artist's ferocious temper. A year on, in 1995, when Blackman suffered a large stroke and was unable to walk without assistance or leave the house on his own, he could no longer gain access to alcohol. But the stroke exacerbated the Korsakoff's syndrome and Blackman became unable to paint or care for himself.

Lowenstein organised Blackman's remaining assets and set up a trust to provide for his full-time care, but after three divorce settlements the artist's situation was vastly diminished. 'Charles said, "Promise me you'll never put me in a nursing home; I'd rather die,"' says Lowenstein.

The Blackman family and friends disagree mightily on many things, particularly on Barbara's determination to gift Charles's paintings to public institutions instead of to her family, or indeed to Charles. 'We won't go there by a long shot,' says Barbara, dismissing the topic. 'They've all had their share along the way.' But all are in agreement about Fred O'Brien, who's been on duty 24/7. The man's a saint, an angel; he's keeping Charles alive in this last stage of his life's journey, and doing it in a way that gives the artist dignity.

I'd spoken to many in the artist's family and circle of old friends before I first went to see Charles. I'd been warned to expect the worst.

'It's a miserable little afterlife he's living now,' declares Barbara.

'Most people say the Charles we all knew died at the time of his stroke. He's incontinent now and in nappies. You can't have a real conversation with him.'

Former restaurateur Sue Burrows, Blackman's loyal friend and most regular visitor, explains, 'It's best to go with the flow of whatever Charles is talking about. Don't ask questions on another topic or he'll become agitated as his brain can't locate the answer. A while ago I lay under a flame tree in the park with him and he said, "I think I'm looking up into my brain."' Others advise me not to take books on Blackman's paintings; he doesn't want to talk about his work. I take some Blackman art books in a bag anyway, and flowers in the colours he'd often painted, hoping it might help develop a conversation.

Charles is sitting on the veranda reading a book. Ignoring the flowers, he walks me straight down the hall to the sunny kitchen, directing, 'Sit down, my dear. Ask me questions. But let me first tell you something: the future is knowing that what happens today doesn't happen tomorrow. And what happens tomorrow is what didn't happen today.' Yes, absolutely true, I nod. O'Brien, beaming while putting the flowers in vases, gives the thumbs-up sign, whispering, 'Go for it. Charlie's in a good mood today.'

So I bring out the art books. He turns the pages and talks happily about his art, way better than I'd anticipated, for a couple of hours before he tires. 'What's for lunch, Fred?' he calls. 'What movie are we seeing this afternoon?'

O'Brien helps Blackman to sit in the courtyard while he prepares lunch. Every day he has outings planned. 'Charlie loves movies, especially comedies and children's films,' explains O'Brien. 'I take him to art galleries, the park, we chat about what we see, then go to a coffee shop. He loves car trips, so I take him to the countryside and beach. He reads, watches DVDs and likes chess.' Sometimes Blackman makes small drawings. I find a white-rabbit one that he's captioned 'Everything suddenly disappeared.'

Family members visit intermittently and a few loyal friends still come, but many have stopped. The limelight life is long gone. 'We'd love more visitors; it always cheers Charlie up,' admits O'Brien. 'He's not as angry and frustrated as he was in the earlier years after his stroke, when I really copped it as the kicking board.

He's more accepting and seems quite contented most days.' I ask O'Brien why he does this wearying job, and for a frugal wage. With bare honesty, he replies, 'I suppose it's become something of a co-dependency after all these years. I don't have a family, so looking after Charles lets me nurture someone.' Another carer, John Grant, now shares the full-time role.

Some seven years ago, as Blackman and O'Brien were out on a stroll, they bumped into Judy Cassab, the grand dame of portrait painters. Cassab asked Blackman if he was still painting, and he despondently replied no; he could still draw a little, but had lost interest. Warm-hearted Cassab hatched a rescue mission. A model came to Cassab's home each fortnight, as Cassab liked the discipline of life-drawing. She invited Charles to join her, and so the ritual visit began each fortnight. Charles arrives in his artist's beret to sit at his easel beside Cassab and draw their regular model, Marina Finlay, while classical music plays. They break for coffee, continental biscuits and a chat with Marina, then resume drawing for another hour.

But there's an added poignancy to the life-drawing sessions these days. Two years ago, Cassab's once meticulous mind drifted into dementia. So now the two senior artists sit side by side in Cassab's studio, drawing their model's pose, their eyes and hands moving steadily above their sketchbooks, their minds in another elusive dreamzone. It's a strange and gentle bond that these painterly companions now share, and Blackman takes Cassab's hand to kiss her fingers as he departs.

'Drawing is an act of the hand, the eye and your dreams,' Blackman was fond of saying. 'Drawing is fearless; it's about wrapping a line around your dream.'

As O'Brien helps Blackman slowly walk back along Cassab's driveway, I think of a paragraph I'd read the night before in Lewis Carroll's *Alice's Adventures in Wonderland.*

'It might end up in my going out altogether like a candle … Oh, how I wish I could close up like a telescope! … the words did not come the same as they used to do … I'll stay down here till I'm somebody else.'

Good Weekend

The States of the Nation

David Malouf

Back in 2000 when the centenary of federation was looming, I was inclined to joke that we had to make a song and dance about it because the thing itself had never really happened.

It had of course, in history and in the history books, and we had a constitution to prove it, but not in the many places where Australians actually live: in Cunnamulla or Queenstown or Port Hedland, and not in those even more numerous places, the hearts of those of us who, without hesitation or doubt, call ourselves Australians, and have a vivid sense of what the country itself is, but in our daily lives, and in the place where our feelings are most touched, have little interest in the idea of nation.

The day of the centenary came and went like any other. Flags were raised, medals struck and distributed, speeches made, but there was little excitement. The country returned next day to life as usual. Boat people arrived and asked to be taken in, life-support systems were turned on or off, a new generation of five-year-olds posed and were photographed in their school uniforms.

Federation may have established the nation and bonded the people of the various states into one, but nations and peoples, unless they arise naturally, the one out of the other, rather than by referendum or by edict, are likely to be doubtful entities, and the relationship between them will be open to almost continuous question. Of course when they arise *too* naturally – that is, when they claim to belong to nature rather than human choice – they are dangerous.

Our federation is on the whole an easy one. We take it lightly as suits our cast of mind, which is pragmatic (anti-theoretical), wryly offhand, and sceptical of big ideas and their accompanying rhetoric. The union works, and we can be proud of the society it has created, but we don't care to talk about it, and unless the country is under threat as it was in 1941, or involved in conflict overseas, we take it as given – and even then, as with Vietnam, the Gulf War, Iraq and Afghanistan, there are some who will remain doubtful, or embarrassed, or openly hostile. We are easiest with 'Australia' when what we are referring to is a national team.

To quote the authors of *The Oxford Companion to Australian History* (2001 edition), the states remain 'set in their ways and as suspicious of one another as they were before the union was declared' – though we should be as wary of making too much of the suspicion as of the union.

These days the suspicions between the states are as low-key, except when it comes to water management, and as intermittent, as our sense of nationhood. A lot of the rivalries are joking ones and when they are formalised in such institutions as the State of Origin rugby matches between Queensland and New South Wales, might just as easily be read as bonding. Most people, like men and women everywhere, are concerned with local questions and local affairs. Their lives take place within a few square kilometres and are determined by local conditions: local needs and customs and habits, local opportunities for schooling and shopping and entertainment, local forms of speech. They turn to community rather than nation when they ask themselves where they belong, and think of those they share their days with as neighbours rather than fellow Australians. 'Fellow Australians' carries with it an air of fake familiarity that belongs to the political platform, the political speech. 'Fellow Queenslanders,' on the other hand, or 'fellow Tasmanians,' is another matter.

*

Federation, as we might expect, came to us in a very Australian way, one that is consistent with the rather offhand manner in which it has been received and is still considered. Not the flowering of a great utopian ideal, or the coming together, after a long period of yearning, of a people that had known the anguish of division, or the achievement, through national unity, of a 'manifest destiny' – though there were some, especially in the latter case, who felt that way.

After thirty-five years of intermittent lobbying and resistance, and a lot of bickering over such non-idealistic questions as preference versus free trade, the opposition lapsed and the federationists took advantage of a moment of unexpected agreement to pop the question. The popular election that voted for union was not based on universal suffrage, was not uniform throughout the states, and the turnout itself was low: 30 per cent of eligible voters actually went to the polls in 1898, 43 per cent in 1899. The areas of control granted to the new federal government were limited, chiefly to defence and trade; the rest remained reassuringly with the states. Of course, the central government was expected to evolve over time and has done so. In the 109 years since 1901, the Commonwealth government has replaced or duplicated state powers to the point where it can be argued that in our present, three-tiered system state governments are not only redundant and wasteful but also obstructive, and should go. The federal government alone would be left to govern, with a system of regional bodies beneath it. The states, with no effective powers, and no visible reason to exist, would wither away.

Given our preference for practical solutions, and the tendency these days for all problems to be presented and resolved in terms of economy and good management, it is inevitable, I suppose, that this question too will be reduced to what is the best value for money, and the most efficient way of bringing uniform practice to what is now a set of multiple authorities: roads, railways, social welfare and health systems, and seven different police forces and courts of law – as if the real goal of federation had all along been uniformity, and the only criteria needed for justifying it were efficiency and cost. But if uniformity from ocean to ocean is what we are to have, then that represents a radical change from what the fathers of federation intended and what the people of the various states, with their strong histories and their 'set ways,' believed they were getting. And what about us? Is this really our preferred choice?

If the argument is couched solely in economic and management terms, then clearly there is no argument at all. But perhaps we need other terms altogether that have to do not with efficiency and cost but with the sometimes untidy and diverse and contradictory needs of those who are to be managed.

So what does it mean to be a nation, and how is that large concept related to place and land – or, as we experience it personally, on the ground as it were, as *locality*, a particular tract of land: a town or a few streets in a town; a church hall, a local pub, a school, a football ground, a shopping precinct? And how is nation related to that other large and emotionally charged concept, a people?

In most places, the transition from people to nation is clear, or is at least presented as clear. A single people, inhabiting a particular tract of land, is at last politically united and becomes a nation.

It is never quite clear of course. The borders of the land may be open to dispute, and no people is entirely pure. But this is how it happened over three or four centuries among the Greeks, when a scatter of independent city-states became an empire, and among the Romans, the French, the Russians and, in the mid-nineteenth century, the Germans and Italians. Australia, like other settler nations, did it in reverse. Having declared that we were a nation, we had still to attract the people to fill it and decide who those people might be.

What defined our nation was not people but geography. The various states – all settled at different times by different groups and classes, and, within the British political system, under different conditions and with different aims – happened to occupy a continent whose borders were fixed because it was an island. Once the British eastern-half of the continent and the Dutch west were declared a single possession under an undisputed (British) claim, political unity became first a possibility and then an imperative, though a mild one. For all the talk in some quarters in the late nineteenth century of a New Britannia that would carry forward the torch of British civilisation when the old country had fallen into decay, there was little of the fervour here, or the passion for political theory, that characterised the great constitutional conventions of 1786–87 in America. We produced no political thinkers of the quality of James Madison or Thomas Jefferson or Alexander Hamilton or Benjamin Franklin. Our fathers of federation, practical men of the late nineteenth century, level-headed traders and politicians and lobbyists, good Christian gentlemen but of a secular bent, *did* want to create a free and fair society but, unlike their counterparts in a more radical and utopian age, they had no feeling for rhetoric of the French or American variety. A 'fair go' is a very down-to-earth version of 'Liberty, Equality, Fraternity,' and no one here expected, or wanted, the 'tree of liberty' (or the wattle) to be refreshed even occasionally with blood.

This down-to-earth quality extends to the land itself. In other places, and to other peoples, the land has presented itself as sacred or holy. This, as we know from Russian novels, is the way Russians have seen it, how indigenous people, including our own indigenous people, see it and how the Nazis saw it when they articulated the philosophy of *Blut und Boden*: as a deep ancestral tie between a people and the soil they inhabit.

A settler population can hardly make such a claim. I have suggested elsewhere that the Roman and British imperial cultures, with their founding myths of an arrival from 'elsewhere,' offered a different model: one in which nation was transportable and national identity or citizenship transferable. If Australians see in the land something they might feel as transcendent or mystical, it is land in its form as space rather than soil, an almost infinite openness; and that is a very useful notion if you are a settler. It suggests that there is always room. That just as the land made room for you, so, with no threat or pressure, it will find room for others.

The idea of nationhood was embodied, in 1901, in a constitution, but the question of who the nation's people were to be remained open. White and British in the first draft: no more Chinese; the Queensland Kanakas to be sent back to the islands; no black Africans of any kind; no Muslims; a language test (European) to be applied against the rest. Then, increasingly, after the wave of European, including southern European, migrants after World War II, it was to be a mix; then, after the lapse of the

White Australia policy in the late 1960s, a *multi-ethnic* mix, then a mix that would be both multi-ethnic and multicultural – an interesting experiment, but not so easy to make work. Just as well that the idea of nation was a light one, and that lightness in the approach to difficult questions, an anti-theoretical stance, easygoing and humorous, should be the temperament of the people who had to live with it.

I called the imperative to nationhood geographic, as if the continent itself, once it found a single name ('Australia' in 1804) made the emergence of a single nation the obvious next step. But this is about as far as our notion of the 'gift outright,' as Robert Frost called it in the case of the United States, would ever get. Very few of us here have ever fallen for the notion of manifest destiny; it's not our style.

The odd thing in our case – but odd things are apt to be the most revealing – is that our earliest appearance as a single people was on the sporting field, as a team rather than a nation. 'Australia' first presented itself to the world (that is, to the British) in the form of the combined cricket teams that toured Britain in the 1880s (the earlier Aboriginal team was too exotic to be representative) and created the myth of the Ashes. What they brought news of was a new tribe, a new 'type,' a new society. The qualities they represented were ones the British could recognise and respect because they were looser versions of their own, the product of a later and different history in a new place, and it helped that sport, and especially cricket, was already seen as the proper sphere for the creation of a moral and social elite – the challenge in this case being that these 'colonials' were *not* an elite. The other sphere of course was war.

Following on from what the cricket teams had created in the national consciousness, the image of Australians as a single tribe and a new and original 'type,' it might be best to ignore the usual evocation of our national coming of age in 1915–16 as a baptism of sacrificial fire and blood, and consider the diggers at Gallipoli and in France as a team rather than an army. Once again, what was being demonstrated, this time on the larger stage of history, was a national character and style: courage, certainly, endurance – the extended campaign at Gallipoli, the fifty-three continuous days in the frontline trenches at Villers-Bretonneux – but also a licensed indiscipline that was not quite anarchy, the 'civilian' triumph among the professional army generals of John Monash, and at home the refusal, in two referenda, of conscription.

The observers of all this may have been the world at large, but when we speak of it as the moment when nationhood itself was confirmed, what we are really registering is the reflection back from outsiders to the players themselves, and even more importantly to their people back home, of what, against all the usual class and colonial prejudices, Australians were now seen to have achieved.

That is the original Anzac story, but it is only half the story. The other half has to do with something else altogether: the understanding that war is *not* sport. That it involves injury, trauma, death, and to wives and parents and children and fiancées, in hamlets and towns and working places all up and down the country, a sense of irreparable loss that was made actual, in the years after the war, in thousands of war memorials, small and large, from one side of the continent to the other.

These are mourning places that mark a national tragedy: a recognition of loss and grief as being central both to the community or nation – 62,000 men, mostly young men, lost from a population of fewer than 4 million – and to individual families and lives. That, a binding of the people at every level in a shared grief, is what 'coming of age' might be about, and explains the power of Anzac Day, and how it has come to be chosen, by the people themselves, as our day of national unity.

When young people these days are drawn to Anzac, it is partly, I think, because they are moved by the drama of youthful death, and partly because, in a nation that makes so little of public ceremony, this day offers a larger and more solemn view of what life may be than is general in a culture whose norm is chatter, noise, almost continuous sensation.

What Anzac Day offers is quietness, contemplation. It appeals, in the young, to what is serious in them. Asks them to attend. Invites them to take part in an occasion that speaks, at both a personal and communal level, for continuity. And this may be what attracts another group that might otherwise see this day as an occasion from which they are culturally excluded: recent migrants.

What Anzac Day offers them is the possibility, which may be rare, of seeing what it is that these people they have attached themselves to are moved by. As an occasion whose commemoration of loss is something they too feel for, Anzac Day becomes, for recent migrants, a way of entering emotionally into the life of the community at large. As W.H. Auden puts it in the very last of his poems: 'Only in rites / Can we renounce our oddities / And be truly entired.'

These are delicate matters. At an individual level, difficult questions of identity or belonging, of what it is that might bind us as fellow citizens, may be resolved more simply than we believe. Where argument, however open and enlightened, may get nowhere or lead only to complications without issue, a moment of 'drama,' of empathy and understanding, will simply annul the question at a stroke. And one might add here – and by no means as a mere footnote – that a wounding sense of loss, and a perception, deeply felt, of the place of the tragic in our lives, does not strike a community only in one place or on one occasion. We already have a Sorry Day. It is meant to mark the sufferings inflicted on indigenous people in the establishing of a nation whose existence we, as I said, take lightly, but which has been a heavy fact in indigenous lives. If this were to become, over time, like Anzac Day a moment of shared identity and real understanding, we might find in it yet another point of national unity.

It is the fragility of such moments of cohesion, of shared emotion and presence, that alerts us to equally fragile but no less significant moments of difference. It is not only unity that characterises a nation or a people.

For most of the time what distinguishes a nation, like any other community, is the variety provided by difference; variety of need and interest, of response to such local factors as climate and land and water use; forms of domestic architecture and language, local custom and lore – even local forms of suspicion and potential conflict; all those conditions, that is, that will have grown up over time among people who live in a particular place and have created their own version of the nation's history.

Nations, as I suggested earlier, grow out of the desire of a single people to be one. It is a historical imperative driven by ties of language and culture but also of shared experience. Federation on the other hand is a political union made on practical grounds, though the hope is that state loyalties and affiliations will in time be supplemented at least by national ones, and may even grow to replace them.

In a federation where separate tribes and people come together, as in most African states, and as has happened in ex-Yugoslavia, ex-Czechoslovakia and Belgium, the two loyalties will often pull against one another and the tension between them may not be capable of resolution.

Our case is unusual, because for all the difference in class and style of their founders, the different environmental conditions they faced and the economies they created in response, the Australian colonies had for the most part the same demographic make-up, spoke the same language, inherited the same culture and legal and political system, and were accountable, in the matter of aspiration and restraints, to the same authority, the British Colonial Office. There is little danger here of the federation's collapse. We have none of the deep-seated cultural and religious divisions that broke the old Yugoslavia and, in a less violent way, threaten Belgium. Our threat is the more insidious one of a tidy uniformity.

Is it only, I wonder, because I grew up in what I hear referred to as one of the 'outlying states' – outlying from where, I ask – that I am so keenly aware of the different styles of our state capitals? The subtle or not-so-subtle difference in the way people deal with one another in Brisbane and Melbourne, for example, or Brisbane and Adelaide, and what this represents of different ways of thinking and feeling. The variation from place to place of building materials and domestic habits that have created the houses people live in, the way they move about and dress. The turn of mind that has created our various education systems. The demographic mix that has shaped not only the forms of speech we use but our different ways, from state to state, of addressing one another and establishing intimacy and ease or the opposite. It isn't sentiment alone that might make us want to preserve these distinctions, but a belief that variousness is also richness, and that different ways of solving a problem or meeting a difficulty might make possible a new or a more original or creative way that would otherwise fail to emerge.

We need to be discriminating here. It is entirely proper that control of all cross-border issues – interstate highways, railway links between the capitals, water management of our river systems, workplace conditions, banking – should be in the hands of a single authority and that decisions in these areas should be made on a national basis and in the national interest, overruling if necessary the interests of individual states. But I wonder if those parts of our lives that involve individual needs and are shaped very largely by local conditions – distance from a major town or city, availability of transport, weather (seasonal floods for instance) – or by local ways of doing things and word-of-mouth contacts that are socially or culturally based, are really best managed from a centre that may be thousands of kilometres off, and by decision-makers who, however well-intentioned, may have little grasp of how differently people see things in Lindsay Tanner's electorate in inner Melbourne, Wilson Tuckey's O'Connor in Western Australia and Bob Katter's Kennedy in far north Queensland.

Cost and efficiency cannot be the only consideration here. These are bureaucratic criteria that speak only for one side of the contract. The other, the human side, is about how close people feel to those who are dealing with them; how comfortable they feel with the style and language of the transaction. People act in ways that suit their needs, and follow the unpredictable and sometimes irrational lines of their own nature and habits. They live in places within themselves that know nothing of jurisdictions or borders. This is not necessarily a perversity. It is a fact, and a society of the kind we mostly support, and would hope to achieve, should remain open and flexible enough to make provision for this, so long as it is not obstructive to others. The last thing we want, however gratifying a vision it might be to a federal minister for education, is an entire generation of five-year-olds singing sweetly from the same page.

The Monthly

Secret Women's Business

Shelley Gare

In 1975, Truman Capote's story-telling took him into dangerous territory. A notorious gossip who loved the socialite life, Capote had decided to share with his readers a number of confidences that his gal pals, the privileged matrons of New York's upper crust, had passed to him as he nestled with them on the plump banquettes of La Côte Basque, then on East 55th Street.

These women were social legends, daughters or wives of the rich and famous: fashion icon Slim Keith, Marella Agnelli, Carol Matthau, Gloria Vanderbilt. Capote, with his sly tongue and early fame, amused and flattered them. They responded with invitations and secrets about their set which Capote was now about to relay to his readers.

Capote was hungry for material. For years, the author of *Breakfast at Tiffany's* and *In Cold Blood* had been promising his readers and friends he was writing a novel. That late New York autumn of the mid-'70s, *Esquire* magazine published a tantalising excerpt from this supposed work in progress, *Answered Prayers.* Capote called it 'La Côte Basque 1965' and it featured, among other notorious incidents, a wealthy Jewish businessman made foolish by infidelity.

A colossus of the newly dynamic corporate world, the businessman had invited a woman to his suite at The Pierre hotel for a nightcap of rumpy-pumpy while his wife was out of town. The woman, an East Coast Brahmin socialite, had bled all over his sheets. It turned out she had her period. Capote makes it clear in his story that her indiscretion had been a calculated gesture of casual contempt.

No one has ever known, for sure, the real identity of the woman. The man, however, was William S. Paley, founder of television and radio network CBS, employer of newsman Edward Murrow. In haste and horror, Paley the mogul spent the rest of the night, once his visitor had left, trying to wash and dry the sheets before his wife came home the next morning. Sluicing them in the bathtub using a tiny cake of flowery Guerlain soap, shoving them in the oven to dry ...

The wife was Babe Paley, one of the most elegant women of her day and a close chum of Capote. Once the story was published in *Esquire*, and people had worked out who was really who, Capote's goose was cooked. Paley and her friends, stung by his betrayal, shamed by the revelations, excommunicated the writer from New York society. He was never allowed back in.

It was little wonder the immaculate Babe was so mortified. Her husband's adultery was one thing; his lover's female functions spread out over her bed's linen sheets – and the pages of a popular newsstand magazine – were another.

I can still remember that issue of *Esquire*. I was a very young newlywed in Perth, buying smart American magazines and dreaming of sophistication. What floored me about Capote's story was the plot's pivot – menstruation – and that such an anecdote was appearing in a magazine usually devoted to men, power, black tie and martinis.

After all this time, I can think of only two other occasions when menstruation has made it into pages that have become as widely read. Anne Frank, on the verge of puberty, wrote wistfully about periods in the diary she kept while hiding from the Nazis in Amsterdam. 'Oh, I am so longing to have it too; it seems so important,' the doomed teenager wrote on 29 October 1942.

In 1978, American feminist Gloria Steinem wrote her astoundingly funny send-up essay, 'If Men Could Menstruate,' first published in *Ms. Magazine* and republished countless times since. She argues that if men had periods, they would see bleeding as a sign of power; they would set up national research institutes into monthly cramps; maxi-pads would be named after swaggering cinema heroes. Sample: 'Menstruation would become an enviable, boast-worthy, masculine event. Men would brag about how long and how much … Street guys would invent slang ("He's a three-pad man") …'

But men don't menstruate and proscriptions against menstruating women – what they are permitted to do and not do – can be found in most religions and cultures. The warnings go back to Pliny the Elder in Ancient Rome, who claimed with a straight face that contact with menstrual blood turned new wine sour, led to barren crops, dulled ivory and even disgusted ants. Something of that oppressive idea of contamination has lingered on forever.

Menstruation, a normal condition which affects half the world's population for around half their lives and which is a vital part of the process that allows human life to flourish naturally on Earth, is mostly invisible in our literature, culture, art, politics, social life, interchanges and journalism. In an age where nothing seems to be taboo, *this* is taboo in mainstream society: acknowledging that menstruation happens.

The world slides by that fact the same way most of us gracefully ease past the giant displays of sanitary products in supermarkets. In 2007, a national survey conducted for Stayfree discovered that 92 per cent of the women surveyed confessed they would rather talk about the intimacies of their sex lives or childbirth than about periods.

Sanitary product manufacturers recently came up with a bright new idea: noise-free tampons. Now, when a woman is using a public restroom and has to take a tampon out of its cellophane wrapper, no other woman in the next-door cubicles – that is, no other woman who has been menstruating since she was twelve or thirteen and been using tampons forever – will hear the tell-tale crackle of the covering and *know* that *that* woman has her period. A Tampax website advises young girls, 'Practise with tampons at home. See how quiet you can be.'

A couple of years ago, Melbourne writer Monica Dux, the 37-year-old co-author of *The Great Feminist Denial,* was at the Brisbane Writers' Festival queuing for a coffee. Suddenly a woman slid up to her, tapped her shoulder and pointed surreptitiously at the floor. There lay a panty-pad which had fallen out of Dux's wallet. 'And it had been in my wallet forever,' says Dux, cheerfully forthright, 'so, you know, it was a bit dusty and ink-stained ...' What she remembers is the cloud of mortification that instantly settled not just over her but over everyone around her. She says, her voice breaking with mirth, 'It was as if half the café was going, "Someone's going to have to *tell* her!"'

In her book *Capitalizing on the Curse*, about the massive products industry surrounding menstruation, American academic Elizabeth Kissling argues that how a society deals with menstruation can reveal a lot about how that society views women.

Oddly, there are signs that the embarrassment, far from receding in our emancipated times, is actually growing. Doctors report a recent, but growing, fad for something they call 'super-hygiene' among their young female patients. It's a fastidiousness about cleanliness, a kind of airbrushing of any bits of femaleness that might hint at the unpleasant realities of our biology.

Periods are seen as messy, shameful. One Melbourne gynaecologist tells me of young female patients complaining bitterly even about their vaginal discharges although she tries to tell them these are normal and are what keep the vagina healthy. 'They just don't want them; they think they're disgusting,' she says. She is intrigued by the disjunct between the sexual sophistication of her young patients and their inhibitions and lack of knowledge about their bodies.

Meanwhile, the menstrual cycle itself may virtually disappear in the light of new medical science. Researchers now claim that modern women who, unlike their ancestors, mostly have few or no children and spend little time breastfeeding, menstruate far too often for their own good.

Already, women, aided by the big pharmaceutical companies, can choose ways to have periods only four times a year, or even just once. Or not at all. Many medical experts argue this will save not just discomfort, but lives.

*

Last year, an unlikely book forced its way out of the close-meshed silence around women's bodily functions and onto the *New York Times* bestseller list and Amazon's top twenty-five in its first month. It's called *My Little Red Book* and it's an anthology of first-person pieces: women writing about their first period.

It sounds like a conversation stopper but the anthology's young editor, Rachel Kauder Nalebuff, and her publisher, Jonathan Karp, the wunderkind creator of the exclusive imprint Twelve, part of the extensive Hachette publishing group, knew what they were doing.

Nalebuff, now nineteen and at college, with a new edition just out, has been collecting the stories since she was twelve. On the phone from San Francisco, she was tart. 'Periods themselves don't really interest me … It's what they signify to different women. That's where I think there's power.'

Nalebuff had been stunned when, after she'd had her own first period in excruciatingly embarrassing circumstances that turned – more excruciatingly – into family dinner-table anecdote, her great aunt Nina confided her own story. She had got her first period in 1942 as she and her family were fleeing Poland, and the Jewish deportations under the Nazis, by train. At the border crossing with Germany, the train was halted and the family ordered to strip for a search. Thirteen-year-old Nina had her yellow star of David secreted in her shoe. In terror, she peed herself and then discovered – more fear, more panic – that her pee was bloodstained. Heedless of the guns and uniforms, she raced for the privacy of the train, her mother behind her. The disgusted guards retreated. The family got to Belgium.

Nalebuff couldn't believe her relative had never related this riveting story to anyone before. Sensing hidden treasure in such untold tales, Nalebuff approached first her friends and other relatives for their experiences; then later, strangers, writers, including Steinem who, eventually, gave her an updated version of her classic essay.

In several of the ninety-two pieces, the writers confess they were convinced they were dying when their periods arrived. Amy Lee, now a social justice educator, was panicked when she saw the small stain on her cartoon-printed underwear. She had no idea what a period was: her Korean parents had never let her go to sex-education classes. 'My parents spoke limited English and they only needed to understand one word: *sex*. So while the girls learned about periods, pads and puberty, I sat with the boys and watched *Big Ben*, a movie about a brown bear.'

At her toney private school, Choate Rosemary Hall in Connecticut,

Nalebuff became known as 'Period Girl.' Undeterred, and unfazed by early knock-backs from various publishers, the unstoppable Nalebuff got herself an agent. Within a week, she had her publisher, young Mr Karp, whose imprint chooses to publish and promote just twelve books a year.

She says astutely of her triumph that, 'It says something really important about how our media works and the way women's roles end up playing out in large companies. All the women [publishers] I pitched it to, they think, my male boss isn't going to like this or my male readers are going to be grossed out by this. But the male bosses, if they feel fine about it, they're going to go for it. [Men] are not going to be worrying about what the other half is going to think.'

Years of feminism and the new in-your-face go-grrrrl raunch don't seem to have been able to change attitudes one jot. The videos on the book's website, www.mylittleredbook.net, where young girls talk about their recent first period, are an eye-opener. These teenagers of the coolly knowing iPhone and Facebook era still seem to be as awkward and sweetly abashed and shamed as girls fifty years ago, 100 years ago, 1000 years ago …

Meanwhile, when I first pitched Nalebuff's book to staff at a local young women's magazine as a possible subject – it was published here mid-2009 – they were genteelly appalled. Why would anyone want to read about *that*, they asked.

Nalebuff tells me exasperatedly, 'The stories [in *My Little Red Book*] let women relate a moment they haven't been allowed to talk about. Menstruation should be viewed like blowing your nose or childbirth, as a fact of life, something that happens and that may be physically unappealing but which has a deeper meaning and it's something important that unites all women.'

*

But maybe women don't have to menstruate after all.

In 1999, Brazilian endocrinologist Elsimar Coutinho co-authored the book *Is Menstruation Obsolete?* He argued that, in history, women menstruated far less because of a later onset of puberty, many more pregnancies and longer periods of breast-feeding. Those women might have menstruated around 100 times in a lifetime; the modern woman has her period 400 to 450 times.

Coutinho believes, as do many others, that this constant cycle means women are vulnerable to a range of physical disorders from anaemia to arthritis to uterine and ovarian cancer.

Coutinho's point was taken up by Malcolm Gladwell in a March 2000 piece for the *New Yorker*. Gladwell also found a medical statistician and cancer researcher, Malcolm Pike, who connected constant monthly ovulation – and the consequent cell division caused by the hormonal surges – with a higher risk of breast cancer. The professor exclaimed, wrote Gladwell, that 'the modern way of living represents an extraordinary change in female biology. Women are going out and becoming lawyers, doctors, presidents of countries ... They ovulate from twelve or thirteen until their early thirties. Twenty years of uninterrupted ovulation before their first child! That's a brand-new phenomenon!'

For the past several years, the billion-dollar pharmaceutical industry has been working on ways to turn menstruation into an anachronism, encouraging women in the United States with marketing and repackaging to adopt the contraceptive pill to stop 'periods' for ever-longer lengths of time. (The pill actually stops ovulation so the fourth week of bleeding in the cycle is not a real period; it occurs because of withdrawal from the hormones. The withdrawal week was only included in the pill cycle by the creators so the process would appear 'normal', and reassure both women and the Catholic church. The latter remains unappeased.)

Women have often manipulated pill packets, running them on, to avoid having a period at key times or to treat severe menstrual pain, endometriosis or migraines. Now some women just want control over their wayward, messy, unpredictable bodies, and medical science is giving them an out.

In 2003 in the United States, one company – Barr Laboratories – took the low-dose oestrogen and progestin contraceptive pill and repackaged and remarketed it as Seasonale, a pill to be taken continuously for three months at a time by any woman who wanted less frequent periods. 'Fewer periods, more possibilities' was the marketing line. Three years ago, in 2007, Wyeth introduced another 'new' pill to the United States, Lybrel, which can be taken for 365 days of the year, eliminating periods altogether.

In more pragmatic, down-to-earth Australia – where the pill is the most popular choice for women using contraception –

medical advice for years has been to simply take the existing low-dose pills for three cycles without stopping. Family Planning Australia (FPA) has been teaching women the practice since the 1980s. Many women don't even bother to ask a doctor; they work it out for themselves.

It has been a quiet revolution. To many of us, it sounds radical. To plenty of others, those in the know and who aren't trying to get pregnant, it's old hat. 'Is menstruation obsolete?' asks FPA's Dr Christine Read rhetorically. 'It can be. You don't have to have it.'

Sexual health physician Dr Terri Foran, who lectures at the School of Women's and Children's Health at the University of New South Wales, and is a former medical director of Family Planning NSW, is matter of fact: 'The only reason for menstruation is to set up the uterine lining for the next possible pregnancy, so if we're only having one or two babies in our lives, there's no need for that to be happening constantly.

'When I say to patients that it's not biologically necessary, you can see the lights go on. Managing menstruation is a drag. Many feel: why bother having periods at all? Young women are more active; they want control of their bodies.'

Will the choice not to menstruate become as accepted as say, women deciding to shave their legs and armpits? Perhaps it will soon be considered 'gross' to be the kind of woman who chooses to still have a period thirteen times a year.

Foran says around a quarter of the young women on the pill she sees at her inner-city Sydney clinic are using it to suppress menstruation. Dr Elizabeth Farrell, of Melbourne's Jean Hailes Foundation for Women's Health, says she has noticed increased interest in the last ten years in the practice and while she might have to tell older women about it as a treatment for medical problems, it's the younger women and teenagers who come to her independently, asking about it. Read says approximately 10 to 20 per cent of FPA patients on the pill, of all ages, extend their cycles. But, surprisingly, there are no official statistics and nor have any long-term studies of continuous pill use been done anywhere. Seasonale and Lybrel only conducted year-long studies because they were using an already-approved drug. For that reason, there is now intense, sometimes vehement, debate about the effect of extended contraceptive pill use on a woman's health.

The arguments from each side are persuasive and often directly contradictory. Foran, like others, argues the pill has been used safely for forty to fifty years and that, in effect, *is* a long-term study. But there is a much-cited quote from the staunch critic, American psychiatrist and author Dr Susan Rako, founder of the activist group Women's Health On Alert, who says, 'Manipulating women's hormonal chemistry for the purpose of menstrual suppression threatens to be the largest uncontrolled experiment in the history of medical science.' She lists possible risks running from heart disease, stroke, osteoporosis and cancer to lower libido due to lower levels of active testosterone.

Canadian endocrinologist Dr Jerilynn Prior of the University of British Columbia tells me she believes her research and data show a link between non-ovulation – occurring either naturally or through use of the pill – and lower bone mineral density. Controversially, she pins it down to lower levels of progesterone, and is especially concerned about the effects of the pill on young women who would normally still be laying down bone tissue. She also worries about what effect the pill's hormones could have on developing breast tissue in young women, and also on the ovulation cycle when it hasn't had time to become established.

A colleague of Prior talks of the 'hubris' of tampering with the endocrine system. 'In complex systems, it is very hard to do just one thing,' researcher Christine Hitchcock explains. But, argues one of Australia's foremost experts in the area of menstrual suppression, Professor Ian Fraser, professor in reproductive medicine at the University of Sydney, our society has been unknowingly tampering with the reproductive system for the last 100 years, in the way women have their babies much later and do little breastfeeding.

'Women now have many more periods than previously, and that means big swings in hormones which occur repeatedly every month.' That, he says, dramatically increases the risk of breast, ovarian and endometrial cancers and other reproductive diseases in women who are susceptible genetically. 'These hormonal swings lead to frequently repeated cycles of cell growth and regression, which can eventually lead to uncontrolled changes in cell growth and function – and therefore, sometimes to cancer.

'Women aren't really designed to have these swings 450 times in a lifetime,' he points out. 'The idea that regular menstruation is a good healthy clean-out is a myth. So then you've got to say: are there any adverse consequences of that "tampering" by society in the way in which reproductive experiences have changed, and should we do something to reverse those consequences or ameliorate them without doing harm? A lot of women would be better off having fewer periods.'

An impressive list of benefits is also claimed for the pill as a result of recent studies: dramatic reductions in lifetime risk of ovarian and endometrial cancer; reductions in colorectal cancer; lower incidences of benign breast disease, fibroids and endometriosis; while conditions like acne, period pain and premenstrual syndrome can be helped substantially. Fraser does not believe there is evidence the pill affects bone density one way or the other.

'Major, long-term studies that examine effects around the body would help clear the conflicting claims between the two camps, but big funding would be needed and resources are always limited. It's also very difficult to get women to stay on studies that might last thirty years,' says Fraser.

Kaisu Vartto, CEO of Sexual Health, Information Networking Education, South Australia, or SHine SA, confided frankly, 'Nobody thinks it's sexy enough to do research on it. It's women's business.' Meanwhile, the idea of suppression still plays uncomfortably close to the notion that a woman is trying to rid herself of something she feels – or has been made to feel – is vaguely disgusting, burdensome or unclean.

American health groups were worried, when Seasonale launched, about the effect on impressionable teenagers and young women. A study conducted four years after the product's launch in the States found that the most common reason American physicians prescribed extended pill use to women aged fifteen to twenty-four was not for medical treatment but the patient's personal preference.

While many doctors believe tri-cycling is safe – 'fantastic,' as Farrell puts it, for treating her patients with severe menstrual disorders – the trend towards super-cleanliness amongst young women may be acting like an intersecting riptide.

Doctors and specialists describe young women patients practising a kind of sanitisation process on themselves. Many young women now don't just shave their underarms and wax their legs and their bikini-lines; they wax their forearms as well and any other bit that looks hairy. Foran says of her patients that she hasn't seen anyone under thirty with pubic hair in a long time. 'Most of my younger patients wax, either completely or maybe just leaving a tiny strip.'

If Foran hands them a pad after a procedure, they'll look at it in wonder. What's this? They've been using tampons forever. Like Farrell, she is bemused by the way her young patients, squeakily clean, are horrified by their discharges. Many insist on routinely wearing a panty-liner each day. 'It's not a healthy thing to do,' she says. 'The vagina can't breathe, they can get dermatitis. But when I say that, these young women will ask, "But how do I stay clean and dry?" I have to explain that a discharge is how the vagina cleans itself; it's what allows you to have sex. But,' she adds memorably, 'they want to be as dry as a chip down there.

'Women are fairly sensitive. A lot of this careful cleanliness is actually driven by women themselves, like the craze for high-heels. We're socialised from a very early age that our worth is to do with how other people think of us.'

In fact, many women manage their period easily, can feel energised by it and see it as a reliable monthly indicator of their general health. The irrepressible Nalebuff provides her own view at the end of our interview, chirping in her sing-song American accent, 'It's hard to say this scientifically … but having a period every month and knowing that your body is healthy and in tune, and that you're not pregnant? That's priceless.'

She has included her younger sister Zoe's first period story from 2005 in her anthology, and it snappily demonstrates how things change, but don't:

> Glittergrrrl007: OMG did u get ure period????
> BananabOat: Yea, I'm pissed.
> Glittergrrrl007: LOL
> BananabOat: Well only 40 more years 2 go!!

Or not.

Good Weekend

Prayers, Tear Gas and Terror

Paul McGeough

The Israeli attack was timed for dawn prayers, when a good number of the men aboard the *Mavi Marmara* were praying on the aft deck of the big Turkish passenger ferry as it motored steadily through international waters in the eastern Mediterranean Sea.

The call to prayer could be heard across the water – haunting chords made tinny by the ship's PA system, yet haunting enough amid tension sparked several hours earlier when the six ships' captains in the Free Gaza flotilla rejected a demand radioed by the Israeli navy – change course away from the Gaza Strip or be confronted with lethal force.

Pacing the *Mavi Marmara* at a steady 8 knots and just 150 metres to its port side, we were aboard the 25-metre *Challenger One*, the fastest but also the smallest boat in the flotilla. It was a front-row seat for the opening to Israel's Operation Sky Wind which, despite confident predictions by a gallery of Israeli officials, was about to go horribly wrong.

In the blackness before the rising of a burnt-orange moon, all that could be seen of the Israelis around us were pinpoints of light, as warships sitting a kilometre or more each side of the flotilla inched in – seemingly to squeeze the Gaza-bound humanitarian convoy.

Then, the tightening noose. Sneaking up and around every boat, there were bullet-shaped hulks which soon became impossible to hide as the moonlight made fluorescent tubes of their roiling wakes. First one, then two and maybe four could be seen sneaking in from the rear.

They hunted like hyenas – moving up and ahead on the flanks; pushing in, then peeling away; and finally, lagging before lunging. But as they came alongside the *Mavi Marmara*, the dozen or so helmeted commandos in each assault craft copped the full force of the ferry's fire hoses and a shower of whatever its passengers found on deck or could break from the ship's fittings.

Suddenly sound bombs and tear gas were exploding on the main aft deck, where prayers were held five times a day. The life-jacketed passengers on the rails at first seemed oblivious as those behind them donned the few gas masks that were on board and others, wearing asbestos gloves, sought to grab the devices and hurl them back at the Israeli commandos before they exploded.

In failing to get their grappling irons to hold on the rails of the five-deck ferry, the commandos in their Zodiac-style assault craft continued to be an irritant, or perhaps a decoy because at this point the Israelis opted for a critical change of plan – if they could not come up from the water, they would have to drop from the sky.

On hearing the machines, activists on the upper decks rushed to the top level of the ship – grabbing the commandos even before they landed, disarming them; beating them until, according to some who were present, leaders demanded the Israelis not be harmed; but in one case, one of the Israelis was hurled from one deck of the ship to the next.

The death toll stands at nine of the ship's activists and maybe thirty injured – and there were claims from some on the ship that some of their comrades were missing, unaccounted for since the battle at sea and the chaotic arrest and deportation by Israel of the estimated 700 activists aboard the six vessels.

Four of the ships carried 10,000 tonnes of emergency supplies for Gaza, which Israel has kept under blockade since 2006 when Hamas won electoral control of the Palestinian Occupied Territories. A year later Hamas retained control of Gaza in the face of an Israeli- and US-backed bid to oust the Islamist movement from power.

The flotilla drew on funds from NGOs in Turkey, Malaysia, Ireland, Algeria, Kuwait, Greece and Sweden. The international coalition of Palestinian support groups is determined to prove the

Israeli blockade of Gaza is a Western-backed exercise in collective punishment – something that will be maintained until Gazans turn on Hamas. Tel Aviv claims it is vital to Israel's security.

As distress flares launched from the ship cut through the steel-beam spotlights on Israeli helicopters hovering overhead, the first Israeli commandos who slithered down ropes from the choppers were easy pickings for the waiting activists.

At this stage, *Challenger One*'s British skipper, Dennis Healey, opted to gun the engines, hoping to break from the Israelis swarming the rest of the flotilla.

The following account of what happened on the decks of the *Mavi Marmara* is based on interviews with activists while they and the *Age* news crew, which accompanied the flotilla as non-participating observers, were held in an Israeli prison for more than two days. People were also interviewed on Wednesday on board one of three aircraft sent to Israel by the Turkish government to ferry all the near-700 captured activists to a rousing 4 a.m. reception by tens of thousands of cheering Turks at Istanbul's airport.

There were conflicting accounts of the first commando landing – some activists said he was injured and was being carried inside the ship for treatment by the flotilla doctors. However, a Serbian cameraman, Srojan Stojiljkovic, said some of the activists had armed themselves with lengths of chain and metal posts that had served as cordons around the ship's lifeboats.

'Some of the people caught the first commando before he touched the deck – a few started to hit him, but a lot of people moved in to shelter him with their bodies,' the cameraman said. 'Another soldier with a bleeding nose was brought in ... a few people threw punches, but not as many as I would have expected.'

Matthias Gardel, a leader of the Swedish Palestinian support group, confirmed the soldiers had been beaten, but insisted those involved were unarmed and in keeping with the ship's non-violent charter, the soldiers' weapons were thrown overboard.

Soon after the soldiers had been treated, injured and dead from among the boat's passengers were brought in. Stojiljkovic said: 'Some were not badly wounded, but then a guy was brought in with a point-blank shot between his eyes – he was dead and I was told that another person was killed in the same way.'

The Turkish actor Sinan Albayrak said he had witnessed one of the most senior of the Turkish activists ordering passengers to cease beating two of the Israeli soldiers.

Later, he saw a Turkish photographer who had been shot in the back of the head; while he and others had been attempting to assist another injured activist, 'Israeli troops had opened fire on them ... we ran away from the injured man.'

Gardel said the bulk of the passengers had remained in the second-deck saloons and had not been involved in resisting the Israelis – 'but a bunch of people tried to protect the bridge, the engine-room and the point from which we streamed the live video.'

Another activist, a Turk, lifted his shirt to reveal ten puncture marks in a rough and black-bruised circle, about the circumferences of a teacup. He said the marks were inflicted when he was bitten by an Israeli security dog – while he had been assisting the Israelis by acting as a translator.

The dead include a Turkish journalist, Chetin Genghis, whose head wounds suggested he had been shot from above – possibly from one of the helicopters. After witnessing his dying moments, his colleague Hisham Goruney said: 'I want to forget – I still don't believe that I saw it.' Another of the dead was said to be an Indonesian cameraman, Sura Fachrizaz, shot in the chest. Also among the dead was a Malaysian doctor who, activists said, was shot while treating the wounded.

It took the Israelis about eighty-five minutes to capture the *Mavi Marmara.*

As the 100-plus reporters and other media workers on board followed orders to return to the ship's press room after being told by the captain his vessel was now under Israeli control, many were crestfallen by the sense that an Israeli blanket of 'white noise' had prevented them from getting the story out.

But then someone flicked the switch on a big flat-screen TV on the wall. It burst into life with a Turkish channel, running the live-feed video which the ship had been transmitting to websites run by the Free Gaza Movement and the flotilla's other sponsors – it was scenes of the Israeli takeover of the *Mavi Marmara.* A resounding cheer went up.

*

In Their Wake

When he recounts the siege, 33-year-old Londoner Mustafa Ahmet is quite irreverent. Having done his ablutions, he joined a big group engaged in morning prayers on the aft deck of the *Mavi Marmara* as it pushed south in the Mediterranean. But then a cry went up: 'They're here! They're here!'

'They' were Israeli commandos coming alongside the lead protest vessel in their assault craft. But the imam leading the prayers was unmoved. Instead of cutting proceedings, he seemed to go on forever. As Ahmet observed the commandos' arrival, 'it was like a scary movie – their helmets were shiny, the sea was shiny and battle ships sat off on either side. But the imam just kept on, holding us in position – it was bonkers.'

But then Ahmet becomes perplexed. 'We were a convoy of peace. But the Israeli choppers overhead, the smoke grenades … all the screaming, all the noise. People were running all ways and there was blood everywhere. But before we could do anything it was all over.'

The protesters had been preparing for the raid. People were distributing lifejackets and taking up positions on the rails. Groups had been rostered through the night to sleep or be at the ready, and electric angle-grinders were brought in to cut steel bars from the lifeboat bays along the main decks. Once the attack began, others would be ready to throw Israeli sound bombs and tear-gas canisters back to where they came from.

Despite thoughts of what might lie ahead, there was good humour. Matthias Gardell, a key figure in the Swedish delegation, was getting used to his lifejacket, unaware that even though it was 3 a.m. back home, his twelve-year-old daughter was out of bed and watching a live video-feed from the ship on the Free Gaza Movement's website. Seeing him in the video, she shot him an email: 'Dad, take it off – you look ridiculous.' To which he fired back: 'It's past your bedtime.'

In an interview aboard the *Mavi Marmara* two days before the Israeli assault, Bulent Yildirim, head of the Turkish NGO IHH, which effectively ran the flotilla, said he believed Israel could not afford to pay the price of what he predicted would be a disaster if it intercepted the convoy. The Jewish state was still smarting from international backlash over the use of passports from allied nations in the Mossad's January assassination of a Hamas operative in Dubai. Now European diplomats in Tel Aviv have denied the Israeli government's claim that the flotilla organisers had ties to Al-Qaeda.

Both sides are documenting their case. The flotilla organisers accuse the Netanyahu government of hijacking their vessels in international waters, killing nine and wounding about thirty people in the process; of then taking almost 700 humanitarians and peace activists prisoner and forcibly taking them to Israel – and then charging them with illegal entry to the country.

The organisers will face government allegations that steel bars were used to beat troops; that weapons confiscated from captured commandos may have been used against their comrades.

Israel argues that sixty to 100 'hardcore' activists had been embedded in the *Mavi Marmara*. They included Turks, Afghans, Yemenis and an Eritrean who were experienced in hand-to-hand fighting.

Yesterday, the Israeli navy claimed three commandos had been dragged unconscious into one of the ship's hulls 'for several minutes' before regaining consciousness and escaping. It was not clear if any of the three were among the three commandos who the activists on board the *Mavi Marmara* have said were beaten, then sheltered and given medical treatment.

However, the flotilla crisis is not just about Israel. The virtual takeover of what was a coalition of groups from a dozen countries by Turkish NGOs plays into regional politics. Long an Israeli ally, Turkey is flexing its muscles regionally, bonding with Syria, Iran, Iraq, Qatar and Hamas – and at the same time, awkwardly exposing the Arab world's flip-flops on the Palestinian cause and, by its demonstrable actions, almost shaming them to do more.

Tucked in under all that is Washington's role in the region. The rest of the world was quick to criticise Israel in the aftermath of the flotilla fiasco, but the Obama White House called for an Israeli inquiry, the kind of response that placates Israel but erodes US credibility in the region.

Some on the ship thought the Israelis did not put enough into their opening shots. Espen Goffeng, a Norwegian, said: 'I looked over the rail and saw the zodiacs. It seemed hopeless for the Israelis – they tried to lock-on their grappling hooks, but they were hit by the fire hoses and their own projectiles going back to them.' He wondered if the boats had been a decoy to draw passengers to the rails while helicopters were used to land Israeli commandos higher in the ship. But that proved difficult too, with the first two lots of chopper-borne commandos being captured by the activists.

'The first ammunition I heard striking the ship sounded like paint balls,' Goffeng said. 'But some people said there had to be glass in them, because of the wounds they caused. There was a lot of blood in the stairwells and then the sound of the ammunition hitting metal changed again – I decided that was the live ammunition. People were yelling, "Live ammo! Live ammo!"'

He said that people in the TV broadcast area on the aft deck were being targeted. 'I helped to carry one of the dead down to the second deck, and as I returned, a man who had been shot in the leg was being carried down. And when I moved to the press room, one of the men who worked there was dead, with a hole in his forehead and half his head missing. Then there was an announcement on the PA system telling us, "Keep calm; it's over ... they have taken the ship and we have lost."'

Soon after, Israeli soldiers smashed the doors to the press room, the *Age* was told, and then called the media workers forward one at a time. 'They searched us,' said a cameraman who had managed to unpick the waistband of his underpants sufficiently to create mini-pockets in which he successfully secreted most of his camera discs – a strip search revealed just one of them. 'They took cell phones and hard drives ... and anything else that was capable of capturing or storing images.'

On the open decks and in the salons lower in the ship, conditions were far less pleasant than the press room. Matthias Gardell, the Swede with the fashion-conscious daughter, complained of people being forced to kneel for hours on the open deck where prayers were held. But with an Israeli helicopter hovering constantly near the deck, its downdraft sprayed the prisoners with wind and water, in the circumstances a freezing combination. 'Keeping the choppers there seemed to be deliberate, as though they wanted to enfeeble us by holding us in such unpleasant conditions,' he said.

People were not allowed to go to the restrooms. But Gardell

was especially horrified by seeing the experience of a badly wounded man in his late fifties, whom the Israeli troops forced to remain on the open deck. 'Suddenly, his right eye exploded in a gush of blood – and a blob of something fell out of it.'

The Israeli troops did come prepared. Canadian activist Kevin Neish found a booklet he believed had been dropped by one of the Israelis – it contained images of the key leadership figures, including IHH leader Bulent Yildirim and the nerves-of-steel Palestinian lawyer who headed the Free Gaza Movement, 34-year-old Huwaida Arraf. On being offloaded at Ashdod, she was last seen by the *Age* being frogmarched away from the detainee processing centre where her activist confreres were being processed through a chaotic maze of bureaucratic and security checkpoints.

By the time the ship reached Ashdod, the passengers complained that most of their cases and other baggage had been strewn on the inside decks. But there was an infectious camaraderie among the protesters on the flotilla – bound by politics, prayer and song; it was a finishing school for almost 700 new and articulate ambassadors from dozens of countries for the Palestinian cause. And the Netanyahu government has given them a story to tell. Like the Dubai assassination, halting the Free Gaza flotilla has been a tactical success but, in hindsight, appears to have been a strategic disaster. The cost to Israel's international credibility may be great. And these new advocates for Palestine were going home prepared – many were observed recording detailed accounts of their experience, with timelines and explanatory graphics.

Back home they may be better received than they might have been last week because of the tone of the trenchant international criticism of Israel. The images broadcast around the world, despite Israel's best efforts, dovetailed with the forthright account of the likes of Anne Jones, a former American diplomat and US army colonel.

'The Israel Defence Forces acted as pirates in shooting at us and stealing our ships in international waters,' she told the *Age*. 'They kidnapped us and brought us to Israel; they arrested and imprisoned us; they paraded us before cameras in violation of the Geneva Conventions.'

Blonde-haired and just twenty-one, Jerry Campbell awoke at 4 a.m. to attend dawn prayers, but she had hardly bowed her head before she was dragged off to a nursing station to help treat four gunshot victims. Worse was in store for this young woman from Queensland's Gold Coast. 'I looked up as I was caring for a wounded Indonesian and saw my husband being carried in.' That was twenty-year-old Ahmed Luqman Talib, who had been shot in the leg. She cut his blood-soaked clothing from him but then followed his instructions to tend to others. 'I'm okay,' he told her.

She lost count of the number and nationalities of those she tended to. 'I saw two men die out there … the floor was covered in blood and the IV units were tied to the ceiling with bandages.'

Campbell went to and from her husband, who seemed to be deteriorating. 'One man's stomach was opened – his intestines were out and the doctor reached inside and pulled out some bullets, before pushing everything back in and wrapping him up,' she said. 'I don't know if he survived.'

Late on the second day in detention, Israeli officials showed 45-year-old Gigdem Topcuoghe, a Turkish woman, a picture of her dead husband – she became catatonic. At the Ella prison in Beersheba, she recounted to her fellow inmate and Fairfax photographer Kate Geraghty how, during the dawn prayers that heralded the attack on the *Mavi Marmara*, she had found her husband on the floor. He had been shot in the forehead and was bleeding from his mouth and nose.

'I think of first aid – I need to help him. I checked his breathing … he was bleeding faster. I gave him some water and started praying for him – I held him in my arms. He wasn't conscious – I held him tight, but I realised he was gone when he didn't react in any way, but my husband is not dead – he will live with and among us.' Several witnesses have recounted in awe how Topcuoghe accepted condolences briefly – before leaving her husband's body to throw herself into helping the injured.

Later, in Israeli detention, the new widow addressed her tearful friends, turning to the state of Israel. Describing the assault on the *Mavi Marmara* as inhuman, she urged Allah to show the people of Israel the right path, but then added: 'May they face more cruelty than we have, and when this happens we'll be there to help them – and to take humanitarian aid to them, just like centuries back when the Ottoman sultan sent aid and ships to rescue the Jews from Spanish cruelty.'

Time, brief as it was, spent inside the Israeli apparatus was revealing. Whenever the flotilla prisoners were processed, security and other workers gathered to gawp, frequently producing mobile phones to shoot happy snaps of themselves in front of the prisoners. As a big group of men – your correspondent included – waited in Block 5 at the Ella prison to be bussed to Ben Gurion Airport for deportation on Wednesday, a big group of security cadets was wheeled in to stare in wonderment, licking ice-creams as they did.

Several Europeans were distressed by the distinction the Israelis made between prisoners. The Norwegian activist Randi Kjos was genuinely shocked by what she observed. 'They treated us with hatred – the old were made to kneel for long periods and women had to sit with their arms crossed. Some of the wounded were naked to the waist … many were in shock. Palestinians and Arabs were treated very differently to Europeans or Westerners. Palestinians who asked for anything were belted, pushed around or treated with contempt. People warned me of the hatred I would see – but still, I was shocked.'

The Norwegian observed that many of the women prisoners were denied a phone call on the grounds that a functioning telephone 'was broken.' Others were furious on behalf of many Turkish women who were denied a call home because they could not satisfy their guards' demand that they converse in English.

At Ella prison it quickly became clear that the guards were under strict instructions not to inflict physical violence on the prisoners. The detainees taunted the guards. 'We're all Palestinians,' one of the prisoners delighted in telling an officer, over and over; while another guard became visibly upset when one of the prisoners told him, when he was already upset about another matter: 'You're not really cut out for this job – you should have been a school teacher.' Whenever an officer clenched his fist in such exchanges, a colleague would move in and take him away. But amid much taunting by prisoners, the refusal to lash out could last only for so long and at the airport a brawl erupted between deportees and their keepers, with several of the activists getting on the planes bruised.

As they left a detention system in which some had been subjected to more than half-a-dozen body searches, many still were subject to a humiliating, painfully slow strip search by smirking airport staff as they quit the country.

As the Israelis continued to hold Bulent Yildirim till late into Wednesday night, a group of fifteen detainees still being processed through the airport staged a protest when they observed Yildirim being put in a cell. 'So the security guys just attacked us,' said Mohammed Bounoua, an Algerian who complained that he had been beaten three times during his less-than-72 hours in Israeli custody.

The ten-hour wait on the Ben Gurion tarmac and the late-night flight to Istanbul was joyous. Three Turkish aircraft were parked adjacent to Terminal 1 and as the Israeli authorities processed passengers at snail's pace, each was welcomed onto the aircraft with clapping, cheering, crying. There was a festive mood as friends who had been separated were reunited and pensive tears for those waiting for husbands, siblings, friends who had not been seen for days.

After several hours on the tarmac, the pilot announced that Turkish prime minister Recep Tayyip Erdogan had insisted that none of the aircraft would leave until all the Turkish activists and the bodies of the dead had been loaded.

There were bursts of song.

The Age and *The Sydney Morning Herald*

The Only Things I Remember from School

Murray Bail

1) the geography teacher, Mr Sullivan, loose cheeks, throat and bottom lip, and trousers too loose – always hitching them up; a general worn-out appearance in clothing and eyelids. The nicotine-stained fingers, his short-sleeved shirts. Talking about the tropics and coral, he said he had been up in the islands during the war, where he found the coral too sharp to walk on. He had to wear sandshoes.

2) the science teacher, who told us the piston of a car engine stops each time it reaches the top and bottom of each stroke – stops each time, even when high-revving. He said the greatest discovery yet to be made was perpetual motion.

3) Mr Kenny, his thick straight hair, combed and parted, his horn-rims. He also wore stout tan shoes. As he talked he smiled, or almost smiled. It was his way of imparting knowledge. When for no reason I let out a laugh he came between the desks and without a pause slapped me across the face. I looked up; I saw how he was unsettled by what he had done. He was perhaps the best teacher.

4) large numbers of students with buck teeth. One called Venning. Coming downstairs in a crowd he liked to give a shove from behind. Turning around, there'd be his good-natured, grinning teeth. His father was a panelbeater.

5) the art teacher, forget his name, who was small and thin, wore beige waistcoats. His way of teaching was to remain seated

behind his desk, sometimes at an angle, his cheek on his hand. He had a slow, exhausted delivery. It was as if he was talking to another audience. His hair fell across his forehead. Someone began calling him Adolf (Hitler). On that hot afternoon, unable to control the class, he appeared to be ignoring the noise – until he jumped up and raised his fist at someone talking in the front: 'You, by Christ, I'll knock your block off.' Sitting down just as suddenly he put his face in his hands, 'I can't stand this any longer.'

Once he brought in another teacher, Mr Lewis, who was an artist. Quite stout, a solemn manner, a dark moustache. He wore a tweed jacket buttoned up. If he was an artist he looked like anybody else. He told us that in a painting of a white sheet hanging on a clothesline there might be half-a-dozen different colours, possibly even more.

6) the moment mathematics made sense. It fell into place, the logic of it. I could see the reason for it.

7) Mr 'Lenny' Blaskett, pink all over, bald, which drew attention to his teeth – his hardworking, prominent teeth. We could not avoid his teeth as he tried his best to introduce classical music. With his gramophone from home placed on the desk, he'd put on a Beethoven symphony and close his eyes. On Sundays he played the organ at his church. Sitting down at the school piano, which was between the desk and the door, he adopted a hurried, anxious manner more suitable to the keyboard and stops of an organ. He enlisted the boy who could read music to sit beside him, as if it was an honour; the class waited for the tentative page-turner to lose his way, which he soon did, and the music to be snatched away from him. The most unpopular teacher – he took it upon himself to teach the importance of hygiene in and around the genitals, erasing diagrams of foreskins on the blackboard just as quickly as he drew them. He used the cane – a length of dowelling, which could draw blood – and for this he took the victim down to the lavatory, away from the class. There he became almost friendly, making light of it, before raising his arm and, eyes bulging, suddenly bringing the cane down on the hand, and repeating, depending on the offence.

I told no one we were distantly related – on my mother's side.

8) reading aloud in class *The Shadow Line*; when someone else was doing it, getting ahead of them. Small book with red cover.

And *The Odyssey* (in prose). Or was that in the earlier school?

9) teachers in the lunch hour strolling in pairs, smoking pipes.

10) Leslie Roach. His mother died. The scabs on his knees.

11) Mr Gemmel was popular, mostly because of his uninterested, almost bored manner. Unlike every other teacher he called us by our Christian names. Also, in the lunch hour he played tennis with one of the older boys, without changing out of his long trousers. And he formed the Photography Club. I was elected president, only because no one wanted his favourite, an English migrant in brown specs, who went around with both hands in his pockets and knew far more about photography than I did.

12) the woodwork and metalwork teachers. Being surrounded by timber, lengths of metal, hammers, tinsnips and loud machinery gave them authority. Bits of yellow sawdust in the hair of the woodwork teacher. He was never seen out of his grey workcoat. He was a teacher, yet hardly ever opened his mouth. He pointed and nodded, or else slowly shook his head. A mostly silent, likeable figure. On the wall behind him was a long strip of varnished wood inlaid with the different timbers of Australia. Next door, the metalwork teacher was plump and bald. He had the thin silver moustache. His unpleasant way of washing his hands, which he did four or five times a day, a soft soapy motion. His crisply ironed, short-sleeved shirts. Never a tie. When something had been dropped into a lavatory bowl he marched everyone in and ordered a boy, one who had the most pimples, possibly the poorest, to put his hand into the water and fish it out. The expressionless humiliation of this boy (at other times, his furtive look). For lunch, the metalwork teacher sat at his desk and cracked open a boiled egg, with cheese and a tomato on a plate, a serviette to wipe his mouth. He used his pocketknife to peel an apple. Years before, he had spent time in the goldfields. He still went out prospecting with his pan. For this he had a Ford V8, green, covered with a canvas hood tied down with white rope. It too was immaculate. Everything about him said he was a bachelor, even his excessive cleanliness, and if such a man could afford a large American car and drive to wherever he liked, it followed that it

would be best not to begin an interest in girls, who would turn into women.

13) the school on Kensington Road, Adelaide, was barely two years old. With its new cream-brick look it was assumed to be a good school. The main building of two or three storeys was set back, parallel to the road. In front was the oval – in summer, the steady metallic insect-hiss of its sprinklers. Behind the main building a creek ran through the grounds. Now and then a boy slipped in, or was pushed. It sometimes flooded and we lined the bank, throwing things into the torrent or just stood watching it, joined by some of the teachers. It felt odd to see nature rushing past, while lessons consisting of facts and possible figures were being taught in rooms.

14) Roger somebody, taller and better looking than the rest of us. He had black curly hair, and one lazy eyelid. The word went around that he had managed the night before – while the rest of us were doing our homework – to put his finger inside a girl. A small group gathered on the oval to see the victorious unwashed finger, and those still curious were allowed to bend forward to have a sniff, not knowing what to expect. In the three years at the school, the only presence of a girl I recall.

The Monthly

Tears of the Sun

Kathy Marks

As you fly out of Perth, heading east, the wheat and sheep country cushioning the world's most isolated capital city quickly recedes. The already sparse signs of settlement diminish, and soft yellows and greens give way to the harsh rust-reds of the continent's interior. But this is not the mostly flat, mostly featureless landscape characteristic of much of central Australia – not nowadays, anyway. This is a landscape pockmarked with man-made hills, and gigantic holes gouged out of the earth. This is gold country.

Of all those holes, none other compares with the Super Pit, one of the biggest craters ever dug by man – so vast that it can be seen from space, and is even reputed to influence the weather in Kalgoorlie, the hard-bitten town crouched on its rim. One of the richest goldmines on the planet, the open-cut pit will be 3.6 kilometres long, 1.6 kilometres wide and 650 metres deep when a current expansion program is completed. The creation of Alan Bond, it is the thrusting symbol of the Australian mining industry, an industry that has shaped multiple aspects of the modern nation, while underpinning the economy and, recently, enabling the country to weather the global financial upheaval with little more than a scratch.

It was in this remote and desperately arid corner of Western Australia that Paddy Hannan and two fellow Irish prospectors made camp in 1893, after one of their packhorses threw a shoe. Ever alert to the potential of virgin ground, they kept their eyes firmly down and spotted several nuggets in a gully. Before long they had collected a hundred ounces of gold, and within three days hordes of men were pegging out claims on what became known as the Golden Mile. It was the beginning of Australia's last and greatest gold rush – 'the rush that never ended,' as they call it in Western Australia, after the title of Geoffrey Blainey's classic history of the mining industry.

More than a century on, the goldfield that Hannan discovered – and the hundreds of ore bodies in and around Kalgoorlie – is still being worked with the same intensity: by thousands of lone prospectors, hoping for their own lucky strike, and by companies large and small. At the Super Pit, where hundred-metre-high slag heaps loom up against the horizon, the blasting, shovelling and crushing go on twenty-four hours a day, 365 days a year. As I watched the oversized dump trucks, laden with rock, toil up the pit face, then descend, empty, to be loaded again, it struck me that this hole, evocative of unbridled ambition and perhaps even hubris, also represents something quite primal: man's millennia-old mania for digging up the treasures in the Earth's crust, and the gamble upon which the mining business has always been predicated.

When Blainey's book was first published, in 1963, gold was in long-term decline, and by the mid-1970s headframe lights were dimming across the Golden Mile. However, new technology and the emancipation of the gold price resurrected a dying industry, and in the early 1980s another boom began. In recent times the price of gold has risen spectacularly, and all over Australia drill holes are being sunk, mothballed mines are being reopened and existing ones are being enlarged. Meanwhile, after a blip lasting barely a year, other mineral and energy resources are being shipped overseas as fast as they can be scooped out of the ground.

In Perth, the cafés are bursting and the traffic is beyond belief: a sure indication that the good times have returned. With China barrelling ahead in its industrial revolution and India not far behind, demand for Australia's raw materials is expected to climb even higher. Yet amid the euphoria – felt most keenly in Western Australia, the nation's resources powerhouse, but also beyond – there is an undercurrent of disquiet. How wise is Australia to stake its future on an industry reliant on finite reserves and fickle commodity prices? How sustainable is mining, with its colossal environmental footprint? And just who is reaping the rewards?

*

Soon after 2010 dawned, I stood calf-deep in a tranquil creek, swishing gravel and sand around a dish while carefully watching for 'colour.' At this same spot in April 1851, John Lister and William Tom noticed gold glistening in a rock crevice, then, a little way downstream, came across a two-ounce nugget. Three years after the start of the California gold rush, they had found Australia's first payable goldfield, thirty kilometres north-east of Orange, in the undulating countryside beyond the Blue Mountains. The site was christened Ophir, after the biblical city of gold, by the man who had identified the area's promise: Edward Hammond Hargraves.

Gold. No other element on the periodic table – not platinum, nor carbon, the source of diamonds – has seized the imagination in the same way, nor ignited such passions. The Incas called it 'the tears of the sun'; the Egyptian pharaohs were buried with it; for thousands of years it has occupied a unique place at the heart of civilisations. Deposited in quartz veins hundreds of millions of years ago by fluids surging up from the Earth's molten core, gold has driven people 'to travel the globe … to lie and cheat, to suffer and speculate, to risk their lives, to move mountains and reshape the landscape,' according to *Gold: Forgotten Histories and Lost Objects of Australia*, edited by Iain McCalman, Alexander Cook and Andrew Reeves. Symbolic of wealth, power, beauty and immortality, gold has tantalised and tormented men, fuelled and funded wars, propped up currencies, permeated languages and spawned innumerable myths and legends.

Like most people, I'm familiar with the glamorous metal. But the first time I held a chunk of raw gold in my hand, fresh from the ground, I felt a little dizzy. It was so shiny, so yellow, so solid, and as I turned it over I caught a faint glimpse of what sends folk crazy. The shy, lanky man who showed it to me had sold his home and business in Perth in order to move to the Eastern Goldfields, around Kalgoorlie, and prospect full-time. I met Brad Parslow outside a shop in Boulder, Kalgoorlie's faded twin town; he was heading back out bush, and when I asked him if he'd had any luck, he reached into his canvas shoulder bag and took out a Tupperware box containing a three-ounce nugget – which, on that day in early December 2009, was worth US$3624: not bad for an afternoon's work. (One troy ounce is 31.1 grams.)

In central New South Wales shepherds tending their flocks had been picking up gold long before Lister and Tom, but the metal's existence was apparently hushed up; according to one tale, Governor Sir George Gipps, on being presented with specks of gold by a geologist and Anglican clergyman, the Reverend William Branwhite Clarke, spluttered: 'Put it away, Mr Clarke, or we shall all have our throats cut.' His fears proved unfounded; however, when news did get out, 'a great excitement unhinged the minds of all classes of the community,' writes Manning Clark in *A History of Australia*.

There's not much gold left at Ophir; in fact, there's nothing much at all – just a commemorative obelisk; a few crumbling headstones in the overgrown cemetery; a landscape pitted with old shafts, mullock heaps and wide tunnels carved out of the hillsides; and the once richly endowed creek, still blithely babbling in the shade of gracefully inclined casuarinas. In 1851 there was a chaotic township, complete with school, post office, police station, apothecary, hotels and sly-grog sellers, while the diggings, according to a letter to the *Bathurst Free Press* in June that year, were so crowded that 'in some spots the miners stand so close together that their picks have to be very carefully used to prevent them from striking each other.'

An estimated 3000 people worked Ophir's stony ground at its peak; the frenzy was short-lived, though, and many miners decamped to the more promising Turon River, to the north-east. In August 1851 the bountiful goldfields of Ballarat were discovered, followed by those of Bendigo and Beechworth. Australia's first real gold rush was on, with fortune-seekers from around the globe converging on Victoria's so-called Golden Triangle. At home, police and soldiers deserted their posts to dig for alluvial gold; ships docking in Melbourne were abandoned by their crews. Geoffrey Blainey writes in *The Rush That Never Ended*: 'Shopkeepers and employers found the relationships of society reversed. Calling at the blacksmith to shoe their horse they found his door locked ... Their children returned from school to report the master had gone ... Preachers looked down from pulpits and denounced avarice to congregations empty of men.'

Although the rush was mostly over within twenty years, Victoria – and its capital city, which metamorphosed into 'Marvellous Melbourne' – would never be the same. For the other colonies, too, it was a turning point: the country's population nearly tripled during the 1850s, to more than a million, as migrants arrived not only from Britain and Ireland but China, the United States and all over Europe. At last Australia had the massive influx of free settlers it coveted; breakneck economic growth boosted the living standards of a society until then largely dependent on agriculture, and as major gold seams were located, in turn, in Queensland, the Northern Territory and Western Australia, each received an injection of wealth and people. Far-flung regions were opened up, with inland towns established and linked by railway to the coast. And Australia's international image was transformed: rather than a dreary outpost of Britain or a convict dumping-ground, it became a promised land.

Today it is the world's second-largest gold producer, behind China, and gold is its third-biggest export, after coal and iron ore, worth $17.5 billion in 2008–09. Yet gold, notwithstanding its allure, has relatively few practical applications, unlike, for instance, that most basic of industrial raw materials, iron ore. In the Pilbara region of Western Australia, iron ore is mined in prodigious quantities – and it is in the Pilbara that the reality of Australia being a quarry for Asia really hits home.

*

The skyline in Port Hedland, 1630 kilometres north of Perth, is dominated by towering red stockpiles: iron ore, awaiting shipment to China's steel mills. Red dust coats pavements and lawns in the small, somewhat unprepossessing town, where every other building seems to be a gleaming mine company headquarters. Port Hedland is often referred to as the engine room of the Australian economy; visiting for the first time, I found it hard not to think that the iron ore companies, particularly Rio Tinto and BHP Billiton, own the Pilbara. Need a motel in Tom Price, the spick-and-span mining community rising from a baked landscape

430 kilometres south of Port Hedland? You'll have to call Rio Tinto's reservations service. (All rooms are booked up months in advance.) Want to drive from Tom Price to the port of Dampier? Sorry, that road is owned by Rio Tinto, although they might let you use it if you ask nicely. Fancy a walk in the fresh air? Try the BHP Billiton Marapikurrinya Park in Port Hedland, where you can also ogle the enormous bulk carriers. Or, you could go hiking in Rio Tinto Gorge.

The rust-coloured gorges of the Pilbara's Hamersley Ranges caught the eye of the late mining magnate Lang Hancock in 1952, when stormy weather forced his plane to fly low over the area. One of the most significant deposits was unearthed at Mount Tom Price, where, three or four times a day, a 2.5-kilometre-long train departs for Dampier, carrying more than 16,000 tonnes of iron ore. (The railway is privately owned, naturally.) If that sounds like a lot of ore, consider this: Tom Price is only one of eleven Rio Tinto mines in the Pilbara, producing 220 million tonnes a year. Then there are BHP's seven mines – another 100 million tonnes – as well as the lesser players, chief among them Andrew 'Twiggy' Forrest's Fortescue Metals, which exported 27 million tonnes in its first year.

Tony Dekuyer gave up his job as a maths teacher at a private Catholic boys' school in Perth in 2006 to drive trucks at Rio Tinto's West Angelas mine. Set against a billowing backdrop of saltbush, spindly trees and red sandhills, West Angelas consists simply of the mine, an airstrip and an accommodation camp. The nearest town, Newman, is 110 kilometres away. Dekuyer's wife, Janette, also worked at the site; for two years, the couple occupied adjacent huts at the camp, returning to Perth one week in three to watch their adult sons play sport, catch up on the gardening and enjoy the café lifestyle. Dekuyer, fifty-one, has now gravitated to a position in the operations centre in Perth, where he earns 'just over double' his teacher's salary.

Everyone at West Angelas has signed up for the 'fly in, fly out' (FIFO) regime that is increasingly the norm in the Australian resources industry, as new mines, many with short lifespans, open up in isolated spots. For the workers, FIFO means long periods away from home and life in a camp which, despite being well equipped – canteen, wet mess, gym, tennis courts, internet access

– has no frills. The wages help to compensate (truck drivers earn about $150,000, including allowances; train drivers up to $210,000) – so much so that some miners commute from Brisbane and Sydney. Tony Dekuyer, who has bought himself a Ducati motorbike (Janette has a convertible sports car), reflects: 'Teaching was very rewarding in many ways, but mentally it was quite exhausting. Here, when the day finishes, it finishes, and you don't have to think about the job at all.'

At Rio Tinto's mines, nearly a third of truck drivers are women. Kylie Piggott spends her waking hours perched eight metres off the ground, driving back and forth to the West Angelas pits. Each trip she collects 240 tonnes of drilled and blasted rock, then, following instructions on a computer screen, transports it to the crusher, stockpile or dump. Piggott, twenty-five, has to climb three metal staircases to reach her cab; the vehicle's tyres alone are twice her height. She says: 'The cabs are air-conditioned and you can play your own music. It's like a little world of your own up there. It's pretty relaxing, although it can be lonely too.'

Young women like Piggott are the new face of the industry, according to mining executives. But you don't have to look far for a more familiar face. On a Sunday afternoon in Tom Price – 340 kilometres from the hottest town in Australia, Marble Bar – I meet Ross, Digger and Pirate in the crowded beer garden of the Tom Price Hotel Motel. Ross is a boilermaker from Queensland with a long, shaggy beard, grey ponytail, beer belly and eye-catching array of tattoos. He spends nine days of each month in Perth with his partner. 'Do I miss home? Hell, yeah,' he says. 'But it's very good money: that's the trade-off. I'm prepared to do the hard yards in the short term in order to pay off the mortgage and create a bit of wealth. But it can be really hard on your relationship, and the evidence is all around you.'

Digger, a short, voluble man who disappears to buy a round of drinks and returns with a blowsy girl on his arm, has three broken marriages behind him. A miner since the 1970s, he believes the industry is far more civilised nowadays. 'It was rough back then. It was all single men, and the wet mess was open twenty-four hours, and there were fights breaking out the whole time.'

What about the lifestyle now? Ross sighs. 'It's a small town in the middle of nowhere. It's stinking hot in summer and freezing cold in winter. If I could make the same money at home, I wouldn't be flying away.'

*

At the turn-off from the Albany Highway to Bannister Marridong Road, 115 kilometres south-east of Perth, a sign states: 'Boddington – A Golden Opportunity.' Another fifteen kilometres on is a country town that is holding its breath.

Boddington is a farming community sitting on Australia's biggest goldmine. The mine, owned by the American giant Newmont, opened in 1987 and was decommissioned in 2001; after the gold price rose, Newmont decided to restart operations, mining and processing lower-grade ore. The first bar was poured last October at the site, which was upgraded at a cost of US$3.2 billion and has a projected life of at least twenty-four years; the plan is to produce a million ounces of gold annually for the first five – even more than the Super Pit. The inhabitants of Boddington are, mostly, thrilled: investment is flowing into the once dozy town of 1600, new businesses have been set up, and new health and recreation services are in the works. The jobless rate has dropped to almost zero (the mine will employ nearly 900 people), and the property market is boiling. In 2009 Newmont ploughed more than $70 million into the local economy.

Over the next four years the population of the town, situated in the Darling Ranges, on the banks of the Hotham River, is forecast to double: a trend that most rural communities can only dream of. However, residents are wary. They recall the high hopes of Ravensthorpe, six hours' drive south, when BHP opened its US$2.2 billion nickel mine in 2008. Eight months later, after the nickel price fell to below $11,000 a tonne – it was above $50,000 in mid-2007 – BHP walked away and 1800 people lost their jobs. In Boddington, many miners have chosen to rent houses, or to live at the camp just outside town, leaving their families behind in Perth. And it is not only they who are hesitant. 'The problem we're having now is to convince the state government, the businesses and, particularly, the financiers that we're not Ravensthorpe,' says Paul Carrots, president of the shire council.

Yet mining has traditionally been a precarious business: for prospectors and companies, for mine workers and their communities, for investors and speculators. Booms are inexorably followed by busts; bubbles always burst. Of the hundreds of new Western Australian companies floated on the London Stock Exchange after Kalgoorlie's riches came to light, only a fraction survived. In 1969 the excitement whipped up by the discovery of nickel at Windarra, north of Kalgoorlie, spurred thousands of Australians to invest in a company called Poseidon; shares soared from eighty cents to $280, but the field did not live up to its hype, and Poseidon's stock, along with other mining shares, crashed. Despite such debacles, a gambling mentality has infused Australian mining since the early days. Geoffrey Blainey calls the gold rushes 'a gigantic lottery in which all had a chance … the magic formula in an age without football pools or state lotteries'; he also relates how, after their board meetings, the directors of Broken Hill Proprietary would play two-up with gold sovereigns.

For today's companies, the gamble is twofold: will the immense capital staked in the quest for new deposits pay off in the shape of a viable mine, and if so, will the commodity price be sustained long enough – and production costs remain low enough – to guarantee profits? Although the odds can be shortened through drilling, geophysics, aerial photography and the study of geological maps, they are still daunting. 'You back yourself to find stuff,' agrees Chris Banasik, exploration director of a small, recently formed goldmining company, Silverlake Resources. 'As a punter, you read the form; as a geologist, you look at rocks and data and make an interpretation about where the gold is.' Campbell Baird, chief executive of Focus Minerals, which owns land at Coolgardie, forty kilometres south of Kalgoorlie, says: 'The high value of gold makes it a high-risk, high-reward business: that's the attraction. But only one in 500 deposits makes it into production. It's reasonably easy to find gold mineralisation, but to prove up an economic deposit – that's the challenge. There are hundreds of companies out there, still looking after ten or fifteen years, and the faith and belief they have in themselves and the land is quite extraordinary.'

Tiny quantities of most minerals are found almost everywhere (even seawater contains minute amounts of gold); the difficulty is to identify abnormal concentrations. The line between success and failure can be fine – particularly with gold, where 'you're mining ounces in a vast landscape,' as Chris Fraser, executive director of the Minerals Council of Australia's Victorian division, puts it. Chris Banasik observes: 'The hardest thing in mining is to stop, because there's always the chance you might have missed it. It's always, "Jeez, can we give it one more shot? Because look at the rocks – it's got to be here somewhere."' Jim Beyer, Boddington's general manager, says: 'You're putting drill holes down, and you could be centimetres away and you wouldn't know. The difference between a dry hole and a bonanza hole can be tiny. Then someone else comes along and finds it. It's heartbreaking, but that's the way the game goes.'

*

'Our skimpies this week: Holly, Sarah, Jamie, Danni,' announces a blackboard sign outside the Exchange Hotel, one of the imposing gold-rush-era buildings that line Hannan Street, in central Kalgoorlie. Across the road, outside the equally historic Palace Hotel, with its stone façade and wraparound balconies, an electronic board flashes up the latest gold price. It is December 2009, and gold is about to hit US$1217.40 per ounce – its all-time peak.

'The price is absolutely unbelievable,' exults Ashok Parekh, whose sprawling accountancy firm occupies almost an entire city block. He boots up his computer to check it yet again. He beams. 'Everyone in Kalgoorlie is happy; you can feel it in the air. I drink in the Tattersalls Club every Friday night with my friends – builders, taxi drivers, businessmen, pensioners – and we all talk about the same thing: the gold price and gold shares; which companies are doing well.' He rummages in a cabinet and brings out a 22-ounce nugget. 'That's worth US$26,000 today,' he confides. I suppress an urge to shrug; after a few days in Kalgoorlie, I've seen so much gold that, like everyone else, I've become blasé. In one pub, the barman produces a nugget as we chat; no one else looks up from their drink.

The gold price smashed record after record in 2009, as nervous investors sought a safe haven. The Perth Mint could not turn out coins fast enough, and even its souvenir shop was packed with people 'desperate to give us their money and buy gold,' recalls Edward Harbuz, the Mint's chief executive. Six hundred kilometres inland, the global recession barely registered in this community of 30,000, or 32,000, or 35,000 – no one seems quite sure what the Kalgoorlie population is. A new $10 million retail development opened, Harvey Norman moved to more spacious premises and work proceeded on a $20 million golf course. 'The global financial crisis?' remarks Russell Cole, the Super Pit's general manager. 'We watched it on our new plasma-screen TVs and heard about it as we drove to work in our big new cars.' Across Western Australia, in fact, apart from the closure of Ravensthorpe and a clutch of other nickel mines, it was almost business as usual. 'The boom hit a speed bump. There was a hiccup, that's all,' says Tim Treadgold, a Perth-based mining journalist. Now, once again, all the talk is of skills shortages, and Perth airport is congested with men and women in steel-capped boots and orange shirts, waiting to catch charter flights to far-flung mines.

An effervescent character with thick grey hair and chunky gold jewellery, Ashok Parekh owns the Palace Hotel, as well as extensive mining interests. Keen to distance Kalgoorlie from its hard-drinking, hard-fighting, Wild West image, he declares: 'I've operated hotels and nightclubs here for twenty-two years, and the whole scene has become a lot more family-oriented. There are thirty-two hotels in Kalgoorlie, and only seven would have skimpies [scantily clad barmaids].' Parekh whisks me across to the Palace, to show me its restaurant ('The pepper steak is superb') and the newly renovated Gold Bar, a nightclub. 'Yes, we do have adult entertainment a couple of nights a week,' he says. 'But you're catering for different crowds, like anywhere.'

No doubt the miners of yesteryear would find it difficult to credit that book clubs, wine clubs and repertory theatre are now part of Kalgoorlie's social scene, or that the West Australian Ballet can fill the 750-seat Goldfield Arts Centre – or that the commercial sex business has become so sanitised that the few surviving brothels earn more from showing tourists around than from prostitution. Yet this is still a community with a preponderance of transient, cashed-up single men, and it retains a hard edge: alcohol-fuelled violence persists, and those who transgress Kalgoorlie's unwritten codes are quietly run out of town. Hannan Street on a Saturday night is not a place for the faint-hearted.

Families such as the Mahoneys avoid the pubs. 'The town's got everything for the kids, all the sports facilities you can think of,' says Lecky, who manages a gold dealership with her husband, Ted. Ashok Parekh, who is of Irish and Indian descent, feels 'the people are very welcoming of outsiders ... They don't care who you are, or what you have or don't have.' Perhaps because of its remoteness – seven hours from Perth, four hours from the port of Esperance – Kalgoorlie has acquired the reputation of a resourceful, can-do place. In the early 1990s, frustrated at government delays in building a bypass road to divert heavy vehicles and equipment, residents got together and built it themselves over a long weekend.

Isolation, a common mission and the challenges of living in a semi-desert environment have forged a strong communal spirit. 'It's harsh conditions, and it attracts a certain type: a person who doesn't mind a bit of adversity,' says Ted Mahoney. But there are chasms within this society: between black and white; between 'old Kalgoorlie' and newcomers; between the beneficiaries of mining and those left behind. Propping up the bar of Boulder's decrepit Grand Hotel, a refuge from the forty-degree heat scorching the deserted wide main street, one old-timer, Malcolm Olden, laments: 'In the past everyone was born here, and we worked shoulder to shoulder at the mines. We were a harmonious community. Nowadays we've got a lot more itinerant workers, and they've brought their own morals and code of ethics.'

And while Kalgoorlie flaunts its multiculturalism, the legacy of migration from Italy and the Balkans, relations have not always been peaceful. In 1934 a miner died after a fight with an Italian barman; locals burnt down the pub, along with houses and shops belonging to southern Europeans; two people were killed as two days of riots climaxed in an onslaught on Dingbat Flat, an immigrant neighbourhood. It was one of Australia's worst outbreaks of racial violence, excluding the frontier wars between whites and Aborigines, and it is still remembered as Kalgoorlie's 'day of shame,' according to Bill Bunbury in *Gold: Forgotten Histories and Lost Objects of Australia*.

Elsewhere, Chinese miners bore the brunt of the xenophobia. The Chinese, who landed in Victoria in the early 1850s and pursued the gold rushes anti-clockwise around Australia, were resented for their industriousness, the thoroughness of their mining methods, and their adherence to their own language and culture. The *Ballarat Star* warned in 1866: 'If these heathens who came here to pollute our blood and debauch our young children are not put under severe regulations we may reckon an epidemic sooner or later that may be as deadly as leprosy.' Colonial governments took steps to limit immigration, and the Chinese were banned from new goldfields. However, anti-Chinese protests escalated, and attacks by white miners culminated in a series of riots in 1861 at Lambing Flat (now Young), in central New South Wales.

The hostility unleashed by the presence of the Chinese miners, in particular, reached a high-water mark with the passage half a century later of the *Immigration Restriction Act 1901*, which formed the basis of the White Australia policy. That policy was not formally jettisoned until 1975, and the issues surrounding it – immigration, multiculturalism, racism, Australia's desired ethnic composition – continue to generate profound ambivalence. It seems ironic that China, as the biggest market for Australian minerals, and as a major investor, has become the backbone of the country's mining industry.

*

Rod Wilson is driving back and forth across a patch of red dirt, shovelling up earth with his front-end loader. After stripping off a good layer, he jumps out and walks over the plot, slowly waving his metal detector. When his headphones squeal, he investigates with pick and shovel, but today the only spoils are scraps of lead and a rusty nail. 'That's the way it goes,' says Wilson, a former fox shooter from Deniliquin, in New South Wales. 'You find nothing for a week, then all of a sudden it's payday. I'll never be a multi-millionaire, but as long as I can feed the animals and pay the bills, I'm happy.'

We're in a parched terrain dotted with stunted white gums, just outside Coolgardie, and the earth-moving machinery – not to mention the metal detector – seems about as far removed from the romance of gold as you could get. Wilson, though, is the contemporary embodiment of a tradition dating back to ancient Egypt, and probably before. So long as men have valued gold they have prospected, and the yellow metal has influenced exploration and settlement on every continent – indeed, mining of all kinds has been so important that the prehistoric ages of man are named after the principal tool-making materials. In Australia, there would be no mining industry without the individuals who discovered the great ore bodies subsequently exploited by companies: Kapunda, Mount Bischoff, Mount Lyell, Broken Hill, Mount Isa and, of course, Kalgoorlie. But Wilson's predecessors not only located the first copper, gold, lead, silver, tin, iron, coal, diamonds and so on; they also, some historians believe, helped to mould the national character. Enterprise, optimism, rugged individualism, 'mateship,' lack of deference to authority, belief in a fair go – such qualities, sometimes defined as quintessentially Australian, crystallised, so it is said, on the nineteenth-century goldfields.

And the love of a flutter – which, along with the hope of winning a fortune, drove people to forsake home and family for the hardships of life on the diggings. The early goldminers gambled with each swing of their pick, and for the diggers of today the motivations are not much different. Rod Wilson, who lives in a simple house shaded by peppertrees with his wife, Donelle, and one dog, three cats, two rabbits and a lorikeet, explains: 'We do gold prospecting during the week and Lotto at weekends, so we've got to have a win somewhere along the line.' One of Australia's most successful prospectors, Mark Creasy, spent two decades in the wilds of the Western Australian interior (on one occasion nearly dying of thirst) before uncovering an immensely rich lode, which he sold in 1991 for $115 million. He says: 'It's the game that counts, not the actual pot that you get at the end of it. You just chuck the pot straight back on the table.' Creasy, who is still exploring, although nowadays he employs teams of geologists, adds: 'It's the ambition to succeed at what you've set yourself. It's an intellectual pursuit – you wonder if there's something out there. It's like doing a crossword puzzle or a quiz and getting all the answers right.'

The ground where Wilson forages is only metres from the site of the lucky strike that unleashed one of the world's final gold stampedes. In September 1892 Arthur Bayley rode into Southern Cross, 190 kilometres west of Coolgardie, with 540 ounces of gold, which he and a mate, William Ford, had collected in an afternoon. Prospectors who followed the pair's tracks 'picked up gold as easily as mushrooms,' according to Geoffrey Blainey, and despite Coolgardie soon being eclipsed by Kalgoorlie, the Eastern Goldfields had burst into being. The population of the Golden West, as the colony called itself, nearly quadrupled within a decade, and in 1900 migrants from the east swung an otherwise reluctant Western Australia into voting for federation – a decision that many in the state, with its disproportionate share of the country's mineral wealth, still rue today.

Such was the lure of the new gold that men disembarking from ships walked cross-country from the coast, pushing a wheelbarrow of possessions through thick scrub for hundreds of kilometres. Many were seasoned prospectors, but here, in one of Australia's most distant and inhospitable regions, they encountered the harshest conditions yet. Unlike elsewhere, these goldfields had, for the most part, not been settled by pastoralists; they were thinly populated by white men, and quite apart from the dust, flies and punishing heat, water was so scarce that it was almost as precious as gold. Malcolm Olden, the long-time Boulder resident, says dryly: 'If you asked for a Scotch and water in those days, the publican would pass you the Scotch and keep his hand on the jug of water.' There were recurrent typhoid epidemics, and a visitor in the 1890s reported that 'one half of Coolgardie is kept busy burying the other half.'

The goldminers – whose lives were transformed by the construction of a water pipeline between Perth and Kalgoorlie, recently recognised by the American Society of Civil Engineers as one of the world's great engineering feats – had much in common with the early pioneers; indeed, one of the nation's most noted explorers, Ernest Giles, took to prospecting later in life and is buried in the Coolgardie cemetery. While the new generation of prospectors might be better equipped, the desert environment is just as tough, and the work is still backbreaking. 'But I'm a lot more fortunate than the old-timers: imagine digging a hole in this heat,' remarks Rod Wilson, who wears dirty jeans, a ripped checked shirt and no hat. Occasionally he finds old bully-beef cans. 'You can see where they [the first miners] had their little camps.'

Unlike iron ore, say, which involves huge capital investment, gold can still be mined by individuals. At its most basic, prospecting requires little more than a pick, shovel, panning dish and dolly pot (mortar and pestle); gold has a high value, and it can be liquidated straight away. (When I visited the Perth Mint, a slightly dishevelled man dressed for the bush wandered into the grand limestone building with a nugget for sale.) Not for nothing is gold known as the 'democratic mineral': a creator of hierarchies, it is also a great leveller. For similar reasons, it suits small companies. Silverlake's Chris Banasik says: 'We decided to go into gold – I'm pretty sure the decision was made over a flat white and a plum muffin in a Perth coffee shop – because, from a mining perspective, it was one of the least complicated things to turn into cash. You don't need squillions of dollars and a railway line; the beauty of gold is that within two days of seeing it underground you can pour a bar of gold, and the next day you can sell it to the Mint. There are very few industries or commodities that afford you that kind of instant karma.'

A century and a half after Ophir, gold continues to enthral; some prospectors still dream about Australia's El Dorado, Lasseter's Reef, claimed to have been found in Central Australia in the 1930s. Gold can be hammered into leaf so thin you can see through it. An ounce can be stretched for eighty kilometres without snapping. Nineteen times heavier than water, gold does not rust or tarnish, and it is almost indestructible: most of the gold mined to date – according to the Perth Mint a total of 160,00 tonnes, which could fit into an average family home – is still in circulation. Both currency and commodity, its primary use – apart from in jewellery – is as a store of wealth; much of the gold removed from the ground, at considerable expense, ends up back underground, in vaults.

And although most of the easily accessible gold has been dug up, it is still possible to hit the jackpot. Bill Powell prospects the old-fashioned way: loaming (tracking a gold source by sifting soil); panning off; dollying (crushing rock); and dry-blowing, using air to separate fine gold from dirt. In 1984 Powell made international headlines when he discovered McPherson's Reward, said to be the most significant find for forty years in the Eastern Goldfields. Powell turned down offers of up to $25 million (including one from Alan Bond) but eventually had to sell the mine, and recently resold it to Ashok Parekh and another Kalgoorlie businessman. Now seventy, Powell lives in a modest house in Coolgardie and drives a decade-old ute.

*

Powell is something of a hero to members of the Eastern Goldfields branch of the 105-year-old Amalgamated Prospectors and Leaseholders Association, who gather monthly in a dusty premises in Boulder. The December 2009 meeting, held on a swelteringly hot evening, is sparsely attended; as the APLA's president, Sean Ashcroft, explains: 'A lot of the guys are out in the field, because the gold price is so high.' As flies buzz around, the dozen men and one woman discuss the latest metal detectors and swap rumours about outrageously sized nuggets. 'Anyone else heard about a thirty-ouncer found near Lake Carey?' enquires one veteran prospector, Stuart Hooper. I ask Hooper if he has ever stumbled across anything noteworthy himself. He shrugs and looks embarrassed. 'Not really,' he says. Later, back at my hotel, I notice a newspaper clipping about Hooper's discovery of a 56-ounce nugget, Little Darling, near Coolgardie in 1979.

Bill Powell's father was a prospector who gambled his gold away on the horses; were it not for the kangaroos and rabbits that Powell shot as a boy, his family would have starved. By the age of fourteen, he had his own little mine. 'I never worried about getting rich,' he reflects. 'At different times I've had quite a bit of money, but flash homes and flash motor cars never really interested me. All I wanted was to get a big mine off the ground. I've been wound up by that all my life. If you find a major ore body, you've really achieved something. It's in your blood and you can't leave it alone: you have to keep digging.'

Last year Powell announced he was hanging up his boots. A few months later he put them back on. 'A lot of my old prospector mates are in the cemetery,' he says. 'I used to see them sitting around, and the next thing you knew they were dead. I thought to myself: Don't do that. Get out there and look for a bit more gold.' Does he have gold fever? 'Christ, yes. That's what's wrong with me: I can't get rid of the gold fever; I can't shake it; it's like a bloody disease. I've often said to myself: Why don't I get a little boat and go fishing? But I never do, I just keep going out prospecting. When I finally get to the cemetery I'll still be digging, so long as they bury me standing up.'

At the APLA meeting, much of the conversation is about the array of fees facing prospectors – 'before you can even put your spade in the ground,' Sean Ashcroft complains. There is no open talk of insurrection, but I'm reminded of the tumultuous events at Ballarat, on the Victorian goldfields, 155 years earlier. Heavy-handed policing of the licence system, in a place where the alluvial gold was particularly tricky to mine, is thought to have sparked the 1854 Eureka uprising, which saw diggers draw up a list of political demands, burn their licences, build a stockade and raise the Southern Cross. Up to thirty of them were killed during a dawn attack by the military, along with five soldiers; such was the strength of public feeling that juries refused to convict the thirteen men charged with treason.

White Australia's first and only armed rebellion against colonial authorities, Eureka led to the licence being replaced by a miner's right and miners being given the vote. Mark Twain declared: 'It was a strike for liberty, a struggle for principle, a stand against injustice and oppression.' Over the years Eureka has become loaded with meaning: hailed as the birth of Australian unionism, a milestone on the road to democracy and nationhood, and as the first stirring of republicanism. Some think it speeded up the process that saw every colony bar Western Australia gain 'responsible' self-government between 1854 and 1859. And at Ballarat another layer was added to the myth-making already inspired by the gold rushes. 'For many the diggers stand between the convicts and the Anzacs as landmarks on the road towards a national self-image,' the editors of *Gold* write, and they quote the historian Sir William Keith Hancock's observation in 1930 that Australians 'have acclaimed the diggers as their Pilgrim Fathers, the first authentic Australians ... the fathers of their soldiers.' Australian soldiers are still known as diggers, reflecting the miners' heroic aura, but the navy and white Eureka flag – a version of which was brandished by the Europeans who drove the Chinese off Lambing Flat – has increasingly been commandeered by extremists. In January this year the indigenous filmmaker Warwick Thornton, speaking just before Australia Day, expressed concern that the Southern Cross, used as a guiding beacon by Aboriginal people for 40,000 years, was being deployed as a 'racist nationalist emblem.'

Eureka is a white, male story, and so is the story of Australian goldmining, and of mining generally. Yet there were women on the goldfields, if in relatively small numbers, and there are plenty of female prospectors nowadays. As for the continent's Aboriginal inhabitants: they had been mining the land, for ochre and flint, for tens of thousands of years before the First Fleet arrived. Almost certainly they encountered gold, but since it did not appeal as an ornamental material they left it be. At first perplexed by the Europeans' passion for the yellow metal (according to Derek Elias in *Gold*, the Walpiri people called it 'white man's Dreaming' and equated its subterranean veins with Dreaming tracks), they soon realised its trading potential. Aubrey Lynch, a prospector and Wongatha elder, says: 'As a child in the 1940s I can remember walking around with my mother, speccing for gold, with our hands behind our backs, stooping down to look at the ground. We were speccing for gold to live on, to go and buy tucker. My mother, one of the old tribal ladies, had been doing that most of her life. We also told the mining companies where our people had been picking up gold, then the companies went out and got themselves tenements.'

Although indigenous Australians are scarcely mentioned in accounts of early goldmining, they made some key finds, and no doubt others went unrecorded. In 1871 a stockman, Jupiter Mosman, came across gold-bearing quartz at Charters Towers, which became, for a while, Australia's largest goldfield; in 1932 a cattle hand found gold near Tennant Creek, in the Northern Territory. In addition, as Henry Reynolds writes in *With the White People*:

> Frontier prospectors were often accompanied by, and dependent on, Aboriginal assistants in the same way that explorers and pioneer squatters had been before them. Their bushcraft, tracking ability, and skill at finding water, were all invaluable assets in the interior of the continent and could be directed at seeking evidence of mineralisation in the same way that they were used to find good pastoral country and easy tracks across unknown country.

In a broad sense, the gold rushes were disastrous for indigenous people, bringing them into ever worsening conflict with European settlers. They had already been displaced from their lands by the pastoral industry; now, that process accelerated as waves of fortune-seekers surged inland. In Western Australia, the migration of prospectors from the depressed east in the 1890s led to indigenous workers losing their jobs on stations. By the mid-twentieth century some were employed in mining; Aubrey Lynch worked underground at the Sons of Gwalia mine, 230 kilometres north of Kalgoorlie, in the late 1950s. 'They were only employing non-Aboriginal people at the time,' he recalls, 'but me and another Aboriginal person turned up and asked for jobs and we were taken on. There were a lot of Italians and Greeks there; we were teaching them English.'

Until quite recently, Australian companies made little effort to engage with communities adjacent to mines. Instead, closed towns such as Tom Price – and, more recently, FIFO camps – were built, housing well-paid workers imported from urban centres. The traditional owners of the land that was being dug up were not consulted; sacred sites were mined willy-nilly, and people were prevented from entering leases to take part in ceremonies. Since the mid-1990s the culture has changed, chiefly as a result of the *Native Title Act 1993*, and nowadays companies, as well as negotiating land-use agreements, establish community partnerships and set targets for indigenous employment and training. However, employment levels are still low, and many native-title deals have proved divisive, with just a few families receiving royalties. According to Simon Hawkins, chief executive of the Yamatji Marlpa Aboriginal Corporation, the Pilbara's native-title representative body, payments to titleholders represent less than one-eighth of a per cent of total mining profits; moreover, royalties are paid only on post-1993 mines. 'Iron ore mining in the Pilbara had been going on for thirty years [before that], without any compensation for the impact on Aboriginal country and culture,' he says.

Projects such as the Ranger and Jabiluka mines, which are enclosed by Kakadu National Park, and the recent five-kilometre diversion of the McArthur River, in the Northern Territory's Gulf Country – designed to enable Xstrata to enlarge a huge zinc facility – were approved against the wishes of traditional landowners, and despite massive protests by environmentalists. Decades of uranium royalties from Ranger, amounting to more than $200 million, have failed to improve the lives of the local Mirrar people. As for the McArthur decision, Charles Roche, of the Minerals Policy Institute, which campaigns against environmentally and socially destructive mining, asks: 'Would a mine that involved the diversion of a river with a substantial white community next to it have happened in southern Australia? Would it even have been contemplated?' Just as the Howard government was endorsing the scheme, Roche notes, it was intervening to scupper a proposed mine in Papua New Guinea because it threatened the Kokoda Track.

In Kalgoorlie, not far from the Super Pit and the ceaseless excavations taking place below, is the community of Ninga Mia, with its run-down houses, packs of stray dogs and rusting abandoned cars. It is hard to imagine a greater divide between black and white, haves and have-nots, mainstream and alienated. Ninga Mia is not marked on town maps; no one from the community works at the pit and, according to Geoffrey Stokes, an Aboriginal pastor, the benefits of living next door to one of the world's biggest goldmines consist of 'sweet nothing, beside the pollution and the dust and the noise.' Stokes says, 'Every week we have a funeral in Kalgoorlie: that's our reality. We die of common diseases while the rest of the community gets fat and rich on our inheritance, our birthright.'

Bryan Wyatt, executive director of the Goldfields Land and Sea Council, was roundly condemned in 2001 when he called Kalgoorlie the most racist city in Australia. Wyatt says he was quoting a Murdoch University survey, and he is convinced that, despite a string of reconciliation-based measures, 'not much has changed.' He mentions a 2010 community calendar published by the Kalgoorlie-Boulder Shire Council, full of glossy photographs, not one featuring an indigenous subject. The *Kalgoorlie Miner*, meanwhile, ran a cartoon last year portraying an Aboriginal man as a violent, drunken paedophile. Although I knew a little of the region's hard-boiled attitudes, I was unprepared for the casual – and sometimes brutal – racism of many of the white people I met there. One otherwise genial man told me, 'When I was a boy, niggers had to be out of town and they knew their place. Then they made them equal, gave them drinking rights, and look at the spin-off now. They breed like flies; they are totally non-contributing; they are unemployable.'

In Western Australia many indigenous people feel that the industry, abetted by a royalty-hungry state government, is trampling their rights. Aubrey Lynch, the Wongatha elder, says, 'Exploration is killing a lot of our country, and our cultural ways are being destroyed. Wherever you go in the bush, you see mining pits and the land being cleared for miles around. They destroy our sites; the Super Pit was developed over Dreamtime tracks. Our people are afraid to go out hunting, because they think the kangaroos and goannas are being affected by mining activities – they think the meat will be poisoned.'

Aboriginal employment levels will remain dismal, Brian Wyatt predicts, unless a more imaginative approach is adopted. For instance, working hours in mining – typically, twelve-hour shifts for two weeks, then a week off – effectively exclude indigenous people, who need to participate in cultural business. Wyatt adds: 'But you have to remember there are two different cultures here. For Aboriginal people, it's never been about gaining maximum economic benefit from the land. People don't see why they should have to dig up the ground when they've lived on it and hunted on it and just want to be there on it. And it's very difficult to say to them: "You're living on a goldmine; dig it up, and all your worries will go away." Yet if they don't, someone else will come along, grab all the minerals and become quite wealthy.'

Robin Chapple, a Greens politician who represents the Mining and Pastoral Region in the Legislative Council, believes mining companies have 'never really engaged with the Aboriginal psyche.' By contrast, he says, on the Gove Peninsula, in Arnhem Land, an Aboriginal corporation contracted to truck waste from the Nabalco bauxite mine has many more drivers on its books than it requires – a recognition that some work only intermittently.

Yet the likes of BHP and Rio Tinto have made determined efforts in recent years to build constructive relationships; at the latter's Argyle diamond mine in the Kimberley, indigenous workers make up about a quarter of the workforce, the highest proportion at any Australian mine. Then there are success stories such as that of Daniel Tucker, from the Eastern Goldfields, who – inspired by the High Court's *Mabo* decision – set up a mining and civil contracting firm, Carey Mining, in 1995. Tucker has become one of Australia's few Aboriginal millionaires; more than half of his employees are indigenous, and he has contracts with some of the world's largest companies, including AngloGold Ashanti. Out in the bush, small bridges are built. Aubrey Lynch says: 'We sometimes make camp with the white prospectors. There's a bond between you, regardless of colour.'

*

Sons of Gwalia, where Lynch was employed, opened in 1896 and was, for a long time, the biggest goldmine in Western Australia outside the Golden Mile. Beside it was a flourishing township, with a general store, butcher, bakery, barber shop, guesthouse, swimming pool and state-run hotel. The underground mine was in its early years managed by a young Herbert Hoover, at that time an engineer with a London firm, later to become the thirty-first president of the United States. Shortly before Christmas 1963 the mine closed down, and Gwalia, home to about 1500 people, emptied almost instantly; with no other work available, the miners and their families left on a special train sent up from Kalgoorlie, taking only what they could carry.

Today Gwalia, three hours' drive from Kalgoorlie, is all but a ghost town, its peeling shopfronts and deserted cottages an evocative reminder of the transience of mining. Inside the corrugated-iron dwellings, with their sagging bare floorboards and rotting furniture, the remnants of lives lived half a century ago are preserved, thickly covered in dust: a transistor radio, a patchwork rug, an oil lamp hanging on a wall, a twisted iron bedstead, a cracked mirror, a child's bicycle.

The Eastern Goldfields are strewn with such towns: places like Kookynie, a red-dirt wasteland dotted with the smashed ruins of brick buildings, and tiny Broad Arrow, which in 1900 had eight hotels, two breweries, a stock exchange, two banks and a hospital; only one pub and a few houses remain. These 'shooting star' communities sprang up overnight and, as the gold-seekers moved on, died almost as swiftly. The larger towns have survived as administrative centres but have a similar air of decay: Coolgardie,

Menzies and Leonora, with their broad, silent streets and handsome historic buildings standing next to boarded-up shops and empty lots.

Wandering through them, you marvel not only at the ruthlessness of boom-and-bust, but that this unforgiving region was settled at all. Much as the locals rave about Kalgoorlie ('It's only four hours from the beach,' several told me), they also admit it would not exist were it not for the gold in the ground. 'There'd be no cause to pitch a tent here; you would just keep on riding your horse past it,' declares Malcolm Olden. The same could be said of Mount Isa, Tom Price, Broken Hill and all the other remote towns established solely because of the presence of minerals, and where, over the decades, those born in or drawn to such places have learned to make the best of things. Without mining, the map of Australia would look quite different, and it is unlikely that the nation would have grown at the same pace, or enjoyed such prosperity. Resources accounted for 41.5 per cent of exports, worth nearly $160 billion, in 2008–09. The country is the world's biggest exporter of iron ore, black coal, lead, zinc and alumina. 'If Australia wasn't mining, it would be bankrupt,' says Tim Treadgold, the Perth-based journalist.

The average lifespan of an Australian mine is ten to twenty years. Gwalia's longevity was unusual, and so is the Golden Mile's, but even the Super Pit will not last forever – it is forecast to shut down in 2021. Communities such as Ravensthorpe know the risks of being a one-company town; while Kalgoorlie has diversified into tourism and the supply of mining services and equipment, and while there are dozens of lesser mines within a fifty-kilometre radius, Kalgoorlie Consolidated Gold Mining – KCGM, which manages the Super Pit on behalf of its joint owners, Newmont and the Canada-based Barrick Gold – wields enormous clout. At least twice it has threatened to close operations unless allowed to proceed with controversial plans: to enlarge a tailings dump, and to build a 3.5-kilometre-long conveyor belt.

Both times the company got its way: no one wants to jeopardise the future of a town which, despite laying claim to the richest square mile of earth in the world, has a history of wildly vacillating fortunes. The gold industry lost its gleam early in the twentieth century and, apart from a mini-revival in the 1930s, it ebbed steadily as other commodities took precedence within the Australian economy. In Kalgoorlie, rising production costs led to mine after mine closing, and in the late 1970s the Golden Mile was on the verge of extinction – saved only by the abolition of the fixed gold price and new processing techniques, which made it profitable to mine much lower grades. Mines reopened and the Super Pit was born in 1989, after Alan Bond conceived of buying up all the old underground leases. (Bond was forced to sell his stake when his business empire crumbled.) Bill Powell still recalls goats wandering through empty houses in Boulder; one of his contemporaries, Doug Daws, was among the nearly 800 people who lost their jobs one black day in 1978. 'It's a bloody devastating feeling,' says Daws. 'You got married in the church, you've got kids to bring up – where the hell do you go when you've got a town that is so overwhelmingly consumed by this giant set of mines on your doorstep?'

*

For now, the Super Pit remains Australia's largest open-cut mine; on the opposite side of the country, Newcrest Mining's Cadia Valley gold facility, near Orange, is poised to be the biggest underground mine after an expansion plan was endorsed in January 2010. Generously endowed with minerals and metals, thanks to the age and nature of its rocks and the geological forces at play, Australia had, as of December 2009, the greatest known reserves of uranium, brown coal, nickel, silver, zinc and lead, while its stores of copper, gold, black coal, iron ore, bauxite and industrial diamonds were in the global top five. If a $20 billion development proposal is approved, BHP's Olympic Dam in South Australia – site of the world's largest uranium deposit, as well as gigantic quantities of copper and gold – will become the biggest open-cut mine on the planet: 4.1 kilometres long, 3.5 kilometres wide and up to a kilometre deep. Also on the horizon is the monumental Gorgon liquefied natural gas (LNG) project, off the Pilbara coast, expected to employ 10,000 people and channel $64 billion into the economy over three decades. The coalfields of central Queensland are humming, and geological surveys point to a new Golden Triangle in northern Victoria, with reserves of up to 70 million ounces: nearly as much again as the state's total output since the gold rush began. There is talk of mining space, and the seabed, for gold and minerals. Australia's future is secure, thanks to its natural resources. Or is it?

To say that mining is unsustainable seems to be stating the obvious. If only it were as simple as calculating what is left in the ground and how long it can last – although even that, as it turns out, is far from simple. Resources, clearly, are finite: the moment a mine opens, it begins to die; every ounce of gold mined is an ounce subtracted from the total stores. In its most recent report, Geoscience Australia estimates that stocks of five minerals – diamonds, gold, zinc, lead and manganese ore – will be exhausted within ten to forty years, at current production rates. Those figures could rise (or fall), however, depending on exploration, scientific advances and fluctuating prices; they are also based on identified resources, and it appears likely that Australia will yield more underground riches, even if they are hidden much deeper down. The Perth Mint's Edward Harbuz considers it 'perfectly feasible' that another Super Pit could be found in Western Australia. 'Much of the state is under sand and has never been explored properly,' he says. 'I think we've only just started to extract the minerals of Western Australia.'

Gavin Mudd, a civil-engineering lecturer at Melbourne's Monash University and the author of a study on the sustainability of mining, is convinced that very few commodities will run out in the conceivable future. Nevertheless, he argues: 'It's not how much you've got left; it's the environmental costs of getting it out of the ground and using it. Then you get to the heart of whether the industry is sustainable or not.' As ore grades decline, according to Mudd, increasing volumes of rock have to be moved, consuming ever more energy and water, and creating bigger waste dumps, tailings dams and carbon emissions. In Queensland, ten tonnes of dirt are excavated for every tonne of coal. At Boddington, Newmont is mining ore with less than a gram of gold (the size of a grain of rice) per tonne; a hundred thousand tonnes of rock will be dug up, processed and dumped daily when the site reaches full capacity later this year. Mudd says: 'The pattern of mining for the last hundred years has been bigger trucks, bigger shovels, bigger processing plants. We can't sustain that pattern for the next hundred years.'

Scandals over toxic emissions in towns such as Mount Isa hint at the underside of the mining boom. The Super Pit was one of Australia's largest emitters of cyanide in 2007–08, according to the National Pollutant Inventory, and it topped the league for mercury. Cyanide-laced dams have been blamed for the death of wildlife, including 60,000 budgies in a single incident in the Eastern Goldfields in the 1980s. Waste rock contains sulphides which, when exposed to air and water, turn into sulphuric acid and drain heavy metals into waterways. The Mount Lyell copper mine in western Tasmania is a notorious example: there is no aquatic life in the nearby Queen and King rivers.

In Western Australia waste dumps are vulnerable to erosion by winds sweeping across an arid, mainly flat terrain, according to Robin Chapple, the Greens politician, while the open pits – apart from being eyesores – are a hazard for cattle. Disused pits fill up with groundwater, which can become hyper-saline, contaminating aquifers and killing vegetation. There is no legal requirement to fill in pits and, so far as the Eastern Goldfields are concerned, Chapple believes: 'It's a case of out of sight, out of mind. The perception is it's a desert and it doesn't really matter.' The Goldfields were once well forested, but they were clear-felled for sixty years to supply the mining industry with fuel.

On the other side of the equation, environmental standards, along with worker safety, have vastly improved – although some companies apply different benchmarks overseas; the infamous Ok Tedi mine in Papua New Guinea, for instance, was majority-owned by BHP until 2002. The Minerals Council of Australia says mining disturbs just 0.26 per cent of the landmass, and companies spend at least $200 million a year rehabilitating slag heaps and tailings dams. The new dam at Boddington, set amid incongruously bucolic scenery, is said to have been designed to world's best practice standards; Newmont is also part-funding a program to conserve endangered cockatoos in the surrounding jarrah forest. Some in the industry describe their interaction with the land in intriguingly positive terms. Campbell Baird, of Focus Minerals, calls mining 'creating something ... building underground,' while Silverlake's Chris Banasik speaks of the 'privilege' of observing a rock face before it is blasted. Banasik says: 'You've got to treat it with respect, because what you see will never be the same again, and because those rocks are giving you a sneak peek of processes you can't even imagine. Most ore deposits are formed at between 600 and 1100 degrees Celsius. Most are formed under thousands of metres of rock. Most are made from fluids that have come from twenty-six kilometres down. They've tapped the mantle, the Earth's molten core.'

*

For two weeks in 2006, Australians were transfixed by attempts to rescue Brant Webb and Todd Russell, trapped underground at the Beaconsfield goldmine in Tasmania. A century earlier, the nation had been equally gripped by the fate of Modesto Varischetti, an Italian miner who spent nine days in an air pocket in the flooded Westralia mine, near Coolgardie, before staggering out alive with the help of two divers. Fascination, fear, awe, revulsion: the mining business has always aroused strong emotions in people living in urban and coastal areas. It is viewed as dangerous, dirty, brave work; mining has a mystique, but it also has a poor image because of its effects on the environment, and its questionable ethics in some developing countries. John Bowler, the independent state member for Kalgoorlie, says: 'A lot of people in the cities hate mining, and the industry doesn't sell itself very well; it just gets on with the job of creating wealth. People in the Middle East have a far more positive image, and greater knowledge, of the oil industry than Australians do of mining. The vast bulk wouldn't know and wouldn't care, and some would say: "Close it down; it's raping the landscape."'

Unlike farming, mining is not part of the Australian psyche, nor is it a sacred cow. Competition for limited resources brings it into conflict with farming and with the wider community; in Orange, fruit growers fear the Cadia Valley expansion will jeopardise their water supplies – in 2007 the town had to donate 450 million litres of water to the mine after Newcrest warned that otherwise it would have to shut down. In Western Australia companies complain that the approvals process is slow and cumbersome, and environmentalists claim the industry almost always gets its own way eventually. Barrow Island, off the Pilbara coast, often called 'Australia's ark' because of its profusion of species that are extinct or endangered on the mainland, is to house a massive plant processing LNG from the Gorgon field, despite the state's Environmental Protection Agency expressing grave reservations. On the Pilbara's Burrup Peninsula, the home of Woodside Energy's Pluto gas scheme, ancient rock art remains at risk. On the Kimberley coast Aboriginal leaders are split over plans to build another LNG processing plant, north of Broome, for the Browse Basin field. At other locations around Australia the delicate balancing act between mining, the environment and the rights of communities, particularly indigenous people, continues.

Meanwhile, the digging frenzy goes on, along with the debate about Australia's economic future and such issues as clean energy, water scarcity and a carbon tax. Robin Chapple, who has worked for both BHP and Western Australia's Mines Department, is one of many voices disputing the notion that the country's resources are infinite, or as good as. 'Our problem is that we actually believe mining will last forever,' he says. 'What are you going to be doing as a nation when you can't mine, or make mining equipment, or do all the other things associated with mining? Do we have a plan? We don't, because governments of the day can't think beyond the next election.'

The flipside of gold fever is greed, and in the nineteenth century some commentators were perturbed by the rampant materialism associated with the rushes. A letter to the Melbourne *Argus* in 1852, quoted by David Goodman in *Gold*, demanded: 'Should Gold, Gold, Gold, be our only desire? … Was man made merely to acquire glittering metal … Is there no higher object, no more noble aim?' In rather more sober language, the Minerals Policy Institute's Charles Roche questions the philosophy behind modern mining practice, which he describes as 'ripping the minerals out of the ground as quickly as possible, without lasting benefit to local communities.' Roche suggests that deposits could be mined sequentially, rather than all at once, enabling people to move to a place and build lives, assured of long-term job prospects. He says: 'I believe that the minerals belong to all of us, current generations and future generations, rather than to a particular mining company. Often the benefits leave the site and the problems remain there.' A May 2009 report by the Australia Institute, a left-leaning think-tank, reached a similar conclusion: 'Overall the mining boom seems to have had very little positive impact on the wellbeing of the majority of Australians other than those directly affected by the expansion in the mining industry.'

A few decades ago, Kalgoorlie was peppered with headframes, and the town consisted of separate neighbourhoods, each one centred on a mine. Over time they were all consolidated into what became Kalgoorlie-Boulder – except for one, Williamstown, which sits sandwiched between the Super Pit and Mount Charlotte, the sole surviving underground operation. A bleak, sunbaked spot, Williamstown is Kalgoorlie's other forgotten community – although, unlike Ninga Mia, it does appear on the map, and is even pointed out as a curiosity to visitors on bus tours.

Callers to KCGM's 'Public Interaction Line' are greeted by a recorded message advising them to 'please press 2 … for today's blasting times.' In Williamstown, Keren Calder points to widening cracks in her living-room wall. 'When there's a big blast, the whole house shakes and it feels like the floor's going to cave in,' she says. 'All the pictures are at an angle, and I've had ornaments fall off the shelf and smash. Visitors get a hell of a fright. The dust is diabolical, too – if I don't sweep my floor every day, it's like someone has emptied a vacuum cleaner over it.' Cheri Raven hears drilling beneath her feet when she takes a shower. 'Sometimes it sounds so close you think a miner's going to pop up the plughole.' Like her neighbours, Raven is certain that KCGM – which has already bought and bulldozed houses in the suburb – would like Williamstown to fade into history. 'But I'm not moving; it doesn't matter how much money they offer me,' she vows. 'My grandparents lived here; my husband and I were both raised here; I've got history here.'

Tony Cooke, an adjunct professor at the John Curtin Institute for Public Policy in Perth, was commissioned by the Western Australian government to report in 2004 on the gold industry's impact on Kalgoorlie. He says that valuable ore bodies lie beneath residential streets, and he predicts some households in Boulder will have to move as mining activity creeps closer. (KCGM denies it.) Cooke also maintains that the area is unstable because of decades of shaft mining: one person 'lost their washing and Hills Hoist into a hole that just opened up in the back garden,' he says, and even cars have been gobbled up. Seismologists, meanwhile, blame mining activity for some of the tremors that periodically shake Kalgoorlie. 'It feels like the Super Pit is swallowing up the town,' says Steve Kean, a Williamstown resident.

Others, in Kalgoorlie and beyond, remain dazzled by gold and its seemingly limitless potential. Tyler Mahoney, Ted and Lecky's fourteen-year-old daughter, found a sliver lying in a puddle in Hannan Street recently, a few hundred metres from the site of Paddy Hannan's strike. In 1995, near Coolgardie, in ground that had been intensively worked for more than a century, the second-largest gold nugget in existence – the Normandy Nugget, weighing more than 800 ounces – was discovered. The mine at Gwalia, already reborn once in the 1980s, reopened in 2008, and historic mining towns such as Bendigo and Charters Towers are once again producing gold. Boom and bust, winners and losers, elation and heartbreak: Australia's love–hate relationship with the mining industry shows no sign of waning.

Griffith Review

John Masefield's Attic

Alex Miller

'This is curious,' said M'sieur Pierre. 'What are these hopes, and who is this saviour?'
'Imagination,' replied Cincinnatus.
—Vladimir Nabokov, *Invitation to a Beheading*

In an email to a friend last year I wrote: 'I'm struggling to move my novel forward. It's giving me a hard time at the moment. But they always make us pay our dues sooner or later. So this is not really unexpected. After all, I've been having a good run with it for quite a while. Now for some deeper probing. The problem with the book is my own doing. I can't bear to take the material for granted; and having written a draft, I have to begin questioning it and erasing it. I don't seem to be able to do it any other way. I'm not as persistent as Giacometti in erasing my works in progress, but I do understand Giacometti's visceral reluctance to believe in what he had created until it had begun to shine for him with a kind of light that was not his own. Without this sense of surprise about what we have done there is no mystery in what we do. And I happen to agree with the spirit of Lorca's "only mystery makes us live." So here I am again this morning attacking what I've done so far with this book as if it were the work of my deadly enemy and I were determined to tear it to pieces.'

We are all born with an imagination. Imagination is not the preserve of a few. Sidney Nolan's muse and mentor, Sunday

Reed, reminded us that 'childhood means creativity.' And it was Coleridge – in T.S. Eliot's view the greatest critic of the imagination – who said in his 'Dejection: An Ode': 'What nature gave me at my birth / My shaping spirit of imagination.' The image of children in a kindergarten sitting on the floor surrounded by their creations is not new. 'Behold the child among his new-born blisses,' Wordsworth wrote. 'See, where 'mid work of his own hand he lies.'

What happens to the imagination in adulthood – the degree to which we are unable or unwilling to forget our childhood liberties – is crucial to our mature creativity. For most adults their creativity is no match for the demands of daily life; or its relatively mild demands are satisfied by daily life, by work and family.

The imagination of the writer or artist, however, persists into adulthood and continues to demand full attention. It's not surprising, therefore, that we often find something childlike in the petulant and self-centred world of the artist, the poet or the novelist.

Creative people often seem compelled to strive to become their own universe, even though they know such a state is not achievable. They have an idealised inner world that demands expression. The artist's attempts at a modest conventional life often fail in the face of the demands of the imagination, combined with ambition and ego. Nolan abandoned his first wife and child to live at Heide, where he was as dependent on the Reeds as the child they did not have, and where they gave his creativity an absolute value. It was just too good an offer to pass up and the conventional morality had to give way. At Heide Nolan became an indulged child, his only remaining responsibility to create art.

In his *On the Aesthetic Education of Man in a Series of Letters*, the German poet Friedrich Schiller makes the point that in dealing with a subject such as aesthetics, 'one is compelled to appeal as frequently to feelings as to principles.' Beauty, aesthetics, art, the products of the creative imagination, depend in great part on our education and cultural situation, even though they are often manifestly in dispute with it. But most deeply our creative products depend for their effects, as Schiller suggests, on our emotional response. Education is essential in matters of the imagination but a search for critical or theoretical objectivity in art is profitless. When artist and critic Adrian Lawlor famously claimed that Nolan's painting *The Boy and the Moon* was not art, he put himself 'into the impossible position of having to demonstrate what is not art,' as art historian Richard Haese put it.

So, given the deeply subjective nature of any appreciation of what the creative imagination does, this essay will be a personal meander rather than an attempt to mount an argument for a particular aesthetic.

The word 'meander' takes its meaning from the name of a winding river in ancient Phrygia, now part of Turkey. Many of the most suggestive and fruitful ideas that strike our imagination, and which have a durable currency in our cultural reference, are based on observations of nature. In referencing nature there is a feeling that we are touching on truth.

Nolan expressed this need to stay in touch with reality when he said: 'There is an unbreakable reality of situations; a need for some immersion in reality to escape the trivial, fanciful and obsessive.' It was Nolan's early response to the rural landscape, to the natural world and not the urban landscape of his upbringing, that gave him his material for the rest of his life.

The human imagination, even in a digital post-modern world, finds sustenance in the assurance of nature's reality. In even the most fanciful of work there must be a bedrock of reality from which the imagination takes flight. There is a kinship between nature and the human imagination and it is deep, enduring and real. This is an aspect of our humanity and extends beyond nature to the facts of human history and culture. Nancy Underhill, in her splendid 2007 collection *Nolan on Nolan: Sidney Nolan in His Own Words*, writes of Nolan's imagination activating 'the ambiguous space between history and myth.' This is almost always what serious novelists attempt. To see the familiar face of their life and times as unfamiliar. And in this, the response of the creative person is necessarily inward. For the artist and the writer address themselves finally in the act of creation.

The novel, no matter how realist its manner, is not a blueprint for 'real' life but is artifice. Fiction is finally invention, no matter how realistic or 'truly' historical its claims to represent reality. The novel is a work of the imagination. Movement in art and literature is never forwards or backwards but is always towards a centre. Each age not only encourages and celebrates certain forms of art and literature but also suppresses regions of the psyche and the imagination. In its seeking, our imagination is never wholly free from the fashionable forms of representation. Creative autonomy is a myth. Perhaps an ideal. But no matter how 'original' a work, it is always of its own time and the passage of time reveals its complex dependency.

Forms of representation are as fundamental to literature as they are to the visual arts. The greatest critic to have discoursed at length on this is Erich Auerbach in *Mimesis: The Representation of Reality in Western Literature.* 'Dante,' Auerbach writes, 'used his language to discover the world anew.' That is, Dante did not create a new world but revealed the unfamiliar in the familiar world.

Writing a novel is rewriting; it is revisiting a familiar place time and again and seeing it anew each time. Beginning the writing of a novel is entering a puzzle, a maze whose centre is unknown to the author. In the beginning the novelist's world is without form. This does not mean the novelist is without subject or is without material, but only that the novelist cannot know what he or she is going to come across before the intricacies of the work have been witnessed and it has assumed its final shape.

With a novel, as with the exploration of a maze or a labyrinth, it is not a matter of reaching a conclusion, but of finding the centre. It is the centre that satisfies us. When it is reached the novel is abandoned. It may look finished but that is artifice, craft.

*

You want to write, you want to make art, but what is to be your subject? How are you to know your subject? When I was a young would-be writer I knew I had a statement to make, but what was it to consist of? Having the desire to be a writer but not knowing what to write about is the principal dilemma of many young writers. But what does the imagination have to do with knowing your material? It was all a mystery to me. I thought that if my desire to write was authentic then I ought to know what it was I wanted to write about. If I were going to write, I believed I should not only have something to say but should know what it was I wanted to say.

All the great novelists I was reading – Proust, Dostoyevsky, Iris Murdoch, Doris Lessing, Patrick White and so on – seemed to have known what they wanted to write about from the beginning. This of course was my misunderstanding. *The Grass Is Singing*, Lessing's astonishing first novel, read – and we all read it – as if it had been written in her heart before she attempted to set it down on paper. What did I have to say, I asked myself, that might correspond to such a work? I stared at the blank page and saw nothing written in my heart, except a yearning to write. Was I really a writer? The question tormented me. I needed an answer.

On the perennial debate about the death of the novel, it's worth remembering that the novel is just another way of telling our stories. We will always find ways to tell our stories, if not through the form of the novel then through other forms yet to be imagined. I grew up in a family where storytelling, though not story writing, was a nightly occurrence. Telling a story is an improvisational form, like jazz, whereas the written story is the product of reflection, like written music. Although it may contain long passages of spontaneous composition, the written story, especially in the long narrative form, is essentially the product of endless rewriting and reconsidering.

From early childhood I had been a storyteller but as an adult it took me a long time to find my material as a story writer. I discovered it wasn't a matter of simply deciding what to write about. There had to be something else or the written work lacked a life of its own. As Simone de Beauvoir said, 'We cannot arbitrarily invent projects for ourselves: they have to be written in our past as requirements.'

The reason we can't simply invent projects for ourselves is that the imagination is ignited by something other than our conscious decisions. I think of writing as a conversation with the unconscious; being open, that is, to the prompts of the imagination. Like Klamm in Franz Kafka's novel *The Castle*, no matter how hard we try we are never going to meet this elusive entity face to face, but we know its influence rules our lives. The prompts, however, are not always forthcoming. 'My work is resisting me at the moment,' I wrote recently to a friend who had asked how things were going. 'I dwell with it in a kind of anteroom of the imagination. I know it's down there but I can't force it.' The imagination will not be coerced.

It took me years to find my authentic material. One of my English tutors at the University of Melbourne in the early 1960s was the academic David Moody. I admired David and he and I became friends. Later I visited him at Oxford, where he had gone to take up a tutorship and where he lived with his wife, Pippa, who was some kind of medievalist. I liked Pippa but I never understood what it was that she did, and I think there was something of the Oxford spirit about this generous vagueness; the encouraging sense that motives and intentions didn't have to be clear or well-planned to be interesting. I had not encountered this before. It was my first inkling of the importance of the spirit of the meander: an openness to the unexpected prompt from the imagination.

David and Pippa were living in John Masefield's cottage. Pippa told me the attic was filled with old stuff that had been accumulating for generations. One afternoon she suggested she and I explore the attic. David, with his New Zealander's cautious excess of propriety, wouldn't permit it. I am still fascinated by thoughts of what Pippa and I might have discovered together in Masefield's attic. Klamm retains his fascination so long as we don't come face to face with him. Instead of exploring the attic, David reminded us that Eliot was reading 'Burnt Norton' on the BBC that afternoon. There was some discussion about where they had put the wireless since they'd last used it. Eventually it was brought out of a cupboard, where it had been found under some blankets.

When the wireless was plugged in and switched on and had warmed up, David was able to get only a hissing sound from it. Pippa reminded him that he needed to set up the aerial. Another search of the house. I suggested I might look in the attic for the aerial but was politely ignored. Eventually the aerial was found and David attached it and tried various positions for it. Hissing and sounds of voices in distant rooms.

A cryptic chord or two of Wagner, was it? Then, suddenly, the clear upper-class voice of the announcer telling us that Mr Eliot would read his poem 'Burnt Norton,' the first of his great *Four Quartets.* So Eliot's sepulchral tones began to enunciate the exact perceptions of his arresting lines, 'Time present and time past / Are both perhaps present in time future.' Even then he seemed to read to us from the tomb.

Like Coleridge 100 years before him, Eliot was impressed by Schiller's ideas of aesthetics. Yet though he ranked Coleridge with the greatest literary critics, Eliot was not a romantic himself but a modernist symbolist who believed the artist should engage with the political actualities of the day. But Eliot was also possessed of that complex humility that acknowledged the debt his work owed to the work of others. Coleridge, he wrote, 'was rather a man of my own type, differing from myself chiefly in being immensely more learned, more industrious, and endowed with a more powerful and subtle mind.' Like Nolan, Eliot believed in 'the need for some immersion in reality.' Eliot also believed in the need to know history. Facts and accurate observation, in play with his imagination, provided the material of his social philosophy as well as of his poetry. Sunday Reed, speaking of Nolan's Wimmera paintings, recognised that the strength in this new work 'was because it was beginning to root itself in fact.' Imagination alone, Nolan was discovering, is not enough to render our imaginative creations convincing to others.

David, Pippa and I sat in front of the wireless in reverent silence, our hands clasped, our heads bowed, and we listened to the great man reading to us. I'm no fan of Eliot's social criticism but the force of his poetry is not to be withstood. After the reading Pippa and I began to toss out hints about the attic again, but David insisted we all go out into the field behind the cottage, with Eliot ringing in our minds, and imagine Coleridge's great friend, Wordsworth, being inspired to write about daffodils. The sloping field behind Masefield's cottage was, David told us, the very place where Wordsworth had been inspired to write his poem.

David wished to remind us we were in the kingdom of the great British romantics, those beneficiaries of Kant and Schiller, and eventual inspirers of M.H. Abrams's great book on romantic theory and the critical tradition, *The Mirror and the Lamp*, itself the inspiration for many of the wonderful essays in Harold Bloom's *Romanticism and Consciousness*, particularly those on Blake, Wordsworth and Coleridge, and of course Mary Warnock's books and a thousand others. There is a library of such books and their derivatives, and some of them are even fun to read. But no one has read them all. The creative imagination, as an idea, has a library to itself. We stood in the field behind Masefield's cottage staring at the grass and imagining; it was the middle of summer and too late or too early for daffodils. I saw only grass and the emptiness of my own imaginative nest.

David knew I was reading English and history in order to become a novelist. He knew I was at the university not so that I could qualify for a job in the real world but because I wanted to have some knowledge of the history of the culture to which I belonged, and of the great works of literature that had been written within and preserved by this culture. After a long meditative silence in the field, he turned to me and asked what it was that I wanted to write about. I dreaded this question from him. It exasperated David that I couldn't answer it. 'I don't know,' I said helplessly, not even inspired enough to lie.

Pippa smiled at me and that made me feel a bit better. She never asked me what I wanted to write about. She was an Oxford person and seemed to understand that it was as important to not know some things as it was to know some other things. Pippa was the first person I had ever met who seemed to think it perfectly proper and authentic of me not to know what I wanted to write about. Life, I might have said if she had asked. But she didn't. Not knowing, however, made me fear I was a charlatan. Especially with Eliot, Wordsworth and John Masefield all singing their enchantments in my ears in the field of the famous 'Daffodils.' I just wanted to find a pub for the afternoon.

*

The discovery of one's material and the awakening of one's imagination are indivisible. It is Proust, in *Time Regained*, who most beautifully deals with this complex event in an inspired passage of something more than 100 pages, of which I will quote just a bit:

> And then a new light, less dazzling, no doubt, than that other illumination which had made me perceive that the work of art was the sole means of rediscovering Lost Time, shone suddenly within me. And I understood that all these materials for a work of literature were simply my past life; I understood that

> they had come to me, in frivolous pleasures, in idleness, in affection, in unhappiness, and that I had laid them up in store without divining the purpose for which they were destined or even their continued existence … And I began to perceive that I had lived … without ever realising that my life needed to come into contact with those books which I had wanted to write and for which … I had been unable to find a subject.

Proust's frivolous meandering has brought him unexpectedly, and by means of a brilliant prompt of the imagination, to a realisation of his material and at once his imagination is ignited and his lassitude and boredom are forgotten. That the novel is about the intimate lives of us holds true from Proust to James Joyce to Georgette Heyer. The novel may be about everything else as well as us, but at its heart it is about us and the trivial intricacies of our private lives.

It was through other writers, Peter Mathers and the Melbourne poet and bookseller Kris Hemensley among them, but in particular my friend Max Blatt, that I eventually located a confident sense of my own material and began to know the joy of writing. Max was a central European intellectual of the kind J.P. Stern and W.G. Sebald write about with such beautiful nostalgic elegance and familiarity. Max interpreted modern European history to me in ways I was not encountering at the university. His confidence that my desire to write was the sign of an authentic vocation despite my confusions about my material was critical to me. It saved me from despair.

Some years later I bought a farm in the Araluen Valley in New South Wales in order to make a living in a way that would enable me to write more or less full-time. While I was on the farm, and over a period of years, I wrote three pre-novels. Max used to catch the train to Goulburn, then a taxi the 150 kilometres or so from there to my isolated farm. He would stay with me for a week or two at a time. I had other friends and visitors, but I looked forward to Max's visits with a special kind of joy and dread. The dread was that my writing would not please him.

He arrived one wintry day and soon asked me about my writing. I had just finished the 400-page manuscript of a novel. He asked to see it. When I handed him the great wad of A4 sheets

I knew this was not a novel Max would admire, and I felt a sense of failure and dismay. I had spent the previous two years largely in isolation, working on the book ten hours a day, six days a week. For the rest of the day and well into the evening, Max sat on the closed-in back veranda reading my novel. Pacing up and down the kitchen, unable to put my mind to anything, I thought I would never hear the last page being set beside his chair. Max read every word. My anxiety exhausted me and by the evening I was slumped at the table with my head on my arms. I was woken by the thump of the 400 pages landing beside my head. I sprang up. Max was lighting a cigarette. With a mixture of disappointment, frustration and regret, he said, 'Why don't you write about something you love?'

And here is Proust again: 'It is sometimes just at the moment when we think that everything is lost that the intimation arrives which may save us.' It was as if Max had opened a door in my kitchen that I had not noticed before, and had revealed to me the vast landscape of all that I loved waiting for me to get on with the job of writing about it. I had been writing for years about what I thought I ought to be writing about. Max could not understand why I was so overjoyed with his angry dismissal of my book. But he had freed me. For the first time in my life I knew myself to be at liberty to write about the most precious and intimate things in my life and in the lives of those I cared about, instead of being required to write about the important social issues of the day. It was a huge relief.

Why did I believe Max? I did believe him, that's what's important, not why I believed him. Why did he believe in me? These are questions without answers.

Visitors arrived later that day and there was a lively discussion around the kitchen table about anti-Semitism. When the visitors had gone, Max told me the story of his escape from an anti-Semitic attack in Poland at the beginning of World War II. He told me the story so that I would understand that anti-Semitism had not been for him a matter for idle intellectual debate in his youth but one of daily survival. He told me the simple bones of the story in a few sentences. I did not sleep that night but wrote the story in detail and in the morning I gave it to him to read. This time, when he took the pages from me, I knew he would like it. I loved Max and had written through the night with a feeling of intense joy in the necessity of the story. When he had finished reading it, he said with feeling, 'You could have been there,' and embraced me. The story was published in *Meanjin* with the ironic title 'Comrade Pawel.' It was my beginning.

But what was it that enabled me to write that story convincingly? The setting, a trench in Poland at the beginning of World War II, was outside my experience. I had no references for the detail, and yet the story is filled with detail, even to the type of woollen cap worn by the men. What did Max mean, 'You could have been there'? I took him to mean, and I am confident he did in fact mean, that my account of the events that had happened to him when he was a young communist in Poland at the beginning of the war was for him an authentic account, one that conveyed the truth of his experience. It was the first occasion on which I had written above myself, and my surprise and gratitude were great. I had yet to understand Paul Valery's remark that 'Every individual is inferior to his most beautiful work.'

Why did I believe, and why do I still believe, that this story was mine? What made it mine? The short answer, and a good one, to this question, was given by the Indian poet Rabindranath Tagore, quoted in Simon Leys's wonderful little book, *Other People's Thoughts*. 'As soon as a thing gives me pleasure,' Tagore said, 'it becomes mine, whatever its origins may be.' And Nabokov, in his novel *Laughter in the Dark*, says memorably of his character Albinus, 'he made it his own by liking it, playing with it, letting it grow upon him, and that goes to make lawful property in the free city of the mind.'

The spirit of amplitude in Tagore's and Nabokov's responses is not to be understood by the literal-minded, but can only be sensed amply. The gift of story is finally mysterious.

*

When it is facts and the truth that are being talked about by historians and philosophers, the creative imagination is sometimes seen as problematic, if not downright suspect. A journalist interviewing Bruce Chatwin about his book *In Patagonia* asked him where the division lay between fiction and non-fiction. I like Chatwin's answer: 'I don't think there is one. There definitely should be one, but I don't know where it is.' V.S. Naipaul, in his inspired memoir on becoming a writer, *The Enigma of Arrival* – which he called a novel to alert us to the fact that he was not including all the facts of his situation – would surely have agreed with Chatwin. Fiction bows to the imagination and bends the truth in order to get closer to it, and in bending the truth it creates distortions and transgressions, but it also arrives at perspectives on ourselves not otherwise available.

When we read Sebald's books we are never sure whether we are reading fiction or non-fiction. But who would care to find out? The best questions need no answers but are insights in themselves. The rich spirit of Sebald's work lies within an almost infinitely flexible dimension of reality and dream, and we are mesmerised, transported, convinced and grateful.

*

We can't consciously call up the ability to write above ourselves, however, and often the opposite, the lassitude and boredom, prevail. I wrote recently to a friend, 'When I try to think of the work I know I must do on this book there is a total silence in my head and I can find no motivation for doing it. I have experienced this imaginative lethargy before; it is as if the imagination has left and has closed the door. A psychologist friend says these empty periods are the precursors of good stuff making its way up out of the dark. I wish I could believe her. It's hard not to panic.'

Since 'Comrade Pawel' I've continued to write about what I love and have always written to be worthy of Max's expectations. If you write about what you love, and you love widely, life and people, you will never run out of material. As Christina Stead noticed, 'It is an ocean of story.' Unlike David, Max didn't ask me impatiently what I wanted to write about, he asked me why I didn't write about what I loved.

Enthusiasm, joy, energy and imagination, the vividness of memories, all are necessary to each other and are inseparable from one another in the creative act. And when we look back on what we have written, the best of it, we ask ourselves, 'How could I have done that? How could I have written that? It's beyond me.' Just as it was beyond Proust when his mood of lassitude and boredom was in the ascendancy. Getting beyond ourselves is what the creative imagination is all about. Wordsworth – whose work in one sense focused so much on himself – expressed it when he said, 'He waxeth wiser than himself.' Wordsworth's whole epic project, as he announced loudly, was to make the growth of the self the subject of epic. My point is that even someone whose epic ambition was to write the story of the self knew that to do it he had to get beyond himself.

Inspiration, that igniting of the imagination that enables us to write beyond ourselves, so that our work shines for us with a light that is not our own, is most often an inner response to a stimulus from outside, some trivial event that triggers memory and alters our mood. It is the source of Lorca's mystery. It is what sustains our interest. But when we consciously go in search of inspiration, it stubbornly eludes us. I'll let Proust have the final word on this:

> … one knocks at all the doors which lead nowhere, and then one stumbles without knowing it on the only door through which one can enter – which one might have sought in vain for a hundred years – and it opens of its own accord …

Australian Literary Review

The Angry Country

Melissa Lucashenko

This is what we know about the death of Jai Morcom.

On the morning of 28 August 2009, Jai, a fifteen-year-old Year 9 student, was involved in a fight at Mullumbimby High School, in far northern New South Wales. After being knocked to the ground in an argument about a lunch table just after eleven, he lost consciousness. Other kids told reporters that Jai, lying collapsed on the ground outside the girls' toilets where the fight ended, was 'frothing at the mouth.' First aid was given by a nurse and 000 was called. An ambulance then took Jai to hospital on the Gold Coast.

Two days later the popular young student, never having regained consciousness, was taken off life support. The school went immediately into crisis management, issuing a script for teachers to read out in class concerning the incident, as an urban media pack poured into the quiet rural town, whose population normally hovers around 3000.

Nearly four months later, in December, police issued a statement asking the Mullumbimby community to come forward with more information. Despite a protracted investigation, with Gold Coast detectives interviewing more than seventy MHS students and staff, no clear picture has yet emerged of why Jai left for school that morning assuring his mother that yes, he had his lunch money, and never returned home.

Despite the fight (variously reported in the national media as a 'brawl,' a 'bashing' and a 'savage attack') having occurred during recess, with up to 200 witnesses in the immediate vicinity, no mobile-phone coverage of the fight – as opposed to its aftermath – has been handed to police. Few in the small hinterland town of farmers, hippies and tree-changers are saying anything, and Jai's anguished parents still have no way of knowing exactly how, or why, their son was killed.

A child's death at a school – any school – is a particular kind of tragedy. Schools are meant to be special places for children. It is the essence of a school, at least in theory, that it nurtures and supports young people as it educates them; aggressive acts are more of an affront at schools than in most other settings. This notion of schools as scholarly safe havens must be tempered by the reality, though, that all high schools contain volatile young teenagers, and that school – particularly schoolyard – conflicts are inevitable. Kids have always clashed in the playground and probably always will. Six short months after Jai Morcom died, another eruption of adolescent conflict saw twelve-year-old Elliot Fletcher fatally stabbed at St Patrick's school in bayside Brisbane. Elliot's death, over which a thirteen-year-old straight-A student has been charged, starkly raises the question of whether adolescent boys may have most of the reasons of adult men to clash, but very few of the negotiating skills which adults are supposed to have developed to avoid disaster.

The harsh reality that no school can ever wholly protect our kids from those who would harm them was abruptly swept aside in the torrent of reaction to Jai's death. Journalists evicted from the Mullumbimby school grounds perched at its gate with telephoto lenses, and headlines blazed 'Schoolboy Beaten to Death During Recess.' Speculation and outright fabrication was published as fact; some of the reportage was sufficiently mendacious to prompt an episode of ABC TV's *Media Watch*.

Unsurprisingly, many in the town and in the media took the line that the death was an outcome of pure thuggery. Bullying became the hot topic that week. Facebook ran wild with hang-'em-high writers urging the cane, military service and the gallows as solutions to endemic 'gang violence' in schools.

Gossip and speculation also whirled about Byron Shire as the school strove to maintain some semblance of authority. In an odd coincidence, the MHS grounds, which border Saltwater Creek, were being fenced with standard-issue black six-foot spike-topped panels when Jai's death occurred. This immaculate new security fence was handy in keeping the school grounds – previously unfenced and frequently deserted by MHS students streaming to and from the town centre, a few hundred metres away – inviolate from media and other unwanted scrutiny. The irony of a highly visible six-foot steel fence keeping out the dangers of the world, when it was inside the school grounds that Jai had been killed, was not easily missed.

In the immediate aftermath of Jai's death, the security fence kept out everyone but staff, investigating police and those few students who turned up to class (school attendance records show entire classes absent the following week, with 'unexplained' marked against dozens of names). A friend of mine who tried to sign his son in to the school was stopped at the gate by quickly imported security in the first week of September. Eventually the security guard realised he was a genuine parent, not a predatory journalist, and allowed him, fuming, into the grounds.

What the new security regime couldn't possibly stop, though, was the rumour mill, which continues to grind away months later, with devastating results for community morale. With no charges laid, and an open finding at the preliminary inquest, Mullumbimby still has nothing concrete to draw upon to explain the tragedy. An undercurrent of fear is present; I was warned by one concerned mother close to the incident to 'be really careful' in researching this story. Every possible scenario to explain Jai's death is being canvassed throughout this small and once close-knit community. A representative sample:

One former Mullum High parent told me the kids believed to be the perpetrators include 'real head-cases going fast down a real bad road'; another local added that some are from families suffering mental illness, 'really off with the fairies.'

No, I was told by a junior MHS staff member, it's impossible to know who was responsible, since it was a melee – nobody knows exactly what happened, nor will we ever.

A common conversational thread is that the fight erupted between a gang of football thugs and a bunch of younger Emo kids. Jai was hit once, say some, his head striking the wall as he fell, and that was the end of it. Or perhaps Jai was knocked to the ground and then assaulted multiple times, kicked and punched by a gang of older boys while unconscious. The autopsy showed multiple blows to his body, others claim – including Jai's father, Steve Drummond, in an open letter to the local newspaper, the *Byron Shire Echo*. Alternatively, the body was unmarked.

One former teacher told me with rolling eyes that the conspiracy theories have gone so far as to suggest that the Gold Coast Titans football club, based an hour to the north, has, along with police, had a hand in suppressing the truth about the death, in order to protect some budding Rugby League talent in the town.

A disaffected Year 10 student I picked up hitchhiking towards his new life as an apprentice in a nearby town was strongly attached to the fantasy he recounted: the boy responsible for killing Jai had already been charged, and was now locked up in juvie (neither is true). Furthermore, he said, outlining a sensational picture of hard drug use by students, 'the teachers don't care – they've just given up. They can't control anything.'

What the staff of Mullumbimby High certainly can't control is the demographic mix which turns up on their doorstep each year with the new intake. My daughter attended Mullum High for four years in the mid-2000s. She learned in classrooms where the children of fifth-generation cane and cattle farmers sat next to kids whose parents had fled the cities to find cheap hilly land on which to smoke dope and build permaculture gardens while awaiting world peace. This group is still relatively small in Mullumbimby, which is equidistant between Narrabri and Nimbin on the Rainbow Scale, and is a demographic increasingly squeezed out by the arrival of cashed-up southern yuppies doing a sea change. (House prices in Mullumbimby more than doubled in the past five years.)

Nevertheless, the hippies have imparted a distinct countercultural flavour to the town centre, with Santos Wholefoods selling organic everything a couple of doors up from the booming real estate offices, and yoga classes and spiritual healings a dime a dozen. Dreadlocked buskers are common in the main street, and the Mullumbimby Medical Centre may be the only doctor's surgery in the world whose staff – yes, the doctors – have happily posed naked (in a 2003 calendar to raise money for the local hospital). And I somehow think it was a hill-dweller, not a cane farmer, who wrote in the school's condolence book that the attitude of Steve Drummond – in the early days after his only son died, one of forbearance and forgiveness – was 'surely the action of the Buddha and the Christ and the love of the Angels made manifest.'

A good percentage of local alternative lifestylers – who live in the isolated hills surrounding Mullumbimby, popularly supposed to mean 'rounded hills' in Bundjalung, up to half an hour's drive from town on potholed dirt roads that wreck your cheap car – send their kids to the Shearwater Steiner school. The Steiner school sits on its own pretty acreage five kilometres further inland, but it is a private school, and it costs. Those parents who won't, or can't, pay the fees have no other convenient high school to turn to. Once at MHS, the twelve-year-olds from, say, Upper Main Arm are asked to leave behind their primary-school uniform – a tie-dyed rainbow T-shirt, shoes optional – and meld into a school population of close to a thousand jostling kids of all descriptions.

*

Up until December 2009, Richard Heazlewood-Ross was the avuncular and well-liked deputy head of Mullum High. When I spoke to him, he was on the cusp of retirement, looking forward to getting more heavily involved with the marginalised kids who are his passion through the Byron Community College. With the support of Southern Cross University in Lismore, the college operates much like alternative schools in the cities. It remains strongly linked to MHS and delivers its courses through distance education modules. The community college began in Byron Bay, but also operates now through 'The Hut' youth centre in Mullumbimby, staffed part-time by Deb Pearse (a woman who struck me as not so much burnt out as close to incinerated). What kind of kids, I asked Heazlewood-Ross, are shifting across from MHS to study at The Hut? 'The BCC kids are those with mental health issues. Anxiety, agoraphobia. There are sexually precocious girls.' He speaks of teenagers, once capable of seriously destructive behaviour, turning around, finishing Year 10. 'It's a beautiful thing, really – one boy's made a table in woodwork that he wants to donate back to Mullum High.'

The college, Heazlewood-Ross explained, runs on 'the smell

of a smell of an oily rag' and is an avenue – realistically the only avenue – for the teenagers who arrive at the school without the skills to survive, let alone succeed, in the classroom at Mullum High. 'They are victims of their home life, and so they come along to us and become victims of the classroom, and that leads to them … well, I don't like to use the word "failing." "Hexagonal pegs" is how one parent described them to me. A lot of them are kids that are difficult for their parents to control. They go out partying, and then it's hard to get to school the next day, so they don't come, and then they get marginalised even more. You've got daughters with AVOs out against their mothers, and the mothers have got AVOs out against the daughters. I mean we've got kids here who go into town at lunchtime and see their mums drunk underneath the Scout Hall. It's no wonder they have trouble fitting in.'

Heazlewood-Ross's deep concern for these struggling kids is palpable. Talking to him, I was reminded of the shock that ran through the school community when he was not awarded the vacant principal's position in 2005. Everyone thought he should have gotten it, my daughter told me at the time – everyone likes him. The job went instead to an outsider to the school, Ian Graham, a quiet, reserved man who in December 2009 took to wearing a red, black and yellow Koori wristband on his right arm, and when asked to describe the mood of the school, told me, 'Settled. Settled – but impacted.'

*

Impacted is the word, all right. Tensions ran very high in Mullumbimby in the weeks following the death. Students in the first furious days marched en masse in the street, demanding Ian Graham's resignation, only to be countered by a group of parents and staff vocally supporting the principal. Steve Drummond berated the protesting students, telling them they should be remembering his son in a quiet, respectful manner, instead of having their 'stupid, petty little fights.'

A teenage Halloween dance organised in the Drill Hall a fortnight after the death was marred by brawling outside and in the streets of the town; a boy arrived stoned and carrying a bottle of whisky.

Back at MHS, as floral tributes and graffiti mounted up against the brick wall of the girls' toilets ('We will never forget you Jai'; 'We'll party again don't you worry bro'), the school canteen became a bizarre side issue. A tuckshop revolution ensued when it was found to be tens of thousands of dollars in debt. New managers were appointed in the weeks following Jai's death, and a revised menu of healthy food was promoted by some as the answer to the school's problems.

Much of the local discontent since 28 August 2009 has centred on whether bullying contributed to Jai's death. It could have happened anywhere, say some; table wars are the norm, not the exception, and all schools have fights at some time or another. It was a freak accident, that's all. The town is now deeply split between those who argue that Mullum High is just like every other public high school in Australia and those who see Jai as victim of a 'born-to-rule' football clique clashing with a subgroup of younger kids.

The footy crowd make up their own rules as they go along, some argue, including the mother of a close friend of Jai's: 'It just makes me sick. They think they're above everyone else, just because they play footy. I told [her partner] if he wants our boy to play for the Giants then he's gonna have to take him and sign him up himself and drive him to all the games, 'cos I don't want anything to do with that lot. I didn't want my son to get like they are – to learn to treat women like shit. And I've seen what it's done to relationships between sons and mothers when they do join the club.'

My daughter similarly described the Mullum High pecking order when she was last a student there, in 2006: 'About half the kids were the footy heroes or else they're hangers-on. They're the so-called popular people, loud people that I would avoid and not want anything to do with mostly. Then there was an overlap between them and the surfer kids, and the rest were a pretty diverse bunch. There were a few Emos and some gamers, and the more arty kids, and they all hung together and got called the Emo group.'

Most people from the top echelon – the 'popular' kids – would deign to talk to the ones on the bottom, my daughter told me, but those in the bottom layer were excluded from a particular kind of social life. They weren't necessarily bullied overtly; they just didn't get invited to certain parties. But a small minority of really aggro guys – and their girlfriends – were different again. They would never speak to anyone outside the football clique 'unless they wanted something from them.' My daughter paused here, and then added matter-of-factly, 'or unless the guys wanted to bash the shit out of someone.' This normally happened away from the school buildings, often on the oval across the road when school was over. And while push-and-shove altercations were fairly common at school, serious fights were rare, occurring, she told me, perhaps twice a year.

*

At Mullum High Jai Morcom was involved in the so-called 'table war,' where ownership of seating at a long aluminium table was highly contested between groups of boys during recess and lunchtimes. At these relatively unsupervised times, the student population at Mullum divides itself not just by age but also by demographic.

As Heazlewood-Ross explains, this is atypical: 'It's a bit different to other schools, I think. They kind of hang together across grade levels, so you get younger-grade kids mixing with the older ones. The Emo kids hang out in one corner of the school and play cards … you've gotta love that bunch of kids. They're a little bit more sensitive, maybe – the kind of kids who've experienced some harassment … They don't buck the system – they ignore the system. And then there's other groups who have their own particular areas. But it's not strictly a grade division like in most schools …'

What happened on 28 August, he went on to say, was probably that a group of older students had taken offence when the younger Emo group took 'their' table at recess. A spitting match ensued, which quickly escalated. Punches were thrown. After that it gets blurry. Very blurry.

Depending on who you talk to, the table war had been going for a couple of days (the official school line) or for a month or more. The table would be carried in triumph from location to location by the rival groups of kids, and I was told by students that the table war was seen not as bullying, but rather as a big joke. One Year 8 boy – call him Thomas – told me that he had been sitting on top of the table one August lunchtime when a bunch of rivals 'lifted the table up with me on it and carried it to where they thought it should be.' Not only that but, in the weeks leading up to the death, Thomas (who belonged to neither clique) had been spat on by a member of Jai's inner group. What had his reaction been to having been lifted into the air on the table? 'I just went – oh, great, woo-hoo!' he explained, grinning a wide attractive grin. 'You know, I made a joke of it.' And to being spat on? 'I just ignore it. People try to pick fights with me all the time, 'cos – I don't know why. Maybe 'cos I'm tall. Even tiny little guys' – and here his palm hovered around his waist in demonstration – 'they come up and hit me. People try and start fights with me all the time. It happened in town on Saturday night. I just ignore them.'

For fourteen-year-old Thomas, a stable, loving home and engaged parents have given him the capacity to laugh off his assailants, and to clown, not rage, when the table war erupted beneath him. But stable, loving homes and engaged parents are hardly universal; they may no longer even be the norm. And for older boys accustomed to having their authority recognised on and off the football field, it must have seemed outrageous to be spat on by the school's outsiders – by one of the nerds, Emos and Koori kids who hung together in a distant corner, playing cards, ignoring the system, avoiding the jocks. Male pride can be a terribly dangerous thing and, once unleashed, almost impossible to put back in the bottle without adult help. As an anonymous statement made by one kid the police interviewed reads: '… and we went back to find out why [the spitting had happened] and ask for an apology … an all-in brawl invoked [sic].'

While the author of this statement claims to have been ten to fifteen metres from Jai at all times during the fight, the text also contains the words 'sorry' and 'regret.' The statement, which was published in a Sydney paper, and later posted on Facebook, is adolescent, confused and reeks of expediency. Penned in the highly charged atmosphere of those early weeks, when revenge attacks threatened, it ends in pathos: 'Two wrongs don't make a right. Peace.'

*

Professor Ross Homel teaches criminology at Griffith University. Big schools, he told me over coffee in a Brisbane café, are bad news. Building friendly relationships is paramount in maintaining order among young people, and in big high schools with lots of small feeder schools, these relationships may simply be too many and too hard to manage effectively.

Inside schools and out, youth violence is on the rise in Australia's eastern states, and the figures in the ten-to-fourteen age bracket make for sobering reading. While overall crime rates, including for violent crime, are in decline, probably due to years of sustained economic growth, the youth figures are going in the other direction. The figures are bad but there is plenty of room for optimism, Homel countered, since 'the gap between what we know and what we don't know is much smaller than the gap between what we know and what we actually *do* on the ground.' Atomised modern families are a big part of the problem, as are rampant alcohol abuse, illegal drug use and income inequality, all starkly worse in Australia than in most comparable countries. While the causes of youth violence are multiple and complex, we know a great deal about what helps at-risk teenagers to stay engaged at school and stay out of trouble. Simple interventions like those made by Deb Pearse and others at The Hut can have dramatic effects; where young people feel listened to and valued by adults, tensions quickly dissipate. Kids stay at school.

As much as anything, Professor Homel says, troubled kids need schools they can connect with and then jobs to go to – 'meaningful activity' – just like adults do. And if their dysfunctional families fail them and institutions can't take up the slack, kids need to be provided with a range of different connections to the wider society, avenues they can take into citizenship and belonging. Failing this, they are likely to drift into a downward spiral of grog, drugs, fights, crime. These connections needn't cost a fortune. Sport is one traditional way of bringing young people into generally safe contact with each other (notwithstanding footy's alleged role in Jai Morcom's death) and there are others means, like gaming clubs and art activities, some of which have been offered by Deb Pearse at The Hut over the years.

There is no escaping the hard data showing the need for more interventions such as these. Australian boys – and to a lesser extent, girls – are frequently involved in violent conflict with their peers. Forty-four per cent of Brisbane teens surveyed in 2007 had attacked another person in some way during the previous year (though some of these attacks consisted only of 'throwing something,' presumably in some cases innocuous objects like fruit or pens). But in an environment where young men feel cut adrift, abandoned by their fathers especially, a hurled apple can be the only trigger necessary for serious conflict to erupt. 'Some of these kids,' Heazlewood-Ross told me of his Year 9 boys, 'seem to have such a deep well of anger in them.'

Be it drugs, family breakdown, socioeconomic inequality or some other mix of factors at work, there is a cohort of angry young men and women in the eastern states who apparently regard violence as acceptable, or at least unavoidable, in their young lives.

On the Facebook memorial site 'RIP Jai Morcom,' scathing responses to adult bloggers sermonising about kids' violent behaviour brand adult suggestions for reform naïve. One boy wrote, 'Kids will never learn we are brout up getting bashed by our rents and watchin our mums get bashed by our faget dads.'

*

In the final quarter of 2009, threats of payback flew around the town as Steve Drummond began to call not for calm but for better explanations, and the police commenced what would turn out to be a tortuously slow investigation. A small group of Jai's young friends – both Kooris and other boys – were taken away by the school's Aboriginal Support Worker, Scotty Sentence, for a weekend camp. The boys came back to town far more settled, most of their talk of revenge evaporated. (Some of this group have since shifted to Byron High, unable to stomach the bad memories at Mullum.) When I visited the school in December, Scotty's predecessor, Steven Strong, showed me plans to have respected local Koori men visit the school and work weekly with all the boys in the younger grades on conflict resolution and identity issues. But interventions to benefit young people and save lives cost money, money that is scarce and hard to find in the public school system. Kings School in Sydney can offer its adolescent boys a top-class education and facilities that include an air-conditioned underground rifle range, but Strong's excellent proposal to give time to troubled boys – one that made Professor Homel nearly leap out of his seat with enthusiasm when I described it to him – remains, as yet, a grossly underfunded dream.

A large mural now decorates the brick wall where Jai lost consciousness on 28 August. The graffiti memorialising him is hidden beneath a songline and kangaroo dreaming painted in mustard and red ochres by Bundjalung leader Uncle Lewis Walker, who along with Maori community leaders held a smoking ceremony for Jai in September. 'It was just an incredible event,' Heazlewood-Ross told me, clearly still moved four months later. 'The most striking thing about it was the presence of Uncle Lewis. He just walked into the school that morning and said: This is what's going to happen here today. This, this and this.' He paused. 'And the *authority* of the man.'

Jai was of Maori descent through his father, and both his parents agreed that an indigenous ceremony was the best way to remember their son and to help heal the fractured school. More than 600 staff and students chose to attend the Sorry Business that September morning, sitting in the concrete quadrangle close to where Jai struck his head. The gathering maintained complete silence for the best part of an hour while the white-ochred Uncle Lewis smoked the area, and solemn Maori rituals were carried out. At one point, sitting among tearful friends and students, Steve Drummond broke down, keening in anguish. Uncle Lewis went immediately to kneel at his side and comfort him; as he did so, the male Maori elder stepped forward and sang 'Our Father' to the motionless gathering. Later, staff and students shared a ritual meal of kangaroo and damper, served as per Maori custom, first to the family, and then to the others.

'If you'd told me that our students would sit there with complete attention for an hour, then line up and eat *kangaroo* and damper – well, I would have said you were mad,' Heazlewood-Ross told me, shaking his head. 'What I remember the most was this little ADHD boy of ours who I've never seen be still for more than about thirty seconds. He just sat there' – pointing to the corner of a garden bed – 'and he didn't move a muscle for the whole thing. He was just riveted to the spot. We all were.'

*

Deb Pearse, operating The Hut with three functional computers told me that she found it a bit curious having to go to Maori and Koori cultures to memorialise Jai. It was as if, she told me, mainstream Australian culture didn't have the right ceremonies to do the situation justice. Aboriginal myself, I was not about to argue with her. I remembered as she spoke that there are no specific words in English for a parent who has lost a child. 'Widow,' yes, and 'widower.' And 'orphan' – for one who has lost their parents. But no name for a mother or a father who has had to put a child in the ground. No equivalent to that heartbreaking status label in more than one indigenous language for a mother whose baby has recently died, which literally translates: she is only empty hands.

Each culture deals with death differently, of course. But across every culture – and probably in every Australian country town of several thousand souls – there remain strong men and women of outstanding leadership ability with the capacity to care for young people, and the willingness to guide them into adult society. Heazlewood-Ross, Scotty Sentence, Deb Pearse, Steve Strong and many others – these people have for years extended an umbrella of deep concern over the troubled young boys and girls of Mullumbimby. It is grossly unfair to think, as did my disaffected hitchhiker, that they don't care, or have given up. They do, and they haven't.

But things are different in Mullumbimby now. A young life is gone, and the town has changed as a result. Angry posters by Steve Drummond (*Truth 4 Jai Part Three*) are plastered on windows and flat surfaces throughout the town: 'There are people responsible. They are not coming forward … the next day after the Drill Hall fighting, two of Jai's friends were attacked by carloads of youths from Mullum … Early this year a boy at Mullum High got taken away by ambulance with concussion, someone had put his head through a brick wall. Jai was not so lucky.'

Innocence has gone from the incense-scented township, and been replaced by a lingering suspicion between two tribes. And the language of the school has been forced to change as well. 'When things blew up in the past, I used to use the throwaway phrase *Well, it's not life-threatening*,' Richard Heazelwood-Ross told me soberly as we walked past the spot where Jai had lain unconscious that August morning. 'I don't use that phrase anymore.'

In early March, Steve Drummond delivered 1400 letters to the Coroner's Court in Sydney, calling for an inquest into his son's death. Still refusing to heed police advice to halt his investigations, Drummond alleged that boys had brought spanners, chains and padlocks to school in August 2009 in an attempt to win the ongoing table wars that culminated in Jai's death. 'It's quite possible that he's been thrown out of the fight and that he may have hit a brick wall,' Drummond concluded. The coroner will decide whether to recommend an inquest into Jai Morcom's death when all submissions have been considered.

Griffith Review

On Being Odd

Lorna Hallahan

Odd to start by quoting P.G. Wodehouse: 'She was a girl with a wonderful profile, but steeped to the gills in serious purpose.' Bertie Wooster is complaining, in 'Jeeves Takes Charge,' about Lady Florence Craye, who has forced upon him *Types of Ethical Theory*. 'Odd' because anyone steeped to the gills in serious purpose would not take Wodehouse as a literary starting point. Wodehouse confessed himself uninterested in politics and affairs of the nation, and people in general. He saw himself in Bertie and all the other fellows from the Drones Club, with the possible exception of Psmith, who was a dabbler in socialism. So the self-contrived scrapes of an indolent young English gentleman and his valet's ingenious rescues would probably not make it onto the must-read list for people of serious purpose.

Although no longer a girl, I am a bit like Florence. I have been, since early youth, steeped to the gills in serious purpose. My shelves are loaded with books on ethics, social and moral philosophy, and some on theology. I confess I am likely to lend books bearing suffering, pain or alienation in the title. It is the wonderful profile that gives me pause. Wodehouse probably pictured a woman with a shapely figure, long legs, fine skin, pretty face and excellent styling – hair and clothes. Not me. I claim a wonderful profile because my body is mutilated and odd, and I get around unconventionally. I inhabit what Rose-Marie Garland-Thomson calls 'a stareable body.'

Although over the years I have come to modify my internal, reflexive gaze to recognise my new body-self, I remember the first few times that I took this stareable body out in public – after I had made my own tentative explorations in front of a mirror. Wondering at my new form, shocked and interested, repelled and compelled to gaze again. It was like that. *I* did not go out; I *took* the body out. The internal body-frame no longer matched the one I saw. I had to learn how to look anew at myself. And those early encounters did not help. In the eyes of those I dared to meet (starers), I saw my own shock and titillation, the same desire to look away and the craving to focus and take apart and put together again. Even after almost thirty-five years, I still catch myself doing it.

Michel de Montaigne, in the sprawling rave 'Of Cripples,' reveals that 'the more does my own deformity astonish me, the less I understand myself.' He also tells us why, persuaded by the ancients, he has come to convince himself that 'I have formerly made myself believe that I have had more pleasure in a woman by reason she was not straight, and accordingly reckoned that deformity amongst her graces.' He is convinced of the increased vitality of the genitalia when the limbs are deformed. I will return to this: but first, a more serious purpose.

Counting deformity as one of our graces is precisely the task. And the path to this is via wonderment and its concomitant: becoming wonderful. Wonderment is often connected to beauty and grace, like Florence's profile, something to inspire rapture and awe, or, better, erotic, even carnal, contemplation. One stands on a precipice of attraction, desire and uplift – made more delightful because of its precariousness; you totter unprotected by repressive rationality. You are exposed to a life-altering encounter, one that might be the turning point in a loveless or cheerless life. Some people are better at it than others. Children, having yet to learn repressive rationality, and older people, having forsaken it as too tiresome, seem more open to the wonderful than are those of us filled with serious purpose. Perhaps they are concerned with the thing, not so much the reason why. Montaigne goes on:

> I was just now ruminating, as I often do, what a free and roving

> thing human reason is. I ordinarily see that men, in things propounded to them, more willingly study to find out reasons than to ascertain truth: they slip over presuppositions, but are curious in examination of consequences; they leave the things, and fly to the causes.

Perhaps this too-soon flight to the causes deprives us of the lessons to be found on the precipice of wonderment.

Much has been said about staring in all its baroque forms – looking, gazing, ogling, eyeing off, goggle-eyedness, lasciviousness, gawking, gaping, watching. A fresh taxonomy will not help us here, but we can agree that, in extravagant looking and elaborate avoidance in the encounter with the mutilated as well as the gorgeous, we cross the threshold of the precipice of wonderment. This is Rudolf Otto's *mysterium tremendum et fascinans*, the dual numinous forces of fear and fascination. Otto is describing our encounter with the Holy Other; I am talking about our encounter with a definitely unholy other – not the polar opposite of the divine (the demonic), but the unsightly, unfamiliar, odd other. So, no, I do not think that when I enter these baroque moments I embody divinity for my starer, but I am taking them, initially at least, to a place that most of the great psychoanalysts would agree we all want to avoid: a confrontation with the ghastly certainty that life is fragile, easily wrecked and fleeting. (Being a goddess is the other matter to which Montaigne alludes.)

A wonderful profile is particularly troublesome in certain places. Indeed, a companion once complained that he hated going out with me because in the stares I attracted he felt his capacity to pass anonymously through the crowd was compromised. *He* didn't like the attention. The symbolic interactionists make sense here when they argue that contexts construct our perceptions. My body is not overly stareable in a hospital – it is what people expect there. Hospitals are, after all, gathering places for the horrible and those approaching death. Casinos are not. A telltale sign of 'this is a place where the wonderfully horrible do not belong' is the presence of staircases. Perhaps ironically then, the stage for Encounter One is a lift foyer.

*

My friend and I, both dressed up, had swanned off to a casino, not so much for gambling but for the lure of glamour, an uncommon pursuit for toilers in the sisterhood of purposefulness. We were young, not goddesses, but more than presentable and completely ill-prepared for the exaggerated, externalised verbal reaction of a group of young men disembarking from the lift we were about to enter. Their insults and faux vomiting, their staggering about in revulsion, their loud assurances to each other, placed me centre stage in a scene that embroiled my friend and other innocents in a drama about the drunken solipsism of young men searching for female sex partners. It was a moment of mutual horror, the frozen-in-time quality broken by my friend propelling me out of their sight. I shook for ages; it took the fun right out of the evening: the numinous *fascinans* lost in their sexism, and my shame. (I take comfort in the retributive fantasy that some sublime beauty rejected them before the night was out.)

Erving Goffman and his fellow symbolic interactionists use dramaturgy to help us work out what is going on here. In simplified form their theories are well known. Individuals marked for stigma must first possess spectacular differences and then attract adverse social reactions. Some targeted people manage to get away with it. Even though they belong to a stigmatised group because of their sexuality (for example), they may conceal their choices and pass as 'normal.' Many of us who are physically impaired cannot. We are 'out' whether we choose to be or not. And so we have to learn ways of managing our attractiveness in the wonderment staring (and shaming) stakes. This process is called impression management. The early symbolic interactionists said that those of us with spoiled identities select various masks in this drama of managing our stigma. In short, they said we choose from ingratiation, intimidation and supplication. All these strategies advance our desire to get something out of the other: perhaps recognition and inclusion; a space to be ourselves; or a service. Drawing on social psychology, they also argue that the person with the wonderful profile also acts to protect herself from the pain of the internalised or introjected horror at the self.

Using this framework, the encounter in the casino had me moving away self-protectively and seeking reassurance from my 'wise' friend. She is considered wise because she is not marked by my stigma but is knowing and accepting of it. Most galling is the fact that I had employed an impression management strategy to enter that fun palace. I had attempted to ingratiate myself by dressing à la mode, by going with a normal and by paying my own way. For most patrons it worked, but no ploy could distract the boozy boyos from the image of oddness that so captured their attention. They stumbled off the precipice into horror.

I want, at times like that, to affirm Emily Post's etiquette rules enjoining others not to stare but to turn away politely and to pass by on the other side. Yet Encounter Two reminds me that such politeness is really only another form of socially sanctioned abandonment; another pathway to shame.

Processions in cathedrals come with all manner of pomp and pomposity, of hierarchical huffing and episodes of episcopal self-elevation. The organ music and choir, the standing congregation, the space, the distance from door to stalls, the whish of gowns, the creak of seldom-worn leather shoes, the clutter of cross and thurible, all floating over the mundane mutterings of the processants. I, as chaplain, was the least among them and the last in line. When I arrived at the stalls no seats were left. While I clambered around (lots of stairs) trying to find a spot to settle before retreating to the pews, nobody moved or spoke or looked or yielded. Tactful inattention, smugness or abandonment? Next day I received a formal apology, which only slightly eased the sting of being out of place. (I resisted another retributive fantasy in which the clerics, stripped of their vestments, noted their naked ordinariness with a touch of disappointment.)

These two vignettes are illustrative of multiple encounters in the thirty-five years of my oddness. Taking the stareable body out in public never ceases to challenge and provoke me. Just being out means dealing with wonderment. So if wonderment leads to a rejection based on horror or denial, how can I, following Montaigne, count deformity amongst my graces? Goffman and Co. would have me protectively and self-deceptively wearing a mask and hanging out with the wise. My colleagues in the disability movement would have me taking up a form of cripple in-your-faceness. This might be viewed as intimidation or as an effective disruptive strategy in the classic drama. And I confess

I have enjoyed myself on many occasions confronting others with the oddness.

Or, I could take up being a goddess.

John Steinbeck points the way when, in *The Grapes of Wrath*, he has the Joad boys telling the one-eyed mechanic to stop crying, to fill in the hole and get out there – just like the one-legged whore who is being paid more than her intact colleagues. It might be tacky, but, if you are interested, you only have to do a simple internet search to enter the worlds of the devotees. It is a playground for the contemporary Montaigne – those people who, for reasons disputed by all players and the psychiatrists, are convinced of Montaigne's conclusion that sex is better with a crippled woman. Though I am not going to explore the proclivities of others here, I must acknowledge that, for some, the arrangement seems to please all players. I have had completely benign and essentially uninteresting contacts with those who see in me a goddess of gorgeous deformity. This also takes the fun out of the evening. And I do not indulge in any fantasies!

At this point, it is tempting to condemn those with unreconstructed attitudes and low brows, but I want to stick with Montaigne's suggestion that we should stay with the thing and not fly to the causes (or other elegant makings of meaning). Yet it seems I am running out of options here. All the identified responses to wonderment – revulsion, ignorance and worship – are too intense and do not match the emotions of the simple social encounters of the daily round. They do not offer a pathway to a quiet transformation.

So the daily challenge remains: when I take the body out in public, am I conscious, confident, proud, courageous and competent? Is there something authentic about this, or is it simply my latest mask? And when the day is done and the technology stacked against the wall, I must ask: can my mother look upon me with delight and not with sorrow? Can my children see me just as I should be? Can I dance naked in the bright, desiring gaze of my lover? Can I know myself as beautiful as well as strong? Can I gawk at myself with love and not with horror or sadness? Must I accept the moral enjoinder of Shirley in Charlotte Brontë's novel of the same name?

> You held out your palm for an egg and fate put into it a scorpion. Show no consternation. Close your fingers firmly upon the gift; let it sting through your palm. Never mind, in time, after your hand and arm have swelled and quivered long with torture, the squeezed scorpion will die and you will have learned a great lesson – how to endure without a sob.

Nineteenth-century Brontë builds on a long philosophical tradition about the place of sorrow and social isolation. Am I condemned to live with the impaired happiness of Aristotle's ugly man? Aristotle wrote at length on happiness, work that is receiving renewed attention from those who can see that justice is important to life satisfaction. If Montaigne sees the deformity as a grace, Brontë as a lesson in silent affliction, does Aristotle help us to see it as a good, as contributing to the proper equipment, as a virtue? Here, to these interlocutors at least, is another odd thing. Although I look unfortunate and continue with the loss, I enjoy all the external goods: good education, good job, good children, good lover, good house, good health, good friends, good community. This disjuncture in impressions simply serves to illustrate the point that wonderment seems to get in the way of seeing the full story of me. Yet it persists.

I am interested in the transforming potential of these encounters, not only for my own sense of dignity but also for that of others. This is the point of being steeped to the gills in serious purpose. If we only focus on the etiquette of encounters between those of us with wonderful profiles and those who find themselves in a state of wonderment, we miss identifying opportunities to reduce shame, to increase life-honouring social connections and to help us all transform our relationships with our own bodies. In saying this I am mindful of Montaigne's caution as he reflects further on cripples:

> Great abuses in the world are begotten, or, to speak more boldly, all the abuses of the world are begotten, by our being taught to be afraid of professing our ignorance, and that we are bound to accept all things we are not able to refute: we speak of all things by precepts and decisions.

This makes the task even harder. If I take Montaigne's caution to heart, I must try, for as long as possible anyway, to put aside the precepts that come so readily in these discussions. Precepts I have already mentioned: etiquette, dramaturgy, pride (or anger), tearless resignation and erotic appeal. I cannot make this encounter work unless I confess that I do not know at the outset from where the mutual meaning might emerge.

*

In 1980, for four months, I worked as a student social worker in a legal agency for Aboriginal and Torres Strait Islander people. On my first day I met Monny. All my contact with her happened in my office, on the street, in the watch-house, the jail or the psychiatric ward of a large hospital. Monny never came to my house, had a meal with me, drove in my car or went shopping with me. I introduced her to only a couple of my friends. Encounter Three occurred in this context.

Monny was born in the late 1950s, in north Queensland. She died in Brisbane in 1983. When I met Monny, her life was the antithesis of all that I thought was decent. As a member of Australia's indigenous nation, the travesty of life offered her was even more disturbing. And she knew why. She urgently, plaintively, proudly, desperately, defiantly – almost like a mantra – cried out, 'Why are we fucking black?'

To many, the cause of Monny's pain was her consumption of massive quantities of alcohol, her reluctance to settle, her provocative dancing, her swearing, her love of popular music and bright clothes, her anger, her violence, her self-destructiveness, her rowdiness, her contempt for the police, her non-compliance with white doctors, lawyers and social workers, her childhood, her lack of moral strength. She was a person to pity, to recoil from; whose death under the wheels of a truck was a release, a timely end to a life going nowhere, the most effective conclusion to so much suffering. But Monny knew her pain came from being homeless in her own land.

As a social worker, you are kitted out with some slick personal skills that should take you into the world of any person in poverty and despair. You help the person change, but only if they want to. You set life goals, assist people to rechannel their anger and to acquire life skills and self-esteem. Having honed your skills, you move on to other fellow citizens. You assess, refer, problem solve, advocate, counsel, report and terminate – ever professional, non-judgmental, confidential, empathetic, self-determining – staying distanced, non-collusive, never personally involved.

That is where I got into strife. I liked this feisty woman and was repelled by the chaos of her life. The remnants of my Anglican schoolgirl persona could never quite wrap themselves around the horribleness of it all. It was worse: I knew I had nothing to offer.

It was a bitter lesson that one who had lost all was urged to rely on one who had gained much and still ended up empty-handed. I just did not know what to do. All my training demanded that I act to effect change, but I had neither the ideas nor the skills nor the emotional strength to do any of it. In the end, all I did was hang around with Monny when I could, charmed by her humour and her pathos, appalled that a life could be lived this way. Honestly, I think our professional contact gained her nothing. If the purpose was to change Monny, it didn't work.

One very hot afternoon, Monny turned up at the office, ill, drunk and agitated. Had she remained on the streets, she would have been picked up by the police and put in the watch-house. So we began to walk two long city blocks to the drying-out centre. Every time a police car drove by – and there were many, for we were near the police headquarters – Monny abused them loud and long. Fearing retribution, I tried to calm and quieten her. But she was fuelled for a fight and wanted to make an impact.

A crowd waiting for the peak-hour buses watched this rowdy duet advancing. Many people permitted themselves to stare. Monny stopped and inspected the group. Their curiosity was not lost on her. I could only stand there, waiting for the abuse and rebuke from a clean-living, racist crowd.

'How dare you fucking stare at this woman just because she is like that? She is a good woman and I know her.' Monny addressed them in a practised, provocative voice, arms raised importunately.

Then, in the silence that followed, we continued into the sun, towards the respite of a few alcohol-free hours.

It was on that street, almost where the Speech of Commendation was delivered to the commuters, that Monny died. That woman never knew how my devotion to her grew from that time on. I who promised much and delivered little was spoken for by her, the discarded woman, who with the intuition of one accustomed to rebuke knew how to defend with fire and, yes, dignity.

*

By contrast, Michel de Montaigne was of noble birth, educated in Latin and Greek under the direction of a humanist father, generally of good health ('entire,' as he puts it) and widely recognised by the leaders of sixteenth-century France. This recognition included being awarded the Collar of the Order of St Michael, the highest order of French nobility. He seems an unlikely interlocutor for someone like me. In his day I would not have survived. But let's imagine for a moment that I *did* live then with the same deformity I now possess. Aristotle would have seen in me the unhappy person, deprived of all external goods to ensure my happiness and possibly virtueless as I sought a way to get through the day.

At best, Montaigne would have seen in me a tantalising partner; at worst, someone worthy of condescension and pity. Our fates could not have been more divergent. A crippled woman would never have dared to speak of these serious matters with a powerful, intact man (sex is clearly another matter altogether). Yet Montaigne endured the losses of his closest friend and five of his six daughters. At thirty-eight, he withdrew from public life to write his essays. Seeking only the stimulus and consolations of his many books, he struggled with the sure knowledge that he was sad, that he knew little and that what he knew was of uncertain value, quipping at one point that, 'Not being able to govern events, I govern myself.' It is with this sentiment that Montaigne finally persuades me of the clearest and best path.

Being of wonderful profile is oddly potent. I do not pass anonymously. In places like the university where I work, many people claim to know me even though they have not met me. They know me because they have seen me and, flying to causes and meaning, have worked out things about me. It is a perversely powerful position to hold, like wearing the Collar of St Michael. I wear the collar of obvious deformity. Perhaps I too cannot govern the smallest of events and, believing that I can only govern myself, I am tempted to retreat to my family, my home and my books. The real challenge is to take the power and use it well for serious purpose. In these ways I can satisfy my quest for public and private authenticity.

In this I must face the impression that the more I explore deformity – others' and my own – the less I understand myself. Years of being stared at have taught me that the moment of uncertainty – of grasping for civil straws that fail us, of trying to remember what our grandmother told us to do when faced with unsettling things – is not a moment for self-abnegation or for vengeful fantasy. It is at best an opportunity for kindness. When I gawk at my oddness in a shop window or the mirror, I need to be kind, for I face my own oddness and fragility. When I see that same gawking in a stranger, I need to be kind, because they too face fragility and loss. This is not a moment of distance, but of groping for understanding, of solidarity and of unity. Surely this is what it means to be wonderful. Surely this is a description of mutual wonderment.

Montaigne's voice reminds me from the roots of Renaissance humanism (curiously so contemporary) to perceive that, in wonderment, even though it seems that my oddness drives the reactions and reactions of unwise strangers, I do not have access to their experience, their dreams or their fears. I cannot sum up this person as they would sum me up. It is the same folly for me to think that I understand the starer's losses as it is for them to assume that they can discern what is important to know about me. The interaction of wonderment is not clarifying: it is opaque, and the more we gaze, the more opaque it becomes. These moments of swinging on the edge of the precipice of wonderment, of enquiry, of openness, of trying to face the thing and not fly to meaning, are not crystal moments. They are moments when our sureness is lost, illumination is dimmed, our fix on reality darkened, and mystery reasserted.

Mutual wonderment relies on suspending my own repressive rationality and entering the social intensity of a staring moment, of recognising in my starer a person of wonderful profile. I can govern my own reactions, stay with the gaze, not look away in shame, but seek a mutual recognition – poignant and potent. I no longer attempt to understand the motivation of my starer, but to share in the discomfort and delight of a fractured anonymity, where in peculiar ways we become fleetingly naked to each other, stripped of some aspects of Emily Post's civil pretences; where we jointly confront Montaigne's truth of the thing – in this case, the fragility of our biological selves. And here, because of my long association with the idea, I can offer a degree of reassurance.

*

The Adelaide Central Market on Saturday morning is fertile ground for moments of mutual staring. In our civvy attire we are equal, stripped of the sartorial pretensions of the workday week. Recently, head down, weaving my way through a mobile crowd in search of my favourite pork bun, I found myself captivated by the ugliest, most painful-looking feet I had ever had the misfortune to observe. I confess that I thought, 'Thank God I don't have to get around on those.' As I picked my way through the crowd, these toes, black, gnarled and disfigured, came closer and closer until they stopped dead in front of me. I looked up into the eyes of a woman perhaps twenty-five years my senior. She said, 'I am sorry this happened to you, but I think you are beautiful.' I looked into her eyes for a long time and said nothing other than 'Thank you.'

Have I been caught up in encounters tinged with *mysterium tremendum et fascinans*? In a simple everyday sort of way, I think so. The yuck-factor is palpable, yet the fascination is quietly comforting. Transforming moments? Yes, again. I have rediscovered that in stigma lies survival, that in ugliness lies beauty, that a woman with gross, gangrenous feet is kind and that I need not feel bad about the way that she recognised in me a fellow who shares the anguish of being not normal.

Is it translatable to those without obvious or spectacular oddness? I am not sure, but this I can assert: those without obvious deformity do not lack the pain that seems to accompany all. That suffering is apparent if you take the time to look into the eyes of the other or to feel their breath upon your cheek. If nothing else, Montaigne's losses tell us that. I am prepared to risk the rejection of the gang of lads, reminded that goddesses do not wait in lift foyers and that they too will be knocked back. I am prepared to risk the turning aside of prattling prelates afraid of their own irrelevance. I am prepared to stand exposed in front of a curious crowd. I am willing to be considered virtuous or to be taken for a sex goddess, if this means that I open myself to moments when I can return the gaze of a stranger with enquiry and kindness.

To Garland-Thomson I want to say, 'Thanks for making me think about the power in a stareable body'; to Goffman and Co., 'I have discovered the troubling beauty of mutual wonderment. I have forsaken being a staree. I have become a respondent starer'; to Montaigne and Brontë: 'Thanks for showing it as an alternative, but withdrawal (with or without a scorpion) is not a lasting option for me'; to Aristotle: 'Happiness is born in connection to others, not just in beauty'; to Homer: 'I agree that, though in my mutilation, much was taken, so much more remains and even more has been given'; and, finally, to P.G. Wodehouse: 'Thanks for sending up a serious purpose. I need that most of all.'

Perhaps this is why Bertie couldn't contemplate a life with Florence: her gaze was too direct for a man dedicated to minor dramas on an illusory (though amusing) stage. Perhaps Goffman and Co. would conclude that I have simply found another script by which to live. Perhaps this is what Aristotle saw as a virtue in the service of happiness? Or perhaps this is what Montaigne meant when he said that there is more pleasure to be found in a woman whose body is not straight.

She does not look away.

Australian Book Review

Born in Vietnam, Made in Australia: Getting the Fish Sauce Recipe Right

Pauline Nguyen

My parents are known as members of the 'first generation' of Vietnamese refugees, who came to Australia after the Vietnam War. I, however, am known as part of the '1.5 generation.' Born in Vietnam, made in Australia. We are the children of defeated warriors who have tried to come to terms with the present life, and the act of negotiating the past with all its rules and traditions, in the hope that the two very different cultures could blend into one well-adjusted whole. This always seemed better in theory than in practice.

When Saigon fell to communist rule, in 1975, my father realised that he had no choice but to escape Vietnam. And the only way that he could do this was to build a boat and smuggle his family out to sea. I was three at the time and my brother Lewis was two. My grandmother begged my father not to leave. She couldn't understand how a parent could risk perishing at sea. But my father is a very determined man.

He stands at just five foot one, a little shorter than me, but what he lacks in height he makes up for in fearlessness and determination – and he had already made up his mind. He would rather die trying than risk imprisonment. Or a fate far worse, the re-education camps. 'It's not enough that they want to take our freedom,' he would tell me. 'They want to take our thoughts as well.' My father was determined that if we died, we would all die together.

So in October 1977, armed with only a rudimentary map and a compass, my father steered our tiny vessel out into the South China Sea. We spent days drifting and waiting and praying. We prayed that a foreign ship might come and save us. We prayed that we might find friendly shores. We prayed that the pirates wouldn't attack us. We prayed that our supplies would not run out.

Our prayers were not always answered. Ship after ship ignored our SOS, and at gunpoint a group of Malaysian soldiers pushed us off supposedly friendly shores before we landed in Thailand, where we spent a very difficult year in a refugee camp. Australia finally accepted us and put us up at the Westbridge Migrant Hostel, in the Sydney suburb of Villawood. My father quickly found a job working on the production line at the Sunbeam factory in Campsie – on the graveyard shift from 2 p.m. to 2 a.m., the job nobody wanted.

The train ride home was the worst, he would later tell me. Every night was dangerous. The locals threatened to beat him and the worst bigots threatened to kill him. 'Go home to your own country, you bastard,' they would yell.

My father cried every day going home on that train. We all cried a lot in those days. We came into a new country with nothing: no job, no house, no money. We didn't know the laws, the language or the systems. My father had nightmares – the same dream, over and over. He's back in Vietnam, preparing for our escape. He's back in the water, drifting day after day with nowhere to go. And then he wakes up.

*

Most Vietnamese who came to Australia during this time settled in either Melbourne or Sydney. My father chose Cabramatta, in Sydney, for its strong sense of community. He liked the idea that a number of his friends had already set up a life for themselves in such a short time. He understood that the secret to their success was hard work and unconditional dedication, often fuelled by underlying desperation. It didn't surprise him that many of them had become astute business people, showing great aptitude as shopkeepers.

In the mid-1980s, my father fed his sudden urge to open a video library. 'Asians love action movies,' he would say. The blockbuster releases at the time were *Full Metal Jacket, Platoon, Born on the Fourth of July* and *Good Morning, Vietnam.* My father found a prime location in the centre of bustling John Street, the spine of Cabramatta's thriving commercial centre.

'But why a video library, Dad?'

'Same as the driving school,' he said. 'No one else in Cabramatta's doing it.'

My father was considered a pioneer in the business community. Before opening a restaurant, he had dared to approach the local council about outdoor seating and shop renovation – a considerable feat for a new Vietnamese migrant. He became the first to offer alfresco dining, which proved a huge success.

Our restaurant offered a place for lonely migrants to meet and chat in their new and native tongues over a shared meal or coffee and ice-cream as they sat and watched the world go by. It made my father happy that his contribution and participation had helped so many rebuild their lives with confidence and hope.

Everybody works hard in Cabramatta. Seven days a week, the commercial centre is at full steam. Rest time comes once a year, in February, to celebrate the Lunar New Year. For most of their lives, my parents have worked seven days a week from 6.30 a.m. until 10.30 p.m. My father has closed the restaurant only once, when my grandmother passed away.

*

My father had constant flashbacks to the war. Part of his job as a lieutenant in artillery was to go back to the scene and count the dead bodies after a kill. One shell killed so many. The scars from his own bullet wounds resemble a question mark down the length of his spine.

Determined to succeed, my father took on a second job and then a third. At home he was always angry. He had an anger that none of us could explain. He would throw and smash things, and yell. Sometimes, he would just stand there and scream.

It wasn't long until he started to offload his anger on my mother, then on us, his children. My father was determined to raise four high-achievers. He wanted to make sure that the sacrifices he and my mother made were honoured.

If someone were to ask me what I remember most about my

childhood, I would tell them it is overwhelming fear. Fear followed me everywhere, every day. My father kept three instruments of torture: a stiff and shiny billiard stick, a flexible cane whip and his most effective weapon, fear.

Twice a year we would bring home our school reports with dread. For every B, he caned us once. For every C, he caned us twice. We had to lie flat on our stomach and not budge until he finished, blow after blow hacking at the flesh on our buttocks and thighs. When he was done, he threw us a dollar for every A.

He used to say, 'I created you and I have the power to destroy you.'

At seventeen, I ran away and spent many years hiding from my father. I would look over my shoulder everywhere, paranoid that familiar faces might follow me.

*

There comes a time when you need to conquer fear. For the sake of my mother and my brothers, and for all the shame I brought my family while I was away, I reluctantly reconciled with my father. I would go home to visit out of duty. I hated those visits. I hated the sense of claustrophobia and suffocation I felt in his presence. Our meetings were stifled, false and tense.

What I hated the most was the realisation that I had grown up to be like him. I too was angry all the time. Angry at my loved ones, my friends, my work colleagues; angry with the world. Angry at myself. Angry people are very skilled at noticing all that is wrong.

Later, when my partner and I decided to have a child, I was determined that this cycle would end. I was determined not to be the same person I had always been, because I was frightened, frightened of history repeating. Frightened of treating my own child the way I had been treated.

Towards the end of my pregnancy, I landed a book deal to write a memoir about my family. As I wrote, my fears returned. I worried: How could I possibly survive my father's reaction to the story?

There are ten chapters in my book. It's not meant to be a scathing account of my father's behaviour, but a beautiful story about personal freedom, family and hope. But in order to talk about the good things I had to talk about the bad things. I planned to finish the book and give it to him, so that he could see the full arc of the story. As I wrote, a cloud of dread hung over me.

By the time I finished the seventh chapter, my father demanded to read it. I freaked out. The seventh chapter was the most confronting, the most scathing about him – the most difficult chapter to write. I thought, *He can't read it now.* But you don't say no to my father: I had no choice but to hand over my unfinished manuscript. The story of his life, written by his prodigal daughter.

I didn't hear from him for two months. I needed to finish my book and move on, so on Father's Day I decided to go home and face the music. With my beautiful baby daughter, Mia, I drove home to Bonnyrigg to confront my parents. I was so nervous and scared I could hardly breathe.

*

I'm not scared that he's going to hit me; we've passed that stage. I'm scared because my writing exposes him and our family stories and secrets to the world. I'm scared because he might give me some ridiculous ultimatum and say, 'I forbid you to publish this book.'

I'm scared because I'm about to do something that's never been done before. I'm about to take responsibility to end this family's pattern. I'm about to confront my father to make things better.

So Mia and I wait at the front door. I've brought a case of my father's favourite red wine as a peace offering. When the doors open they take Mia, kiss her, cuddle her; they're so happy to see her. I see that they've made a feast for me. When we sit down to eat, I ask, 'Dad, what do you think about my story?'

'It's good, it's good, but there's just one thing wrong.'

'What's that, Dad?'

'The fish-sauce recipe's wrong.'

'What do you mean, the fish-sauce recipe's wrong?'

This can't be happening.

Later, I ask him again: 'Dad, what do you think about my book?' I get the same answer about the fish-sauce recipe. I'm frustrated that we're never going to define our relationship. We're never going to connect; I'm never going to finish my book;

I won't be able to move on. I get Mia ready and gather our things.

I'm just about to leave when I ask him one last time. 'Dad, what do you really think about my book?'

And in a voice sad and serious he says, 'Do you know why Buddha sits on a lotus flower?'

'No, Dad. Why does Buddha sit on a lotus flower?'

'There is nothing as beautiful as a lotus flower. Out of watery chaos it grows. Emerging from the depths of a muddy swamp, and yet remaining so pure and unpolluted by it. So pure you can eat it, all of it, the leaves, the roots, the seeds, the petals. But the lotus flower has another characteristic. Its stem you can easily bend, but you cannot easily break. It has tenacious fibres that hold the plant together.

'My children are lotus flowers. You have grown out of the aftermath of war. You have grown up in Cabramatta during its murkiest time. And you have grown out of me. I am mud, I am dirt, I am shit. I am very lucky to have you all.'

With those words he gave me everything I had been waiting for. He never apologised, but he acknowledged the harm he had inflicted. Now, when I think about my father, I think about forgiveness; I think about redemption, and about hope, and about unfailing courage in the face of adversity.

*

In October 2007, Murdoch Books published *Secrets of the Red Lantern*. It has been translated into two languages, won numerous awards and touched the lives of many people. This made my partner, my brother and me realise that as restaurateurs, business people and human beings, we have a social responsibility to make a difference.

At Red Lantern we have embarked on a journey to promote ethical eating. We use the freshest in local sustainable and organic produce, and aim to leave as light an environmental footprint as possible, while staying true to our Vietnamese origins. We have transformed Red Lantern's backyard into a 'garden of tranquillity' where we grow our own herbs and vegetables. We recycle everything, even our food scraps. Our aim is to reduce our garbage waste by at least two wheelie bins a week.

*

When I was asked to write a second book, my initial answer was no. I had to face many personal demons to write the first book. As I was about to decline the offer, I received three letters. It was a Friday morning, and I spent most of it in the back shed of our restaurant sobbing.

The first was from a woman who lives in Western Australia. She wrote that after reading *Secrets of the Red Lantern*, she felt an incredible sense of loss and guilt. Loss, because before reading the book, she never knew what it meant to be an immigrant, refugee or boat person. And guilt, because she had mistreated the immigrant kids at school. Now, twenty years after leaving school, she needed to make amends.

The second letter was from a couple living in Woollahra, in Sydney. They celebrated the wife's birthday at Red Lantern and bought a copy of the book. They wrote that some onions must have got caught in the pages, as they both sat up all night reading and crying tears of applause. They said that although it was a Vietnamese migrant story it was also their story, and their story had never been told in such a way before. They had fled Nazi Germany.

The third letter left me speechless. A man from Cecil Park, in Sydney's outer west, wrote eight pages. He too was a victim of child abuse, and after reading the book he was inspired and determined to return to his home country to try to find the reasons for his father's behaviour. He wrote that he was inspired to go back to Ireland to try to find answers and compassion and peace.

The next thing to do was to ask my parents, and my nervousness and fear returned. When I told my father about the second book, his answer threw me. 'How can you say no? You cannot. There are so many people out there with stories to tell but no voice to tell it. You have been given this opportunity and you must say yes.'

So with the blessing of my parents and the powerful words of others, I have agreed to write a second book, another *Secret* …

Griffith Review

The Ace of Spades

Carmel Bird

The ace of spades is the highest card in the deck, and is also the death card, used as such by American troops during the war in Vietnam. When an artist places this card in a painting, the viewer does well to take notice. And when a publisher puts on the cover of a book an image of a man with an ace of spades in his breast pocket, the reader must pay attention.

My personal library used to contain a paperback copy of *The Lucky Country* by Donald Horne, published in 1964. I am not sure when I first got the book, but it was probably a few years after it was first published. The library has travelled with me for nearly fifty years and has shed some books while acquiring others. The image on the cover of the lost book stays with me – a painting of a man's head by Albert Tucker, a head brutally carved from some hideous yellowy-brown substance, perhaps metallic, with a hawk nose and a grim, humourless prognathous jaw, wearing a battered Stetson with a cockatoo feather stuck in the band. The man is holding a mug of beer in his paw-like hand, and there in his top pocket is the ace of spades. He is a gambling man; he's an Australian. Years after the appearance of the man on the cover of *The Lucky Country*, Malcolm Fraser became the prime minister of Australia. I thought the image of the man resembled Fraser, while he in turn resembled an Easter Island statue. I expect all that says is that the man on the cover has a recognisable Australian face, but it was a nice comparison.

Behind the man shimmers a bright blue sky – heaven, you might say – and there are sails of yachts that suggest sharks while also repeating the crisp white collar of the man's open-neck shirt. The sun in the top left-hand corner looks quite pale and small and benign. How I hated that picture when I got the book. Has the great thick blight of the dominant drinking-gambling man with his back to the sea blotted out the carefree summer's day? I am afraid it has. The picture nicely sums up the ironic twist of the title, which arose from the sentence towards the end of the book where Horne says that Australia is a 'lucky country, run by second-rate people who share its luck': fighting words that have been largely forgotten. The title and the cover image play on each other to deliver the cry of the book, which was a wake-up call to Australians to start to understand the 'distinctiveness' of their own society in order for that society to remain 'prosperous, liberal and humane.' In a double irony, the title was taken up as a mantra intended to prove once and for all that Australia is so lucky that it can just sit back, produce the ace of spades, drink up, reap the benefits of luck and enjoy life.

In November 2009, when the federal Opposition was in disarray just before the bill on carbon emissions trading was about to go to the Senate, the image of the Tucker painting kept coming into my mind, and the phrase 'lucky country' kept ringing its hollow ring. Was the very luck on which the country relied finally running out, like sand through the floorboards of each house? In 2009 Australia was being described as the hottest and driest country on the planet, and a great deal of second-rate behaviour and thinking was coming to the fore as the critical vote on the carbon-tax bill drew closer. I searched the bookshelves for *The Lucky Country* and that was when I realised it had gone.

I wanted an old copy, one with that man on the cover. So I went to a place called Book Heaven in Castlemaine, Victoria, and there it was. I confess I had forgotten about the beer and playing card. How could I have forgotten the ace of spades? The sweet irony of the second-hand bookshop's name is obvious: Book Heaven. But what was I doing in the old gold-mining town of Castlemaine?

*

Two years ago I left Melbourne for Castlemaine, shedding a thousand books, among which perhaps was *The Lucky Country*. I have spent much of my life writing (in both fiction and non-fiction) about aspects of the distinctiveness of Australia, generally seeking to uncover on the one hand, beauty and goodness; on the other, those forces that play against humanity, often in the very name of prosperity and liberality. I have had a particular interest in policies regarding indigenous Australians, and also in the racial and religious fabric of this country. I can to an extent trace these interests to having been born in Tasmania during the Second World War.

When I was a child I was conscious that the island state of Tasmania was a kind of abject Australian joke, not part of a 'lucky' country at all, a place of negative importance nationally and internationally. How interesting it is to see how this perception has changed, with the advent of green politics and powerful political activism of various kinds, as well as clever tourist campaigns. Tasmania is now a destination of choice for people seeking clean air and beautiful wild scenery. My leaving of Tasmania was thus: I was twenty-two, a teacher in the Education Department, going along in lucky-country fashion teaching French and English. Then suddenly I received a transfer to go to a tiny island in Bass Strait, King Island. Now, King Island is world-famous for cheese, but in 1962 it was seen as the young female teacher's gulag. Yes, it could have been a challenge to the brave person I was not. To me, it was a call to arms – I left the state, packing my library of Racine and Voltaire and Rimbaud and Yeats into a big old cabin trunk, and went to teach in a private school in Victoria. I had, in a small way, rebelled. I had gone, as Tasmanians used to say, 'over the other side,' meaning mainland Australia, not the afterlife.

I thought of this act of, if you like, disobedience when I read recently in a newspaper the story of a young Melbourne priest who was musing on his vow of obedience. He reportedly said that if his bishop ordered him to move from Brighton to Castlemaine, he would have to go. Perhaps I am reading too much into this, but it seemed to me that he was putting the pleasant life among the sanitised mansions and rose gardens and tennis courts of Brighton against the grim spectre of the bacon factory and the prison of Castlemaine, and was feeling challenged. Of all the places he could have chosen to put up against Brighton, he chose Castlemaine. He caught my attention by that little slip of the pen. Perhaps he was just working his way through the alphabet.

Anyway, he got me thinking about places of obedience and places of choice. I chose to come here to live, making, as it is cutely said, a 'tree change.' Simply stated, since I can pursue my profession of writer just about anywhere, I followed my daughter and her young family here. But why did *they* come to Castlemaine? Well, she and her husband got teaching jobs here, and they thought it would be good to raise children in the country. I shed those thousand books and a lot of furniture and clothes, sold a house and bought a house, and here I am. It has been a short enough journey, from Tasmania to Melbourne to Castlemaine, with a year in LA and a year in Paris thrown in. Most of my life has been spent in Melbourne, and now that I look around at Castlemaine I can see – in the terrain, the size of the town, the winter cold, the old houses, the old gardens, the pear trees and the prunus trees, the stars in the clear night sky – vestiges of Tasmania in the 1950s.

Perhaps I am just projecting childhood scenes and feelings onto it, but that is my perception. I suppose I am fulfilling some childhood dreams of having a place with a lily pond and a covered walk draped in wisteria – like entering the images on some of my favourite swap cards. The choice of location was made for me by my family, but the choice of residence was my own. In fact, there was very little choice, and ending up with the lily pond and the wisteria vine was a matter of chance. That favourite Australian quality, chance.

The streets of Castlemaine soon tail off into forests and wild places. The town is two hours from the city of Melbourne. Civilisation here winds through the countryside in fairly thin slivers. I can lie in bed and glimpse the Melbourne train as it flashes through the trees in the near distance, running over an old arched brick bridge. I watch the black cockatoos perch in a crackle on the blue spruce outside the bedroom window, and listen sometimes in dismay to their throaty cacophony. Green parrots habitually dangle and twitter on the slender branches of the grey box. Sometimes a kangaroo hops down the road beside the house or takes a short cut through the front garden. And once I found a bewildered koala lurking in the branches of a tall dark cypress. I am reminded at every turn that I have exchanged the streets of Melbourne for life on the edge of the forest, have exchanged the waters of the bay for the dry inland.

In early spring the streets are lined with the dreamy clouds of pink prunus blossoms, and a little later on the verges are washed with waves of the dark golden stars of gazanias. The air is often sweet with the perfumes of many aromatic plants. The drought here is severe and long-lived, so there is an obsession with water. I am obsessed. I grew up in a state that was obsessed with water, to begin with. One of the first things I did here was install a water tank, and then I restored the empty lily pond, removing a dense, dry infestation of dead irises. Living among the irises was the biggest, blackest, knobbliest toad, which I relocated to a deep dark corner of the garden. Since then I have not seen it. I filled the pond and stocked it with water plants and with goldfish which disappeared into the depths, seen only occasionally as a lovely flash in the sunlight.

One day, as I was sitting with friends beneath the wisteria vine beside the pond, I noticed that many of the fish had suddenly decided to swim out in the sunlight and I later discovered that the level of the water in the nearby swimming pool was rapidly dropping. Some of the water from the pool seemed to have moved through the pond, killing off the fish, which had multiplied since I had put them there, and which now floated sadly on the surface after their final desperate moment in the sun. Throughout the winter the level of the swimming pool kept falling, owing to the failure of the plug that holds the water in.

During the months when the pool was out of action, the filter pump was turned off. Came the day in late spring when the pool was refilled, I turned on the pump. With a horrible whine the pump, useless, began to give off smoke, for curled up inside it was a dead bluetongue lizard which had been in residence over the winter months. Stiff and cold and stripy. I buried the bluetongue and ordered a new pump.

Meanwhile, I restocked the pond with goldfish, in time for the mosquito season. The buds of the waterlilies were just beginning to break the surface of the water. So there I was again sitting happily beneath the wisteria with friends, when a tall heron came swooping gracefully down, silent, alert. He landed on a rock beside the pond, paused, took a quick inventory, but perhaps because we were now watching, flew off. He would be back for the goldfish in due course. The wire mesh below the surface of the water can stop a small child from drowning, but can't stop a heron from fishing.

One of my favourite lines in literature comes from *Alice's Adventures in Wonderland*: 'There was a table set out under the tree in front of the house.' I think of it often when I come out and have tea under the plum tree: the round red teapot and the red-and-white-striped milk jug with its beaded cover to keep out the bugs that might tumble in. There is a cloth on the table, a bowl of red roses, and yes, we sometimes have cucumber sandwiches. Such civilised rituals so close by the busy industry of birds and fish and lizards and toads and bugs. Not to mention spiders and snakes. There is of course no paradise without a serpent as standard issue, whether real or metaphoric. And I realise that Alice was walking in on a *mad* tea party.

I spend a lot of time reading, writing or taking tea under the wisteria's sweet dreamy purple drifts in spring, and under the green umbrella of its leaves in summer. Well, there I was again. It was the day I buried the bluetongue, and as we sat there, a black swarm of bees moved swiftly overhead, a loud thrumming shadow. For an instant the air was humming with threat; then it was gone. It is a relief and pleasure to see bees, though, since they are endangered, and without them human life will not survive. So if they are going, everybody is going. There are all kinds of superstitions about bees: some say that a swarm overhead is an evil omen; some say it is good. Let's say it's good, then. Will the omen of the bees have the power to counteract the evil promise of the single silent crow – the biggest, blackest, shiniest crow – that took up residence the following day on the bluetongue's resting place? As I backed away from the crow I saw, among the poppies that were almost flowering, the first ladybird I have seen in two years. It was tiny and shiny and bright, bright glittering scarlet. A busy little bead on the grey-green poppy leaves. Now these bugs *are* a good omen, and the sight of one always lifts the spirit. Except the rhyme you must say if you accidentally kill one is distinctly unsettling as spring turns to summer and the threat of bushfire haunts the heart. Close to the surface of everyday life in rural and not-so-rural Australia lurks the fear of fire. So who wants to hear the words in the rhyme 'Fly away home. Your house is on fire'? The rest of the verse is something I have always found unspeakably awful: 'Your children are gone.'

Something else I have missed since I have been here are the snails. In late spring there was a burst of fierce hot weather. The hardy gazanias by the roadside were suddenly all burnt by the sun. Then there were days and days of black thunderclouds and lightning and lashing rain. And then, one grey day, crawling up the bricks by the front door came a small snot-coloured garden snail. One. I do not wish for snails, but this little creature inching up the wall was the possible harbinger of more sweet rain. Dams and tanks were full and overflowing, and everyone attended public meetings to discuss strategies for the coming fire season. It is so obvious that the patterns of weather in Australia, like elsewhere, have changed, and that extremes of drought, heat and storms are becoming more frequent and more dramatic, and that human behaviour must change accordingly and quickly. Restrictions on the use of water apply not only in the country towns but also in the city. People in the city also now have water tanks. In the 1970s in Melbourne I wanted to put in a tank because it seemed such an obvious thing to do, but council laws forbade it. Times change.

As hot, wet November moved on to December, and summer drew closer and closer, the reports of tragic stories of the early 2009 bushfires kept coming, offering a dreadful background of truth and detail to the hourly twists and turns of the power struggles in the Opposition, mingled with the government's struggle to pass the bill on the carbon emissions tax in the Senate. The two stories seemed to me to be entwined, each embedded in a narrative where the weather is the real villain and chance is driving the plot.

Bushfires are more fierce and more common than they used to be, and I am more alert to them now because I live close to the forest and have a fire plan for the summer. The level of the sea is rising. The polar ice is melting. I have re-read *The Lucky Country*, which I rescued from Book Heaven, and I feel the deep wisdom of Donald Horne's simple enough message of a call to consciousness. But every time I close the book I see the image of the man in the hat and I wonder about the plot. Who will reap the benefits? What are the benefits? What's the weather doing? Is the ugly Australian still holding the highest card, and does he realise it is the death card?

Griffith Review

Magic Island

Nicolas Rothwell

Just off the marshy coastline of the Northern Territory there lies a magic island, unknown to most Australians, where spirits walk, spells and incantations course through the humid air, and rival bands of traditional doctors wage a constant struggle for supremacy.

Elcho Island – better known these days by the name of its main settlement, Galiwinku – is home to almost 3000 Aboriginal people, members of the hyper-cerebral Yolngu group of clans. It is a place of lush natural beauty: the curving beaches are surrounded by deep-red cliffs; the forests of acacia and stringy-bark stretch away.

But the community itself is at once remote and overcrowded; it is under-resourced and afflicted by grave medical challenges. Only a single Elcho local is famous in the wider world: Geoffrey Gurrumul Yunupingu, who grew up there, and sings its songs. Once, a Christian mission shaped the island's trajectory; today, the ever-changing plans for its development are set by shire managers and Canberra bureaucrats. The different phases of this history are still visible. Tall crosses dot the roadside graveyards, alongside traditional funerary carvings, sacred flags and the Intervention's 'prescribed area' warning signs. Cows graze in front gardens, dog packs maraud hungrily, vast card games unfold as lightning flickers in the sunset sky: it is a surreal stage-set – indeed, almost anything seems possible, yet the armies of service providers stationed here remain blissfully unaware of the metaphysical currents seething beneath the placid surface of Galiwinku life.

So it has been for years; so it was, too, in the early 1970s, when an inquiring transcultural psychiatrist named John Cawte began making dry-season visits to Elcho, and exploring the mysteries of its spirit life. Cawte's portrait, titled *Healers of Arnhem Land*, uncovered a world almost unknown to the missionaries and managers of the North: a world where the fear of sorcery was omnipresent, and a constant paranoia about spells, cursing and malign witch-doctors shaped the pulse of life.

In Cawte's account, a kind of arms race of traditional medicine was in place across the Yolngu clan realm of north-east Arnhem Land all through the years when he was in the field. Two forces seemed to be contending, and their techniques were always shifting, escalating, in a fluid adaptation to new circumstances. On one side were the 'good' doctors, or 'Marrnggitj' – figures of seniority, able to comfort and to heal. On the other were the shadowy 'Galkas' – malevolent, murderous, responsible for all deaths and sicknesses, sowing terror and anguish in every heart. Some Galka men would use spells, or killing stones, or they would whip up dry, strength-sapping poison winds. Others stole up on their victims secretly, and inserted sharp spines in their bodies. Death would follow, inexplicably, a day, a week or a month later. There were scores of ways for a Galka to kill a man – and just as many methods the Marrnggitj could use in defence. But it was difficult back then to study healers – as Cawte remarked: 'They do not run a clinic, or put up a brass plate' – and the secrecy that surrounds traditional medicine is even more entrenched on Galiwinku today, though its grip on the Yolngu population is just as strong.

How, then, to make inroads? There are surface aspects of this magic world: many healers use plant medicines. Gradually, over recent years, a handful of traditional bush remedies have been incorporated into the Western medical service, and at the sprawling Ngalkanbuy Clinic in Galiwinku, health education worker Helen Guyupul prepares a large batch of stringy-bark tea for distribution at the start of each week. It is a bright-green decoction, astringent: it removes pain, cures asthma, serves as a tonic, and, in large doses, induces sleepiness. A tree-gall fungus is used to combat vomiting and internal problems, another tree's leaves heal the liver, another still yields jet-black ash that takes fevers away. Down a nearby side street, two visitors from Mapuru outstation, Roslyn Malngunba Guyula and Ian Wuruwul Gurrumba, are brewing their own remedies from paperbark and vines.

'When we get sick,' says Roslyn, 'we dig a long hole in the ground, and cover ourselves with wet paperbark and hot ant-bed sand. You lie there for seven hours. After that time, after that fight with moisture, you're healed, you feel like a newborn.' Indeed, newborn children are themselves carefully smoked over gum-leaf fires to give them strength. Behind traditional healing methods of this kind lies a philosophy, one Roslyn explains to some of the more troubled patients who come her way: 'You have to heal people, see they need to be healed. You tell them it's all about stories: good is good. Live the right way, and if you live in the good way, bad forces wouldn't touch you.'

Here, still well-masked, is a faint hint of the elaborate belief system that holds sway on Elcho and across Arnhem Land: a balanced, complex set of ideas and values that provide a framework for interpreting the joys and the pains of life. It is tempting to paint it simply as a form of dualism: light does battle with dark, good contends with evil. Much in this schema involves hidden forces, spirits and ancestral power. Most of it is kept veiled from outside eyes.

Of course, the Westerners on Elcho understand the island is a fairly unusual place, where the locals perform ceremonies, carve totemic animals, make hollow log coffins and conduct dance-glutted funerals that last for weeks on end. The largely mainstream-staffed medical services at Galiwinku are the membrane where Yolngu and Western ways of thinking come into closest contact. Nurses are often warned in dark tones about increased witch-doctor activity: 'Lock your doors,' they are told, in peremptory fashion. 'No questions!' Or the instruction comes to conceal all the syringes and needles at the clinic, because the Galka sorcerers like using them, or there is a sudden need to count the store of body bags, in case the Galkas have been secreting them away.

Fear of the Dark

Are the Galka real, or not? To visitors or new arrivals, belief in them may seem mere superstition – but the consequences are real, and deep. One of the island's best-known ceremonial leaders vanished a few years ago, while walking on a quiet beach: the body was never found. Police assumed he'd been taken by a crocodile, but his family were devastated, and the tensions caused by the disappearance and the ensuing recriminations linger to this day.

Deaths are always followed by blaming: the attempt to find a meaning and a cause for death is pervasive in the Yolngu world, where so many die young, without obvious cause. And the deceased linger, long after their funerals, in the form of Mokuy, or spirits, who can be seen from time to time on distant promontories and sensed very often as presences in rooms they once frequented. You can smell the scent of their cigarettes, or they make themselves felt by mischievous pranks and little jogging gestures: the mysterious removal of keys, for instance, is a constant problem. Given this state of affairs, it is natural for men of prominence to arm themselves with healing magical authority, or the air of it; and it is very widely assumed in Galiwinku that senior men have special powers.

'It's a culture of anxiety and paranoia,' says Michelle Dowden, manager of primary health care at Ngalkanbuy. 'There's constant worry in people's lives: worry about who might come in the night.' Fear of the dark is universal among the Yolngu, and intense, so in the days before street lighting families tended to stay together, clustered, bonded, telling stories. It was only with the arrival of streetlights that young people began roaming around at night, and drugs and social anomie took their present hold.

But even the noontime is no sure guarantee of safety. The mere suggestion of the presence of Galkas is enough to strain the health of the sick, or induce suicidal thoughts – and given their grip on the popular imagination, it becomes essential to devise counter-measures. One Yolngu health worker likes to explain the problem in terms of a mafia. Today's Galka man is no longer believed to be just malevolent: he is also a mercenary. Thus it is said that one can buy the services of a Galka, and once such threats are invoked, desperate steps are necessary. It is helpful to find a Marrnggitj, a good doctor, for your defence. Such protection, though, is hard to come by, for the great healers are much sought after, and they tend to live far from town, on remote outstations in the vicinity of the Arafura swamp. Procuring a Marrnggitj can be like finding a top-notch lawyer: you have to ask around. Maybe there's one down at First Creek, a silent man, wearing a tall hat. But at First Creek, the news is bad: the Marrnggitj went back to his home in Milingimbi Island a week ago. And anyway, who's asking, and why, exactly?

Curses in the Digital Age

At such a juncture, it helps to bear in mind the multiple pathways that lead to medicine, as well as the close parallels Yolngu people like to trace between traditional doctoring and modern technology. In John Cawte's days, Marrnggitj and Galka powers were often compared to the magic of the radio telephone, or to radiation from uranium mines in far west Arnhem Land. Today, the strong link is with mobiles: they can send words from afar, and make the hidden visible. Take the mystic water snake that swims from Milingimbi across to Elcho once every seven years. It has just made its latest spirit journey, and an aerial photo, snapped by mobile from a Mission Aviation Fellowship flight, shows its long, sinuous shadow, immersed in the wave-caps as it heads towards its destination.

The Galkas seem to favour the mobile network. It offers instant dissemination, and visual proof of their disquieting powers. With this convenient method of information transfer available, the inevitable has happened: magic force can now be transmitted by phone, and indeed by text. Curses, the bane of Galiwinku life, can be sent with the push of a button from Darwin, where increasing numbers of Yolngu have taken refuge from the wild affrays of the local spirit realm.

Since daily life has become so full of hazard, it pays for each clan to have its own set of healers, curse-lifters and specialist magic doctors: a spiritual defensive cadre. Responsibility for plant remedies tends to fall on women; the tasks of the doctor, though, are often seen as male, and they are strongly linked to clan authority. In the world of the Gumatj, perhaps the best-known of the clan groups on Elcho, the dominant figure for the

Burarrwanga family line is Charlie Matjuwi, now in his late seventies – blind, profoundly deaf, yet still grand and regal in his bearing, and still one of the region's chief ceremonial singers. Matjuwi had several sons, among them George Burarrwanga, lead singer of the Warumpi Band, who died three years ago; the prominent artist Peter Datjing; and the subtle, tradition-minded Layilayi, who serves now as his father's daily healer, protector and guide. Layilayi is a striking figure, even by the histrionic standards that prevail on Elcho. Tall, thin, mantled by a dust-pink peaked cap, eyes veiled by white-framed wrap-around dark glasses, he can generally be found at the Galiwinku aged-care centre, where his natural bent for therapy finds free expression. But his ceremonial responsibilities are increasing, as are his medical tasks.

A Yolngu doctor's procedures can seem, by Western standards, unusually personal. The healer and his patient enter into a close, wordless bond, for illness is understood primarily as an affair of spirits: disturbance of the afflicted body by a spirit substance, which must be found and taken out. The patient lies prone before the healer, and explains in detail the nature of his symptoms. The healer, whose hands have been dipped in fresh, cleansing water, begins his assessment. He sees an aura, as much as a corporeal form: 'I touch, and heal,' says Layilayi. 'If I touch that spirit, I take that sickness into me. That man before me, when I touch him he feels something like a cold fire going into his body; he feels light, and then the pain will go away. It is real, for the whole world, when we believe with heart and soul: that spirit is always there.' The healer takes the distemper from the patient into himself, then he vomits it back out, in the form of blood and bile.

When he was younger, Layilayi kept a small dillybag with healing accoutrements, a familiar feature from descriptions of Marrnggitj practices in years gone by. Among them were spirit stones, and stones that gave the power to see far, and carved objects that ward off evil spells. Layilayi, though, left the magic dillybag in Yuendumu, in the Central Desert, where members of his family live, and embarked on a medical path largely unaided by such props.

Treatment at his hands makes a strong impression: the patient feels the healer at his side, feels the touch of fingers, moving upon his skin. They press inwards, they probe. How cold they are! And then a lightness comes, a dizziness, a depleted tiredness, a need to sleep, which persists for almost an hour, only to give way to clarity, balance, a feeling one has a new path ahead. This sensation explains the demand for such services: the healer holds the keys to coherence, to a sense of order amidst the chaos of community life. He can also gauge the emotional climate around him, and Layilayi is constantly advising his father to stay within his run-down, crowded dwelling in the heart of town; not to go outdoors, where spells and curses threaten. 'This is the worst place, here, Galiwinku,' Layilayi says, with intense feeling. 'People do anything; they do cruel things. There's always jealousy in the Yolngu background. Too many divisions! They're doing Galka way, people killing each other. It's the jealousy at the heart of it – trick stories. We know, we can read people's heads.'

Layilayi and other members of his clan have just returned from Maningrida, from the funeral of a young Elcho man who committed suicide. The death is firmly ascribed to magic 'cruelties,' and the collapse of moral standards in the region's life. Hence, undoubtedly, the strong emphasis on healing in recent times, across the communities of north-east Arnhem Land, as the upholders of tradition attempt to ward off the black-magic plague. Healing ceremonies are the natural defence, and younger Marrnggitj doctors have been flocking to large, secret gatherings where they can gain access to the higher aspects of their craft. Those mysteries lie buried close to the core of the Yolngu world. What are the powers? Where do they come from? How did the dark side grow so predominant?

Instrument of Payback

When explorers, missionaries and anthropologists began probing the remote beaches of Elcho Island and its surrounding archipelagos they were struck, of course, by the complexity of the religious system and the influence it wielded over day-to-day affairs. The pioneer researcher in the region, Donald Thomson, was quick to spot the ambiguous relationship between the 'good' Marrnggitj doctors and the forces of Galka. He reported, in a very early paper, that black magic seemed to be a recent, cultic import, which had its origins far to the west, in the swampy country where Maningrida lies today. But healer-magicians have long been a feature of the Yolngu realm, and Cawte's book includes a striking cameo of his encounter with Djipuru, the great Marrnggitj of the Arafura Swamp. Djipuru shows Cawte his instrument of payback, a carved wooden amulet with two projections that represent the horns of the buffalo. Cawte is surprised: the buffalo, after all, is an introduced species in Arnhem Land, though it now runs wild in vast numbers. But eventually he accepts the logic: why not choose 'the long strong horns of this powerful animal' as a symbol of retaliation in the magic wars?

The shadow of Djipuru looms over Galiwinku. He died recently, but his descendants and relations revere him, and his memory is still very much present in their world, as are the lessons he taught about the Marrnggitj power and its place in the social order. Djipuru was 'second father' to Ian Wuruwul Gurrumba of Mapuru. Wuruwul was raised by him, in happier times, when Yolngu men were healthy and strong, and lived quite free from Western medicine. Indeed, when Djipuru passed away, aged 100, Wuruwul received 'a half spirit' – half the old man's Marrnggitj powers. 'That's why,' says Wuruwul, 'if someone has a cough, or headache, today, I can put my hands in water and then heal them, with nothing, without any spirit tools. I can touch the body and make it better.'

Djipuru's own gifts, however, were of a quite different order: he was a 'bush clever man.' Everyone came to consult him and receive treatment from him; Milingimbi people used to make the trip by plane, and car, to see him at his remote home and have their devil spirits removed by his hands. When Roslyn Malngunba was struck by lightning fifteen years ago, and she found herself convulsed by sickness and constant pains, it was he who healed her. 'He concentrated all his power in the palms of his hands, he took water into his mouth, he touched me, then he expelled what was inside me. He spat it out,' she says.

There is a sense, often, in accounts of such treatments, that the blood of the sick patient is recycled, purified, by the doctor, who serves much the same function as a dialysis machine. But the healing process, at its highest level, is also emotional: it relies on insights, courage, will. Djipuru, in fact, was something more than merely human: he could manifest as a pig or a jabiru, an emu or a stone curlew, but above all he chose the buffalo as his favoured form, and still today when a buffalo comes towards Wuruwul's outstation house he knows it is his second father's spirit drawing near. There was proof of Djipuru's persisting presence in his old haunts only recently, when a local at Naliyindi homeland was taking a quick video with a mobile phone in the bush. When the clip was replayed, there, on screen, in clear definition, was Djipuru, standing, wearing a hat, his camp-dog at his side – inevitably, for Naliyindi lies in country shaped by dingo ancestors in the far-off creation times.

The most spectacular instance of Djipuru's shape-shifting is, oddly, the best documented. In the 1970s, he manifested near Nhulunbuy, the mining town just down the road from the Yolngu community of Yirrkala: he was wallowing, in buffalo form, in a billabong when he was spotted by a member of the Gumatj clan, Nyapanyapa Yunupingu. She swore at the buffalo; Djipuru charged and gored her – but then felt, apparently, a rush of contrition. The buffalo proceeded to gather up Nyapanyapa on his long horns, much like a forklift, and conveyed her gently to the nearby hospital and lay there, docile, as the nurses and doctors gathered round. Nyapanyapa went on to become a prominent bark painter, and her autobiographical picture of the attack, accompanied by a dramatic video reconstruction, won the 3D prize in the 2008 Telstra Aboriginal Art Award.

Power of Life and Death

The capacity to travel great distances instantaneously, the ability to see spirits and assume the guise of totemic animals, these are distinctive gifts, and the way Djipuru acquired them was also distinctive. Indeed, the story gives a clue to what lies behind the skills of traditional medicine. Mitjarrandi Wunungmurra, who knew the old man well, explains how one day, when out hunting with a group of men near Oenpelli, Djipuru became lost. He was camped alone beneath a rock overhang when he heard a strange flapping sound. It drew near, nearer, until a giant spirit, a birdman, with flying-fox wings, pounced on him, picked him up and carried him away to a distant mountain. He was kept there by the birdmen. 'His language was changed,' says Mitjarrandi, 'so he could speak their words, and understand them. That's the place where the winged spirits offered him the magic stones. One makes you invisible, one can turn you into an animal, one heals you. Each stone had a name.' Possessed of these powers, Djipuru was able from that time on to sense marauding devil-spirits from far away. He held the power of life and death distilled inside him: Mitjarrandi's mother once saw him kill and then revive a man. And if one probes a little deeper it becomes plain that he was both a Marrnggitj and a Galka – the two roles were mingled in complex ways in him; the power he held to heal was also the power that could kill.

Here, at last, we break through to the heart of things. In the Yolngu cosmos, light and dark belong together – they should support and define each other. The doctor's gift partakes of both; it is simply life's force, channelled, intensified: the strength of nature, passed through man. It seems clear that when the Galka men first made their appearance in Yolngu life, they had their natural place, they served as a regulatory power; far from being dread black magicians, skulking in the shadows, they were a form of sanction, they were almost agents of the law. People who infringed key social rules were confronted by them and told, openly, to conform or die. And even today, men or women with magic powers can choose which way to use them: for good or ill. Marrnggitj and Galka, then, were not at first opposing forces at all; they were once in harmony, and should still be in equilibrium – balance, in north-east Arnhem Land, being everything.

But the system has broken down on Elcho; the stresses of modernity are in the ascendant: drugs, kava, violence between men and women. Life on a large Yolngu community today is a life of troubles, and the surge of Galka magic can be read both as symptom of the collapse of the old, strict social order and as contributing cause. The rise of the Galka also parallels the growing sense among the Yolngu that they have lost power and control over their own lives. Galka magic has gone from being a force wielded by a handful of well-known individuals to being a noxious, terrifying mood in the social landscape, a state of generalised fear that keeps men and women locked indoors in fright.

What lies behind this shift? For centuries, the Yolngu lived by their own, hard laws; for decades, they lived under missionary control; then – nothing well-defined, no rules, no work, a flow of welfare, minutely administered, indefinitely prolonged. It was several years ago that Galiwinku first emerged as the capital of cursing and spell-casting – perhaps because of its isolation and its crush of population and the resultant social strains. There were strange tales of anti-Christ cults and hidden sects. The fear of Galka became almost as important as the phenomenon itself. And, as a natural counter, a fresh revival of tradition began. Elcho had always been an island of ceremonial dance, much loved by anthropologists. Under the surface layers of community life, that trend intensified. Marrnggitj healers gained in prominence. 'We all go to them, quietly, of course,' says one Yolngu teacher. 'We all use them these days. All the time.'

The light is softening in the eastern sky; blue cloud-banks ride far out to sea. The waves are lapping at the rocks; a ramshackle troop carrier, laden with young dancers, pulls up. Several fan out through the sandy bush, clutching axes, and begin felling pandanus trunks. Others prepare the white clay needed for their body paint. Old Charlie Matjuwi, head of the Burarrwanga Gumatj line, feels the salt breeze on his cheeks, and at once begins to sing, and tell stories; it is his first visit to this beach in the six years since he went blind. Gum-leaves are gathered up and lit; a sturdy platform of branches has taken shape in the scrub, and on it lies a young man, white-painted, ready for traditional medicine to take its course.

From the shadows of the forest, dancers converge, step by step, their movements full of grace. Full of menace, too, for this is the crocodile dance: the Gumatj dance of cleansing fire. The clapsticks are sounding, Matjuwi is singing, chanting, smoke billows into the air; it envelops the patient. Now the Marrnggitj healer approaches: Layilayi Burarrwanga himself, elaborately painted, transformed into a new creature, sinuous in his movements, reptilian. His head and his arms are festooned in feather-bands of red and orange; he holds clan symbols and two decorated spears. Nearer he draws, nearer, with spasmodic steps; a sacred bag is clutched in his teeth. He makes smooth gestures with his hands; everything is balanced, the voices and the clapstick rhythms join together and swirl into the air. From a distance, the gathered women look on. The sun quivers on the horizon. The ritual takes its course. Night descends. The dancers gaze out, quiet now, and calm. The sea breeze drops away. All ills have been healed, at least for the moment: the Yolngu universe is calm and whole again.

The Weekend Australian

Asylum Seekers and Australian Democracy: What Do We Fear?

Robert Manne

The first boat in Australian history with asylum seekers on board reached our northern coastline in April 1976. Over the next thirty-four years a further 24,000 boat people, as they came to be called, arrived. One of the most intriguing and puzzling questions of Australian politics is how so apparently minor an issue has had such an impact on our national life for such a protracted period of time. No political question has more clearly separated Australia's 'battlers' from the inner-city 'elites.' No ideological issue has more sharply divided the left from the right. The asylum-seeker issue dominated the 2001 election. It cast its shadow across the 2010 campaign. It has blighted the careers of two Labor leaders, Kim Beazley and Kevin Rudd.

The first boat people were South Vietnamese fleeing from the communist victory of 1975. Between 1976 and 1982, 2000 reached our shores. In order to stem the flow, the Fraser government accepted more than 50,000 Vietnamese from the archipelago of refugee camps in Thailand, the Philippines, Malaysia and Indonesia. Australians were easily panicked by the spontaneous arrival of a small number of boats. They were comfortable and relaxed about a far larger refugee program under government control. In the history of Australia and boatpeople, these were the halcyon years. The Fraser government treated all these refugees, including the spontaneous boat arrivals, with exemplary generosity.

There was no talk of mandatory detention or temporary protection visas. Fraser could not have accomplished this alone, however. The success of the settlement relied on the existence of a bipartisan consensus within the Australian political elite. With the boat arrivals, the Labor Opposition under Whitlam, and then Hayden, resisted the temptation to exploit underlying racist or anti-refugee sentiment for party-political gain. Even the Cold War ideological divide was blurred. The right supported the refugees as escapees from communism; the left as part of the project of burying White Australia.

No boats of asylum seekers arrived for several years after 1982. In the early 1990s, however, a new wave of mainly Cambodian asylum seekers landed in the north. In response, the Keating government erected Australia's first anti-asylum-seeker deterrent – mandatory detention. In the mid-1990s, a larger number of boats arrived bearing mainly Chinese or Sino-Vietnamese. The asylum claims were rejected. The repatriation process was so swift, ruthless and efficient that few Australians are even now aware that it took place.

In 1999 boats with asylum seekers mainly from the Middle East began arriving. The overwhelming majority were indisputably genuine refugees who had fled from the Taliban regime in Afghanistan, from Saddam Hussein's Iraq and from the Iranian theocratic state. While the left in general welcomed these asylum seekers on humanitarian and anti-racist grounds, the right reacted with undisguised hostility. The Cold War was over; the Bush-led wars against the Taliban and Saddam Hussein had not yet begun. Although, as a signatory to the Refugee Convention, the Howard government was obliged to assess the asylum claims of the Afghans, the Iraqis and the Iranians, it made their lives as unpleasant as possible. The asylum seekers were described as 'illegal immigrants' and as 'queue jumpers.' Under the already existing system of mandatory detention, men, women and even children faced indefinite periods of imprisonment behind razor wire in desert camps. Mental illness, hunger strikes, self-harm and suicide attempts became common. For those whose asylum applications succeeded, a system of temporary protection visas was introduced. The new refugees were unable to build secure lives or even to apply to have their wives or children join them.

Gradually the asylum-seeker issue moved to the centre of Australian political life. It divided Australian society into two relatively clear groups. The mainstream was overwhelmingly hostile to the Middle Eastern asylum seekers; a smaller number of well-educated and well-heeled inner-city dwellers were their friends. Since the 1996 election, the Howard government had been searching for a way to ride the populist wave Pauline Hanson had created. In late August 2001 it discovered how, when it refused to allow a Norwegian vessel, the *Tampa*, to unload its cargo of 433 mainly Afghan asylum seekers on Christmas Island. Mainstream opinion responded with delight at the boarding of the *Tampa* by SAS troops. It reacted with anger at even the slightest sign of Labor opposition to the anti-asylum-seeker course that Howard had chosen. With *Tampa*, Howard simultaneously satisfied the appetite for an aggressive populist politics One Nation had stimulated and threatened to tear the Labor Party apart along the seam dividing its two core constituencies: the professional middle class and the traditional working class. Having forbidden the *Tampa* to land, the government swiftly improvised a system for preventing the arrival of any further asylum-seeker boats. The government excised both Christmas Island and Ashmore Reef from Australia for the purposes of the operation of the *Immigration Act*. Asylum seekers would no longer need to be dealt with according to the legal obligations of the Refugee Convention. It mounted a naval and air operation, the purpose of which was to intercept all asylum-seeker boats heading towards Australia – to drive the seaworthy ones back to Indonesia and to dispatch the passengers of the non-seaworthy ones to hastily improvised offshore processing detention camps on Nauru and Manus Island, Papua New Guinea. It called the anti-asylum system it created the Pacific Solution.

Since the early 1990s Australian governments had been searching for an effective anti-asylum-seeker deterrent. The old system of deterrence begun under Keating and completed under Howard – indefinite mandatory detention in desert camps, temporary protection visas, anti-people-smuggling operations – had comprehensively failed. Between 1999 and 2001, some 180 boats bearing around 12,000 asylum seekers reached Australia. The new system of military repulsion and offshore processing in detention camps on godforsaken Pacific Islands was an equally comprehensive 'success.' In the six years between 2002 and 2007, eighteen boats arrived with fewer than 300 asylum seekers. The liberal political imagination finds it difficult to accept that political ends are often achieved through the use of brutal means. History is however full of such examples. The Pacific Solution was one. Through a combination of military force, diplomatic bribery and legal chicanery, the Howard government was able to solve Australia's 'problem' with asylum-seeker boats.

In the six years between the *Tampa* and the election of the Rudd government, the friends of the asylum seekers seemed incapable of thinking clearly about the meaning of what had occurred. It was one thing to condemn the Pacific Solution as immoral. It was an altogether different thing to pretend that Howard's anti-asylum-seeker deterrent barrier had not succeeded. The friends of the asylum seekers found it impossible to accept the main reason that asylum-seeker boats had stopped coming to Australia, namely that no one was interested in paying people smugglers thousands of dollars for the privilege of languishing in misery in the hellhole on Nauru. This failure of intellectual honesty was not costless. By the third year of the Rudd government, there would be a heavy political price to pay.

*

In 'Faith in Politics,' an article written for the *Monthly* prior to his bid to lead the Labor Party, Kevin Rudd wrote passionately about the question of asylum seekers.

> Another great challenge of our age is asylum seekers. The biblical injunction to care for the stranger in our midst is clear. The parable of the Good Samaritan is but one of the many which deal with the matter of how we should respond to the vulnerable stranger in our midst.

Rudd was true to these words. In 2008 his government abolished temporary protection visas; it pledged to try to settle all asylum-seeker claims within three months; it formally ended offshore processing by closing the nearly empty detention camp on Nauru. Softening mandatory detention and ending temporary protection were unproblematic. Neither measure had succeeded as a deterrent. Abandoning the Pacific Solution was not. It had been the creation of the offshore processing camps that was primarily responsible for stopping the asylum-seeker boats.

In retrospect it is clear that the government would have been wiser to move towards the kind of regional offshore processing centre that Julia Gillard suggested on the eve of the 2010 election than simply to close the detention camp on Nauru. What reason did the government have for believing that if the Pacific Solution was simply abandoned asylum-seeker boats would not return? If the Rudd government wanted to help asylum seekers, it could have increased substantially its annual quota of refugees. As in the days of the Fraser government with its intake of Vietnamese, a generous refugee resettlement program would have posed no danger for Rudd. Dismantling Howard's Pacific Solution and presiding over an apparent loss of control at the border carried grave political risk.

The risks it ran were always obvious. In November 2008 I argued in the *Monthly* that the Rudd asylum-seeker policy was morally admirable but politically perilous:

> The hope of the government is … that because of the success of the Howard government's brutal deterrence policy, people smugglers will continue to give Australia a wide berth. The new humanitarianism of the Rudd government's asylum-seeker policy is free-riding on the 'success' of the Howard government's inhumanity. Rudd is gambling on the fact that the shaky logical and moral foundations of its asylum-seeker policy will not be tested.

Other friends of the asylum seekers probably found this an inconvenient truth too unpleasant to face. As we now know, that gamble failed. During the course of 2009, almost 2800 asylum seekers reached Australia by boat. During the first eight months of this year, 4000.

*

Less than a year ago, the question of boat arrivals became a serious political problem for the Rudd government. Rudd now spoke rather incoherently of his determination to find an asylum-seeker policy that was simultaneously 'tough' and 'humane,' that is to say, which expressed a Good Samaritan's sympathy for asylum seekers but treated the people smugglers who served their interests by bringing them to Australia as 'vermin.' He sought to convince the public that changes in the international situation rather than the abandonment of the Pacific Solution explained the return of the asylum-seeker boats. Unfortunately this defied common sense. In 2008 and 2009 there had been an identical number of asylum-seeker claims lodged in Western countries – 377,000. By contrast, in 2008 some 160 boat people had reached Australia and in 2009, as we have seen, some 2800. Sensing the danger the return of the boats posed for his government, Rudd struggled to save the situation by attempting to improvise what became known as the Indonesian Solution. In return for the funding of detention centres, intelligence sharing, cooperative naval searches and joint anti-people-smuggling operations, Indonesia, it was hoped, would prevent the onward movement to Australia of asylum seekers. The hope was almost instantly stillborn. Corruption ensured that anti-people-smuggling operations would be partially successful at best. Moreover, Indonesia had unpleasant memories of the international criticism it had attracted from the West over conditions in the Galang detention camp it had agreed to run during the period of the outflow of Vietnamese refugees. Two attempts were made to institute the Indonesian Solution. Two hundred and fifty Sri Lankan asylum seekers were intercepted on Australia's behalf and brought to the port of Merak. Seventy-eight Sri Lankan asylum seekers were rescued by Australia at Indonesia's request and transferred to the customs vessel the *Oceanic Viking* in preparation for their detention in an Australian-financed camp, Tanjung Pinang. Both attempts ended in tears. In October 2009, following the *Oceanic Viking*'s failed attempt to unload its human cargo, Newspoll discovered that Labor's primary vote had dropped by 7 per cent in the space of a fortnight. With this poll, the longest honeymoon in Australian political history had come, rather abruptly, to an end. The *Oceanic Viking* was *Tampa* in reverse. *Tampa* convinced the Australian people that John Howard was strong; the *Oceanic Viking* that Kevin Rudd was weak.

At the time of the *Oceanic Viking*, Rudd faced a Liberal Party moderate, Malcolm Turnbull. Turnbull's asylum-seeker policy did not go beyond a return of temporary protection visas. By 2010 he faced a completely ruthless opponent, Tony Abbott. Abbott captured his argument with the prime minister's asylum-seeker policy in a witty aphorism: Labor had inherited a solution and created from it a problem. He advocated far more than a mere return to temporary protection visas. Boats should be turned round by military force. Nauru should be immediately reopened. Turnbull's asylum-seeker policy had been no more popular than Rudd's. That was the price of decency. Abbott's hit the spot. In the first six months of this year every opinion poll taken on the question of asylum seekers strongly favoured the Abbott policy. By now, the asylum-seeker issue had clearly weakened the Rudd prime ministership. At the time of the Gillard challenge, Rudd spoke of his refusal to conduct 'a race to the bottom' over the question of asylum seekers. His unwillingness to participate in this race was one of the reasons he lost the Labor leadership on 24 June.

Julia Gillard did not refuse such participation. The game was on. At the Lowy Institute, she argued that it was wrong to characterise those who were fearful of the return of the asylum-seeker boats as 'rednecks,' or to try to smother legitimate debate under a blanket of 'political correctness.' (Pauline Hanson was delighted. As she pointed out, that was precisely what she had argued in her 1996 maiden speech.) Even her own migrant parents, Gillard told us, were appalled at the thought of special privileges for refugees. Although she was opposed to moving backwards to the Pacific Solution, she advocated moving forwards to the establishment of a regional offshore processing centre on the territory either of East Timor or some other country that had signed the Refugee Convention. The evil people smugglers had to be deprived of a product to sell; asylum seekers needed to learn that a successful boat trip to Australia merely bought them an air ticket to an undesirable offshore processing centre. This was the Pacific Solution with a human face. When Gillard travelled to Darwin, she boarded a coastal patrol vessel in the presence of the member for Lindsay, David Bradbury, to reassure the voters of western Sydney that they now were safe. Like Abbott, Gillard was now committed to stopping the boats. All that distinguished her asylum-seeker policy from his was an unwillingness to restore temporary protection visas and stop the boats by reopening the detention centre on Nauru. An overwhelming majority of both Labor and Coalition voters welcomed Gillard's tough new stance. Labor knew, in the words of the immigration minister, Senator Chris Evans, that the asylum-seeker issue was 'killing the government.' Following Gillard's policy reversal, the danger had at least been significantly reduced.

*

The central puzzle in this story is why Australians are overwhelmingly hostile to asylum seekers who reach our shores by boat. There are probably too many plausible explanations rather than too few.

It is difficult to believe that the deepest patterns of the political culture play no role. For a century or more Australian immigration policy was dominated by fears about a small white population being overwhelmed by the hordes of Asians to our north. If the majority of the asylum seekers had been white Zimbabwean farmers and their families fleeing from the regime of Robert Mugabe, rather than Hazaras fleeing from the Taliban or Iraqis fleeing from Saddam Hussein or Tamils fleeing from the Sri Lankan civil war, it is improbable, or so it seems to me, that public opinion would have tolerated their detention behind razor wire or their transportation to Nauru. It is revealing that, in many suburbs of Australia, African immigrants are thought to be asylum seekers.

Yet there is more to the hostility towards asylum seekers than ancient anxieties of race. For many Australians the spontaneous arrival of asylum-seeker boats offends the central political virtue of the nation – the idea of the 'fair go.' Lacking a history that makes it easy to imagine the kind of desperation borne of political oppression and fear, many Australians are genuinely disturbed by the disorderly nature of the refugee scramble for safety and receptive to the idea that those who reach Australia have done so at the expense of others by jumping the queue. On fair-go grounds, even recent immigrants are unlikely to be more sympathetic to asylum seekers than Australians who have been settled here for generations. Many have struggled unsuccessfully to bring family members to Australia. Why should asylum seekers be allowed to enter Australia, they argue, when their own family members are not?

Nor should ordinary selfishness be ruled out as a reason for mainstream resentment of asylum seekers. It seems to me no accident that the voters most hostile to the asylum seekers are those that John Howard called the battlers and those that Kevin Rudd christened working families: that is to say, those who believe they are doing it tough and who bitterly resent the supposed privileges given to outsiders. Downward envy is a potent force in all Western societies. Nor is it an accident that entirely fanciful urban myths about asylum seekers being treated more generously by the state than ordinary citizens continue to circulate persistently and widely. In 2009, in addition, the asylum-seeker issue became a surrogate for battlers' hostility to Rudd's enthusiasm for a Big Australia. Even though the population impact of successful asylum claims is zero – for every successful onshore refugee claim one fewer refugee is accepted from abroad – as a result of this frightful muddle, voters seething in traffic jams in western Sydney are able to point the finger at asylum seekers.

Even more deeply, we live in an era when Western societies are barricading themselves against the claims made upon them by perceived outsiders. European politics is increasingly dominated by fear of being swamped by Muslims; the politics of the United States is presently being shaped by hostility directed towards the millions of illegal immigrants from Mexico; and Australian politics is being moulded by resentment of the tiny handful of asylum seekers who arrive uninvited on our shores. Australia's borders are more or less impenetrable. It would seem that no single asylum-seeker boat has ever arrived unobserved. Yet in this atmosphere, as the drawbridge is raised, fantasies about the breakdown of border security seem to exercise an extraordinary and altogether irrational power.

In recent times friends of asylum seekers in Australia have described those who are hostile to asylum seekers, or who support a return to the Pacific Solution, as 'rednecks.' In my opinion, this involves a serious category mistake. Every recent opinion poll makes it clear that hostility to unauthorised asylum seekers represents the opinion not of a small racist minority but of the overwhelming majority of the Australian mainstream. Neither 'education' nor 'leadership' seems likely in the near future to make Australians open their hearts to asylum seekers or to challenge the mood of the conservative populist political culture that crystallised at the time of *Tampa*. As recent political events have rather painfully revealed, no party that wishes to govern Australia can afford to ignore the meaning of what occurred in the spring of 2001.

Bertolt Brecht was responsible for one of the twentieth century's best political jokes. After an incident in which East German troops fired on their own people, he composed what he thought to be the appropriate official announcement. 'The government has lost confidence in the people. It has therefore decided to elect a new people.' A new people cannot however be elected. This is the situation that Australian friends of asylum seekers must now honestly confront.

The Monthly

High Times at the Hotel Desiccation

Sarah Drummond

Mad Dog Rangi

We live in a desert Pilbara hotel with an alcoholic camel, one petrol bowser and no one else for 150 kilometres. We do the best we can with our time off. Rangi, the cook, a wiry brown Maori, disappears between shifts – walking, she says.

The resident geologists surprise her one day, clad only in her boar's tusk, sandals and a string water-bottle bag. Out in the brutal Pilbara sun, she treads the bones of the country, ochre against ochre, her hair wild with red dust and hot wind. She was walking, like she said.

The Wrong Place

Shazza, the reluctant barmaid, was lured out here by The Hotel Owner while she sunned herself on turquoise Cable Beach. The funny, round little woman shows me her tattoos. They look like they've been thrown at her, lucky to have hit her flesh at all. The misshapen bluebirds on each breast are not symmetrical – the cabbage rose sits on her hip, in the wrong place.

'I've gotta stay here for a fortnight now,' she tells me, and her pretty face grows glum. 'I need the money to get back to Broome.'

Skimpies Tonite!

Dorothy (the innocent) is in love with Matt (the yardie). She and her aunt hitchhike in from South Hedland. Dorothy is dressed in a purple tutu, G-string and not much else. She is being tutored in the art of skimpy barmaiding by her aunt Lolita (knowing, blonde, hard body, forty).

Rum-sodden off-duty police from Karratha pick a poker fight with the geologist's lackey. The camel bellows for more beer and is obliged. Matt is out the back, smashing empties and perfectly good middy glasses against the skip bin.

Lolita mutters something to me about The Hotel Owner and 600 dollars. There's money changing hands, lots of it. The moon is full, but I miss the nuances; I don't really understand what is going on.

Dorothy mopes, unattractively. Dorothy is sacked for 'not performing.'

One Night Stand With Ink

Of all the outsiders who stop for beer and fuel, there is one. He rides from the north on an old English motorbike. We walk around the abandoned mine. The late sun makes our copper shadows fall together in long, dark lines. Our shadows, stitched together, become tiger's eye country.

He says goodbye and continues south. He has to return half an hour later because he'd met me. He is all flustered and had forgotten to fuel up.

We crunch over swarming black beetles on the path to my room. I supply the Textas. He draws me.

It is already twenty-two degrees at 4.30 a.m. The man on the old English motorbike leaves and does not return.

In the breakfast room, the geologists drop their cutlery into toast and bacon and eggs, and stare at my technicolour limbs – magenta dragonflies, sunflowers, turquoise scarab beetles with mandala haloes, wild red roses and their thorns, cockatoos, green salamanders, birds of paradise, a tiny blue snake, the Tree of Life.

Wahine Toa, Warrior Woman

Shazza shoots through. She bared her bluebirds to a smitten truckie and found her way back to Broome. This means the cook and the cleaner are the new barmaids, Rangi and me.

Fat, red-faced and horny, a drunken bikie leans over the bar at Rangi. She just laughs at him and he morphs into a fat, red-faced and nasty racist. I watch her turn him to mush. I see her rise to her full six feet. I see her teeth flash as white as that boar's tusk pendant she wears. Her eyes are magnificent. 'Bro, 200 years ago,' she snarls, 'we used to *eat* cunts like you.'

Journey Man

He only stays one night. He walks in off the highway with cracked lips, a blanket and three books. He tells me some fantastic story about a shamanic vision after three days on the bitumen at forty-one degrees. I believe him because of his sunburn. He is gone when I knock on the door to change the sheets in the morning. They smell of lanolin and stale piss. I didn't really like him. He made me feel uncomfortable, but I think about him a lot.

Roadkill Baby

A local (more a regular) walks into the bar and, with a complicit smile, opens his jacket. 'I have something for you.' He produces a roadkill baby, all ears and legs, a scrawny unhappy body, moist, mammalian eyes.

I call her Kai. Rangi snorts into her mashed potato. 'You know that means "dinner" where I come from,' she tells me. But Kai she is, a fey creature and an opportunistic bully. She swivels her ears, rocks back on her tail and goes for any broom or blue heeler that comes her way. She is committed and swift in her delivery of violence.

On Tuesday nights, I hitchhike to Point Samson, to the sea. Each truck I climb into is different. The shock and then delight on the face of every truckie who sees Kai wriggle out of my handbag is the same.

I like to lie in the water on Wednesdays, wash away the red dust and drama of the dry hotel. On Wednesdays, I eat fresh, juicy, coconut-encrusted prawns from the café at Point Samson. I carry Kai down to Honeymoon Cove where I crack oysters off the rocks and suck their salty broth. I wonder how, of all my strange companions at The Hotel, a kangaroo becomes my best friend. We swim and swim in warm northern waters, that mad little roadkill baby and me.

Indigo

A Fine and Public Place

Gerard Windsor

My wife has just acquired three graves. This has been a cause for some celebration. Such is the nature of marriage that I now know where I'll be buried. It's been an unconscious, implicit vote by the pair of us that we'll go on together to the end, a particularly generous gesture on my wife's part. There was no planning about this. Only in passing have we talked about funeral arrangements. It's quite by chance that some of the attendant circumstances of our deaths have now been arranged.

For about ten years I have always read the death notices in the *Sydney Morning Herald*. Every now and again there are wordings and details that astonish and delight me. About five years ago a man whose first name I've forgotten appeared as 'Roots, [Jack] (known to his friends at the Bowling Club as "Seldom").' Just a few months ago I came across an old teacher, 'Gilchrist, Joseph Charles Benedict, Jesuit Priest and Teacher, loving husband of …' The bereaved, however, are rarely in a frame of mind to include jokes in their death notices, so the pickings are pretty slim for anyone looking merely for mirth. But I've got other motives for scanning these columns; above all I pick up names that I associate with my mother, and I pass on these finds to her, and although her short-term memory is bad, she is a whizz on the genealogy and maiden name and rural origins and urban residences of her contemporaries, and so we talk together about the newly dead. Then, at a less detached level, I read the death columns because there is that growing number of my own contemporaries who are appearing there.

So, because I was loitering one morning in the back pages of the broadsheet section of the paper, I couldn't miss a notice whose most immediately eye-catching feature was a long list of names. The notice was headed 'Waverley Cemetery,' the lettering archaic and curlicued. Now I've long had an affection for Waverley Cemetery. In 1982 I published a story, 'In Waverley Cemetery the Faith of Our Fathers,' which was partly a tribute to the 1898 Irish monument there, the most idiosyncratic icon of the Irish diaspora in this country, and a fabulous piece of funerary sculpture, narrative depiction and memorial tablet. The monument however is only one of the cemetery's charms for me. Waverley Cemetery occupies an east-facing hillside that slopes to the cliffs between Clovelly and Bronte beaches. Developers could only alternate between rage and salivation at this exclusion from the market of such prime eastern-suburbs real estate. Instead the place is a democratic necropolis where a century and a half's worth of Australians, without any massive public marks of distinction in wealth or grandeur, tumble towards the Pacific and the hope-inspiring east. Throw in the graves of umpteen of the definers of Australian culture – Henry Kendall, Henry Lawson, Dorothea MacKellar, Victor Trumper, Fanny Durack – and no Australian could have a more desirable long-term residence than Waverley Cemetery. In my 1982 story I find I have a character, a criminal, coming out with the line, 'I'd give the world to be buried in Waverley Cemetery.'

When my father died in 1987 my mother hoped he would go into a plot at Waverley that already held her parents and paternal grandparents, and that in time she would follow him there. But the message she got was that the space was not available. So my father went further south to Botany Cemetery, enclosed by market gardens and the decaying ruins of Bunnerong Power Station. My mother made a payment on two graves.

This gesture put her in a small minority of the population. In fact she's doubly in a minority. She's one of the 40 per cent of Australians choosing burial rather than cremation. But that's not the most interesting statistic about our national funerary habits. In other Western countries 35 per cent of people pre-plan the disposition of their remains. In Australia however only about 8 per cent do so. What's this distinctiveness all about? Are we such a mobile population that we can't predict our penultimate residence, and so never choose an ultimate one? Are we more averse to facing up pragmatically to death? Are we an instinctively grasshopper society where sufficient for today is the pleasure thereof and tomorrow can take care of itself? Are we such convinced secularists that we have absolutely no interest beyond the moment of apparent extinction? Are we so environmentally indifferent that we don't care quite how all the residual blood and bone is distributed? Or are the undertakers of this country just slack in developing new business opportunities? I've no idea; I'm no sociologist. But anyone who thinks of pre-planning – and this includes me – apparently belongs to a sepulchral elite.

I've got some personality-defining decisions to make. As is to be expected from the national dearth of forward-planners, people commonly say, 'It doesn't matter to me where I'm buried,' and that point of view is easy to appreciate. But individuals who take a bit of forethought and don't leave the decision to a family member or an executor or a funeral director will have to invoke some criteria for choosing where they go. The regular articles about the shrinking vacancies in all the older cemeteries are accurate enough, but the situation isn't dire. There are still options. Waverley, for example, can take 150,000 sets of remains, but to date there have only been 68,000 laid there. Among the paltry few who think about it, maybe some will plump for where the family have previously gone, or maybe for somewhere close to home, or maybe somewhere the survivors can easily visit them. Of course the pleasure and satisfaction in the choice has to be all pre-mortem. And a satisfying, far from empty pleasure it can be too. The view you get from Waverley, for example, is so sunny and majestic and fresh-aired and teeming with melodious ghosts that you can't help thinking 'It is good to be here now' – and that delight spontaneously overflows into 'It will be good to be here in future.' And at Macquarie Park, the level greenness of the lawns and the orderly profusion of shrubs and trees might appeal to the gardener or demesne owner that you are, or aspired to be, and that's where you want to go. Or Rookwood – where old Sydney meets new, variegated Sydney, and families come to picnic and play – might call to the yearning in you to live on in a haunt of cheerful, continuing, egalitarian life. Or if a life of instability doesn't worry you, you scatter yourself exuberantly to the wind.

The pleasure, in any of these circumstances, is that of anticipation. Anticipation is a massive ingredient of any pleasure, particularly those that bring experience of another world, not least sexual pleasure or the low-key febrile thrill of travel. The sex or the holiday might be disappointing, but that doesn't nullify all the excitement that preceded them. Ditto for lying in the grave. And, what's more, there's no saying definitively what awaits in the undiscovered country. Marvell might even have got it wrong.

I'm a tidy-minded eldest child, and I've always intended to have the grave fixed up well in advance. But money's been tight, and there have always been more pressing calls on it: the sustenance of life now is more urgent than the comfort of death later. So the issue of graves has been on very low heat on the back-burner for a long time. So much so that when I came across Waverley Cemetery's notice in the paper, I was merely curious. The notice called for 'applications to renew all Rights of Burial Certificates' where the right had lapsed. The list that followed was of persons who had had these rights but had not exercised them, with the result that the rights had lapsed. The notice was carefully legal. What in fact had generally happened was that persons had acquired the rights, buried various family members and then eventually buried themselves. Their subsequent inaction meant that the rights, valid for only fifty years, duly expired. The rights could be renewed 'where the original grantee or their heirs and successors choose to make a claim.'

As a devotee of unusual lists I read down this one. The Ds yielded one George Davidson. I had an uncertain memory that my wife's great-grandfather was a George Davidson. Yes, he was, she told me. It was worth a phone call. My wife was going overseas so I made the running. The cemetery office, the most helpful and patient public body I've ever dealt with, told me there was already one application from a descendant of a George Davidson. How do you decide between the claimants, I asked the manager. We don't, I was told. You work it out between yourselves. I let my wife know all this. Her primary interest turned out to be this chance of discovering an unknown relative. The rights were somewhat secondary, and would involve an immediate gush of barely existent funds.

The priorities changed when she began to collect the relevant birth and death certificates; all these details she hadn't known about her ancestors. Her great-grandfather was about thirty years of age before he arrived in Australia from Scotland via New Zealand. He had ten living children when he died. He was a 'Stonemason' when his daughter Helen, my wife's grandmother, was born in 1885. When he died in 1928 he was a 'Municipal Engineer.' Life as an ascent is the preferred trajectory. My own great-grandfather, in his middle age, was a 'Real Estate Agent and Auctioneer,' but by the time of his death he was an 'Australian Historian.'

Poor George Davidson hasn't had much of a press in his family. His daughter told her granddaughter that of an evening, after his dinner at the family home, 77 Goodhope Street, Paddington, he would leave his wife weeping while he went up the street to visit his mistress. And the woman in tears was the only image of Margaret Davidson that seemed to have survived. Otherwise the family was a blank – with one exception. A son, William, had been killed in France in 1918, and my wife and I had once visited his grave at Jeancourt.

My wife presented her claim and the supporting documentation to the staff at Waverley Cemetery. It was in order; she was a legitimate claimant. The competitors mentioned earlier had been disqualified: their George Davidson was not *the* George Davidson. A cheque was handed over; selling off a set of *Meanjin* covered the cost of the plot. My wife was given the location of the grave – her grave, my grave – and, importantly, a map to find our way to it. Downhill we went.

Most gravestones are severely factual, maybe aspirational, maybe declarative. Some few tell a story, and may do so while actually including all these other features. The Davidson grave tells a story. The allotment, we gathered, had been taken up in 1885, eight years after the cemetery had opened. George Davidson however lived on for another forty-three years – by which time his right to the plot had only seven years to run. The headstone, when we walked down the hill and first saw it, was eloquent. Margaret Anne (d.1920) and George Davidson (d.1928) are buried there all right, but they weren't the first. Margaret's father, 'John Beringer (late of Oamaru, N.Z.) aged 71 yrs,' was laid there in 1889. But the purchase of the plot in 1885 was a matter of haste and urgency, not forethought. The headstone reads '... also our dear children, MARY ANNE d. 5 May 1885, aged 3 yrs and 11 months, LIZZIE, d. 12 May 1885, aged 2 yrs and 9 months, Pte WILLIAM ESTHER DAVIDSON, 4th Machine Gun Coy, Killed at Venables, France, 12 Sept 1918 aged 38 yrs.' So the little girls died within a week of one another. Very likely of diphtheria. Their mother was five months pregnant with her sixth child who was to be Nellie, later Helen, and my wife's grandmother. Margaret Davidson had a lot to cry about in the evenings, and to die of in May 1920, aged sixty-seven, eighteen months after the death of her son in France.

So this is my new family. I'll be spending time with them. The cemetery manager says this allotment my wife has bought the right to can take at least another three burials and two cremations. This advice is somewhat a matter of divination and the combined experience of the gravediggers; high-tech archaeological tools are not yet priority equipment for Waverley Council. But it looks as though I'm in. These are my wife's graves, and she's invited me to share them. These two square metres are another world I had never imagined. For one thing they're Anglican ground, and I regard myself as Catholic to the bone. And then again I've never lived with small girls – not since my sister was one but she was always more or less my age so I never thought of her as a small girl. And I don't know how things are between this married couple; although they are referred to respectively as 'Beloved Wife' and 'Beloved Husband,' I've no idea whether this family is so strongly bound by the public proprieties that it could ever proclaim anything else. And there is so much grief there, far greater than I have ever known.

These are the people I will clamber out with when and if the resurrection comes. I start to see through the eyes of Stanley Spencer – small girls clinging to their mother's dress, and she, a middle-aged woman, supporting her elderly father, and her husband, the patriarch, out first, dusting himself down, taking in the view, before he strides off again into his new life. And some vicarious ghost of a soldier, whose own bones knit and put on flesh as he heaves himself out of a pit in France. And my wife and I tagging along, deferential to such senior generations, looking at George and Margaret and Lizzie and the rest of them in this new light. We shall be changed utterly, the book says. But not our personalities surely? Nor translated completely from Waverley Cemetery, I hope. The satisfactions of this life so drench every nerve in us, so seem to answer, at least momentarily, to our highest expectations of repletion, that the prospect of them being taken away and replaced by anything half so marvellous is such an incomprehensible one.

The whole disposition of Waverley Cemetery is so sunny, such a contiguity of earth and water and the overarching sky. It's easier to be a believer there. There is neither beach nor impassable cliff at its base; nothing hedonistic, nothing forbidding; nothing enticing you to stay here, nothing preventing your progress any further into the deep.

The humpy plains of inland cemeteries, or the small graveyards that huddle beside churches and look for their hope and comfort in that proximity, or the little niches that hold ashes inside walls, none of these have the tight elastic promise of a breakout that Waverley holds. Promise is probably too ambitious a word: the world is full of promise, and when we use the phrase it's most often when we speak of a life or a day that was full of promise and then failed to live up to it. Promises may be kept or broken, but promise seems to be most frequently something that stretches out in front of us, and then, as we go on, it dissipates. But in another context, on another day, in another person, it returns, and we hope again. It is a mirage that time and again will not solidify, but keeps us going till somehow, some day, maybe it breaks out into a great conflagration of light.

*

After I had lingered over the Davidson grave on that first sighting, and taken down all its particulars, I walked down the slope from this 'General' section of the cemetery to the 'Select' section where my own maternal grandparents and my grandfather's parents are buried, to pay them my respects, as I occasionally do. There are parallels here. My great-grandfather, Charles Trimby Burfitt, took out the right to this plot in 1896, thirty-one years before his own death. But before he was laid there he had buried two daughters and a son. In this instance one daughter was still a child, the other barely twenty. The son, my grandfather, had been too sickly to go to war, and instead he had studied medicine and by 1918 he had managed to marry, but by 1921 he was dead. His wife, my grandmother, outlived him by fifty-one years, and was the last person to be laid in this plot, in 1972, thirty-nine years after the previous interment, that of her mother-in-law in 1933. Prior to 1992 the tenure of the right of burial was fifty years from the first interment. So George Davidson's right had expired in 1935, and Charles Trimby Burfitt's in 1946. On my way up the hill to the gate I called at the office. 'Just as a matter of interest,' I asked, 'could you tell me who has the right now to the original C.T. Burfitt allotment?' I have subsequently read the by-laws and understand this is an illicit question – 'Cemetery Management protects the Legal Grantee's Privacy.' But my question didn't have to be rebuffed because in fact no one had taken up the right.

Well, well. How much of this land has not been taken up? I was free to do so. Suddenly, in what I thought was the most closely settled and tightly guarded real estate in Sydney – the land where real estate is emperor – I was being swamped by a surfeit of opportunity. The Burfitt plot is superior to the Davidson one. This primarily means that it is on the final steep slope, about eighty metres from the sea. Whereas the Davidsons are on a plateau, further up the hill – and their site lacks the same magnetic gravitation towards the sea and the rising sun. The Burfitts look down on the fresh stone and timber work of the recently constructed coastal walkway; they can catch the movement of exultant, athletic life flickering silently between them and the vastness beyond.

But I've committed myself to the Davidson plot. A man shall leave his own family and cleave to his wife. If a husband and wife have lasted together to the grave, there'd need to be a hefty reason for them to go their separate ways when they'd got that far. There's a family memory that when my mother wanted her husband in her parents' grave there was only one vacancy. She said no: there had to be room for two. Twenty-three years later the Burfitt residents have settled down: the cemetery manager's opinion is that there's now space for three more burials and eight cremations – even more roomy than the Davidson allotment. But my mother's example carries weight. I'll stick with my spouse. Besides, I've lived with Burfitts and their stories so long that this sudden incursion of new plots has the edge in excitement. The Davidsons might be embarrassing or boring or incapable of inspiring or edifying me, but the chances are against that; I've known enough of their descendants.

All this unlooked-for plenitude, all this expansion of possibilities. The manager says there is so much more on offer. He puts out a list of expirees annually, but if he had the staff he could do so monthly. And if you have an ancestor on the premises you pay just one seventh of what a Waverley new chum would be up for. On my way out yet again I ask him how many descendants of this year's ninety-eight expirees took up the offer.

'Just one,' he says. 'Just you.'

Publication Details

Sunil Badami's 'Country and Western' was commissioned by Campbelltown Arts Centre for *Edge of Elsewhere* (January 2010), a publication for the Sydney Festival.

Murray Bail's 'The Only Things I Remember from School' appeared in the *Monthly*, July 2010.

Carmel Bird's 'The Ace of Spades' appeared in *Griffith Review 28: Still the Lucky Country?*, Text Publishing, May 2010.

David Brooks's 'The Smoking Vegetarian' appeared in *Angelaki: Journal of the Theoretical Humanities*, vol. 14, no. 2, August 2009.

Peter Conrad's 'Something Sacred' appeared as 'Sister Act' in the *Monthly*, September 2010.

Mark Dapin's 'Ten Myths of Australian Crime' appeared in *Good Weekend*, 14 August 2010.

Sarah Drummond's 'High Times at the Hotel Desiccation' appeared in *Indigo 5*, Summer 2010.

Elizabeth Farrelly's 'All Things Being Equal' appeared in the *Sydney Morning Herald*, 12 April 2010.

Tim Flannery's 'Getting to Know Them' appeared in the *New York Review of Books*, vol. 57, no. 7, 29 April 2010.

Shelley Gare's 'Secret Women's Business' appeared in *Good Weekend*, 1 May 2010.

Lorna Hallahan's 'On Being Odd' appeared in *Australian Book Review*, May 2010. It was joint winner of the 2009 Calibre Prize.

Janet Hawley's 'Art and Darkness' appeared in *Good Weekend*, 12 June 2010.

Ian Henderson's '"Freud Has a Name for It": A.A. Phillips's "The Cultural Cringe"' appeared in *Southerly*, vol. 69, no. 2, 2009.

Amanda Hooton's 'Another Universe' appeared in *Good Weekend*, 8 August 2009.

Clive James's 'Peter Porter 1929–2010' appeared in the *Times Literary Supplement*, 12 May 2010.

Christine Kenneally's 'The Inferno' appeared in the *New Yorker*, 26 October 2009.

Jo Lennan's 'On Botany' appeared in *Intelligent Life*, Spring 2010.

Melissa Lucashenko's 'The Angry Country' appeared in *Griffith Review 28: Still the Lucky Country?*, Text Publishing, May 2010.

Paul McGeough's 'Prayers, Tear Gas and Terror' and 'In Their Wake' appeared in the *Sydney Morning Herald* and the *Age* on 4 and 5 June 2010. 'Prayers, Tear Gas and Terror' will be featured in *Infernal Triangle*, published by Allen & Unwin.

Shane Maloney's 'Shoulder-Deep in the Entrails' appeared in *Inside Story*, 28 June 2010.

David Malouf's 'The States of the Nation' appeared in the *Monthly*, August 2010.

Anne Manne's 'Ebony: The Girl in the Room' appeared in the *Monthly*, February 2010.

Robert Manne's 'Asylum Seekers and Australian Democracy: What Do We Fear?' appeared as the 'Comment' in the *Monthly*, September 2010.

Kathy Marks's 'Tears of the Sun' appeared in *Griffith Review 28: Still the Lucky Country?*, Text Publishing, May 2010.

David Marr's 'Patrick White's London' was the 2010 Menzies Lecture, delivered in London in June 2010.

Alex Miller's 'John Masefield's Attic' appeared as 'Waxing Wiser Than Oneself' in the *Australian Literary Review*, 7 October 2009.

Les Murray's 'Infinite Anthology: Adventures in Lexiconia' was the British Poetry Society's annual lecture, delivered in London in May 2010. It was published in the *Monthly*, August 2010.

Pauline Nguyen's 'Born in Vietnam, Made in Australia: Getting the Fish Sauce Recipe Right' appeared in *Griffith Review 27: Food Chain*, Text Publishing, February 2010.

Maureen O'Shaughnessy's 'Rick Grossman: The Trip Home' was previously unpublished.

Nicolas Rothwell's 'Magic Island' appeared in the *Weekend Australian*, 8 May 2010.

Guy Rundle's 'Culturestate' appeared in *Meanjin*, vol. 69, no. 2, Winter 2010.

Andrew Sant's 'On Marriage' appeared in *Meanjin*, vol. 69, no. 4, Summer 2009.

Gerard Windsor's 'A Fine and Public Place' was previously unpublished.

Notes on Contributors

The Editor

Robert Drewe was born in Melbourne and grew up on the West Australian coast. His many novels and short stories and his prize-winning memoir, *The Shark Net*, have been widely translated, won national and international awards and been adapted for film, television, radio and theatre.

Authors

Sunil Badami has written for the *Sydney Morning Herald*, *Good Weekend*, the *Australian*, *Australian Literary Review*, *Cultural Studies Review* and *Meanjin*. His short stories have appeared in *The Best Australian Stories 2007* and in *Growing Up Asian in Australia*.

Murray Bail has written many novels and short stories. His novel *Eucalyptus* won the 1999 Commonwealth Writers' Prize and the Miles Franklin Award. His most recent novel is *The Pages*.

Carmel Bird's books include *The White Garden*, *Crisis* and *The Bluebird Cafe*. *Red Shoes* is a novel in hardcopy and on CD-ROM. Her story collections include *Automatic Teller*, *The Common Rat* and *The Woodpecker Toy Fact*. Her manuals for writers are *Dear Writer* and *Not Now Jack – I'm Writing a Novel*.

David Brooks's latest collection of poetry is *The Balcony* and his most recent novel is *The Umbrella Club*, both from the University of Queensland Press. He is an associate professor of Australian literature at the University of Sydney and co-editor of *Southerly*.

Peter Conrad teaches English at Christ Church, Oxford. A regular contributor to the *Observer*, his many books include works on Orson Welles, Alfred Hitchcock and, most recently, *Islands*.

Mark Dapin is a feature writer and columnist for *Good Weekend*. His first novel, *King of the Cross*, won a Ned Kelly Award in 2010.

Sarah Drummond lives on the south coast and works as a fisherwoman and PhD candidate. Her stories are published in *Shadow Plays* and *Short Stories Australia*.

Elizabeth Farrelly is a Sydney-based columnist and author. A former editor and Sydney city councillor, she is adjunct associate professor of architecture at the University of Sydney. Her books include *Glenn Murcutt: Three Houses* and *Blubberland: The Dangers of Happiness*.

Tim Flannery has published numerous scientific papers, two *Quarterly Essays* and over a dozen books, including, most recently, *Here on Earth*. A former director of the South Australia Museum and Australian of the Year, he chaired the Copenhagen Climate Council.

Shelley Gare is an editor, writer and columnist. She was the editor of *Good Weekend* and *Sunday Life* and deputy editor at the *Australian*, having previously worked for the *Sunday Times* in London. She writes regularly for the *Weekend Australian*. Her first book is *Triumph of the Airheads – And the Retreat from Commonsense*.

Lorna Hallahan is a social worker and theologian working as an academic in the School of Social and Policy Studies at Flinders University.

Janet Hawley is a senior feature writer with *Good Weekend*. Her writing has covered a range of topics, including Indonesian politics and society, the Arab–Israeli conflict, Aboriginal culture, environmental issues and sport. Her arts features and profiles have won two Walkleys and the Gold Walkley.

Ian Henderson completed his PhD at the University of Sydney in 2001 before lecturing at Griffith University in Brisbane. He began work at the King's College, London in 2004 in the Department of English Language and Literature and is associated with the College's Menzies Centre for Australian Studies.

Amanda Hooton is an award-winning journalist who has written for the *Scotsman*, the *New York Times*, the *Times* and the *Daily Telegraph*. She now writes for the *Sydney Morning Herald* and the *Age* and is a regular contributor to *Good Weekend*.

Clive James's latest books are a collection of essays, *The Revolt of the Pendulum: Essays 2005–2008*; his selected poems, *Opal Sunset: Selected Poems 1958–2008*; and the fifth volume of his memoirs, *The Blaze of Obscurity: The TV Years*.

Christine Kenneally is a science journalist. Her book, *The First Word: The Search for the Origins of Language*, was published in 2007. She is currently writing a book about genealogy and genetics.

Jo Lennan was born in New South Wales and studied in Sydney and Oxford. Her essays, stories and reportage appear in disparate places of print, including *Time*, the *Economist*, *Intelligent Life* and the *Monthly*.

Melissa Lucashenko is a writer of mixed European and Murri (Aboriginal) heritage and writes about the lives of Aborigines, women and the poor. Her novels include *Steam Pigs, Hard Yards* and *Killing Darcy*.

Shane Maloney is author of the Murray Whelan series of crime novels and, most recently, *Australian Encounters*, with Chris Grosz.

David Malouf is one of Australia's most celebrated writers. In a career spanning four decades, he has written poetry, essays, fiction and opera libretti. His latest book is *Revolving Days: Selected Poems.*

Anne Manne is the author of *Motherhood: How Should We Care for Our Children?* and *Quarterly Essay 29: Love & Money*. Her latest book is *So This Is Life: Scenes from a Country Childhood.*

Robert Manne is professor of politics at La Trobe University and a regular essayist and commentator for the *Monthly*. His most recent books include two edited collections, *Goodbye to All That?* and *W.E.H. Stanner: The Dreaming and Other Essays.*

Kathy Marks is the *Independent*'s Asia-Pacific correspondent. Born in Manchester, she worked for Reuters and Fleet Street newspapers before moving to Sydney in 1999. She has reported from more than twenty countries, covering stories including the Bali bombings, the civil war in Indonesia's Aceh province and the Boxing Day tsunami.

David Marr is the author of *Patrick White: A Life.* He has written for many years for the *Sydney Morning Herald*, authored two *Quarterly Essays*, been editor of the *National Times*, a reporter for *Four Corners* and presenter of ABC TV's *Media Watch.*

Paul McGeough is a senior foreign correspondent for the *Age* and *Sydney Morning Herald*, specialising in Middle Eastern affairs. He was awarded the 2003 Walkley Award for Journalism Leadership in recognition of acts of courage and bravery in the practice of journalism.

Alex Miller is a multi-award-winning novelist, including in 2008 the Manning Clark Cultural Award for an outstanding contribution to the quality of Australian cultural life. His latest novel, *Lovesong*, was published in 2009.

Les Murray's work is studied in schools and universities around Australia and has been translated into several foreign languages. His latest collection of poems is *Taller When Prone.*

Pauline Nguyen is the author of *Secrets of the Red Lantern*. She is one of the proprietors of Red Lantern, the acclaimed modern Vietnamese restaurant in Sydney's Surry Hills.

Maureen O'Shaughnessy is completing a Masters of Creative Writing at UTS. Her work has appeared in *Island, Blue Dog, Swamp* and the anthologies *Reflecting on Melbourne* and *New Beginnings*.

Nicolas Rothwell is the author of *Wings of the Kite-Hawk, The Red Highway, Journeys to the Interior* and *Another Country*. He is the northern correspondent for the *Australian*.

Guy Rundle is European features correspondent for *Crikey* and the *Sunday Age*. Former editor of *Arena Magazine*, his books and shows include *Down To the Crossroads* and *Your Dreaming*. A book on US politics and TV drama is forthcoming.

Andrew Sant co-founded the literary magazine *Island* in Tasmania and served as editor for ten years. Since 2000 he has been a writer-in-residence at institutions in England and China. In 2007–08 he was Writing Fellow at the University of Chichester.

Gerard Windsor's new book, *All Day Long the Noise of Battle*, a non-fiction account of an Australian infantry company in Vietnam and its defining battle, will be published in April 2011.